The Polish Coal Miners' Union and the German Labor Movement in the Ruhr, 1902–1934

The Polish Coal Miners' Union and the German Labor Movement in the Ruhr, 1902–1934

National and Social Solidarity

John J. Kulczycki

BERG

Oxford ● New York

First published in 1997 by
Berg
Editorial offices:
150 Cowley Road, Oxford, OX4 1JJ, UK
70 Washington Square South, New York, NY 10012, USA

© John J. Kulczycki 1997

Berg is the imprint of Oxford International Publishers Ltd.

Library of Congress Cataloging-in-Publication Data
A catalogue record for this book is available from the Library of Congress.

British Library Cataloguing-in-Publication Data
A catalogue record of this book is available from the British Library.

ISBN 1 85973 158 9 (Cloth)

Printed in the United Kingdom by Biddles Limited.

Cover photograph: Polish migrants in a tavern in the Ruhr in Mengede ca.
1910. Courtesy of the Zakład Badań Narodowościowych PAN in Poznań,
Poland.

For Regina

Contents

Contents

Contents

Abbreviations in Notes

AAN	Archiwum Akt Nowych, Warsaw
APP	Archiwum Państwowe Miasta Poznania i Województwa Poznańskiego
ARPB	Ambasada Rzeczypospolitej Polskiej w Berlinie
ARPP	Ambasada Rzeczypospolitej Polskiej w Paryżu
BA	Bergamt
GR	*Gazeta Robotnicza*
HSTAD	Nordrhein-Westfälisches Hauptstaatsarchiv Düsseldorf
KGRPB	Konsulat Generalny Rzeczypospolitej Polskiej w Berlinie
LR	Landrat, Landratsamt
MdI	Minister des Innern
MfHuG	Minister für Handel und Gewerbe
MSZ	Minister, Ministerstwo Spraw Zagranicznych
OBAD	Oberbergamtsbezirk Dortmund
OP, OPC, OPM	Oberpräsident, -präsidium Coblenz, Münster
RA, RD, RM	Regierungsbezirk Arnsberg, Düsseldorf, Münster
RP, RPA, RPD, RPM	Regierungspräsident, -präsidium Arnsberg, Düsseldorf, Münster
StAB	Stadtarchiv Bochum
STAM	Staatsarchiv Münster
WP	*Wiarus Polski*

Acknowledgments

To see things more clearly or even just differently, we must inevitably stand on the shoulders of others. But not often does a scholar find fellow specialists as willing to put up with his muddy boots as I have: Christoph Klessmann, Jerzy Kozłowski, Valentina-Maria Stefanski, and Klaus Tenfelde, all of whom have written substantial works on the Polish community or miners in the Ruhr, repeatedly assisted, advised, and encouraged me and thereby made the completion of this project possible. Archivists in both Poland and Germany willingly used their expertise to search out documents crucial for my work, but special thanks are due to Edward Kołodziej of the Archiwum Akt Nowych in Warsaw and Leopold Schütte of the Staatsarchiv in Münster. I also benefited from the hospitality and practical assistance of others during long research stays abroad, including the families of Johannes Hoffmann in Dortmund; of Barbara and Rainer Fremdling, Christa and Leopold Schütte, and Richard Tilly in Münster; and of Marianna, Tomasz, and Konrad Knothe in Warsaw. Maria Bowgierd of Poznań did tedious bibliographical work at an early point in my research.

At my own institution, the University of Illinois at Chicago, the bibliographer in the social sciences Stephen E. Wiberley and Kathleen S. Kilian and her staff in the inter-library loan department aided me in obtaining items not available in our library. Richard S. Levy read parts of a draft of my work and made astute suggestions, and I continued to reap the benefits of assistance given earlier in my research by Burton Bledstein and Daniel Scott Smith, all colleagues in the Department of History. Raymond Brod of the Department of Geography kindly produced the maps. I also gratefully acknowledge the generous financial assistance and material support that this project received from the Campus Research Board, the Institute for the Humanities, and the Office of Social Science Research of the University of Illinois at Chicago and from the Joint Committee on Eastern Europe of the American Council of Learned Societies and the Social Science Research Council, financed in part by the Ford Foundation and the National Endowment for the Humanities, which also provided a grant to visit archives in Poland.

In a long-term project, encouragement and psychological support can sometimes play a greater role in the completion of a project than concrete assistance. For the former I am grateful to Peter Brock and Piotr S. Wandycz, mentors in an earlier project closer to their specialties. Friends and family also had their patience tested, and they passed. Deserving of particular mention are the members of the fishing brotherhood and especially Regina Bowgierd, to whom I dedicate this book.

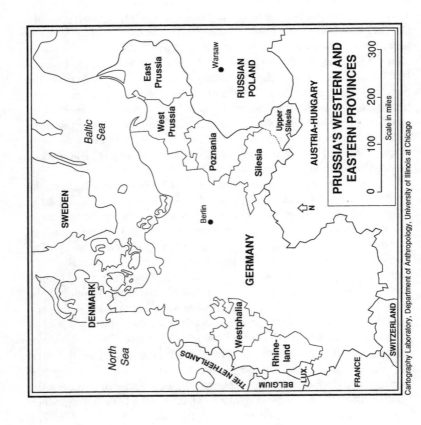

PRUSSIA'S WESTERN AND
EASTERN PROVINCES

0   100   200   300
Scale in miles

Cartography Laboratory, Department of Anthropology, University of Illinois at Chicago

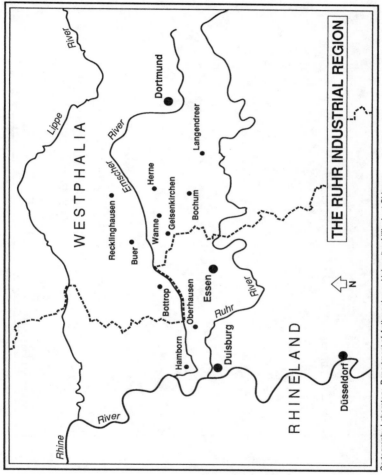

THE RUHR INDUSTRIAL REGION

Cartography Laboratory, Department of Anthropology, University of Illinois at Chicago

Introduction

My previous study of the substantial Polish-speaking minority among the coal miners of the Ruhr region documented its role in the labor movement of the region before World War I.[1] I argued that the militancy of the Polish-speaking miners negates the stereotypes of the foreign worker as invariably an obstacle to the labor movement or a threat to the livelihood of the native worker. Instead, xenophobia on the part of the native worker stood as the main barrier to solidarity between him and the foreign worker. The Polish-speaking miner, though conscious of the cultural and linguistic differences that divided him from the native German worker in the Ruhr, proved quite capable of acting together with his German co-worker in pursuit of their common working-class interests. In practice the Polish-speaking miner in the Ruhr exemplified an ethno-class consciousness that invalidates the analytical dichotomy between national and social solidarity.[2]

Nothing better illustrates this ethno-class consciousness than the *Zjednoczenie Zawodowe Polskie* (ZZP) or Polish Trade Union formed in the Ruhr in 1902. Born in an overwhelmingly German milieu, it emphasized its Polish character in opposition to the other, predominantly German, trade unions. At the same time, it functioned as a genuine working-class institution, modeled after the other trade unions of the region. It quickly became the third most important miners' union and encompassed a majority of the organized Polish-speaking miners of the Ruhr. But it also reached out to workers in the Polish homeland and soon achieved the status of the sole Polish trade union of any significance in all of pre-war Germany. After the war and the re-emergence of an independent Poland, the ZZP united under its banner worker organizations in other parts of Poland to form the largest trade union of

---

1. John J. Kulczycki, *The Foreign Worker and the German Labor Movement: Xenophobia and Solidarity in the Coal Fields of the Ruhr, 1871–1914* (Oxford, Providence, USA: Berg Publishers, 1994).

2. Christoph Klessmann, "Zjednoczenie Zawodowe Polskie (ZZP—Polnische Berufsvereinigung) und Alter Verband im Ruhrgebiet," *Internationale Wissenschaftliche Korrespondenz zur Geschichte der deutschen Arbeiterbewegung*, XV (1979), 68, sees problems of a "double loyalty" and of priorities in the "conflict between class interests and national consciousness."

the early years of the Polish state.[3] The history of the ZZP gives new meaning to Eric Hobsbawm's claim that, "Both immigration and emigration have a bearing on the history of national working classes."[4] Despite its importance in the labor movement in Germany and in the Ruhr region in particular and its relevance to questions concerning the interplay of national and social solidarity, historians of the labor movement in the Ruhr largely leave it out of their accounts.[5] Others frequently misconstrue its essential nature. Hans-Ulrich Wehler, a pioneer in the study of the Poles of the Ruhr among post-World-War-II German historians, characterizes the ZZP as "Catholic-conservative."[6] Christoph Klessmann, who has written the most comprehensive history of the Poles in the Ruhr region, speaks of "the clerical and nationalist traits of the ZZP."[7] The omissions and misperceptions derive basically from two sources: first of all, the national prism through which we tend to view events both in the past and in the present; and, secondly, stereotypes of rural migrants strongly attached to their traditional religious beliefs.

Nationalism divides as much as it unites. If one is writing about the German labor movement in the Ruhr, a nationalist perspective justifies the exclusion of the Polish trade union from consideration even if it constituted a vital part of the region's labor movement. The distortion that such an approach introduces into our image of the past is increasingly

3. Tadeusz Kotłowski, *Zjednoczenie Zawodowe Polskie: Zasięg wpływów i działalność społeczno-polityczna w latach 1918–1939* (Poznań: Uniwersytet im. Adama Mickiewicza, 1977), p. 21.

4. Eric Hobsbawm, "What is the Workers' Country?" in *Workers: Worlds of Labor*, ed. by Eric Hobsbawm (New York: Pantheon Books, 1984), p. 53.

5. For example, Ullrich Feige, *Bergarbeiterschaft zwischen Tradition und Emanzipation: Das Verhältnis von Bergleuten und Gewerkschaften zu Unternehmern und Staat im westlichen Ruhrgebiet um 1900* (Düsseldorf: Schwann, 1986), and Klaus Schönhoven, "Die Gewerkschaften als Massenbewegung im Wilhelmischen Kaiserreich 1890 bis 1918," in *Geschichte der deutschen Gewerkschaften von den Anfängen bis 1945*, ed. by Ulrich Borsdorf (Cologne: Bund-Verlag, 1987), pp. 167–278, take no note of the ZZP; nor does a study of the town where the ZZP Miners' Union had its headquarters, David F. Crew, *Town in the Ruhr: A Social History of Bochum, 1860–1914* (New York: Columbia University Press, 1979); Gerhard Adelmann, "Die Beziehungen zwischen Arbeitgeber und Arbeitnehmer in der Ruhrindustrie vor 1914," *Jahrbücher für Nationalökonomie und Statistik*, Bd. 175 (1963), p. 422, justifies leaving it out of consideration because "The influence of the Polish Trade Union confined itself to a specific part of the Ruhr region."

6. Hans-Ulrich Wehler, *Sozialdemokratie und Nationalstaat: Die deutsche Sozialdemokratie und die Nationalitätenfragen in Deutschland von Karl Marx bis zum Ausbruch des Ersten Weltkrieges* (Würzburg: Holzner-Verlag, 1962), p. 162.

7. Christoph Klessmann, *Polnische Bergarbeiter im Ruhrgebiet 1870-1945: Soziale Integration und nationale Subkultur einer Minderheit in der deutschen Industriegesellschaft* (Göttingen: Vandenhoeck & Ruprecht, 1978), p. 119.

recognized.[8] The same perspective labels the Polish trade union as "nationalist," which reflects the German point of view.[9] It also reflects contemporary sources: the Prussian authorities categorized the Polish trade union as a nationalist organization, not a trade union, and many German trade unionists felt the same way. To the Polish-speaking migrants, however, the predominantly German trade unions seemed nationalist.

The Polish-speaking miners of the Ruhr migrated primarily from the rural areas of the eastern provinces of Prussia. There they practiced a traditional Roman Catholicism and accepted the authority of the mostly Polish clergy. They kept their religious traditions as they filled the ranks of the Polish trade union in the Ruhr, but this hardly suffices for characterizing the ZZP as "Catholic-conservative" or "clerical." In fact, as we shall see, it merits such descriptions far less than the predominantly German Christian trade union in the Ruhr.

Whatever the reason, the ZZP has yet to receive a thorough treatment covering its entire existence in the Ruhr, from 1902 to 1934, and it is this gap in the historical literature that the present study seeks to fill. Histories of the Polish community in the Ruhr have dealt with the ZZP as one of the most important organizations in the community. But, besides devoting only limited space to the ZZP, these histories mostly take as their main concerns the role an organization played in the creation of a Polish community and how it affected the integration of the Poles into the larger society.[10] A proper assessment of the ZZP as a trade union, however, requires that we view it as such and put it in the context of the labor

8. John R. Gillis, "The Future of European History," *Perspectives: American Historical Association Newsletter*, XXXIV, No. 4 (April 1996), 5, calls for "a renewed interest in Europe's multicultural and multiethnic heritages." Some fifteen years ago, Hobsbawm, "What is the Workers' Country?" p. 49, pointed out the fallacy of assuming the national homogeneity of a working class.

9. Geoff Eley, *From Unification to Nazism: Reinterpreting the German Past* (Boston: Allen & Unwin, 1986), p. 65, poses the question if one can write German history "without replicating the cultural preconceptions of the German nationalist tradition?" Thus, even an English author refers to the ZZP as "nationalist": S.H.F. Hickey, *Workers in Imperial Germany: The Miners of the Ruhr* (Oxford: Clarendon Press, 1985), p. 239.

10. Note the titles and subtitles of three of the major studies of the Poles in the Ruhr region: Jerzy Kozłowski, *Rozwój organizacji społeczno-narodowych wychodźstwa polskiego w Niemczech w latach 1870–1914* [The Development of Social-National Organizations of the Polish Emigration in Germany in the Years 1870–1914] (Wrocław: Ossolineum, 1987); Valentina-Maria Stefanski, *Zum Prozess der Emanzipation und Integration von Aussenseitern: Polnische Arbeitsmigranten im Ruhrgebiet* (Dortmund: Forschungsstelle Ostmitteleuropa an der Universität Dortmund, 1984); Klessmann, *Polnische Bergarbeiter im Ruhrgebiet 1870-1945: Soziale Integration und nationale Subkultur einer Minderheit in der deutschen Industriegesellschaft.*

movement in the Ruhr. Some partial studies of this type exist and have proven invaluable sources of information. None, however, tells the full story, covering with equal justice the pre-war and the post-war periods.[11]

This is more than just a question of telling the whole story from beginning to end. The pre-war and post-war situations of the ZZP differed radically, and it responded to them quite differently. Before the war the union and its members lived entirely under German rule, and even though it united its members on the basis of national solidarity, it put this solidarity at the service of the working-class interests of its members, which meant acting together with the representatives of the German working class. But, when the war resulted in the long-dreamt-of independence of Poland, the ZZP and the Polish community in the Ruhr union proved unable to resist—as many before and after—the *ignis fatuus* of living in their own nation-state.

This study, then, naturally falls into two parts. After a brief account of the creation of a Polish working class in the Ruhr region, the first chapter examines the formation of the Polish Trade Union in 1902 and its first years of development. Chapter 2 focuses on the role of the ZZP in the 1905 strike, a milestone in the acceptance of the Polish union within the labor movement. Whereas Chapter 3 gives an account of the internal history of the ZZP in the years before the strike of 1912, Chapter 4 turns to the union's relations with the region's labor movement before the world war. Thus, the first part necessarily covers some familiar ground, such as the Polish participation in the mass strikes of 1905 and 1912. Nevertheless, it presents new documentation for establishing the character of the ZZP and its success in organizing a major portion of the Polish-speaking miners of the Ruhr region. The argument is that one can see the ZZP primarily as a trade union and as such it formed an integral part of the labor movement in the Ruhr. Its Polish character did not impede its

11. For example, Franciszek Mańkowski, "Historja Z.Z.P.," in *Ćwierć wieku pracy dla Narodu i Robotnika* (Poznań: Nakładem Zarządu Centralnego Zjedn. Zawod. Polskiego, 1927), pp. 34–266; Marjan Chełmikowski, *Związki zawodowe robotników polskich w Królestwie Pruskim (1889–1918)* (Poznań: Fiszer i Majewski, 1925); Christoph Klessmann, "Klassensolidarität und nationales Bewusstsein. Das Verhältnis zwischen der Polnischen Berufsvereinigung (ZZP) und den deutschen Bergarbeiter-Gewerkschaften im Ruhrgebiet 1902–1923," *Internationale Wissenschaftliche Korrespondenz zur Geschichte der deutschen Arbeiterbewegung*, X (1974), 149–178, covers the most important years, but its length does not allow for a thorough examination nor does it exploit some of the most important archival sources for the post-war years. Similarly, Jerzy Kozłowski, "Polnische Berufsvereinigung (ZZP). Einflussbereich und Tätigkeit der polnischen Gewerkschaft in Deutschland 1902–1919," *Fremdarbeiterpolitik des Imperialismus*, XX (1988), 43–52, which notes the absence of "a comprehensive description" of the ZZP before World War I, p. 43.

function as a trade union even if it limited the union's potential membership, much in the same way that the character of the other trade unions limited their appeal.

The second part of this study, dealing with the period after 1914, covers less familiar territory. Even a recent major study of the post-war Polish community in Germany devotes little attention to the ZZP.[12] Moreover, in delineating the history of the ZZP in this period, no one made full use of the documentation of the Polish Ministry of Foreign Affairs in Polish archives, which provide previously unpublished material on the Polish community in the Ruhr and the ZZP.[13] This material throws an essentially different light on the history of the ZZP and the decline of the Polish community in the Ruhr region. After a chapter on the world war, during which the ZZP changed direction, Chapter 6 finds that Polish involvement in the labor movement in the immediate post-war years decreased in comparison with the pre-war years. Finally, Chapter 7 turns our attention to the decline of the Polish community in the Ruhr region and the union's role in that decline, which contributed to its own liquidation.

One might take the post-war history as evidence of an innate contradiction between national and social solidarity, but the conflict between these two ideals arose out of particular circumstances and choices. The real dichotomy lies in the pre-war and post-war history of the ZZP, not in the stars.

---

12. Wojciech Wrzesiński, *Polski ruch narodowy w Niemczech w latach 1922–1939* (Wrocław, Warsaw, Cracow: Zakład Narodowy im. Ossolińskich, 1993).

13. Marian Orzechowski, "Z dziejów polskiego ruchu robotniczego w Nadrenii-Westfalii w latach 1918–1933," mimeographed (Poznań: Instytut Zachodni, 1969), relies on some of this material but interprets it in a tendentious manner.

PART I
National Solidarity in the Interest of the Working Class

1

The Formation of a Polish Trade Union, 1902-1905

A Polish Working Class in the Ruhr

The rapid industrialization of the Ruhr region in the second half of the nineteenth century created a greater demand for labor than the population of the region and the surrounding areas could satisfy. In 1871 this led to the first recruitment of a group of Polish-speaking miners from the eastern provinces of Prussia.[1] In the following decades a stream of Polish-speaking laborers—unlike their forerunners, mostly unskilled agricultural workers—from East and West Prussia, Poznania (Posen), and Upper Silesia flowed to the Ruhr region in rhythm with its economic development. By 1893 about 14 percent of the total work force in the mines of the Ruhr spoke Polish or Masurian—an archaic form of Polish spoken by the predominantly Protestant population in southern East Prussia.[2] In the next two decades, the flow of migrants from the Prussian East flooded the region, cresting in the years 1908 when miners born in the East formed 37.9 percent of the work force in the region's mines and in 1913 when they numbered 139,178.[3]

Although not all migrants from the East spoke Polish as their native language, a study found that in these years the number of Poles in the Ruhr grew faster than that of eastern migrants.[4] An increase in the proportion of miners from the East born in Poznania, the sole Prussian province with a Polish-speaking majority and the center of the Polish national movement in Prussia, testifies to the same effect: from 25 percent

1. "Geschichte einer polnischen Kolonie in der Fremde: Jubiläumsschrift des St. Barbara-Vereins in Bottrop" (Bottrop, 1911), in German translation, *Kirche und Religion im Revier: Beiträge und Quellen zur Geschichte*, Vol. IV (Essen: Sozialinstitut des Bistums Essen, 1968), pp. 3–4.

2. O. Taeglichsbeck, *Die Belegschaft der Bergwerke und Salinen im Oberbergamtsbezirk Dortmund nach der Zahlung vom 16. Dezember 1893*, (2 vols.; Dortmund: Bellman & Middendorf, 1895–96), Vol. II, pp. xiii–xiv.

3. Christoph Klessmann, *Polnische Bergarbeiter im Ruhrgebiet 1870–1945: Soziale Integration und nationale Subkultur einer Minderheit in der deutschen Industriegesellschaft* (Göttingen: Vandenhoeck & Ruprecht, 1978), pp. 265–266.

4. Robert Müllers, "Die Bevölkerungsentwicklung im Rheinisch-Westfälischen Industriegebiet (in der Abgrenzung des Siedlungsverbandes Ruhrkohlenbezirk) von 1895 bis 1919" (Unpublished Ph.D. Dissertation, University of Münster, 1920), p. 107.

in 1893 to 41.9 percent in 1914.[5] In addition, children born in the Ruhr to Polish-speaking migrants constituted nearly a third of the region's Polish-speaking population by 1910, and the males among them frequently entered the mines as they came of age.[6] Thus, on the eve of the world war, Polish-speaking miners in the Ruhr region numbered nearly 100,000 and formed about a quarter of the work force; together with the Masurian-speaking miners, they made up perhaps as much as a third of the work force.[7]

The miners of the Ruhr fought long and hard to establish an enduring trade union organization, finally succeeding in the wake of the 1889 strike with the formation of the Union for the Protection and Advancement of Miners' Interests in the Rhineland and Westphalia, later known as the *Alter Verband* (Old Union).[8] Opposition to an increasingly socialist orientation of the *Alter Verband* led Catholic miners to form an alternate organization in 1894, the *Gewerkverein christlicher Bergarbeiter* (Trade Association of Christian Miners), whose statute declared that "by joining the union, everyone professes himself to be an opponent of social-democratic principles and aims."[9]

Historians of the labor movement see the origins of these trade unions in the miners' extensive network of voluntary associations as well as in the traditions that survived among miners even after a series of laws culminating in the General Mining Law of 1865 abolished their corporate status.[10] "The creation of their own highly-developed network of associations," according to one historian, constitutes "possibly the greatest achievement" of German workers in the period before World War I.[11] These associations of workers "made an essential original contribution to

5. Klessmann, *Polnische Bergarbeiter*, p. 266.

6. *Statistisches Jahrbuch für den Preussischen Staat*, Vol. XI (Berlin: Herausgeben vom Königlich Preussischen Statistischen Landesamt, 1914), pp. 30–31.

7. For a more detailed discussion of the statistical base for this estimate, see John J. Kulczycki, *The Foreign Worker and the German Labor Movement: Xenophobia and Solidarity in the Coal Fields of Ruhr, 1871–1914* (Oxford, Providence, USA: Berg Publishers, 1994), pp. 29–35.

8. Klaus Tenfelde, *Sozialgeschichte der Bergarbeiterschaft an der Ruhr im 19. Jahrhundert* (Bonn-Bad Godesberg: Verlag Neue Gesellschaft GmbH, 1977), pp. 512, 590–591, 596–597.

9. Michael Schneider, "Religion and Labour Organisation: The Christian Trade Unions in the Wilhelmine Empire," *European Studies Review*, XII, No. 3 (1982), 351–352; Heinrich Imbusch, *Arbeitsverhältnisse und Arbeiterorganisationen im deutschen Bergbau* (Essen: Verlag des Gewerkvereins christlicher Bergarbeiter, 1908), p. 716.

10. Tenfelde, *Sozialgeschichte*, pp. 345–396, 482.

11. Gerhard A. Ritter, "Workers' Culture in Imperial Germany: Problems and Points of Departure for Research," *Journal of Contemporary History*, XIII, No. 2 (1978), 172.

the emancipation of the proletariat. By taking part in club activities members learnt to express themselves and accept responsibility," and thus "the clubs were a training ground for workers' leaders." Moreover, such organizations helped in "the formation of common beliefs and patterns of behavior and in particular created their own proletarian code of solidarity in the political and trade union struggle."[12] In the Ruhr, voluntary associations formed by miners adopted some of the symbols and forms of the former corporate body of miners, the *Knappschaft*. For the older miners the new societies replaced the old community they lost, while for the many new miners the traditional rituals "cloaked harsh everyday existence in a semblance of dignity" and offered a substitute for customs they had known in the homeland.[13]

Catholic clergymen played a role in the organization of workers' associations, and miners became involved in the Christian-social movement, with its militant advocacy of a Christian, as opposed to a liberal or socialist, solution to workers' problems. Catholic clergy initiated the transformation of the old miner associations (*Knappenvereine*) in the region of Essen into Christian-social associations at the beginning of 1871. The organization of new Christian workers' associations followed, with miners forming a major part of the membership. Their goals included material as well as religious-moral betterment through educational programs and mutual aid. Although the local priest formally headed such Catholic workers' associations, they elected their own officers. These associations took a prominent part in parish life, with special services on the feast day of the association's patron saint and group participation in the annual Corpus Christi procession. In keeping with old customs, members would march behind their association banner wearing miners' caps and insignia. The associations also often had their own choirs, theatrical groups, and libraries.[14]

Despite the importance that historians of the labor movement in Germany have given to these developments among German workers, they have largely ignored similar developments among the Polish migrants in the Ruhr.[15] The migrants formed their first organization, the "Unity"

12. *Ibid.*, pp. 174–175.

13. Klaus Tenfelde, "Mining Festivals in the Nineteenth Century," *Journal of Contemporary History*, XIII, No. 2 (1978), 395–396.

14. *Ibid.*, pp. 396–397; Tenfelde, *Sozialgeschichte*, pp. 464–470.

15. John J. Kulczycki, "The First Migrants' Miner Associations in the Ruhr," in *Essays in Russian and East European History: Festschrift in Honor of Edward C. Thaden*, ed. by Leo Schelbert and Nick Ceh (Boulder, Colorado: East European Monographs, 1995), pp. 114–115.

(*Jedność*) Educational Association of Polish Workers and Artisans, at the end of 1876 in Dortmund, an important center of Catholic organizational activity.[16] The resemblance in character and practices of this and later Polish associations to the German workers' associations suggests the latter served as a model for the Polish associations. But, if the Polish-speaking workers took the forms of their associations from those of native workers and German-speaking miners, the migrants filled these forms with a content familiar to them from their homeland. They built on the tradition of social gatherings on Sunday afternoons in Polish villages. When they met to sing "old" songs and converse in Polish, they behaved no differently than in the homeland.[17]

Additional Polish-Catholic workers' associations did not form, or at least did not endure, until the 1880s. But, by the end of that decade, they numbered more than a score. Under the influence of Rev. Franciszek Liss, who came to the Ruhr in 1890 to minister spiritually to the Polish migrants, these associations continued to multiply. Moreover, at the end of 1890 Liss founded the first Polish newspaper in the Ruhr, the *Wiarus Polski* (Polish Veteran or Old Polish Soldier), which provided a channel of communication among the migrants and their associations. His activities prompted the Prussian authorities to pressure the Catholic hierarchy to recall Liss from the Ruhr, which he finally left in 1894. Nevertheless, the *Wiarus* continued to build and sustain a Polish community in the Ruhr under the editorship of Jan Brejski, to whom Liss sold the newspaper in 1893, and his younger brother Antoni. Like Liss they also promoted the formation of Polish organizations, so that by 1899 116 Polish-Catholic associations existed in the Ruhr with a combined membership of some 9,500.[18]

The first attempt to unite the Poles of the various communities of the Ruhr in a single organization came shortly after Liss's departure with the creation of the Union of Poles in Germany (*Związek Polaków w Niemczech* or ZPwN), in part to replace the coordination and leadership that Liss had informally provided through his meetings with association

16. Jerzy Kozłowski, *Rozwój organizacji społeczno-narodowych wychodźstwa polskiego w Niemczech w latach 1870–1914* (Wrocław: Ossolineum, 1987), p. 76; Edwin Jared Clark, "Industry, Society, and Politics in the Ruhr: National Liberalism in Dortmund, 1848–1913" (Unpublished Ph.D. Dissertation, University of Illinois at Chicago, 1990), pp. 198–200.

17. Johannes Kaczmarek, "Die polnischen Arbeiter im rheinisch-westfälischen Industriegebiet, eine Studie zum Problem der sozialen Anpassung" (Unpublished Ph.D. Dissertation, Cologne, 1922), pp. 32–33.

18. Kozłowski, *Rozwój*, pp. 133, 140.

chairmen. Jan Brejski together with a bank employee Jan Piłowski and a merchant Jakub Żynda drafted the statutes approved at a meeting on 12 August 1894 on the premises of the *Wiarus* with the participation of about 180 migrants, mostly workers. The first officers included Piłowski, Żynda, Antoni Brejski, and the activist and former miner Hipolit Sibilski as deputy secretary.

According to the statute, "The goal of the Union is unification of Poles living in the German provinces to safeguard their moral and material rights, with the unconditional exclusion of social democratic and similar machinations."[19] A further, though negative, indication of the predominantly working-class audience that the primarily middle-class leaders sought to attract came in the provision that excluded political provocations "as well as attacks against particular social classes."[20] Among specific tasks, the ZPwN promised to provide legal assistance, call public meetings, promote Polish language instruction, and concern itself with obtaining sufficient Polish clergy. At one of its first meetings, the ZPwN designated the *Wiarus* as its official organ.

The ZPwN never achieved the broad membership that its creators had intended. Nevertheless, because its ranks included many officers of Polish associations, it did play an influential role, particularly in its first years. It accomplished this primarily by taking up the demand for Polish clergy, using it to rally and solidify the Polish-speaking Catholic migrants into a united community. The ZPwN contributed to a wave of meetings organized in the following years around this demand, which found expression in the accompanying resolutions, petitions, and protests. For example, about 1,500 people attended a meeting in Bochum on 10 February 1895 and endorsed a petition to the bishop of Paderborn requesting a Polish clergyman.[21]

Liss's departure and the resistance of the Prussian authorities and the Catholic Church to the appointment of Polish clergymen to minister to the migrants contributed to a trend toward secularization of the migrants' organizations first manifested in an assertion of their independence from clerical control. On 27 September 1895 a ZPwN meeting in Bochum

19. The statute is reprinted in German in Hans Jürgen Brandt, ed., *Die Polen und die Kirche im Ruhrgebiet 1871-1919: Ausgewählte Dokumente zur pastoral und kirchlichen Integration sprachlicher Minderheiten im deutschen Kaiserreich*, (Münster: Aschendorff, 1987), pp. 89–92; on the ZPwN generally see, Krystyna Murzynowska, *Polskie wychodźstwo zarobkowe w Zagłębiu Ruhry w latach 1880-1914* (Wrocław: Ossolineum, 1972), pp. 95–103; Klessmann, *Polnische Bergarbeiter*, pp. 101–102; Kozłowski, *Rozwój*, pp. 153–156.

20. Brandt, *Polen*, p. 90.

21. *Ibid.*, pp. 104–105; Murzynowska, *Polskie wychodźstwo*, p. 101.

voted a resolution endorsed by the leaders of 37 Polish-Catholic associations, i.e. a majority of them, that defined their relationship with the clergy:

> Our associations are Catholic through and through. Hence we are glad that the local clergy concern themselves with us and also keep watch that we do not deviate a single step from Catholic principles. To the extent that it is a question of purely religious matters, we promise the clergy unconditional obedience. In every other respect, however, we wish to maintain full freedom and independence of action. This freedom and independence we will not relinquish at any price, and threats or hindrances also cannot move us to subservience. Above all we wish to take care that not only the Catholic but also to the same extent the Polish character of our associations remain as so far explicitly guaranteed. Our associations ought to remain for all time Catholic and Polish.[22]

On 23 February 1896 over a hundred ZPwN activists meeting in Bochum reaffirmed these principles and protested against what they claimed was an attempt to introduce a policy of Germanization into the Church.[23]

Discord over the role of the clergy in the St. Barbara Association of Bottrop led to the formation of a new association in Bottrop under the patronage of St. Hyacinth (Jacek) in June 1897 with an initial membership of sixty-one, mostly young people. According to the memoirs of one member, they quit the St. Barbara Association because they did not want a German cleric as their chairman. He recalled, "We called those from the St. Barbara Association 'bootlickers' for doing what the priest ordered."[24] The new association offered its honorary chairmanship to a priest, but he declined. A religious association without a clerical connection, the St. Hyacinth Association found itself excluded from participation in church services. According to a police report in March 1897, this mistrust of

---

22. The resolution is reprinted in Brandt, *Polen*, pp. 107–108, where the date is given as 27 Oct. 1895, whereas Murzynowska, *Polskie wychodźstwo*, p. 101, and Kozłowski, *Rozwój*, p. 157, give the date as 27 Sept. 1895.

23. Kozłowski, *Rozwój*, p. 157; Hans Jürgen Brandt, "Das Kloster der Redemptoristen in Bochum und die Polenseelsorge im westfaelischen Industriegebiet (1883–1918)," *Spicilegium Historicum Congregationis SSmi Redemptoris*, Jg. XXIII, Fasc. 1 (1975), p. 156.

24. Franciszek Połomski, "Ze wspomnień starego 'Westfaloka'—A. Podeszwy," *Studia Śląskie*, I (1958), 260, literally: "paw-lickers"; on the conflict, see "Geschichte einer polnischen Kolonie," pp. 16–18; Richard Charles Murphy, *Guestworkers in the German Reich: A Polish Community in Wilhelmian Germany* (Boulder, Colorado: East European Monographs, 1983), pp. 150, 152–153.

German clerics was widespread in the Düsseldorf administrative district and impeded the development of Polish-Catholic associations there.[25] German miners' associations went through a phase of clerical domination before evolving towards greater secular leadership and concerns. At the end of the century, a predominantly Catholic labor movement among the Ruhr's coal miners struggled against the efforts of the clergy to maintain its control over the German Catholic workers' associations. Here and elsewhere in Germany, many Catholic priests could not accept the idea of such a movement free of clerical tutelage and therefore opposed the establishment of independent Christian trade unions.[26] Thus a conflict over secularization affected both Polish and German worker organizations.

Most of the Polish-Catholic associations retained their ties with the local parish priests, which meant the German clergy.[27] The religious component of their identity restrained the Polish-speaking migrants from breaking their ties with the Church. But many German Catholic workers "had already found in the workplace, and in their relatively democratic Christian union, a haven from the omnipresent, authoritarian church. They had grown more independent and secular in their thinking, cherishing private religious feelings and beliefs but alienated from the organization of the church."[28] So, too, for at least some Polish-speaking migrants, the national component of their identity made them sensitive to claims of clerical authority over their associations made by German priests.

Late in 1897 Polish activists in the Ruhr formed a second organization that sought to encompass all of the Poles of the Ruhr by establishing a separate Polish electoral organization for the region on the model of one existing in Prussian Poland since 1893. With a statute drawn up by the Brejski brothers, the Main Polish Electoral Committee for Westphalia, the Rhineland, and Neighboring Provinces early in 1898 set up a network of county and communal electoral committees at meetings held in Polish-speaking population centers throughout the Ruhr in preparation for the approaching Reichstag elections. Although after the election the Polish electoral committees deactivated until the next election, their creation marked another milestone in the organizational development of the Polish community in the Ruhr. Even such a temporary episode could not help but

25. Klessmann, *Polnische Bergarbeiter*, p. 225.

26. Tenfelde, *Sozialgeschichte*, pp. 361–362; Eric Dorn Brose, *Christian Labor and the Politics of Frustration in Imperial Germany* (Washington, D.C.: The Catholic University of America Press, 1985), pp. 108–109, 127, 129, 131.

27. Klessmann, *Polnische Bergarbeiter*, pp. 96–97.

28. Brose, *Christian Labor*, p. 155.

raise the political consciousness of the community and contribute to its solidarity and integration by demonstrating the possibility of common action on behalf of common goals.[29] Further organizational diversification in the Polish community came at the local level. Choral groups initially formed within the Polish-Catholic associations, at first singing religious hymns and then folk and Polish patriotic songs. These choral groups and even a band provided entertainment at association meetings and celebrations. In 1894 the miner and Polish activist Jan Wilkowski and his brother founded the first independent choral organization, "Lute," in Gelsenkirchen. That same year, at the end of August, the *Wiarus Polski* printed a model statute for choral associations, encouraging others to follow the example of "Lute." By mid-1899 the "Violet" glee club in Bruch had 113 members and its own library and banner. That year the practice began of holding congresses in various locales for the choral groups of the area with singing contests and prizes.[30]

The choral groups illustrated the progress of secularization in the Polish community as they evolved from being part of religious associations into independent organizations and added secular music to religious. At the same time, they increasingly emphasized their national identity, and not only in their choice of music. Initially, they had to rely on Germans as music directors, but gradually self-taught Polish musicians replaced them.[31] In his memoirs, one Polish miner told how he conducted three glee clubs in and around Bottrop and in 1897 formed an "orchestra." He recalled how with the choral groups he liked to slip in selections from a collection of Polish patriotic songs among the religious hymns. For his "orchestra," he ordered special traditional Polish folk caps from Poznań.[32]

Just before the end of the 1890s another type of Polish organization, the gymnastic club, arrived in the Ruhr. Polish gymnastic associations first appeared in Austrian Poland in the 1860s, inspired by the Czech example from which they took the name *Sokół* (Falcon). From there they did not spread to Prussian Poland until the latter half of the 1880s, where in 1893 they formed the Union Falcons of Great Poland. In Great Poland or Poznania, the membership had an overwhelmingly artisan and urban

29. Kozłowski, *Rozwój*, pp. 159–161; Klessmann, *Polnische Bergarbeiter*, p. 125.

30. Anastazy Nadolny, "Polskie duszpasterstwo w Zagłębiu Ruhry (1871–1894)," *Studia Pelplinskie* (1981), pp. 285–286; Kozłowski, *Rozwój*, p. 204.

31. Stanisław Wachowiak, *Polacy w Nadrenii i Westfalii* (Poznań: Nakładem Zjednoczenia Zawodowego Polskiego, 1917), p. 102; Kaczmarek, "Polnischen Arbeiter," pp. 35–36.

32. Połomski, "Ze wspomnień," p. 261.

middle-class character, which may explain why it did not spread quickly to the Ruhr, whose Polish-speaking migrants came mainly from rural areas. Only in April 1899 did the Ruhr's first Falcon Association come into existence in Oberhausen, founded by a miner Andrzej Zielinski, who was chosen its first chairman. Apparently only his membership in the *Alter Verband* led the Prussian authorities to label him a "social democrat." According to the statutes, "Politics and religion as well as public affairs will not be discussed in the Association."[33]

Choral societies and gymnastic associations had formed part of the social structure of German workers since the 1860s. Within this structure, shielded from the threatening forces of the outside world, they found an environment in which they could engage in purposeful social activity centered around their own interests and concerns, which included adaptation to the industrial world and the struggle to earn a living in the new economic conditions resulting from the changes in the mining industry after the middle of the nineteenth century. In concrete terms, the associations served as mutual aid societies, but more generally they also schooled the miners in self-government and organization. Elections of officers and decisions on financial matters could lead to heated disputes but also afforded the opportunity for direct participation that hardly existed for workers elsewhere in German society. Here members could learn practical lessons in the observance of rules and organizational discipline. Despite police surveillance and clerical direction, the associations in addition became a forum for a relatively free exchange of views in a friendly atmosphere, which contributed to the development of individual and collective consciousness. It was in this soil that the miners' trade union movement germinated.[34]

---

33. Diethelm Blecking, *Die Geschichte der nationalpolnischen Turnorganisation "Sokół" im Deutschen Reich 1884-1939* (Dortmund: Forschungsstelle Ostmitteleuropa an der Universität Dortmund, 1987) pp. 42, 72-75, 87-89.

34. Dieter Dowe, "The Workingmen's Choral Movement in Germany before the First World War," *Journal of Contemporary History*, XIII, No. 2 (1978), 269, 272-275; Volker Schmidtchen, "Arbeitersport - Erziehung zum sozialistischen Menschen? Leitwerte und Jugendarbeit in zwei Ruhrgebietsvereinen in der Weimarer Republik," in *Fabrik, Familie, Feierabend: Beiträge zur Sozialgeschichte des Alltags im Industriezeitalter*, ed. by Jürgen Reulecke and Wolfhard Weber (Wuppertal: Peter Hammer Verlag, 1978), pp. 349, 352, 354; Günther Herre, "Arbeitersport, Arbeiterjugend und Obrigkeitsstaat 1893 bis 1914," in *Sozialgeschichte der Freizeit. Untersuchungen zum Wandel der Alltagskultur in Deutschland*, ed. by Gerhard Huck (Wuppertal: Peter Hammer Verlag, 1980), pp. 189-194; Klaus Tenfelde, "Bergmännisches Vereinswesen im Ruhrgebiet während der Industrialisierung," in *Fabrik, Familie, Feierabend: Beiträge zur Sozialgeschichte des Alltags im Industriezeitalter*, ed. by Jürgen Reulecke and Wolfhard Weber (Wuppertal: Peter Hammer Verlag, 1978), pp. 315, 317, 318, 323, 327, 338-339.

The Polish-Catholic associations and the other increasingly diverse secular Polish organizations had a similar influence on the migrant. Developing later, they borrowed elements from the German miners' associations, even without comprehending the traditions that stood behind them, and domesticated them by filling alien forms with a content meaningful to the migrant from his homeland.[35] Thus both his working-class status and his origins marked the character of his associations. Yet they served the same functions as the German associations. The Polish-speaking migrant, coming in the main from agricultural employment, had to make an even greater adjustment to a new world of labor in a foreign environment. Often arriving as a single individual without kith or kin, he faced even greater isolation and insecurity than the miner shorn of his traditional corporate status and privileges.[36] Used to the agricultural world's seasonal rhythms and work from dawn to dusk, the migrant even had to learn how to spend his time to satisfy the need for diversion and social contact. But, from his associations, he could also learn to express and pursue his interests in a collective effort. Because of the friction that developed with at least some of the clergy, Polish-Catholic workers' associations may have developed even greater autonomy than their German counterparts.[37] In any case, by the beginning of the twentieth century, a Polish trade union had the soil in which it too could germinate and find nourishment for growth.

German social democrats created a network of institutions that some argue isolated the workers who joined within a tightly enclosed "class-conscious Social Democratic sub-culture," which strengthened the intransigence of the Social Democratic Party (SPD) and yet afforded inner satisfaction to many workers and helped them to bear exclusion from bourgeois society and treatment as second-class citizens.[38] The SPD's socio-cultural apparatus rendered its working-class constituency impermeable to the surrounding society. As the movement grew, its

---

35. Tenfelde, "Bergmännisches Vereinswesen," p. 329, notes the borrowings; Tenfelde, "Mining Festivals," p. 400, says that they took "very distorted forms."

36. Marcin Bugzel, "Wspomnienia starego emigranta," in *Pamiętniki emigrantów 1878–1958* (Warsaw: Czytelnik, 1960), p. 21, related how at the age of sixteen he left his home in Poznania penniless, worked his way across Germany to Westphalia for three months, and took a job at a mine in a town where he knew no one.

37. Tenfelde, "Bergmännisches Vereinswesen," p. 338, discusses the strength of clerical influence over the associations.

38. Günther Roth, *The Social Democrats in Imperial Germany: A Study of Working-Class Isolation and National Integration* (Totowa, N.J.: Bedminster Press, 1963), p. 315; Ritter, "Workers' Culture," p. 167.

organizations came "to include almost the whole of social life."[39] The SPD politicized everyday life and emphasized the centrality of class to all aspects of the lives of workers, thereby reinforcing their identity with their class. It formed a working class with a shared political outlook, culture, and goals.[40] The Polish movement in the Ruhr performed an analogous function in creating a nationally conscious yet working-class sub-culture. It, too, politicized daily life, as in the demand for Polish pastoral care. It fostered the migrants' identification with the Polish nation by emphasizing the centrality of nationality to all aspects of their lives, which the discrimination and suspicion that they encountered seemed to confirm. By providing a crucible of shared experiences, it also created a working class. The assimilation of the migrants in the Ruhr to the Polish nation contributed to the process. Identification with the Polish nation gave the migrants a long history of political repression to harken back to—like the English working class.[41] The national and social characteristics need not be antithetical. Rather, in the Ruhr the Polish nation and the Polish working class were virtually identical. If the process further divided the workers in the Ruhr, the division already existed and the Polish associations merely enfranchised the dispossessed and gave them a home.[42] The associations integrated migrants from various regions giving them a more broadly based identity. This identity had a rich tradition of resisting oppression. Thus the associations also provided the migrants with the organizations as well as the symbols to combat exploitation and inequality.[43] Yet, in the early twentieth century, a notable gap in their growing sub-culture remained: an expression of their existence as a working class in its relations with their employers.

39. Richard J. Evans, "Introduction: the Sociological Interpretation of German Labour History," in *The German Working Class 1888–1933: The Politics of Everyday Life*, ed. by Richard J. Evans (London: Croom Helm, 1982), p. 19.

40. Geoff Eley, *From Unification to Nazism: Reinterpreting the German Past* (Boston: Allen & Unwin, 1986), p. 183

41. E.P. Thompson, *The Making of the English Working Class* (New York: Vintage, 1966), pp. 198–199, sees the simultaneous intensification of economic exploitation and political oppression as part of the explanation of the formation of the English working class.

42. See Tenfelde, "Bergmännisches Vereinswesen," p. 344, on the question of associations dividing miners. For a theoretical consideration of the combination of national and social consciousness among migrant workers, see Józef Chlebowczyk, *On Small and Young Nations in Europe: Nation-Forming Processes in Ethnic Borderlands in East-Central Europe* (Wrocław: Ossolineum, 1980), pp. 196, 201–203.

43. See Anthony D. Smith, *The Ethnic Revival* (Cambridge: Cambridge University Press, 1981), p. 153, on immigrant ethnic groups.

The Origins of the Polish Trade Union

The roots of the Polish trade union in the Ruhr, the *Zjednoczenie Zawodowe Polskie* (Polish Trade Union) or ZZP, lie in the working-class character of the Polish community in the Ruhr and the community's organizational development before the turn of the century. When in 1919 a clerical activist among Polish-Catholic associations asked the head of the ZZP about the union's attitude toward these associations, he replied that such organizations had existed among migrants in Germany since 1877 and gave birth to all other migrant organizations: "the leaders of the ZZP also drew their first lessons from these associations. All the leaders of the ZZP belonged to these associations and even were their leaders."[44] In fact, the first chairman of the ZZP, Stefan Rejer, had served at different times as chairman and deputy chairman of the Polish-Catholic St. Joseph Association in Wattenscheid. Another future official of the union, Jan Korpus, had been chairman of the Polish-Catholic St. Francis Association in Riemke.[45] One Polish migrant, who worked initially at a mine in Herne, reported that he joined a Polish gymnastic association there in 1903, becoming one of the movement's leaders, and that he was also a "co-organizer of the Polish Trade Union"—presumably meaning the local in Herne, for which he long served as union steward.[46]

The migrants formed their own Polish trade union in part for the same reasons that they formed other organizations separate from German organizations. Jan Brejski, who played a leading role in the creation of the ZZP, later gave a moral sheen to the natural tendency to associate with others that one identifies with when he stated, "We will go hand in hand with non-Polish workers and their organizations—as equals with equals in the struggle for an improvement in material existence, but we do not think of drowning in alien unions, because they would threaten us with the loss

44. Franciszek Mańkowski, "Historja Z.Z.P.," in *Ćwierć wieku pracy dla Narodu i Robotnika* (Poznań: Nakładem Zarządu Centralnego Zjedn. Zawod. Polskiego, 1927), p. 177.

45. WP, No. 138, 18 Nov. 1899, in German translation, *Gesammtüberblick über die polnische Tagesliteratur* (hereafter cited as *Gesammtüberblick*), VIII, No. 47, 27 Nov. 1899, p. 735; Brandt, *Polen*, p. 108.

46. "Lebenlauf des Sokolturners Ignacy Bereszyński," reprinted in Blecking, *Geschichte*, p. 252.

of moral values inherited from our ancestors, that is, our national and religious ideals."[47] The impulse for the creation of a Polish trade union came from a souring of relations between Polish-speaking and German coal miners, particularly as manifested in the attitudes and actions of the trade unions that already existed in the Ruhr as the Polish-speaking migrants flooded the region in the 1890s.[48] If the socialist orientation of the *Alter Verband* turned the traditionally Catholic leadership of the Polish community against it, the Christian character of the *Gewerkverein* boded well for Polish participation. Less than two weeks after the first general meeting of the *Gewerkverein* in 1894, the *Wiarus Polski* commented favorably on its creation.[49] In December 1897, the *Wiarus* warned Polish miners not to join the *Alter Verband* and instead suggested, "Whoever wants by all means to belong to a miner's organization that in fact tries to improve the lot of the miner, he can join the *Gewerkverein christlicher Bergarbeiter Deutschlands.*"[50]

Both of the existing miners' unions, however, reflected the antipathy of their overwhelming German membership to the "foreign migrants," whom German workers stereotyped as "strikebreakers," "wage-cutters," and "rate-busters," and who in any case represented an identifiable group of competitors. In addition, the Prussian authorities and union leaders tended to blame the migrants for a variety of ills associated with the rapid industrialization of the Ruhr, from an increase in mining accidents to the spread of diseases.[51] Union leaders, who regarded the "foreign migrants"

47. Jan Brejski, "Dlaczego powstało 'Zjednoczenie Zawodowe Polskie?'—Bo chciał tego lud polski," in *Ćwierć wieku pracy dla Narodu i Robotnika* (Poznań: Nakładem Zarządu Centralnego Zjedn. Zawod. Polskiego, 1927), p. 514. Similarly, Franciszek Mańkowski, "Związki zawodowe na wychództwie," *Pamiętnik wystawy przemysłowej w Bochum od 19–27 lipca 1913 roku* (Oberhausen: Nakładem Komitetu Wystawowego, n.d. [1913]), p. 30, gives as reasons for forming a Polish trade union that German unions "not only expose Poles to the loss of virtues and customs nursed in numerous Polish associations, but also do not bring Poles the least advantage, because the German unions would have the Poles only as a reserve for paying dues."
48. On the relationship between the migrants and the unions before the creation of the ZZP, see Kulczycki, *Foreign Worker*, pp. 82–93, 147–153; John J. Kulczycki, "Nationalism over Class Solidarity: The German Trade Unions and Polish Coal Miners in the Ruhr to 1902," *Canadian Review of Studies in Nationalism*, XIV, No. 2 (1987), 261–276.
49. Murzynowska, *Polskie wychódźtwo*, p. 140.
50. Reprinted in German translation, Brandt, *Polen*, p. 134.
51. John J. Kulczycki, "Scapegoating the Foreign Worker: Job Turnover, Accidents, and Diseases among Polish Coal Miners in the German Ruhr, 1871–1914," in *The Politics of Immigrant Workers: Labor Activism and Migration in the World Economy Since 1830*, ed. by Camille Guerin-Gonzales and Carl Strikwerda (New York: Holmes & Meier, 1993), pp. 133–152.

as having a low capacity for organization, despite the growing network of organizations in the Polish community in the Ruhr, also made an inadequate effort to reach the Polish-speaking miners in their native language.

After World War I the last chairman of the ZZP, Franciszek Kołpacki, attributed its formation to the refusal of the German unions to satisfy the wishes of Polish members in appointments to union positions or in the use of the Polish language in union publications and meetings. As he summed it up, "the Polish worker had been treated by the German unions in a step-mother-like fashion."[52] This partisan view recently found confirmation in a scholarly assessment of the leader of the *Gewerkverein*, August Brust, whose "greatest blunder was undoubtedly his mishandling of the significant Polish-Catholic minority in the *Gewerkverein*."[53]

Tensions between the unions and the Polish community came to a head over a series of specific issues at the end of the 1890s. In 1898 the *Gewerkverein* and the *Wiarus Polski* quarreled over the number of Polish miners the union would nominate for election as "elders" or officers of the miners' pension and insurance fund (*Allgemeiner Knappschaftsverein*): in the end, the Christian union nominated no Polish candidates.[54]

The next year the Prussian Royal Superior Mining Office (*Oberbergamt*) of Dortmund, which oversaw the mines of the Ruhr, issued an ordinance that mandated a knowledge of German for employment in the mines, including an ability to "speak German and read it in script and in print" to qualify for a dozen specified supervisory and technical positions, even that of head of a mining team, which could

---

52. Quoted in Kaczmarek, "Polnischen Arbeiter," p. 40; Franciszek Kołpacki, "Polnische Berufsvereinigung," *Internationales Handwörterbuch des Gewerkschaftswesens* (Berlin: 1932), II, 1274, reprinted in *Arbeitsmaterialien des XIX. Betriebsräteseminars an der Ruhr-Universität Bochum zum Thema: "Ausländer, Gastarbeiter: Integrationsprobleme und ihre Lösungsansätze in historischer und Aktueller Perspektive"* (Bochum: Ruhr-Universität Bochum and Industriegewerkschaft Metall 1985), p. 23, reiterated this view; Mańkowski, "Związki," p. 30, claims that a Polish union would not have been organized so soon "if the German unions had at that time overcome German pride and treated the Poles impartially"; Christoph Klessmann, "Klassensolidarität und nationales Bewusstsein. Das Verhältnis zwischen der Polnischen Berufsvereinigung (ZZP) und den deutschen Bergarbeiter-Gewerkschaften im Ruhrgebiet 1902–1923," *Internationale Wissenschaftliche Korrespondenz zur Geschichte der deutschen Arbeiterbewegung*, X (1974), 149, 152, 159, questions the validity of this view; for an argument to the contrary, see Kulczycki, "Nationalism," pp. 261–276.

53. Brose, *Christian Labor*, p. 175.

54. Kulczycki, *Foreign Worker*, pp. 85–86.

consist of as few as three or four members.[55] Prussian officials thought that such an ordinance would discourage Polish-speaking migrants from remaining in the Ruhr. Because the ordinance left the testing of German language ability to mine management, it gave management an additional tool for disciplining Polish-speaking migrants. Nevertheless, both the *Alter Verband* and the *Gewerkverein* welcomed the ordinance.[56]

A third blow to the relations between the Polish community in the Ruhr and the trade unions came in their reaction to a strike that broke out among predominantly young, Polish-speaking miners at mines in the vicinity of Herne in June of 1899. Police repression quickly led to violence on the part of strikers and their supporters. But, despite a similarity to earlier strikes, including the strike of 1889 that gave birth to the *Alter Verband*, the strike did not win the support of most of the older, German miners. Moreover, the unions took the line of the Prussian authorities and mine management in characterizing it as a "Polish riot" and used the occasion to repeat all of the negative stereotypes of the Polish-speaking migrant.[57]

Jan Brejski testified to the impact of this event when, more than a quarter of a century later, he spoke of the "wildcat strike in Herne" as the "immediate cause that hastened the founding" of the ZZP.[58] The conflict probably contributed to the *Gewerkverein*'s decline in membership in 1899, its first since its founding in 1894.[59] If the Polish-speaking miners

55. STAM, RA I, Nr. 149, *Górnik*, No. 32, 1898, in German translation; Imbusch, *Arbeitsverhältnisse*, pp. 506–507.

56. Kulczycki, *Foreign Worker*, pp. 90–93.

57. *Ibid.*, pp. 105–153; John J. Kulczycki, "The Herne 'Polish Revolt' of 1899: Social and National Consciousness among Polish Coal Miners in the Ruhr," *Canadian Slavonic Papers*, XXXI, No. 2 (1989), 146–169.

58. Brejski, "Dlaczego," p. 514; Marjan Chełmikowski, *Związki zawodowe robotników polskich w Królestwie Pruskim (1889–1918)* (Poznań: Fiszer i Majewski, 1925), p. 83, dates the movement for a Polish trade union in the Ruhr from a Polish protest meeting against the 1899 language ordinance on 5 March 1899. That the ZZP should owe its origin to a failed strike reflects a common pattern in the history of trade unions: "In sum, workers first expressed their grievances through strikes because this allowed the most immediate and spontaneous protest. As they gained experience and realized how much organization was needed to maintain a successful strike they formed unions or joined existing unions to protect their ability to strike," Peter N. Stearns, "The European Labor Movement and the Working Classes, 1890–1914," in *The European Labor Movement, the Working Classes and the Origins of Social Democracy, 1890–1914* by Harvey Mitchell and Peter N. Stearns (Itasca, Illinois: F.E. Peacock Publishers, Inc., 1971), p. 165.

59. Ullrich Feige, *Bergarbeiterschaft zwischen Tradition und Emanzipation: Das Verhältnis von Bergleuten und Gewerkschaften zu Unternehmern und Staat im westlichen Ruhrgebiet um 1900* (Düsseldorf: Schwann, 1986), pp. 52–53, suggests Poles left the union because of the lack of a Polish-language union organ but made no mention of the Herne strike.

could not look to the German trade unions to defend their economic and occupational interests, then they would have to form their own union.

According to one source, activists among Polish miners, especially Franciszek Mańkowski as well as others who later became prominent in the ZZP, began to discuss the possibility of forming their own union at least as early as 1899.[60] Mańkowski himself in 1913 wrote of such discussions among "loyal and right-thinking leaders of Polish workers" but later credited the Brejski brothers with taking the initiative by convening secret conferences of worker-activists and other leaders of Polish associations beginning in 1900 to discuss the need for a Polish trade union.[61] Michał Lengowski, at the time a miner and an officer in Polish associations in Schalke, recalled more than half a century later that Antoni Brejski invited him and five others to three private meetings to discuss the formation of a Polish trade union.[62]

Certainly, the Brejskis' influence in the Polish community of the Ruhr, particularly through their control of the *Wiarus Polski*, meant no such initiative could have succeeded without their support. But an emphasis on the role of the Brejskis at the expense of that of worker-activists like Mańkowski results in a view that sees the ZZP more as a Polish nationalist organization than a trade union, a view taken by the Prussian authorities and the German unions.[63] According to Mańkowski, he and other worker-activists attached great importance to the union movement and saw the need to educate Polish workers about it in the language they

---

60. Andrzej Wachowiak, "Wspomnienia z polskiej, robotniczej emigracji do Westfalii i Nadrenii oraz do Francji z konca XIX i początku XX wieku" (Typed manuscript, 1965), p. 26, Wspomnienie No. 839, Zakład Historii i Teorii Ruchu Zawodowego, Centrum Studiów Związków Zawodowych, Ogólnopolskie Porozumienie Związków Zawodowych, Warsaw; although he was too young at the time to recall these events as an eyewitness and Mańkowski was his hero, his later involvement in the ZZP and his close relationship with its early leaders suggest that his account be given some weight. The same is true of the account of his brother, Stanisław Wachowiak, *Czasy, które przeżyłem: Wspomnienia z lat 1890–1939* (Warsaw: Czytelnik, 1983), p. 17, which in a reference to the founding of the ZZP mentions only Mańkowski, not the Brejski brothers.

61. Mańkowski, "Związki," p. 30; Mańkowski, "Historja," pp. 52–53; see also Franciszek Kołpacki, "Zjednoczenie Zawodowe Polskie we Westfalji (w Niemczech)," in *Ćwierć wieku pracy dla Narodu i Robotnika* (Poznań: Nakładem Zarządu Centralnego Zjedn. Zawod. Polskiego, 1927), p. 483.

62. Władysław Gębik, *Pod warmińskim niebem (O Michale Lengowskim)* (Warsaw: Ludowa Spółdzielnia Wydawnicza, 1974), pp. 76–77.

63. Chełmikowski, *Związki*, p. 91; Klessmann, "Klassensolidarität," pp. 150–152, emphasizes the role of Jan Brejski as well as the union's nationalist intent; Wachowiak, "Wspomnienia," p. 35, argued for Mańkowski's independence in his relations with Jan Brejski.

understood best.[64] Such considerations and the events of 1898 and 1899 seem sufficient to have stimulated worker-activists to take steps toward creating a Polish union.

The initial public signs of movement toward the formation of a Polish trade union came in the fall of 1900. In Oberhausen on 14 October 1900, at the first of a series of meetings organized by the Union of Poles (ZPwN), Jan Brejski argued that German trade unions, including the *Gewerkverein*, were not for Poles. According to him, all the benefits that these organizations offered Poles could find in their own associations. He announced that the ZPwN would create a trade union division "within its bosom," particularly for miners and metalworkers, as well as a legal aid and information bureau so that no one would any longer have an excuse for joining a German union.[65]

Meanwhile, the dispute between the *Gewerkverein* and the *Wiarus* found its bitterest expression yet, once again over the election of pension fund elders. When the Poles in Bruch chose their own candidates, the Christian union's journal *Bergknappe* snapped,

> If these [Polish-speaking migrants] want to separate themselves, then let them go, and we will also ruthlessly oppose them at every turn. We know well where the Poles are heading. One would also like to have the pension fund statute [*Knappschaftsstatut*] printed in Polish; nevertheless, that will still remain a beautiful wish for a long time. One should after all finally learn to adapt oneself to the conditions as they are in the industrial region.[66]

The *Wiarus* responded with an editorial entitled, "The *Gewerkverein* and the *Alter Verband*, Two Enemies of the Polish Miners," which concluded that the Polish miners of the Ruhr very much needed their own separate organization.[67]

A campaign promoting the idea of a Polish trade union conducted in the *Wiarus* and at public meetings continued for the next two years. For example, at a meeting in Gelsenkirchen on 29 June 1901, the miner and musician Jan Wilkowski, who later became a vice-chairman of the new Polish union, gave a long speech in which he denounced the

64. Mańkowski, "Związki," p. 30.

65. STAM, OBAD 883, *Uebersetzungen aus dem "Wiarus Polski*," WP, No. 124, 18 Oct. 1900.

66. Quoted by WP, No. 141, 27 Nov. 1900, in *ibid.*; also quoted by Murzynowska, *Polskie wychodźstwo*, pp. 140–141.

67. STAM, OBAD 883, *Uebersetzungen aus dem "Wiarus Polski*," WP, No. 141, 27 Nov. 1900.

discriminatory treatment of Polish workers and asked those assembled to approve a letter of protest to the ministry in Berlin. Antoni Brejski then spoke in the same vein. In the ensuing discussion, Wilkowski called for the formation of a Polish miners' organization, and others criticized the existing two main miners' unions. As Wilkowski put it, whoever gives a penny to the two unions cheats his own pocket; instead, he urged, all should join the Union of Poles.[68]

At a meeting on 6 October 1901 in Bruch, prior to a speech by Antoni Brejski on the Polish community's demand for Polish clergy, the chairman of the meeting announced that the ZPwN would open a legal aid bureau probably by the first of the year. Claiming that the two main German unions had lost the confidence of the Poles, he stated that nothing remained for them but to organize themselves, and, to this end, the *Wiarus* published the biweekly supplement *Głos Górników i Hutników* (Miners' and Metalworkers' Voice), and all should join the ZPwN.[69] Finally, at the beginning of February 1902 the *Wiarus* announced the establishment of a trade union division for miners within the Union of Poles; by August so many were coming to the office of the *Wiarus* for advice at all hours that regular office hours had to be established.[70]

Yet a Polish trade union in the Ruhr faced a number of obstacles, including the indifference of many of the migrants: only 30 out of 336 attending the meeting in Gelsenkirchen in 1901 at which Wilkowski spoke of the need for a Polish union cared enough to stay till the meeting's conclusion.[71] "The older Polish workers, before they had come here, had never heard of trade unions. The younger generation was of course raised in the middle of the social movement but held back because this movement had a social democratic character ascribed to it, and the Poles sought to keep it at a distance," according to Mańkowski.[72] In Poznania the Polish national movement, with its upper- and middle-class leadership and growing middle-class constituency, opposed class conflict. "The Polish press...considered the protection of wage interests materialism or socialism."[73] Furthermore, "an independent workers' movement,

68. STAM, OP 2748, Bd. 4, ff. 79–80, Polizei-Verwaltung, Gelsenkirchen, 1 July 1901.

69. *Ibid.*, f. 112, RPM, 16 Oct. 1901.

70. STAM, OBAD 883, *Uebersetzungen aus dem "Wiarus Polski,"* WP, No. 14, 1 Feb. 1902, No. 108, 5 Aug. 1902.

71. STAM, OP 2748, Bd. 4, ff. 79–80, Polizei-Verwaltung, Gelsenkirchen, 1 July 1901.

72. Franciszek Mańkowski, "Geschichte der polnischen Verbände," *Kalendarz Górniczy*, 1913, in German translation, STAM, RM VII, Nr. 36c, p. 111; Kaczmarek, "Polnischen Arbeiter," p. 38, quotes a somewhat different translation.

73. Mańkowski, "Geschichte," STAM, RM VII, Nr. 36c, p. 111.

escaping out from under the patronage of the clergy, smelled somewhat of socialism," at a time when some members of the German Catholic hierarchy, including the chairman of the Prussian Bishops' Conference, Georg Cardinal Kopp, whose diocese encompassed Upper Silesia, still opposed even Christian trade unions.[74] Also, the existing local Polish-Catholic workers' associations in the Ruhr generally continued the practice of choosing clergymen as at least titular or honorary chairmen. The creation of a Polish union in defense of its members' material interests without clerical leadership required careful preparation.

Although some historians have concluded that Polish activists initially aimed at transforming the already established Union of Poles into a trade union, the strategy they followed seems to have been more cunning than that.[75] Less than three months prior to the creation of the ZZP, when plans must have been well under way, *Wiarus* denied the claims of *Gewerkverein* leader Brust that the Poles were building a union and asserted that so far there only existed a trade union commission in the ZPwN.[76] But evidence suggests that the Brejskis and the worker-activists early recognized the need for a separate organization that would have a strictly working-class character, led by and for workers, unlike the Union of Poles, with its middle-class officers and efforts to encompass the entire Polish community in the Ruhr.[77] This departure from the established model of Polish organizations together with the obstacles noted above dictated the more than two years of preparations, which included the creation of a division for miners within the Union of Poles as an intermediary step, with its members constituting the great majority of early members of the ZZP.[78]

By the beginning of the twentieth century, thousands of German workers had joined Christian trade unions "in part to protect and promote their economic interests, in part to eschew the perceived religious abuses of the socialist union."[79] Despite the attacks on the *Gewerkverein* by the *Wiarus* and Polish activists, the German Christian union still counted

74. Quote, Chełmikowski, *Związki*, p. 83; on Kopp, see Brose, *Christian Labor*, pp. 147–149.

75. Murzynowska, *Polskie wychodźstwo*, pp. 141–142; Klessmann, *Polnische Bergarbeiter*, p. 110.

76. STAM, OBAD 883, *Uebersetzungen aus dem "Wiarus Polski,"* WP, No. 122, 21 Aug. 1902.

77. Mańkowski, "Historja," p. 53.

78. On the early membership of the ZZP, see Klessmann, *Polnische Bergarbeiter*, p. 110.

79. Brose, *Christian Labor*, p. 155.

among its members a large number of Polish-speaking miners, including even some leaders of local Polish-Catholic associations.[80] Many Polish-speaking migrants continued to accept the leadership of the German Catholic *Zentrum* Party, which since the end of the 1890s had moved closer to the Christian trade unions, and therefore the promoters of a Polish trade union moved slowly and covertly also out of a fear that most Polish workers would not understand the need to go beyond the existing national organizations into the sphere of the *Gewerkverein*.[81]

Moreover, in response to the preparations for the creation of a Polish trade union, both the *Gewerkverein* and the *Alter Verband* intensified their efforts to recruit Poles. Nevertheless, the German unions and their members exhibited no change in their underlying antagonism toward the Polish-speaking migrants from the East.

After the *Alter Verband* leader Otto Hue reported on the Poles in the Ruhr at a district conference of the SPD in western Westphalia in 1901, it passed a resolution calling on the party "to practice the widest possible tolerance toward the Polish workers living here and possibly to support Polish local organizations, in so far as they stand on the ground of the program of the Social Democratic Party and limit their separateness to the use of the Polish language."[82] If support explicitly required subordination, suggesting suspicion of the aims of Polish socialists, the condition reflected a break in relations between the SPD and the Polish Socialist Party of Prussian Poland (PPS). At a party conference in Lübeck in 1901 the SPD leadership justified the discontinuation of financial assistance for the journal of the PPS *Gazeta Robotnicza* (Workers' Gazette) despite the recognition of the need to overcome the language barrier "to make enlightenment about their class position accessible also to the Polish workers." As for "tolerance toward Polish workers," the report to the conference repeated the stereotype of their being "used by German entrepreneurs from time immemorial as wage-cutters, especially in the Ruhr region."[83]

---

80. Wachowiak, "Wspomnienia," p. 42; Mańkowski, "Historja," p. 51.

81. Mańkowski, "Geschichte," STAM, RM VII, Nr. 36c, p. 111; Kołpacki, "Zjednoczenie," p. 484; Brose, *Christian Labor*, pp. 168–169.

82. *Vorwärts*, 30 Nov. 1901, supplement, quoted by Klessmann, *Polnische Bergarbeiter*, pp. 118–119.

83. Wilhelm Schröder, ed., *Handbuch der sozialdemokratischen Parteitage von 1863 bis 1909* (Munich: G. Birk & Co.m.b.H., 1910), pp. 427–428; on the SPD-PPS split, see Hans-Ulrich Wehler, *Sozialdemokratie und Nationalstaat: Die deutsche Sozialdemokratie und die Nationalitätenfragen in Deutschland von Karl Marx bis zum Ausbruch des Ersten Weltkrieges* (Würzburg: Holzner-Verlag, 1962), pp. 161–163.

Such views posed a direct threat to the interests of Polish-speaking miners when the demand for coal decreased early in 1901.[84] During the recession that followed both the *Alter Verband* and the *Gewerkverein* blamed "foreigners" for the economic plight of miners in the Ruhr.[85] If these developments confirmed the need for a Polish trade union to look after the migrants' interests, it still faced practical problems. The economic downturn that continued into 1902 did not favor the recruitment of members for a union. Mine owners took advantage of the slack in demand to rid themselves of "bad elements," and miners feared risking dismissal when other jobs were scarce.[86] Indeed, soon after being chosen the first chairman of the ZZP, Rejer lost his job in the mines and, black-listed, had to resign from the union and emigrate to France, where he resumed his efforts to organize Polish workers and after World War I became chairman of the Union of Polish Workers in France.[87] Moreover, the Polish community in the Ruhr faced particular obstacles. "One must not forget that at that time except for the Brejski brothers there was no intelligentsia in the West."[88] As one activist found after helping organize the educational association *Oświata* (Enlightenment) in Bochum in 1898, "We lacked people to give lectures and addresses. Brejski would have to give a talk at every meeting, and he did not have that much time."[89]

84. STAM, BA Herne A8, Nr. 16, draft of quarterly report, 13 March 1901, claims that the situation began to worsen in Jan. 1901.

85. For specific examples, see Kulczycki, *Foreign Workers*, p. 156.

86. Gerhard Brauckmann, "Der Einfluss des Konjunkturverlaufs auf die gewerkschaftlichen Mitgliederbewegung" (Unpublished Ph.D. Dissertation, University of Bochum, 1972), pp. 226–227, 250; Elaine Glovka Spencer, "West German Coal, Iron and Steel Industrialists as Employers, 1896–1914" (Unpublished Ph.D. Dissertation, University of California at Berkeley, 1969), p. 99; Hartmut Kaelble and Heinrich Volkmann, "Konjunktur und Streik während des Übergangs zum Organisierten Kapitalismus," in *Arbeiter in Deutschland. Studien zur Lebensweise der Arbeiterschaft im Zeitalter der Industrialisierung*, ed. by Dieter Langewieche and Klaus Schönhoven (Paderborn: Ferdinand Schöningh, 1981), pp. 269–295; STAM, BA Herne A8, Nr. 16, draft of quarterly report, 13 March 1901, notes the firing of "bad elements."

87. Wachowiak, "Wspomnienia," p. 46. It is not known if the Prussian authorities played a role in Rejer's dismissal, but the possibility of mines firing ZZP agitators was raised by the RPD in a draft to the OPC, 9 Jan. 1904, HSTAD, RD 15915, ff. 189–190. Rejer's role as a worker-activist in France is in accord with the conclusion that such people played a role in the Ruhr.

88. Mańkowski, "Geschichte," STAM, RM VII, Nr. 36c, p. 111.

89. *Goniec Wielkopolski*, No. 196, 29 Aug. 1899, *Gesammtüberblick*, VIII, No. 35, 11 Sept. 1899, p. 566; Wachowiak, "Wspomnienia," pp. 27, 34–35, 39, notes the lack of cadres and Mańkowski's role in training them.

The Creation of a Polish Trade Union

Once the ground seemed adequately prepared, Antoni Brejski sent out invitations to two groups to meet to discuss "a very important question," to a smaller group to meet at the editorial offices of the *Wiarus Polski* in Bochum at noon on 9 November 1902 and to a second, larger group to meet at a hall across from the Redemptorist cloister—the so-called "Polish church"—in Bochum at 4 p.m. that same day.[90] At the first meeting, attended by some 25 influential worker-activists who did not need much convincing of the necessity of an autonomous Polish trade union, Jan Brejski presented a draft of the union's statute, which the assembled leaders discussed in detail for three hours and approved unanimously after introducing certain amendments and additions. At Jan Brejski's suggestion, they agreed that union members should call each other *druh* ("comrade" or "friend," but avoiding the socialist *towarzysz*) and use the greeting *Szczęść Boże* ("God bless" or "good luck") as a Polish equivalent of the German miners' greeting *Glück auf*. Finally, they chose candidates for the leading positions in the union.

Antoni Brejski opened the second meeting, attended by some 200 delegates. He spoke of the need for a Polish trade union and cited the 1899 language ordinance and the support it received from German unions: to develop their own industry, the capitalists bring Polish workers for their brawn to ruin their health and lives, and, for this great sacrifice made by Polish workers, the Prussian government wants to wrench away their language and warp the Polish spirit with the help of such laws. In the discussion that followed, the delegates echoed these sentiments, approved with only minor changes the statute read by Brejski, and elected the union's first officers: the miners Rejer and Wilkowski (the latter formerly a member of the *Alter Verband*) as chairman and first vice-chairman respectively, two other workers as second vice-chairman and treasurer, and a non-worker but former miner, the activist of long standing Hipolit Sibilski, as secretary constituted the executive board; the miner Walenty Grześkowiak, who had run as a Polish candidate for pension fund elder, chaired a board of trustees of thirty to forty members, which chose the executive board.[91] For tactical reasons, only at the very end of the meeting

90. Mańkowski probably is the best source on these meetings, "Geschichte," STAM, RM VII, Nr. 36c, p. 111; Mańkowski, "Historja," pp. 53–57.

91. Klessmann, *Polnische Bergarbeiter*, p. 111; Mańkowski, "Historja," pp. 46, 56; Adam Piotrowski, *Powstanie i rozwój polskich związków zawodowych pod zaborem pruskim* (Poznań: Nakładem i drukiem "Pracy" Sp. z ogr. p., 1910), pp. 89–90, gives an apparently complete list of the first officers of the union including thirty trustees.

did Jan Brejski say a few words of encouragement. The ZZP, with its headquarters in Bochum, was formally established.

The ZZP statute gives an indication of the union's character in the eyes of its initiators. The *Gewerkverein*'s statute no doubt served as a model, but there are significant differences as well as similarities between the two. Both cited the goal of moral improvement of its members and excluded religious and political matters while opposing socialism—the ZZP specifically excluded "unconditionally all agitation in a social-democratic spirit."[92] But the national and virtually exclusively working-class character of the Polish community in the Ruhr also had an influence. Thus, unlike the *Gewerkverein*, the ZZP did not declare its loyalty "to the Kaiser and the Reich." Nor did its statute promote national solidarity across class divisions and thereby dull the edge of conflicting interests as the *Gewerkverein*'s statute did by setting as one of its aims "the preparation and maintenance of a peaceful agreement between employer and employee."[93]

Along with moral advancement, the ZZP's statute spoke of "the material advancement of [its] members, assuring them adequate and steady earnings as well as the respect and position in society due them." This was to be achieved by "all means allowed by Christian teaching and not forbidden by law." The concern for respect flowed from the discrimination that the Polish-speaking miners believed they suffered from and which motivated the formation of their own union. Yet they also showed a greater willingness to defend their class interests than the *Gewerkverein* by not explicitly restricting the right to strike, which the statute of the latter all but ruled out. The *Gewerkverein*'s statute even dropped from a draft a reference to the "material and industrial interests of its members," which enhanced its similarity to the "yellow" or company unions later formed by employers.[94]

---

92. Mańkowski, "Historja," pp. 55–56, reprints excerpts from the ZZP statutes.

93. Hans Mommsen *et al.*, *Bergarbeiter. Ausstellung zur Geschichte der organisierten Bergarbeiterbewegung in Deutschland* (Bochum: Berg-Verlag GmbH, 1969) (unpaged), reprints an excerpt from the statutes of the *Gewerkverein* in illustration 88; see also Klessmann, *Polnische Bergarbeiter*, p. 230.

94. Brose, *Christian Labor*, p. 92–97; Klessmann, *Polnische Bergarbeiter*, p.112, notes the differences between the two statutes but underestimates their significance; in "Klassensolidarität," p. 152, by characterizing the intention behind the ZZP "essentially as 'protection against social democracy,'" Klessmann overestimates the significance of one clause of the statute: the *Gewerkverein* also came into existence as "protection against social democracy," and other Polish associations typically banned socialist influences; one cannot assume that "social democracy" or the *Alter Verband* was perceived as a greater threat to the Polish community than the *Gewerkverein*.

The ZZP's commitment to an active defense of working-class interests also set it apart from other similar Polish organizations in the homeland that it would eventually absorb. But the ZZP broke with the tradition of the mutual aid associations only gradually. Out of the low monthly dues of 50 Pfennige, 40 were divided between a death benefit fund and a sickness and self-help fund, which remained the possession of the member, who could under certain conditions obtain a full refund.[95] This led the *Alter Verband* leader Hue to dismiss the ZZP as "a savings-bank."[96] But in 1898 he himself had advocated that his union set up a death benefit fund to make union membership more attractive, and both it and the *Gewerkverein* set up such funds in 1900: without material incentives, the unions could not appeal to the mass of miners, who had no understanding of the purpose of unions.[97]

The leadership of the ZZP soon realized the inadequacy of these provisions in providing a financial base for the union to fulfill its goals, which included the establishment of legal aid and employment assistance bureaus. Little over a year after the union's founding, in January 1904, a general assembly of the union revoked the right to a refund and set limits on the death benefit. Still, this initial defect had its positive side, because it helped draw in members who thought of a trade union as just another self-help association.[98] Out of similar considerations, the *Gewerkverein* had sought to compete by keeping its dues significantly lower than those of the already established *Alter Verband* and took even longer than the ZZP to recognize the need to expand its support funds.[99]

The ZZP and the Union Movement, 1902–1904

The ZZP initiated its quest for members with a flurry of activity, casting its net as wide as any Polish workers' union could. As an early appeal addressed "To our Brother, the Polish Worker" put it, "Brother! Everyone who works in a large-scale industrial concern, be it in a mine, foundry, or

---

95. Chełmikowski, *Związki*, p. 85; Wachowiak, *Polacy*, pp. 118–120.

96. Otto Hue, *Die Bergarbeiter: Historische Darstellung der Bergarbeiter-Verhältnisse von der ältesten bis in die neueste Zeit*, Vol. II (Stuttgart: I.H.W. Dietz Nachf. G.m.b.H., 1913), p. 565.

97. Feige, *Bergarbeiterschaft*, pp. 28–29, 33–34.

98. Wachowiak, *Polacy*, pp. 119–120.

99. Brose, *Christian Labor*, pp. 97, 174–175; Michael Schneider, *Die Christlichen Gewerkschaften 1894–1933* (Bonn: Verlag Neue Gesellschaft, 1982), p. 72.

in any kind of factory or at a construction site, can join us."[100] Mańkowski later claimed that in four weeks the ZZP convoked some 20 meetings at which it recruited 1,800 members.[101] The Arnsberg administrative district reported to the Ministry of Internal Affairs in Berlin on five ZZP meetings held in December 1902.[102] At one of these meetings, on 7 December in Eickel, 68, or about half of those present, signed up as members, which the meeting's chairman characterized as a good beginning though he regretted that not everyone had joined.[103] According to another account, the union held at least 93 meetings by the end of 1903 and reached a membership of 4,616.[104]

Speakers at these meetings usually included the union's officers or Antoni Brejski, editor of the *Wiarus*, which initially served as the union's newspaper. In their talks they sought to recruit members by focusing on both the need for unions and the virtues of the ZZP over the other unions, particularly for Polish-speaking workers. Thus, at a meeting in Oberhausen on 25 January 1903, which opened with the singing of a Polish religious hymn, the 100 (at the meeting's end) to 150 men heard a local speaker and the union leader Rejer warn them that German and Polish workers must hold together until they finally get the wages they really deserve from the capitalists, who do not keep their promises and snatch great profits for themselves. At the same time, both speakers noted the advantage for Polish-speaking workers of a union that holds its meetings in Polish so that all can understand and take part without fear of being laughed at because of a lack of fluency in German.[105]

Jan Brejski, whose role in the creation of the ZZP supposedly demonstrated its nationalist and non-union character, also struck the note of working-class solidarity in the face of the capitalist through membership in the ZZP. At a meeting in Essen at the end of August 1903, the Reichstag deputy presented himself as elected by Polish workers in the area of Toruń (Thorn) but with the obligation of representing Polish workers of the Ruhr as well, and therefore he urged them to send him

---

100. *Dziennik Berliński*, No. 52, 5 March 1903, *Gesammtüberblick*, XII, No. 10, 17 March 1903, p. 184.

101. Mańkowski, "Historja," p. 56; pp. 56–61 provide an account of the union's activities until 1905, on which the following is in part based.

102. STAM, OP 5365, report, 8 Jan. 1903, copy.

103. *Ibid.*, police report, copy.

104. Chełmikowski, *Związki*, p. 90; Mańkowski, "Historja," p. 60, claims a membership of 9,600 by the end of 1903.

105. HSTAD, RD Präs 871, f. 38, Polizei-Verwaltung, Oberhausen, 25 Jan. 1903.

their complaints so that he could come to their aid.[106] But he emphasized that above all workers need a strong organization. While lamenting the divisions among workers in Germany, he defended the necessity of a Polish union, which should not act as an enemy of the German unions but should protect the Polish worker.

Until its statute changed in 1904, the ZZP could claim a financial advantage over other unions as well. A miner speaking at the meeting in Eickel less than a month after the union's founding noted that the Polish migrant lost the dues paid to other unions when he returned to his homeland, whereas in the ZZP the member retained title to the money.[107] At the same meeting, the union secretary Sibilski also emphasized that the money paid in by members remained their property and that the dues were low enough for everyone to be able to afford them. Similarly, a ZZP appeal for members that appeared in the press in March 1903 attributed the provisions with regard to dues to an egalitarian concern "that one member could not take advantage of the other, that the individual could not feather his nest by chance at the cost of the general membership, as happens in so many an institution."[108]

To be sure, speakers at these meetings also made more hostile comments about the German unions, including the claim that Polish membership in any German association posed moral dangers while bringing no material advantage because no account is taken of non-German-speaking members. At the December 1902 meeting in Eickel, Sibilski claimed that the *Gewerkverein* is headed by "Sirs" (*Herren*) who do not know where the worker's shoe pinches and therefore cannot defend his interests.[109] For its attacks on the *Alter Verband*, the ZZP—like the *Gewerkverein*—exploited the widespread antipathy to social democracy. At a meeting in Alstaden on 18 January 1903, the miner Stanisław Kunz, who headed the *Sokół* (Falcon) gymnastic association "nest" in Ueckendorf, gave a long speech about the social democrats as a secret enemy of the Poles, which the audience warmly applauded and frequently interrupted with shouts of "Out with the social democrats," "Social democrats are animals," and other insults.[110]

---

106. *Ibid.*, ff. 112–114, Polizei-Verwaltung, Essen, 30 Aug. 1903.

107. STAM, OP 5365, police report, 7 Dec. 1902, copy.

108. *Dziennik Berliński*, No. 52, 5 March 1903, *Gesammtüberblick*, XII, No. 10, 17 March 1903, p. 184.

109. STAM, OP 5365, police report on the meeting, 7 Dec. 1902, copy.

110. HSTAD, RD Präs 871, f. 35, police report, copy; on Kunz, see Kozłowski, *Rozwój*, p. 202.

The particular vehemence of the hostility expressed at this meeting toward the social democrats stemmed from an attempt by a Polish social democrat to disrupt the meeting at its start. To avoid having the meeting dissolved, Kunz, who chaired the meeting, had the police eject him. At that point some 50 social democratic sympathizers left the meeting as well, a few calling out threats of resorting to knives and guns as they exited the hall. Similar incidents occurred at at least two other ZZP meetings, again provoked by partisans of the social democrats or the *Alter Verband*. In the fierce competition for members that raged at this time, such conflicts between partisans of the two main German unions also broke out at their meetings.[111]

Of course, the conflict between the ZZP and the German unions derived from more than just a rivalry between trade unions. At the meeting in Alstaden in January 1903, the miner Tomasz Kubiak, an activist in the Union of Poles (ZPwN), gave a speech with a strong Polish national accent touching on topics such as official efforts to Germanize the Poles, local examples of unhappy marriages between Poles and German women, the importance of thrift to gather capital for the purchase of a farm in the homeland, and buying only Polish newspapers. But, as a result of the working-class character of the Polish nation in the Ruhr, even Kubiak defined the interests of the nation as those of Polish workers when at the start of his speech he criticized the Polish deputies in the Reichstag, who the previous month had voted for the government's tariff bill, in spite of their claim to be the friends of workers. Indeed, the first of four resolutions passed unanimously at the meeting's conclusion denounced those who voted for the tariff as "enemies of Poles" alongside those who sold Polish land to the Colonization Commission, sought to Germanize Poles, and did not educate their children in the Polish language.[112] Significantly, this tendency within the ZZP to identify the interests of Polish workers as the interests of the Polish nation brought the ZZP closer to the position taken by the *Alter Verband* than to that of the

111. HSTAD, RD Präs 871, f. 33, police report, copy; f. 39, Polizei-Verwaltung, Oberhausen, 25 Jan. 1903; Mańkowski, "Geschichte," STAM, RM VII, Nr. 36c, p. 111. On the mutual attacks and conflicts of the German unions, see Feige, *Bergarbeiterschaft*, pp. 36–37.

112. HSTAD, RD Präs 871, ff. 33–36, police report, 18 Jan. 1903, copy; Kozłowski, *Rozwój*, p. 187, identifies Kubiak as a chairman of the Union but also as a merchant, though the above report refers to him as a miner.

Gewerkverein, whose leader Brust had openly supported the tariff bill despite its great unpopularity among most workers.[113] These meetings also chose local union stewards to collect dues from members. For example, at the meeting in Eickel, a member of the ZPwN was chosen.[114] In addition, new members signed up at the union's office in Bochum, where they came directly from work, initially keeping three or even five people busy at a time, all of whom in the beginning, like the union's officers, served on a voluntary basis. In two months the union collected enough money to pay off its debts to the *Wiarus* for the printing of materials it had needed to begin its activities. According to Mańkowski, the union hired its first paid employee, the miner Jan Brzeskot, to assist members in legal questions in 1903, but the police reported the establishment of a legal aid bureau, in which Brzeskot did the paper work under the supervision of Antoni Brejski, only on 1 July 1904. In its first month, the bureau received 128 cases for investigation, 183 in August, and 212 in September.[115]

The conflict among the unions over the loyalty of the Ruhr's miners became especially bitter preceding the election of pension fund elders. When in a by-election in Habinghorst in August 1903 a Polish candidate opposed ones put forward by each of the other two main unions but then lost by six votes, an article in the *Wiarus* castigated those who did not vote or voted for the "foreigner."[116]

But the main battle came in the general election of pension fund elders in September 1904, which was already mentioned at a ZZP meeting in December 1902.[117] Brzeskot, then chairman of the ZZP board of trustees, initiated the campaign at the union's general assembly in Steele on 17 January 1904 in a speech in which he criticized both the socialist-oriented and the Christian German unions with unusual sharpness at the same time as he urged the need to fight for equal rights for the Polish language in mines and factories and to oppose the exploitation of workers by

113. On the split between the German unions over the tariff, see Feige, *Bergarbeiterschaft*, p. 41; Brose, *Christian Labor*, pp. 159–162, 167–168, 173–174.

114. STAM, OP 5365, police report, 7 Dec. 1902, copy; union stewards apparently received financial compensation for collecting dues, HSTAD RD Präs 871, f. 35, police report on the meeting in Alstaden, 18 Jan. 1903, copy.

115. Mańkowski, "Historja," p. 60, possibly erred in giving 1903 as the year Brzeskot was hired; STAM, OP 5365, RPA, reports, 23 July 1904, 28 Feb. 1905. Brzeskot may be the same person named as recruiting in Polish for the *Gewerkverein* in mid-November 1902, STAM, RM VII, Nr. 18, Bd. 1, Polizei-Verwaltung, Bottrop, report, 17 Nov. 1902.

116. WP, No. 184, 4 Aug. 1903, No. 189, 20 Aug. 1903, *Gesammtüberblick*, XII, No. 34, 1 Sept. 1903, pp. 667–668.

117. STAM, OP 5365, police report on meeting in Eickel, 7 Dec. 1902, copy.

employers.[118] A week later he spoke at a ZZP meeting in Borbeck, where the selection of candidates for the pension fund elder election headed the agenda. He asserted the right of Polish-speaking miners to elect their own pension fund elders by stating, "We are no longer here as wanderers, rather we want to be a nation."[119]

Just three weeks before the election, the attacks on the German unions culminated in a long article in the *Wiarus*.[120] It called Hue and Hermann Sachse, leaders of the *Alter Verband*, parasites and traitors and claimed that their union opposed Polish workers in cooperation with anti-Polish elements. The article also characterized Brust as desperate and his "*Zentrum-Gewerkverein*" (Center Party Union) as nearly bankrupt and a defender of capitalists. The *Wiarus* reminded its readers that both unions were all German and as such awaited with impatience the downfall of the Polish worker, who is for them an inconvenient competitor. In this situation, the article argued, Poles have no choice but to unite in a Polish organization that has shown that their strength is great and that with diligent effort can achieve more for the worker than the socialists and the Center Party people combined.

Unable any longer to ignore the ZZP as it had initially done, the Christian union's journal *Bergknappe* replied to these attacks by suggesting that the ZZP could more aptly be called the "Polish Worker-Betrayer Union" (*polnische Arbeiterverrätervereinigung*).[121] At the same time, the *Gewerkverein* tried to improve its relations with the Polish-speaking miner. In February 1904 Brust stated in the Prussian Landtag, to which he had been elected as a *Zentrum* deputy in 1903, that contrary to his earlier belief he now saw the necessity of mine regulations being posted in Polish because many miners did not understand German well enough, citing the practice in Alsace-Lorraine of publishing mine regulations in French and German as a precedent.[122]

The uncompromising and personal attacks of the ZZP did not essentially differ from those made against each other by the other unions

118. Kozłowski, *Rozwój*, pp. 213–214.

119. HSTAD, RD 15915, ff. 201–202, Polizeiverwaltung, report, 25 Jan. 1904, copy.

120. STAM, OBAD 884, *Uebersetzungen aus dem "Wiarus Polski,"* No. 191, 21 Aug. 1904.

121. Hue, *Bergarbeiter*, Vol. II, p. 564. Herbert Fulde, *Die polnische Arbeitergewerkschaftsbewegung* (Weinfelden: A.-G. Neuenschwander'sche Verlagsbuchhandlung, 1931), p. 89, claims that the *Gewerkverein* regarded the ZZP "in principle sympathetically" but provides no evidence for this improbable response.

122. *Stenographische Berichte über die Verhandlungen des Preussischen Hauses der Abgeordneten*, I, 1117–1118; STAM, OBAD 884, *Uebersetzungen aus dem "Wiarus Polski,"* No. 39, 18 Feb. 1904.

during the 1904 election campaign. Because the *Gewerkverein* chose to align itself with "company elders" rather than with the *Alter Verband*, the Christian union opened itself to charges of being a "company union" and its leader Brust a "traitor." Mutual insults even led in individual cases to brutality between rival German union members. Thus the ZZP reflected rather than created the existing differences among the miners of the Ruhr.[123]

The election ended in a severe defeat for the *Gewerkverein* and for Brust personally, resulting in his replacement as union leader. The *Alter Verband*'s candidates won 170 contests, often by overwhelming majorities, while the Christian union won in 100 instances. By comparison, the ZZP's success in winning five seats seems minuscule and of no consequence.[124] It did not really exceed by far the expectations of the Prussian authorities in January 1904 that the ZZP would garner few if any seats.[125] Yet, at that time, there were no Poles among the pension fund elders, so that the ZZP election victories set a precedent and contributed to the legitimization of the ZZP as an alternative to the German unions.[126]

The ZZP showed other signs of vitality in 1904. Early in the year, the union began to publish a periodical for its members, *Zjednoczenie* (Union), under the editorship of Antoni Brejski.[127] The union also submitted a memorandum to the Polish parliamentary deputies in Berlin proposing a number of reforms in the regulation of the mining industry,

123. On the campaign of the predominantly German unions—no note is taken of the ZZP—for the election of pension fund elders in 1904, see Feige, *Bergarbeiterschaft*, pp. 41, 45–47.

124. Klessmann, *Polnische Bergarbeiter*, p. 284; Fulde, *Polnische Arbeitergewerkschaftsbewegung*, p. 91; according to Mańkowski, "Historja," p. 60, only 4 ZZP candidates won.

125. HSTAD, RD 15915, ff. 188–189, LR des Landkreisen Essen to RPD, 7 Jan. 1904; RPD to OPC, 9 Jan. 1904, draft.

126. According to Mańkowski, "Historja," pp. 45–46, Poles won election as pension fund elders in 1898 and 1899, but, at least for the election of 1898, this is contradicted by archival evidence: see John J. Kulczycki, "Polish Economic Immigration in Western Germany and France, 1895–1935," in *Russian and Eastern European History: Selected Papers from the Second World Congress for Soviet and East European Studies*, ed. by R.C. Elwood (Berkeley, California: Berkeley Slavic Specialties, 1984), pp. 266–267.

127. According to Joh. Victor Bredt, *Die Polenfrage im Ruhrkohlengebiet. Eine wirtschaftspolitische Studie* (Leipzig: Duncker & Humblot, 1909), p. 57, it began on 1 Jan. and was a biweekly; according to Wojciech Chojnacki, "Bibliografia czasopism i kalendarzy wydawanych w języku polskim w Westfalii i Nadrenii w latach 1890–1918," *Przegląd Polonijny*, III, No. 1 (1977), 199, it was a monthly; according to a report of the Erste Bürgermeister, Bochum, to Polizeipräsident, Posen, 14 March 1904, it was a monthly whose first issue appeared on 22 Feb. 1904, APP, Polizeipräsidium 4964, p. 3.

including the limitation of the workday to a maximum of six to eight hours.[128] In November the ZZP established its first union local outside the Ruhr, not coincidentally in Jan Brejski's home base of Toruń, thereby effectively challenging the claim of the Polish trade union in Poznań to the right to organize Polish workers in the homeland. At the same time, the ZZP began organizational work in Saxony and northern Germany.[129] Meanwhile, ZZP membership grew rapidly, despite the change in the statute at the beginning of 1904 revoking the refundability of union dues, which might have been expected to alienate members and prospective recruits.[130] In the first two quarters of 1904, membership grew by nearly 50 percent, reaching 6,845. In the next quarter, at the height of the pension fund elder election campaign, membership increased more than twice as rapidly, bringing the total to 8,733 by the end of September and then more slowly to 10,081 by the end of the year. This total included only 165 outside of the districts of Arnsberg, Münster, and Düsseldorf, where the predominance of miners in the union is clearly evident from the strength of the union in the coal-producing districts of the Ruhr.[131]

Earlier in 1904 a reader of the *Wiarus* wrote to the paper,

Everywhere, be it in the foundry or in the mine, the Polish worker is brought in for the most difficult work and receives the worst pay, for which there is ample evidence. Needlessly, they want in addition to do him the favor of keeping him in hostile "Verbänden" and "Gewerkvereinen." They are not for us. There will we be called stupid Poles, and we of course have our own organization, to which every Pole must belong.[132]

Obviously, not all Polish-speaking migrants were yet ready to agree. If, in a little over two years, the ZZP proved its durability, it still had not organized more than a small portion of the Polish-speaking miners of the Ruhr. Like the other unions, it had to overcome the indifference to unions of the mass of miners. But it also faced special problems due to the nature

---

128. Wachowiak, *Polacy*, p. 153.

129. Kozłowski, *Rozwój*, p. 214; Mańkowski, "Historja," pp. 60–61.

130. On reactions to increases in union dues, see Feige, *Bergarbeiterschaft*, pp. 34, 53.

131. STAM, RM VII, Nr. 35b, Polizei-Verwaltung, Bochum, reports, 8 July, 3 Oct. 1904, 5 Jan. 1905, copies; see also, HSTAD, RD 874, ff. 266–267. Mańkowski, "Geschichte," STAM, RM VII, Nr. 36c, p. 111, claims a membership in 1904 of 11,500, and this figure is given in other accounts: Klessmann, *Polnische Bergarbeiter*, p. 283; Murzynowska, *Polskie wychodźstwo*, p. 144; Kozłowski, *Rozwój*, p. 213.

132. STAM, RA I, Nr. 152, *Uebersetzungen aus dem "Wiarus Polski,"* No. 58, 11 March 1904.

of its potential constituency and to its late appearance within the labor movement of the Ruhr.

A Polish migrant, Jakub Wojciechowski, recalled in his memoirs how he resisted being recruited by the ZZP early in 1905 when he was working at a mine near Wanne, although he willingly joined other Polish organizations, read Polish newspapers, and generally exhibited a high degree of Polish national consciousness. In reference to the supposed financial benefits of union membership, he told a ZZP "agitator," "I didn't pay anything and so I don't want anything, and secondly, you have so many unions, and one just sics on another, and thirdly, I may be here just a short time, too, so that it doesn't pay for me to join this association."[133] Wojciechowski, who wandered far and wide in Germany, did not sufficiently identify with his fellow miners to see the value of a union, especially in the light of the evident lack of solidarity among the unions in the Ruhr. His strong identification with the Polish nation, which implied a commitment to save money for an early return to the homeland, might even have stood in the way of his joining a union, pointing up a potential paradox in trying to combine a commitment to class solidarity in the mines of the Ruhr with a commitment to a separate identity based in Prussian Poland.

Nor were all Polish-speaking migrants who recognized the value of union membership attracted as yet to the ZZP. Some who belonged to other unions did not want to sacrifice the money they had already paid into the union coffers by switching, and others simply were waiting to see if the ZZP would thrive.[134] Then, too, since the founding of the ZZP, the other unions made a greater effort than previously to recruit Polish-speaking miners, as we saw already in 1902.

What role did Polish-speaking miners generally and the ZZP specifically play in the competition between the *Alter Verband* and the *Gewerkverein* that escalated in these years, beginning in 1901?[135] Since the struggle between the two German unions predated the creation of the ZZP, as did even the turning point at which the *Alter Verband* began to gain the momentum that would give it the upper hand, one can see the Polish union as more of an effect than a cause of the divisions within the miners' labor movement.

133. Jakub Wojciechowski, *Życiorys własny robotnika*, Vol. I (Poznań: Wydawnictwo Poznańskie, 1971), pp. 305–306.

134. Wachowiak, "Wspomnienia," p. 45.

135. Feige, *Bergarbeiterschaft*, pp. 42–47, 52–53, discusses the competition without considering the question posed here; indeed, he seems to regard it as irrelevant. Similarly, Brose, *Christian Labor*, pp. 154–158, 173–175, 195.

Presumably, factors that repelled many miners from the *Gewerkverein* affected Polish-speaking miners as well: the enervating internal controversies with the Catholic Church, the deficiency of the union's financial resources, its relative passivity in the face of miners' grievances, and the failures of its leadership, including Brust's support of free trade. Thus, in reporting on a decline of over a third in the membership of a *Gewerkverein* local in the rural county of Recklinghausen in the third quarter of 1904, the *Landrat* explained that besides a supposed dispute over the pension fund elder election "the Poles are gradually seceding."[136] Since the Polish-speaking miners were overwhelmingly Catholic, it is commonly assumed that the *Gewerkverein* suffered greater losses to the ZZP than did the *Alter Verband*.[137] But the *Gewerkverein* certainly suffered still greater losses to the *Alter Verband*, which experienced extraordinary growth prior to the pension fund elder election in 1904, just as the ZZP did.[138] The ZZP did not so much cause the membership losses of the *Gewerkverein* as profit from them.

The *Alter Verband* felt the competition of the Polish trade union as well. According to the recollections of a former Polish miner in the Ruhr, "Social democrats did not like Poles from the 'Zjednoczenie' [ZZP], first, because we were Poles, and secondly, because through the establishment of the 'Zjednoczenie' the 'Altersverband' [*sic*] lost many members."[139] But the *Alter Verband* also recruited Polish-speaking miners. At the beginning of September 1903, the Arnsberg administrative district reported that in the urban county of Gelsenkirchen some 200 Poles had joined the *Alter Verband* in the previous six months, whereas the total membership of the ZZP in that county a month later numbered only 197. Of course, the ZZP was then less than a year old and nearly doubled that total by the end of 1904.[140] Still, a large number of Polish-speaking miners remained in or joined the *Alter Verband* rather than the ZZP, no doubt for many of the same reasons German miners did: the financial benefits and other resources it could offer its members, its aggressiveness in responding to the miners' discontents, its leadership role in the work force

---

136. STAM, RM VII, Nr. 18, Bd. 1, 1 Oct. 1904.

137. See, for example, Emil Schrumpf, *Gewerkschaftsbildung und -politik im Bergbau (Unter besonderer Berücksichtigung des Ruhrbergbaus)* (Bochum: Industriegewerkschaft Bergbau mbH, 1958), p. 16; Hue, *Bergarbeiter*, Vol. II, p. 564.

138. Feige, *Bergarbeiterschaft*, p. 52.

139. Połomski, "Ze wspomnień," p. 260.

140. STAM, OP 5365, RA, 5 Sept. 1903; Nachweisung, 1 Jan. 1904; HSTAD, RD 874, f. 266.

meetings of 1904, and ultimately its size, which suggested greater power and influence in labor disputes than the other unions.[141]

Developments in the Polish community and the German response to them, particularly toward the end of the nineteenth century, led to the creation of a Polish trade union in the Ruhr, the most important and effective institution established by the Polish-speaking migrants of the Ruhr region.[142] On the initiative of the Brejski brothers and of Polish worker-activists, efforts to provide Polish-speaking coal miners with an alternative to the German unions came to fruition in a genuine working-class organization within the Polish community.[143]

Despite the fierce competition that existed at this time within the union movement in the Ruhr, the ZZP succeeded in establishing itself as a viable alternative for Polish-speaking workers thanks to its dual appeal to the national and class interests of the Polish-speaking worker. It was not just a national organization as the Prussian authorities and opposing unions often portrayed it. Furthermore, the ZZP was an organization "in which in any case the national element, in the face of the necessity of defending economic interests, retired into the background."[144]

Yet the national identity of the ZZP also played a role. In explaining why in the ZZP "the proletarian and oppositional feeling remained strong enough to prevent its development into an organization friendly to the mining companies," the *Alter Verband* leader Hue pinpointed two factors: "that the Poles in the Ruhr region, apart from relatively few exceptions, belong to the working class, and further, the brutality of the 'Eastern Marches policy' [*Ostmarkenpolitik*] directed against the Polish population."[145] Similarly, the *Gewerkverein* leader Imbusch wrote in 1908, "The development of the ZZP depends in large part on the development

141. Feige, *Bergarbeiterschaft*, pp. 33; Brose, *Christian Labor*, pp. 173–174, 195.

142. Christoph Klessmann, "Polish Miners in the Ruhr District: Their Social Situation and Trade Union Activity," in *Labor Migration in the Atlantic Economies: The European and North American Working Classes During the Period of Industrialization*, ed. by Dirk Hoerder (Westport, Connecticut: Greenwood Press, 1985), p. 264; Kozłowski, *Rozwój*, p. 210.

143. The Brejskis here played a role analogous to that of the "internal" "pioneer elite" among American immigrants as defined by Victor R. Greene, *American Immigrant Leaders 1800–1910: Marginality and Identity* (Baltimore: Johns Hopkins University Press, 1987), pp. 15–16, "the founding architects of organized group institutions," "enabling immigrants to feel secure about the compatibility of their ancestral heritage and the principles of their adopted country," though here the "adopted country" might be seen as the German labor movement rather than the Ruhr.

144. Mommsen *et al.*, *Bergarbeiter*, unpaged.

145. Hue, *Bergarbeiter*, Vol. II, pp. 564–565.

of Prussian Polish policy and of the radical-Polish political movement."[146] More generally, studies of factors influencing the strength of trade unionism suggest the importance of the degree of social isolation and occupational homogeneity of a group.[147] The Polish-speaking migrants fit this description better than the native population of the Ruhr. A further attribute of the ZZP facilitated the role it would play in the labor movement in the Ruhr. The lack of direct clerical influence over the ZZP, as compared with the *Gewerkverein*, reflected and contributed to a tendency toward secularization among Polish-speaking miners. Despite explicit opposition to "social democrats," this lack of clerical influence made it easier for the ZZP than for the *Gewerkverein* to cooperate with the *Alter Verband* and thereby contribute to the unity of the labor movement that most miners desired.[148] This became particularly evident in the 1905 strike and its aftermath.

146. Imbusch, *Arbeitsverhältnis*, p. 666.

147. David F. Crew, "Class and Community. Local Research on Working-Class History in Four Countries," in *Arbeiter und Arbeiterbewegung im Vergleich. Berichte zur internationalen historischen Forschung*, ed. by Klaus Tenfelde, *Historische Zeitschrift*, Sonderheft, Vol. XV (Munich: R. Oldenbourg Verlag, 1986), pp. 307–308.

148. On the clergy as an obstacle to labor unity in this period, see Feige, *Bergarbeiterschaft*, pp. 42–43; Michael Schneider, "Christliche Arbeiterbewegung in Europa. Ein vergleichender Literaturbericht," in *Arbeiter und Arbeiterbewegung im Vergleich. Berichte zur internationalen historischen Forschung*, ed. by Klaus Tenfelde, *Historische Zeitschrift*, Sonderheft, Vol. XV (Munich: R. Oldenbourg Verlag, 1986), p. 490.

2

The Achievement of Parity: The 1905 Strike

In 1905 a strike broke out in the Ruhr region that exceeded in size and importance any previous strike on the European continent. At the start of the strike, the ZZP had just barely completed the second year of its existence, a tender age for any union to be put to a major test of its ability to rally and lead workers in a conflict with an adversary as powerful as the mine owners of the Ruhr. The ZZP not only passed the test but took advantage of the occasion to grow and achieve acceptance on a par with the major unions of the Ruhr.

The Origins of the Strike

The immediate cause of the strike echoed a dispute that had occurred in Oberhausen a year earlier. In January 1904 the Gutehoffnungshütte Aktienverein für Bergbau und Hüttenbetrieb lengthened the shifts at its Oberhausen and Vondern mines.[1] After a brief strike that began at the newly opened Vondern mine in early February and then spread to the Oberhausen mine, the management rescinded the shift extensions, and peace was restored.[2] Although a large portion of the work force at the Vondern mine consisted of migrants from predominantly Polish-speaking Upper Silesia and Poznania, the miners' meetings held in connection with this dispute included no representative of the ZZP alongside those of the *Alter Verband* and the *Gewerkverein*.[3]

Once the strike ended, the *Wiarus Polski* concluded that the dispute should serve as a lesson for miners, that they should organize themselves

---

1. See Ullrich Feige, *Bergarbeiterschaft zwischen Tradition und Emanzipation: Das Verhältnis von Bergleuten und Gewerkschaften zu Unternehmern und Staat im westlichen Ruhrgebiet um 1900* (Düsseldorf: Schwann, 1986), pp. 136–142, on the following events, though he takes no note of the composition of the work forces involved.

2. HSTAD, RD 15915, f. 228, telegram, 7 Feb. 1904; STAM, OP 2847, Bd. 9, telegrams, 6 Feb. 1904, 7 Feb. 1904.

3. In mid-1905 41 percent of the work force had been born in the East, Franz Schulze, *Die polnische Zuwanderung im Ruhrrevier und ihre Wirkung* (Munich: Josefs Druckerei, Bigge, 1909), pp. 101–102.

better, which for Poles meant joining the ZZP.[4] At the same time, the *Wiarus Polski* advocated a subordinate role for Polish miners, even following the lead of the German unions, though as members of the ZZP. A new organization, it had less resources than the other unions. But of greater concern to the *Wiarus* was the tendency, amply demonstrated in connection with the Herne strike of 1899, to blame the Poles for disorders. Therefore, Polish miners should act together with other miners but, in a favorite metaphor of the period, "not pull chestnuts out of the fire for others."[5]

In the following months, the ZZP continued to develop its organization and to grow in membership, which more than doubled in the course of 1904. In the fall the Polish union also had its first success in the competition for pension fund elder seats. When the next major dispute arose in the mines, the ZZP was more difficult to ignore.

Despite the object lesson offered by the failed attempt to extend the miners' shift in Oberhausen, the industrialist Hugo Stinnes announced on 28 November 1904 a lengthening of the shift at the Bruchstrasse mine in Langendreer as of 1 December. Miners naturally saw this as a unilateral lengthening of their workday. A brief strike forced management to postpone implementation of its directive until 1 February 1905 in order to give sufficient notice of the change in work rules.[6]

According to a local official, a large part of the work force at the Bruchstrasse mine belonged to the *Alter Verband*.[7] Polish-speaking migrants made up a relatively small portion of the work force, and the ZZP had only 85 members in Langendreer as of 1 October 1904 and 109 at the end of the year.[8] Nevertheless, the Polish union took the opportunity

---

4. WP, No. 31, 9 Feb. 1904; STAM, OBAD 884, *Uebersetzungen aus dem "Wiarus Polski,"* No. 31, 9 Feb. 1904.

5. STAM, OBAD 884, *Uebersetzungen aus dem "Wiarus Polski,"* No. 44, 24 Feb. 1904.

6. On the origins of the strike, see STAM, OP 2849, Bd. 1, ff. 5–6, 8, 18–20, 30, LR Bochum, 5 Dec. 1904, to RPA, copy, notice of 28 Nov. 1904, copy, RPA, 24 Dec. 1904, Berghauptmann, Dortmund, 31 Dec. 1904; August Brust, "Der Bergarbeiterstreik im Ruhrrevier," *Archiv für Sozialwissenschaften und Sozialpolitik*, XX, No. 2 (1905), 484.

7. STAM, OP 2849, Bd. 1, f. 7, Amt Langendreer, 5 Dec. 1904, to LR Bochum, copy; Dieter Fricke, *Der Ruhrbergarbeiterstreik von 1905* (Berlin: Rütten & Loening, 1955), p. 61, claims, however, that the *Alter Verband* had only 150 members at the mine in Dec. 1904.

8. On 1 July 1905 28 percent of the mine's work force had been born in Prussia's eastern regions as opposed to 34 percent of the work force of the Ruhr as a whole; 45 percent of the mine's eastern migrants came originally from East Prussia and therefore probably included a large number of Masurians, Schulze, *Polnische Zuwanderung*, pp. 25, 97; on ZZP membership, see STAM, RM VII, Nr. 35b, Polizei-Verwaltung, Bochum, 3 Oct. 1904, 5 Jan. 1905.

offered by the dispute at the Bruchstrasse mine to gain legitimacy and equal status with the major unions. In a speech at a meeting of the Bruchstrasse work force on 27 December, Brzeskot of the ZZP claimed that the Polish union took the initiative in calling upon the three unions to cooperate in the dispute.[9]

At that meeting, Brzeskot won warm applause from the miners by taking a more militant stand than a speaker from the *Alter Verband* and by promising that the ZZP would do everything to see to it that, if a strike broke out, it would end in victory. At the same time, he criticized the *Gewerkverein* for not responding to the Polish union's initiative. Although the *Alter Verband* representative stated that the *Gewerkverein* had agreed to act in concert with the other unions, it sent no representative to the meeting and its executive committee explicitly decided against a strike.[10] Clearly, the Polish union knew how to exploit an opportunity to outshine its rivals in the eyes of the angry miners. The cooperation between the *Alter Verband* and the ZZP also raised concerns among Prussian officials.[11]

The *Wiarus Polski* reported on the miners' meetings in Bruchstrasse and on the ZZP endorsement of the miners' protest. Furthermore, it urged Poles to support the commission elected by the miners that was collecting signatures against extending the shift. The Polish daily warned that, if the management did not retreat, a strike could easily break out. Expressing its understanding for the indignation that reigned among miners and assuring the miners of Bruchstrasse that they had the support of all their organized colleagues, the *Wiarus Polski* added that the dispute should induce all Polish miners to join the ZZP, because only organized workers can successfully "confront capitalist designs of exploitation."[12] Promotion of

9. Brzeskot's speech is summarized in *Bergarbeiter-Zeitung*, No. 1, 7 Jan. 1905; and in HSTAD, RD 15924, ff. 214–216, Bezirks-Polizeikommissar, Bochum, 28 Dec. 1904; STAM, OP 2849, Bd. 1, f. 26, RPA, 31 Dec. 1904. The involvement of the ZZP belies the claim in Donald Rosenberg, "The Ruhr Coal Strike and the Prussian Mining Law of 1905: A Social and Political Conflict of Working Class Aspirations and Industrial Authoritarianism" (Unpublished Ph.D. Dissertation, University of California, Los Angeles, 1971), p. 283, that "the Polish Miners' Federation chose to remain a quasi-nationalistic association that had little in common with the needs, programs, and aims of German trade unionism," which he uses to justify excluding the ZZP from consideration in a chapter on union and political spokesmen of the miners during the strike, pp. 277–332.

10. On the *Gewerkverein*, see Eric Dorn Brose, *Christian Labor and the Politics of Frustration in Imperial Germany* (Washington, D.C.: The Catholic University of America Press, 1985), p. 176.

11. STAM, OP 2849, Bd. 1, RPA, f. 26, 31 Dec. 1904; ff. 28–29, 2 Jan. 1905.

12. STAM, OBAD 884, *Uebersetzungen aus dem "Wiarus Polski,"* Nos. 297–299, 28–30 Dec. 1904.

the ZZP went hand in hand with support for the miners of Bruchstrasse. The January 1905 issue of *Zjednoczenie*, which had replaced the *Wiarus Polski* as the ZZP official organ in 1904, joined the controversy over the lengthening of the shift by including, among other demands, one for limiting the workday to ten hours for surface workers, eight hours for underground workers, and six hours for those working in especially unhealthy conditions.[13]

The ZZP also organized a meeting for the Polish members of the Bruchstrasse work force on 1 January 1905. Attended by 150 to 200, which must have included the majority of Polish-speaking miners at the Bruchstrasse mine, the meeting seemed primarily aimed at shoring up the union's newly formed alliance with the *Alter Verband*. Brzeskot himself stated that the purpose of the meeting was to demonstrate the unity of the German and Polish miners of Bruchstrasse. He virtually admitted that the dispute provided an opportunity for the union to prove itself: "We will show that we are united with German workers and like them strive to improve our lot."[14]

Symbolic of this new cooperation with the *Alter Verband*, a representative of the socialist-oriented union, Stefan Tuszyński of Oberhausen, was invited to speak at this Polish meeting.[15] He in turn explained why the commission elected by the workers of Bruchstrasse, apparently before the ZZP entered the controversy, did not include a member of the Polish union. Before the meeting ended, Brzeskot again attacked the *Gewerkverein* by accusing it of betraying the cause of the miners at the Bruchstrasse mine. Following the meeting, a number of Poles signed up with the ZZP, according to a report in the *Wiarus Polski*, which added its own comment: "The plan of lengthening the workday is improper and unjust, and therefore the miners are only doing their duty when they resist the appetite of capitalist industrialists."[16]

Thus, at an early stage in the dispute at the Bruchstrasse mine, the Polish trade union openly supported the miners in their dispute with management. The issue in the dispute concerned all miners, and therefore could serve to rally support well beyond a single mine. The ZZP seemed

13. Marjan Chełmikowski, *Związki zawodowe robotników polskich w Królestwie Pruskim (1889–1918)* (Poznań: Fiszer i Majewski, 1925), p. 231.

14. On the meeting, see StAB, LR 1277, report, Bezirks-Polizeikommissar Goehrke, Dortmund, 1 Jan. 1905, copy.

15. *Ibid.*, gave the name as Tuschinski, the Germanized form of the name; on Tuszyński, see Jerzy Kozłowski, *Rozwój organizacji społeczno-narodowych wychodźstwa polskiego w Niemczech w latach 1870–1914* (Wrocław: Ossolineum, 1987), p. 224.

16. STAM, OBAD 884, *Uebersetzungen aus dem "Wiarus Polski,"* No. 2, 3 Jan. 1905.

to sense this and seized upon the opportunity to get involved. The lack of any significant number of Polish-speaking miners at the Bruchstrasse mine indicates that the ZZP here was vying for legitimacy as a union in the eyes of all miners. The way its representative spoke to the miners, both in surpassing the militancy of the *Alter Verband* and in attacking the *Gewerkverein*, suggests a self-confidence and a desire to be accepted as an equal of the major German-led unions. Like a reckless adolescent, the ZZP felt that it had come of age.[17] The strike would test the validity of this self-perception.

The Strike Begins

The strike began at the Bruchstrasse mine on Saturday 7 January. The very next day the ZZP joined together with the other miners' unions—the *Alter Verband*, the *Gewerkverein*, and the small liberal Hirsch-Duncker union—in issuing a joint appeal that defended the strike at the Bruchstrasse mine at the same time as it called on miners elsewhere to continue to work. To this, the *Wiarus Polski* added a plea to Polish miners for calm and reflection because any illegal expression of their dissatisfaction would alienate public support for the miners. The ZZP also cautioned Polish miners against accepting work at the Bruchstrasse mine under any circumstances.[18]

Nevertheless, even the personal intervention of leading figures of the labor movement had little success in dissuading other miners from joining the strike. On Monday 9 January it spread to the Kaiserstuhl I and II mines with their combined work force of over 3,500 men, 35 percent of them born in the Prussian East.[19] At a meeting mainly of workers from these two mines on 10 January, the SPD Reichstag deputy and *Alter Verband* leader Sachse, the *Gewerkverein* leader Johannes Effert, and a ZZP representative all tried to persuade the miners to resume work at least until a conference of miner delegates met in Essen on 12 January. Instead,

17. According to Franz-Josef Brüggemeier, "Bedürfnisse, gesellschaftliche Erfahrung und politisches Verhalten: Das Beispiel der Bergarbeiter im nördlichen Ruhrgebiet gegen Ende des 19. Jhs.," *Sozialwissenschaftliche Informationen für Unterricht und Studium*, VI, No. 4 (1977), 158, the German unions tried to prevent a strike in 1905 out of fear that they would not survive it; such fears did not inhibit the ZZP.

18. Otto Hue, "Über den Generalstreik im Ruhrgebiet," *Sozialistische Monatshefte*, Feb. 1905, p. 203; STAM, OBAD 884, *Uebersetzungen aus dem "Wiarus Polski*," f. 188, No. 7, 10 Jan. 1905.

19. Schulze, *Polnische Zuwanderung*, p. 95; a plurality (12.8 percent) came from East Prussia.

five sixths of the 2,000 present voted to continue the strike, and the hostility toward the union leaders reached such a pitch that the police had to summon reinforcements to provide for their safety.[20]

The ZZP, however, seemed ready to continue to play upon the miners' discontent to enhance its own standing. On 11 January, the day after the strike spread to the Neumühl mine (just under a third of whose work force had been born in the Prussian East, mostly in Poznania), Brzeskot attended a meeting in Schmidthorst for the Polish-speaking miners of Neumühl. When speakers urged a continuation of the strike, Brzeskot did not contradict them. Instead, he simply read the workers' demands, which mirrored those of the striking miners at Bruchstrasse, and urged them to avoid provocative behavior. Nevertheless, only about 30 of the 500 miners present responded to his call to join the ZZP by signing up after the meeting.[21]

During this early, wildcat phase of the strike, the miners of the Oberhausen mining district, where the Neumühl mine lay, led the movement.[22] Here it probably also found the largest number of its Polish-speaking participants. Although eastern migrants formed a lower than average percentage of the district's work force (28 percent versus 34 percent for the Ruhr as a whole), it had the Ruhr's second largest absolute number of eastern migrants and of migrants from Poznania.[23] Furthermore, the district had a disproportionately large share of the ZZP's membership in the Ruhr (16 percent of the membership in the three administrative districts of the Ruhr on 1 January 1905 compared with 9 percent of the Ruhr's eastern migrants and 13 percent of its Poznanians).[24]

20. STAM, OP 2849, Bd. 1, f. 119, Oberbürgermeister Dortmund, 10 Jan. 1905; Rosenberg, "Ruhr Coal Strike," p. 44.

21. STAM, OBAD 1843, pp. 368–369, Polizei-Verwaltung, Hamborn, 12 Jan. 1905; on the composition of the work force, Schulze, *Polnische Zuwanderung*, p. 102.

22. Konrad Engel, *Zum Ausstande der Bergarbeiter im Ruhrbezirk* (Berlin: Springer Verlag, 1905), pp. 14–15, 36; on 11 Jan. 1905 the strike also began at the Alstaden and Concordia mines and the next day at the Oberhausen mine, Fritz Mogs, "Die sozialgeschichtliche Entwicklung der Stadt Oberhausen (Rhld.) zwischen 1850 und 1933" (Unpublished Dissertation, University of Cologne, 1956), p. 153.

23. Schulze, *Polnische Zuwanderung*, pp. 94–102.

24. STAM, RM VII, Nr. 35b, Polizei-Verwaltung, Bochum, 5 Jan. 1905, lists union members by place of residence, not by place of employment, and therefore the ZZP membership at the mines in the district is an estimate based on the membership residing in Ruhrort county, Oberhausen, Osterfeld, and Alstaden, all of whose mines lay within the Oberhausen mining district. See also the claim made by the ZZP that it had 12,000 members mainly in Bochum and Oberhausen, Protocol, 17 Jan. 1905, reprinted in Gerhard Adelmann, ed., *Quellensammlung zur Geschichte der sozialen Betriebsverfassung. Ruhrindustrie unter besonderer Berücksichtigung des Industrie- und Handelskammerbezirks Essen*, Vol. I: *Überbetriebliche Einwirkung auf die soziale*

Brzeskot's tacit acceptance of the strike at the meeting of the Neumühl Polish work force meant that for some of these strikers they were taking part in a movement approved by their leaders. The ZZP had only seven delegates among the 151 representatives of the miners' unions that met in Essen on 12 January to forge a common strategy. Waiting to see what positions the larger unions would take, the Polish delegates long remained silent. When Brzeskot finally took the floor, he hypocritically claimed that the ZZP wished to avoid a strike at this time but that it would go along with the decision of the majority. He even referred to the strike at the Neumühl mine as "very ill-advised," though he had done nothing to oppose it at the meeting of the mine's Polish work force.[25]

The union delegates meeting in Essen resolved to give the Mine Owners Association until January 16 to respond to the miners' demands or face a general strike on 17 January. To represent the miners, the meeting created a "Commission of Seven," whose composition signalled the acceptance of the ZZP by the rest of the German labor movement: although the small Hirsch-Duncker union received only one seat on the commission, the ZZP gained representation on a par with those of the *Alter Verband* and the *Gewerkverein* when Brzeskot and ZZP chairman Józef Regulski became members of the Commission.[26]

The Miners' Meetings and Union Growth

Once the strike began, the most conspicuous activity on the part of the ZZP as well as of the other unions was their participation in the miners' meetings held throughout the coal fields of the Ruhr. Between 14 January and 4 February, twenty-nine meetings took place in the town of Recklinghausen alone. According to the mayor, the speakers included fourteen from the ZZP, far fewer than the forty-six from the *Alter Verband* but equal to the number from the *Gewerkverein*.[27]

Betriebsverfassung der Ruhrindustrie (Bonn: Peter Hanstein, 1960), p. 257.

25. HSTAD, RD Präs 841, f. 18, report, pp. 21–22, 30.

26. For the resolution and the demands, see August Brust, "Bergarbeiterstreik," pp. 489–493; WP, No. 12, 15 Jan. 1905, printed the demands. Regulski's inclusion led the Prussian authorities to investigate his origins: he was born in the county of Jarocin, Poznania, in 1869, StAB, LR 1276, Amt Langendreer, 27 Jan. 1905.

27. STAM, OP 2849, Bd. 5, RPM to MfHuG and MdI, 2 Feb. 1905, to MdI, 5 Feb. 1905, copies; another copy of the latter is in HSTAD, RD 15925, f. 140.

On the surface, the meetings reflected the union solidarity symbolized by the Commission of Seven. Thus, those elected to officiate at the meetings, even when they were held in German, usually included a Pole. Although Prussian officials used words such as "malicious," "animosity," and "swaggering agitation" to describe the Polish speeches at these meetings, they generally covered the same ground as the other speeches.[28] As earlier, both Poles and Germans emphasized the importance of maintaining order and avoiding violence to win the support of public opinion and government officials in the dispute with mine owners.[29] Their pleas proved effective, resulting in what the Bochum *Landrat* called an "unnatural peace."[30] Other officials also noted the discipline of Polish miners in following the directives of the strike leaders and the unions, particularly the ZZP.[31]

The Münster district *Präsident* bemoaned the access to meeting halls that the miners' meetings afforded the "social-democrats," something his officials had for years sought to deny them.[32] Thanks to the leading role that the *Alter Verband* played in the meetings, they redounded in particular to that union's benefit, according to officials. But the ZZP also profited from the same exposure, if to a lesser degree. During the strike, no clear distinction existed between meetings of the Polish Trade Union and the miners' meetings held in Polish, even when the speakers included a German representative of the *Alter Verband*.[33] Polish speakers at the miners' meetings avoided specifically mentioning the ZZP when they urged miners to join a union, according to the Recklinghausen *Landrat*.[34] One could, however, easily construe such exhortations by ZZP activists at the Polish meetings as admonitions to join the ZZP.

---

28. STAM, OP 2849, Bd. 7, 26 March 1905, copy; HSTAD, RD Präs 874, f. 3229, 16 Feb. 1905; StAB, LR 1276, 20 Feb. 1905; Stadtarchiv Bottrop, A V–3, Nr. 3, 18 Feb. 1905, to LR Recklinghausen, copy, typed copy provided by the archive.

29. See, for example, the police report on the meeting in Bottrop, 18 Jan. 1905, Stadtarchiv Bottrop, A V–3, typed copy provided by the archive.

30. STAM, RA I, Nr. 63, 25 Jan. 1905.

31. STAM, RM VII, Nr. 35b, 7 March 1905; StAB, LR 1276, Amtmann, 22 Feb. 1905.

32. STAM, OP 2849, Bd. 5, to MfHuG and MdI, 2 Feb. 1905; according to Johann Leimpeters, "Die Taktik des Bergarbeiterverbandes," *Sozialistische Monatshefte*, June 1905, p. 489, during the strike "a freedom of assembly and association began such as we had never known in the Ruhr."

33. Stadtarchiv Bottrop, A V–3, Nr. 3, reports, 18 and 23 Jan. 1905, in Bottrop.

34. STAM, RM VII, Nr. 35b, 28 Feb. 1905.

Furthermore, on 18 January, the ZZP appealed to Poles to see to it that "every Polish miner joins only the Polish trade union."[35] The district police commissar of Essen also reported that Brzeskot gave a long speech about Poles who joined German organizations at a meeting on 22 January, presumably not portraying those Poles in a favorable light.[36] The same official later claimed that a "vehement argument" broke out in the Commission of Seven between the ZZP and the other unions because, contrary to an agreement reached by the unions for the duration of the strike, ZZP officials had told Polish miners at the meetings that they should belong only to the ZZP and urged them to quit the other unions.[37] Even after the dispute, the ZZP leaders supposedly did not change their behavior. But other officials reported that the *Alter Verband* similarly recruited members at miners' meetings during the strike.[38]

The one overt attempt to win over Polish-speaking miners to the socialist orientation of the *Alter Verband* ostensibly failed. Although the editors of the Polish socialist newspaper *Gazeta Robotnicza* planned to organize a series of public meetings in the strike region, only one—in Oberhausen on 29 January—came to fruition, and the police termed it ineffective. A ZZP member who chaired the local *Sokół* nest rebutted the main speaker Dr. Ester Golde's explanation of the social-democratic program, including an end to private ownership of mines, and then led a walkout of about half the audience of 200 before she could reply, leaving an audience equal in size to the membership of the local Polish social-democratic organization Fraternal Assistance.[39]

"So therefore, the *Alter Verband* and the Polish trade union are growing in membership in a way that the leaders at the beginning of the movement could themselves have scarcely hoped and suspected," the Münster district *Präsident* reported on 5 February 1905, before the strike ended.[40] He calculated then that membership in the ZZP had grown since 1 January 1905 by 1,432 in the town of Recklinghausen and by 6,472 in

35. Krystyna Murzynowska, *Polskie wychodźstwo zarobkowe w Zagłębiu Ruhry w latach 1880–1914* (Wrocław: Ossolineum, 1972), p. 150, citing WP, No. 14, 18 Jan. 1905.

36. HSTAD, RD Präs 841, f. 105.

37. HSTAD, RD Präs 874, ff. 326–327, 25 Feb. 1905.

38. See the responses to the request for information, StAB, LR 1276, 26 Jan. 1905, draft, especially Amtmann, Baukau, 26 Jan. 1905, and Amt Langendreer, 27 Jan. 1905.

39. HSTAD, RD Präs 841, f. 106, Bezirks-Polizeikommissar, Essen, 22 Jan. 1905; RD 15925, ff. 1–3, Bezirks-Polizeikommissar, Essen, 30 Jan. 1905; RD Präs 874, f. 49, Polizei-Verwaltung, Oberhausen, 30 Jan. 1905, f. 327, Bezirks-Polizeikommissar, Essen, 25 Feb. 1905.

40. HSTAD, RD 15925, to MdI, ff. 140–141, copy; another copy in STAM, OP 2849, Bd. 5.

the surrounding rural county, surpassing the growth of the *Alter Verband* by 1,000 and 4,790 respectively and of the *Gewerkverein* by about 400 and 6,149.[41] As a result, ZZP membership in the town and rural county of Recklinghausen totaled 10,233, which nearly matched the *Alter Verband*'s 11,492 and exceeded the ZZP's entire membership in all of Germany just a month earlier! Although migrants from the East among the miners of the town and rural county of Recklinghausen numbered 17,579, about 6,800 came from East Prussia and therefore included many Masurians, unlikely candidates for the ZZP.[42] Therefore the police in the town of Recklinghausen observed accurately that, despite the prominence of the *Alter Verband* in the meetings there, during the strike Polish miners "almost without exception" joined the ZZP.[43]

The Polish Trade Union made its largest gains in this period precisely in Recklinghausen rural county followed by the rural counties of Dortmund, Gelsenkirchen, and Bochum, which together accounted for 65 percent of the increase in membership and 59 percent of the ZZP's total membership in the Ruhr on 1 April 1905. Recklinghausen followed closely by Bottrop had far more ZZP members than any other single community; the only other with more than a thousand members on 1 April 1905 was Wanne, where membership had increased by 244 percent from 369 on 1 January to 1,270.[44] Overall, the statistics suggest that a larger percentage of the Polish population tended to join the ZZP in this period where that population was most numerous. Linear regression shows a strong direct relationship between the increase in ZZP membership expressed as a percentage of the Polish population of a county and the

---

41. Based on a comparison of statistics in STAM, OP 2849, Bd. 5, RPM to MfHuG, MdI, 2 Feb. 1905, copy; Bd. 7, RPM to MfHuG, MdI, 18 Feb. 1905, copy. HSTAD, RD 874, f. 266, gave the ZZP membership on 1 Jan. 1905. Citing a report of the RPM to the MdI, 13 March 1905, Murzynowska, *Polskie wychodźstwo*, p. 147, reported still higher growth of the ZZP in the urban and rural counties of Recklinghausen, 1,667 and 6,658 respectively, for a total ZZP membership of 10,454.

42. STAM, OP 2847, Bd. 7, RPM to MdI, 13 March 1905, listed the total as "Polish" miners but here followed the widespread practice of so categorizing all miners born in the Prussian East; compare with the statistics for the Recklinghausen mines on the number of miners born in the Prussian East and in East Prussia on 1 July 1905, Schulze, *Polnische Zuwanderung*, pp. 95–96, 99–102.

43.434343. STAM, RM VII, Nr. 35b, 28 Feb. 1905.

44. *Ibid.*, Oberbürgermeister Bochum, 12 April 1905, lists membership by community.

size of the Polish population.[45] Not surprisingly, larger numbers inclined a greater percentage of Poles to join the ZZP.

Both the *Landrat* of rural Recklinghausen county and the magistrate of Bottrop expected union membership to decline significantly once the strike ended because they believed that many miners joined only out of the expectation of receiving strike pay from the unions.[46] Miners may well have had such expectations, although all strikers, whether union members or not, received strike pay. The Polish migrant from Poznania Wojciechowski, who worked at the coking plant of the Shamrock III/IV mine at the time of the strike, described in his memoirs how his colleagues anticipated that by joining the union they would get 6 marks in strike pay the following Saturday.[47] In fact, by 1 April 1905 ZZP membership in Recklinghausen town and the surrounding rural county declined by 31 percent from the level reported during the strike.[48]

Nevertheless, even in Recklinghausen town and rural county ZZP membership on 1 April 1905 exceeded the level on 1 January 1905 by more than 300 percent. Contrary to the expectation of the magistrate in Bottrop, ZZP membership there actually rose from about 1800 during the strike to 2042 on 1 April.[49] In his report of March 26 on the Poles and the

---

45. The Pearson correlation coefficient is +.63 when using the population statistics in Max Broesike, "Die Polen im westlichen Preussen 1905," *Zeitschrift des Königlich Preussischen Statistischen Landesamts*, XLVIII (1908), 251–274, and +.56 when using those in Karl Closterhalfen, "Die polnische Bevölkerung in Rheinland und Westfalen," *Deutsche Erde*, X, No. 5 (1911), 115–116.

46. STAM, RM VII, Nr. 35b, 28 Feb. 1905; Stadtarchiv Bottrop, A V–3, Nr. 3, to LR Recklinghausen, draft, 18 Feb. 1905, typed copy provided by the archive. Such a loss of interest in the union after the strike would not be unusual: according to Klaus Schönhoven, *Expansion und Konzentration. Studien zur Entwicklung der Freien Gewerkschaften in Wilhelminischen Deutschland 1890 bis 1914* (Stuttgart: Klett-Cotta, 1980), p. 379, membership closely correlated with strike activity, with many of the members who joined during a strike turning their backs on the union soon after the conflict ended; Adam Walaszek, "Emigranci polscy wśród Robotników Przemysłowych Świata, 1905–1917," *Przegląd Polonijny*, XIV, No. 2 (1988), 55, notes that immigrants initiated strikes and turned to unions, but once the goal of the strike was achieved, they did not see the point of union membership. Fricke, *Ruhrbergarbeiterstreik*, p. 145, seems wrong in dismissing this motivation for joining the unions during the strike; even the evidence he presents of continued growth in the membership of the *Alter Verband* suggests many left the union between 1 April and 1 July 1905.

47. Jakub Wojciechowski, *Życiorys własny robotnika*, Vol. I (Poznań: Wydawnictwo Poznańskie, 1971), pp. 305–306.

48. HSTAD, RD 874, f. 267.

49. Stadtarchiv Bottrop, A V–3, Nr. 3, to LR Recklinghausen, draft, typed copy provided by the archive; STAM, RM VII, Nr. 35b, Polizei-Verwaltung, Bochum, 5 Jan. 1905, Oberbürgermeister Bochum, 12 April 1905. According to Richard Charles Murphy, *Guestworkers in the German Reich: A Polish Community in Wilhelmian Germany* (Boulder, Colorado: East European Monographs, 1983), pp. 75, 77, ZZP membership in

strike, the Arnsberg district *Präsident* recorded that ZZP membership had risen since 1 January 1905 by 13,573 compared with an increase of 16,098 in the membership of the *Alter Verband*.[50] In the three administrative districts that encompassed the Ruhr ZZP membership rose by 14,377 to 24,282 by 1 April 1905 or nearly two and a half times the membership on 1 January 1905.[51] If some Janek-come-latelies joined the union during the strike and then quit after collecting their strike pay, many more stayed in the union after the strike had ended. As a result, in the first quarter of 1905, more Polish-speaking miners of the Ruhr came to belong to the ZZP than to the other unions combined.[52] More easily than the other unions, the ZZP could of course appeal to the Polish-speaking miner on the basis of both his cultural ties and his class interests.

Following the strike, the popular West Prussian *Gazeta Grudziądzka* (Grudziądz Gazette) noted the Polish union's growth but belittled it in comparison with the thousands of Polish workers in Westphalia: "They must all as one man join the union...Only then, when the workers advance united, disciplined, and of one mind, can they gain human rights for themselves, and hence, forward—shoulder to shoulder!"[53] Although the ZZP accepted any Polish workers as members and thus included a number of non-miners, its total membership in the Ruhr in 1905 barely exceeded half the total number of miners born in West Prussia, Poznania, and Upper Silesia, let alone East Prussia.[54] Even members of a Catholic Polish Association who took part in the strike in Moers county belonged to the *Alter Verband*, not to the ZZP, which did not have any locals in that county.[55] Other Polish miners, apparently still harboring doubts about the

Bottrop rose from 559 at the beginning of Jan. 1905 to almost 2,100 by Oct. 1905.

50. STAM, OP 2849, Bd. 7, to MdI, copy.

51. HSTAD, RD 874, f. 267; the total membership for all of Germany was 24,611 on 1 April 1905 as compared with 10,081 on 1 Jan. 1905.

52. ZZP chairman Wojciech Sosiński estimated the *Alter Verband* had 15,000 Polish members and the *Gewerkverein* 4,000, Biblioteka Raczyńskich, Poznań, MS. 800, f. 4, *Dziennik Berliński*, No. 74, 31 March 1905. Another source claimed lower Polish membership before and after the strike: 4718 in the *Alter Verband* in 1904 and 8155 in 1906; 2438 in the *Gewerkverein* in 1904 and 3816 in 1906; see Christoph Klessmann, *Polnische Bergarbeiter im Ruhrgebiet 1870–1945: Soziale Integration und nationale Subkultur einer Minderheit in der deutschen Industriegesellschaft* (Göttingen: Vandenhoeck & Ruprecht, 1978), p. 117.

53. No. 22, 21 Feb. 1905, *Gesammtüberblick*, No. 8, 28 Feb. 1905, pp. 175–176.

54. According to Schulze, *Polnische Zuwanderung*, p. 103, on 1 July 1905, 53,736 Ruhr miners came from these three regions; on ZZP membership at the end of 1905, see Appendix I.

55. HSTAD, RD Präs 874, LR, 22 Feb. 1905, f. 321.

ZZP, joined it while continuing their membership in the *Alter Verband* or the *Gewerkverein*.[56]

The Strike and the Polish Community

From the very beginning of the strike and throughout its course, the miners evoked the sympathy of German society (outside of circles closely connected with mine owners) to a degree unparalleled in the history of the German labor movement.[57] The sympathy was even greater within Polish society in the Ruhr, with its predominantly working-class character, which made even nonworkers economically dependent on the miners. No wonder a Polish merchant in Wanne published a denial of a rumor that he tried to force miners to return to work by refusing them credit: "I won't do that, even if the miners were to strike another three months. I am ready to aid them even if I were to become impoverished. I can still now accept 100 decent fellow countrymen as customers."[58] The *Wiarus Polski* of course printed a ZZP appeal for contributions to its strike fund, but so did the *Dziennik Polski* (Polish Daily) founded in 1904 and backed by Polish middle-class nationalists in Poznania to challenge the *Wiarus Polski*, with its working-class orientation, for the position of standard-bearer of the Polish community in the Ruhr.[59] Again, the Polish character of the ZZP served as a source of strength.

Polish newspapers in the homeland also printed the ZZP's appeal to fellow countrymen for financial assistance.[60] Poznania's *Orędownik* (Advocate) printed a long article sympathetic to the strike and warned Polish workers at home and abroad against being recruited as strikebreakers by the "coal barons."[61] But, characteristically, the nationalist daily blamed the Prussian government for current conditions

---

56. Stanisław Drygas, *Czas Zaprzeszły: Wspomnienia 1890–1944* (Warsaw: Czytelnik, 1970), p. 74.

57. Rosenberg, "Ruhr Coal Strike," pp. 76–85.

58. Tadeusz Cieślak, "Pismo polskich robotników w Westfalii 'Wiarus Polski' (1890–1923)," *Rocznik historii czasopiśmiennictwa polskiego*, XI, No. 2 (1972), pp. 235–236, citing WP, 28 Jan. 1905.

59. WP, No. 18, 22 Jan. 1905, *Dziennik Polski*, No. 14, 19 Jan. 1905, *Gesammtüberblick*, XIV, No. 4, 31 Jan. 1905, pp. 84–85.

60. *Orędownik*, No. 18, 22 Jan. 1905, excerpts reprinted in Witold Jakóbczyk, ed., *Wielkopolska (1851–1914): Wybór źródeł* (Wrocław: Ossolineum, 1954), pp. 76–77.

61. 24 Jan. 1905, No. 19, excerpts reprinted in *ibid.*, pp. 74–76.

in the mines whereas the ZZP along with the other unions looked to the government for favorable intervention.

According to one source, contributions to the strike fund from the homeland amounted to less than 7,000 marks.[62] The *Alter Verband* reported that altogether the ZZP collected 8,000 marks, a tiny fraction of the nearly 2 million-mark total contributed to the strike fund.[63] If the national character of the ZZP enabled it to appeal to Polish society in the homeland, its class character limited the effectiveness of that appeal.

Nevertheless, the ZZP and the striking miners received support from the official representatives of Polish society, the Polish deputies in the Prussian Landtag and the German Reichstag. In the Reichstag, the co-founder of the ZZP, Jan Brejski, defended the miners' cause in a speech on 23 January 1905.[64] He and the other Polish deputies did not confine their speeches to issues unique to Polish miners. They also addressed the broader issues of concern to all miners and, along with the social democrats, stood as loyal proponents of the workers' demands.

The Strike Ends

Despite an announcement by the Prussian government that it would propose legislation amending the mining law, the Commission of Seven cited the refusal of the Miner Owners Association to make any concessions and therefore declined to call off the strike. But the government's decision to intervene in the dispute led to the first division within the Commission, with the *Gewerkverein* in favor of an immediate end to the strike. Thus, when on 31 January the strike spread to a mine on the left bank of the Rhine, the *Gewerkverein* instructed its members there to continue working. The *Alter Verband* and the ZZP wanted to prolong the strike until there was more evidence that it had achieved something of benefit for the miners. Still, they also had to face the refusal of the miner owners to negotiate and the depletion of their financial resources to pay

62. Adam Piotrowski, *Powstanie i rozwój polskich związków zawodowych pod zaborem pruskim* (Poznań: Nakładem i drukiem "Pracy" Sp. z ogr. p., 1910), p. 95.

63. Fricke, *Ruhrbergarbeiterstreik*, p. 187; Hue, "Über den Generalstreik," p. 209, states that the ZZP collected about 10,000 marks, the *Gewerkverein* about 200,000 marks, and the *Alter Verband* 1,200,000.

64. *Stenographische Berichte über die Verhandlungen des Reichstags*, 23 Jan. 1905, VI, 3967–3971.

strikers. Moreover, with the government formulating new legislation, the unions did not want to alienate public support by continuing the strike.[65] Thus the Commission of Seven called a meeting on 9 February in Essen to consider ending the strike. The delegates included twenty from the ZZP, seventy-six from the *Alter Verband*, sixty-seven from the *Gewerkverein*, and six from the Hirsch-Duncker Union. Although a number of delegates, including at least three Polish-speaking miners, spoke in favor of continuing the strike, the Commission of Seven had already decided to end it: printed bilingual (German and Polish) fliers signed by the Commission of Seven that called the suspension of the strike simply a truce awaited the delegates as they emerged from the meeting. During the debate, the ZZP's chairman and member of the Commission of Seven Regulski used the same term when he spoke in favor of halting the strike. In the end, the overwhelming majority of delegates accepted the arguments of union leaders and voted to return to work the next day, 10 February.[66]

Nevertheless, the decision to end the strike encountered considerable resistance. Although ZZP activists joined those of the other unions in speaking at miners' meetings in favor of following the lead of the Commission of Seven, the Polish union like the others faced dissension in its own ranks. At a meeting for Polish miners in Bottrop on 9 February, speakers from the ZZP and the *Alter Verband* announced the decision reached in Essen and called on all miners to resume work.[67] The unions had a large following among the Polish-speaking miners in Bottrop. With few exceptions, the 350 members of the *Alter Verband* in Bottrop in 1904 were all Poles.[68] With the growth of the unions during the strike, the ZZP had a membership in Bottrop that equaled two thirds of the number of eastern migrants working in its mines.[69] Like the unions, the *Wiarus Polski* urged miners on 10 February to follow the decision of the Essen conference, saying that nothing gives capitalists greater pleasure than

65. Fricke, *Ruhrbergarbeiterstreik*, p. 131.

66. HSTAD, RD 15925, ff. 183, 238–255, report on the meeting; f. 269, RPA to MdI, 10 Feb. 1905, copy, lists three main speakers for the meeting, one from each of the German-led unions but none from the ZZP. See also a report on the meeting and the immediate reaction to its decision, "Waffenstillstand. Aus dem Streikgebiet," *Soziale Praxis*, 16 Feb. 1905, columns 500–503.

67. Stadtarchiv Bottrop, A V-3, Nr. 3, police report, typed copy provided by the archive.

68. Fricke, *Ruhrbergarbeiterstreik*, p. 53.

69. On the migrants in the work force in Bottrop in 1905, see Schulze, *Polnische Zuwanderung*, pp. 96, 100; according to Stadtarchiv Bottrop, A V-3, Nr. 3, Amtmann to LR Recklinghausen, 18 Feb. 1905, the ZZP had c. 1,800 members in Bottrop.

when miners do not act in solidarity.[70] Nevertheless, on 11 February over half of those still on strike in the rural county of Recklinghausen worked in the mines in Bottrop, and the last miners in Bottrop to resume work were Polish.[71]

A violent clash between a crowd and the gendarmes accompanied the continuation of the strike in Bottrop and may have contributed to the tenacity of the strike there.[72] But, in another case, a ZZP delegate at the meeting in Essen actually spoke in favor of continuing the strike at meetings of the work forces of the Neumühl and Deutscher Kaiser III/IV mines.[73] Elsewhere, however, it seems that the ZZP worked effectively to bring the strike to an orderly conclusion.[74]

The ZZP sought to deflect the miners' anger and dissatisfaction from the union itself. At a meeting of its board, Polish miners' delegates, and other activists on 12 February, the union's chairman Regulski admitted that many miners wanted to continue the strike but a lack of funds made that impossible.[75] He mentioned demands for more strike pay and claimed that without it many who had nothing to live on would have resumed work anyway. Moreover, he argued, the strike had no immediate prospects of victory. Because dissatisfaction with the decision to end the strike resulted in a rumor that Brzeskot had been removed from the Commission because he favored continuing the strike, Regulski explained that his removal resulted from an internal dispute between Brzeskot and the board of the ZZP.[76]

The resolution voted at the ZZP meeting expressed regret over breaking off the strike so unexpectedly, contrary to the miners' general inclination, but argued that otherwise there would have been a split in the miners' organization, their sole means of defense. The resolution also

70. WP, No. 33.

71. STAM, OP 2849, Bd. 6, LR Recklinghausen to RPM, 11 Feb. 1905, copy; STAM, RM VII, Nr. 35b, LR Recklinghausen, 28 Feb. 1905.

72. STAM, RA I, Nr. 66, RPM to MdI, 11 Feb. 1905, copy; another copy is in HSTAD, RD 15925, ff. 294–297; Stadtarchiv Bottrop, A V–3, Nr. 3, Amtmann to LR Recklinghausen, 18 Feb. 1905, draft.

73. HSTAD, RD 15925, LR Ruhrort, p. 254, 10 Feb. 1905; RD Präs 874, ff. 320–321, 3 March 1905.

74. For a discussion of the statistics of the strike at its end, see John J. Kulczycki, *The Foreign Worker and the German Labor Movement: Xenophobia and Solidarity in the Coal Fields of the Ruhr, 1871–1914* (Oxford, Providence, USA: Berg Publishers, 1994), p. 195.

75. WP, No. 36, 14 Feb. 1905, carried a report on the meeting.

76. Brzeskot left the Commission of Seven well before the decision to end the strike; the *Alter Verband* leader Otto Hue intimated to the police that Brzeskot's departure did not constitute a great loss for the Commission, STAM, RA I, Nr. 64, Königl. Polizei Kommissar, Bochum, 2 Feb. 1905.

called on the ZZP to influence the Commission of Seven to consult with miners' delegates before taking important decisions and to report fully on its activities. Thus, the ZZP tried to disassociate itself from a decision taken in common with the other unions in the Commission and sought to curry the favor of those who had opposed that decision. As a result, the ZZP found itself on the same side as German social democrats who attacked the leadership of the *Alter Verband* for ending the strike.[77]

Nevertheless, dissension continued within the ranks of the ZZP. Brzeskot, who had worked actively to support the strike until his break with the board of the ZZP, published a brochure prior to the union's annual general assembly in Steele on 12 March 1905. In it he attacked the leadership of the ZZP, blaming it for the union's disorganization during the phenomenal growth in membership that the strike brought the union and even accusing certain union officials of drunkenness. This led some members to threaten to withhold their dues and to call for the election of new leaders, even in the *Wiarus Polski*.[78] As a result, Regulski declined to seek reelection. To succeed him as chairman, the union chose another coal miner, Wojciech Sosiński, who in his report at the meeting sharply criticized the union's administration and accused Brzeskot of seeking to divide the union during the strike. Jan Korpus, who had replaced Brzeskot on the Commission of Seven after his break with the union leadership, became the new secretary.[79]

The conflict over leadership of the ZZP played out in the wider context of the continuing battle between the *Wiarus Polski* and the *Dziennik Polski* for influence over the Poles in the Ruhr. The *Wiarus Polski* characterized itself as a workers' newspaper and claimed that set it apart from the *Dziennik Polski*, which looked to other circles for support and even sought to create an aristocracy in the emigration, the "Westphalian *szlachta*" as the workers supposedly referred to it.[80] The editor of the *Dziennik*, Ignacy Żniński, exploited the dissatisfaction of many Polish miners with the abrupt end of the strike and its lack of substantive results. He printed Brzeskot's brochure attacking the leadership of the ZZP. At a

77. Leimpeters, "Taktik," pp. 485–495.

78. *Dziennik Polski*, No. 59, 12 March 1905, *Gesammtüberblick*, No. 11, 21 March 1905, p. 255; WP, No. 57, 10 March 1905, *Gesammtüberblick*, No. 12, 28 March 1905, pp. 279–280.

79. Franciszek Mańkowski, "Geschichte der polnischen Verbände," *Kalendarz Górniczy*, 1913, in German translation, STAM, RM VII, Nr. 36c, p. 111; Murzynowska, *Polskie wychodźstwo*, p. 144.

80. WP, No. 41, 19 Feb. 1905, *Gesammtüberblick*, No. 9, 7 March 1905, p. 199; *szlachta* is the Polish term for Poland's historic nobility.

meeting of the Union of Poles (ZPwN) on 12 February in Oberhausen, where most strikers opposed the decision to return to work and some continued to reject it, Żniński seemed to pose the ZPwN as an alternative to the ZZP when he spoke of the need for organization to collect a large fund for a strike.[81] In any case, the 500 present expressed their disagreement with the Commission of Seven. Although at the start of the strike the *Dziennik Polski* printed the appeal for contributions to the union's strike fund, the ZZP later charged that the *Dziennik* forwarded to the union only 14.45 marks of the approximately 300 marks it collected in response to the appeal.[82] Żniński lamely replied that the ZZP continually ignored his newspaper and therefore he did not feel the obligation to provide assistance where it was not wanted.

Defeat of the strike also bred dissension among the unions that made up the Commission of Seven as the search for scapegoats began. Before the end of February, in their presses, the *Alter Verband* and the *Gewerkverein* labelled each other as "traitors to the miners."[83] A miner writing to the *Dziennik Berliński* (Berlin Daily) at the end of March claimed that the ZZP was staying out of the battle between the two German unions, a battle that could only gladden the mine owners, for which workers could thank the leaders of the *Zentrum* and the socialists.[84]

Yet the ZZP got in its licks, too. At a union meeting in Essen attended by 120 on 26 February, Sosiński, prior to his election as chairman of the ZZP, defended the Commission of Seven from complaints that it had accomplished nothing. Comparing the recent strike and the one in Herne in 1899, with its many bloody conflicts and criminal penalties, he attributed the "beautiful order" and behavior of the miners during the recent strike entirely to the unions and the Commission of Seven. Nevertheless, after blaming the brutality of the capitalists for the strike, he went on to hold others responsible as well. Singling out the *Alter Verband*, he claimed that it thought that the strike would win it members and harm the other organizations. Supposedly the Poles constituted the primary target because the *Alter Verband* and the socialists believed they would be the first to need financial support. According to Sosiński, however, the opposite occurred: the Poles wanted to strike another four weeks while the other trade unions pushed for a resumption of work. As

81. HSTAD, RD 15925, ff. 309–310, Polizei-Verwaltung, 13 Feb. 1905. On the strike in Oberhausen, see Mogs, "Sozialgeschichtliche Entwicklung," p. 153.

82. *Robotnik Polski*, No. 37, 9 May 1905, *Gesammtüberblick*, No. 20, 23 May 1905, pp. 491–492.

83. Rosenberg, "Ruhr Coal Strike," p. 311, citing *Bergarbeiter-Zeitung*, 25 Feb. 1905.

84. 30 March 1905, No. 73, clipping, Biblioteka Raczyńskich, Poznań, MS. 800, f. 3.

for the government, he saw it playing into the hands of the social democrats by not acting sooner to allay dissatisfaction among miners.[85]

The leadership of the ZZP deftly exploited the miners' dissatisfaction that found expression in the strike of 1905. As a result, the ZZP became a major player in the labor movement in the Ruhr. By the end of the strike, it included in its ranks a majority of all the organized Polish-speaking miners in the Ruhr and therefore could legitimately pose as the spokesman for a quarter of the work force in the region's mines. Although membership in the other unions also grew, none grew as fast as that of the ZZP. It accomplished this by expressing and supporting the class grievances of the miners at the same time as it identified with the cultural characteristics that differentiated the Polish-speaking miners from the native workers. The ZZP's success in this effort testifies to both its class and its ethnic character. It was no less a union for being Polish than the *Alter Verband* and *Gewerkverein* were for being German. Further evidence of this would come in the years following the 1905 strike from both the internal development of the ZZP and its participation in the labor movement.

---

85. HSTAD, RD Präs 874, ff. 207–208, police report, Essen, 26 Feb. 1905.

3

Consolidation of the Polish Union Movement, 1905–1912

In the decade and a half before World War I, as the trade unions of Germany built up their strength, they evolved from combat formations primarily concerned with higher wages into all-encompassing social-political interest groups.[1] The development of the ZZP reflected this evolution primarily in the period following the 1905 strike. In fact, none of the unions went through a greater transformation than the ZZP during these years. As a result of this transformation, the ZZP contributed to the growing importance of disciplined organizations that characterized both sides of the dispute between management and labor in Germany prior to World War I.[2]

The Growth and Development of the ZZP after the 1905 Strike

The strike and its attendant disputes within the ZZP had resulted in a change in leadership at the union's annual general assembly in March 1905, with Wojciech Sosiński assuming the chairmanship. But a significant change in the union statute came only later in the year. The strike demonstrated the financial weakness of the unions, and the *Gewerkverein* in particular led the way in streamlining its organization and drastically raising its dues from 50 Pfennige per month to 40 Pfennige per week.[3] The ZZP followed suit at a special meeting of its general assembly in Gelsenkirchen on 26 November 1905, raising dues for its

1. Klaus Schönhoven, "Die Gewerkschaften als Massenbewegung im Wilhelmischen Kaiserreich 1890 bis 1918," in *Geschichte der deutschen Gewerkschaften von den Anfängen bis 1945*, ed. by Ulrich Borsdorf (Cologne: Bund-Verlag, 1987), p. 212.

2. Elaine Glovka Spencer, "West German Coal, Iron and Steel Industrialists as Employers, 1896–1914" (Unpublished Ph.D. Dissertation, University of California at Berkeley, 1969), p. 262. No general account of this development in the labor movement of the Ruhr considers the ZZP.

3. Hans Mommsen *et al.*, *Bergarbeiter. Ausstellung zur Geschichte der organisierten Bergarbeiterbewegung in Deutschland* (Bochum: Berg-Verlag GmbH, 1969) (unpaged); Max Jürgen Koch, *Die Bergarbeiterbewegung im Ruhrgebiet zur Zeit Wilhelms II. (1889–1914)* (Düsseldorf: Droste, 1954), p. 109; Eric Dorn Brose, *Christian Labor and the Politics of Frustration in Imperial Germany* (Washington, D.C.: The Catholic University of America Press, 1985), pp. 177–178.

members in the Ruhr from 50 Pfennige per month to 30 Pfennige per week as well as doubling the initiation fee from 25 Pfennige to 50.[4] Furthermore, the ZZP for the first time included strike pay among the benefits of membership, alongside assistance in case of illness and unemployment. The union set aside two thirds of the dues collected for a strike fund and received the right to levy additional contributions on members not affected by a strike. Although the ZZP demonstrated its militancy in the 1905 strike, these changes clearly marked the ZZP as a union ready to use strikes as a means to further the material interests of its members.

Apparently, the increase in dues did not adversely affect the ability of the ZZP to recruit members. By 1 February 1906 its membership in all of Germany reached 32,000, which exceeded the already expanded membership following the strike by some 30 percent.[5] Rapid growth continued until 1908 when an economic downturn affected German industry. The ZZP had 40,962 members (35,863 or 88 percent in the Ruhr) at the end of 1906, 47,926 (39,256 or 82 percent in the Ruhr) at the end of 1907, and 48,952 (40,842 or 83 percent in the Ruhr) on 1 April 1908.[6] At the same time, the ZZP greatly increased its financial strength and thus its ability to provide benefits for its members. Its income in 1906 (192,247 marks from 1 February) exceeded twice the amount in 1905 (95,231 marks including January 1906) and in 1907 rose to 222,954 marks. The economic downturn meant that the union had to pay out more in unemployment benefits, over twice as much in 1908 (7,322.20 marks) as in 1907 (3,312.60 marks).[7] The union's total assets rose from 56,834

4. Stanisław Wachowiak, *Polacy w Nadrenii i Westfalii* (Poznań: Nakładem Zjednoczenia Zawodowego Polskiego, 1917), p. 121; Marjan Chełmikowski, *Związki zawodowe robotników polskich w Królestwie Pruskim (1889–1918)* (Poznań: Fiszer i Majewski, 1925), pp. 89–90, 176, 178, 181, 183–184; Krystyna Murzynowska, *Polskie wychodźstwo zarobkowe w Zagłębiu Ruhry w latach 1880–1914* (Wrocław: Ossolineum, 1972), p. 145.

5. Franciszek Mańkowski, "Historja Z.Z.P.," in *Ćwierć wieku pracy dla Narodu i Robotnika* (Poznań: Nakładem Zarządu Centralnego Zjedn. Zawod. Polskiego, 1927), p. 67, puts the total membership at the end of Jan. 1906 at 32,364; Wachowiak, *Polacy*, p. 132, puts it at 31,680; HSTAD, RD 874, f. 267, put the total on 1 April 1905 at 24,611.

6. Christoph Klessmann, *Polnische Bergarbeiter im Ruhrgebiet 1870–1945: Soziale Integration und nationale Subkultur einer Minderheit in der deutschen Industriegesellschaft* (Göttingen: Vandenhoeck & Ruprecht, 1978), p. 283; STAM, OP 5365, RPA, 18 April 1908, and Joh. Victor Bredt, *Die Polenfrage im Ruhrkohlengebiet. Eine wirtschaftspolitische Studie* (Leipzig: Duncker & Humblot, 1909), p. 52, for 1908.

7. Mańkowski, "Historja," p. 87.

marks on 1 February 1906 to 133,904 marks at the end of 1906 and 234,492 at the end of 1907.[8] This growth in strength made the ZZP an increasingly credible alternative to the *Alter Verband* and the *Gewerkverein*. Indeed, the ZZP organ *Zjednoczenie* claimed that over 3,000 of 5,400 new members recruited by the ZZP between 1 April 1905 and 1 January 1906 came from the *Alter Verband*.[9] Still, substantial numbers of Polish-speaking miners continued to belong to the German-led unions. According to estimates of the Prussian authorities, in 1906 the *Alter Verband* had 8,155 Polish members and the *Gewerkverein* 3,816; in 1908 in the Düsseldorf district, the ZZP had 4,216 members while the *Alter Verband* had 923 Polish members and the *Gewerkverein* 886.[10] Furthermore, the ZZP still encompassed only a fraction of the Ruhr's Polish-speaking coal miners.

Much of the growth in the ZZP in the years following the 1905 strike came outside the Ruhr. Yet the dominant element in the ZZP remained the Polish workers in the Ruhr. This meant above all Polish miners, even though membership in the Ruhr grew among other Polish workers. A miner, Sosiński, headed the union until 1913, and another miner succeeded him. As a migrant from Poznania, Sosiński had contributed to laying the groundwork for the establishment of the union.[11] In 1905 he replaced Antoni Brejski as editor of the union organ *Zjednoczenie*.[12] Another miner who had promoted the idea of a Polish trade union before its realization, Mańkowski, also assumed increasing responsibility in the union following the 1905 strike. At the general assembly in March 1905,

8. Wachowiak, *Polacy*, p. 132. Note that the figures for the union's annual income were inflated by the practice of including funds left over in cash from the previous year, Chełmikowski, *Związki*, p. 169.

9. Cited by Chełmikowski, *Związki*, p. 209.

10. Klessmann, *Polnische Bergarbeiter*, pp. 117; STAM, OP 6351, 26 March 1909. Bredt, *Polenfrage*, p. 53, estimates the Polish membership of the *Alter Verband* and the *Gewerkverein* to be 7,000 and 8,000 respectively.

11. *Wielkopolski słownik biograficzny* (Warsaw: Państwowe Wydawnictwo Naukowe, 1981), p. 687; Andrzej Wachowiak, "Wspomnienia z polskiej, robotniczej emigracji do Westfalii i Nadrenii oraz do Francji z konca XIX i początku XX wieku" (Typed manuscript, 1965), p. 26, Wspomnienie No. 839, Zakład Historii i Teorii Ruchu Zawodowego, Centrum Studiów Związków Zawodowych, Ogólnopolskie Porozumienie Związków Zawodowych, Warsaw.

12. *Zjednoczenie* had a circulation approximately equal to the union's membership, 41,000 copies in April 1907 and 46,000 in March 1908, APP, Polizeipräsidium 4964, p. 12, Polizei Verwaltung, Stadt Bochum, 11 April 1907; p. 20, Oberbürgermeister, Stadt Bochum, 17 March 1908.

he succeeded Brzeskot as director of the ZZP's legal aid bureau.[13] Chosen in 1906 as chairman of the union's board of supervisors, he presided in 1907 over the reorganization of the union into seventeen districts (fourteen in the Ruhr). He served as chairman of the board and of its executive committee created in 1907 until he took charge of office operations as one of the ZZP's few paid officials in 1908. In 1909 he took over as editor of the union organ.[14]

Unification of the Polish Workers' Organizations in Germany

Despite an eagerness to expand, the ZZP proved hesitant when it came to a fusion with two worker organizations based in the homeland. The first public suggestion of such a fusion came in November 1904 from a militantly nationalist source, the *Dziennik Śląski* (Silesian Daily), published by the Polish parliamentary deputy Wojciech Korfanty.[15] A fusion made sense from a national point of view. Not only did rivalry among the three organizations divert resources from competing against German trade unions, but the geographic dispersion of their centers in the Ruhr, Poznań, and Upper Silesia provided the basis for an organization encompassing the major concentrations of Polish-speaking workers throughout Germany.

As we saw, the ZZP sought to expand in the homeland by organizing a meeting in Toruń, Jan Brejski's base of operations, in November 1904. Having achieved prominence during the 1905 strike, the ZZP followed with further recruiting efforts in the homeland, holding meetings in as many as twelve places in September 1905 alone. Although nearly all of these meetings took place in the provinces of East and West Prussia, the ZZP organized one in Poznania in 1905 and another in 1906. By mid-1906, the ZZP succeeded in recruiting over 2,000 members in this region, which almost equaled the total membership of the Polish workers'

13. Krystyna Murzynowska, "Ruch zawodowy robotników polskich w Zagłębiu Ruhry," in *Ruch zawodowy w Polsce: Zarys dziejów*, ed. by Stanisław Kalabiński, Vol. I (Warsaw: Instytut Wydawniczy CRZZ, 1974), p. 493.

14. Mańkowski, "Historja," pp. 69–71, 75, 82; Wachowiak, "Wspomnienia," pp. 52–54; see also *Wielkopolski słownik biograficzny*, pp. 453–454.

15. Chełmikowski, *Związki*, p. 102.

organization headquartered in Poznań, the *Polski Związek Zawodowy* (Polish Trade Union) or PZZ.[16] Formed in 1902 about a half year before the ZZP, the PZZ owed its existence primarily to members of Poznań's Polish intelligentsia associated with the aggressively nationalist National Democrats.[17] The union's first board of supervisors came entirely from their ranks and included not a single worker. Even the first head of the union was the owner of a dyeworks rather than a worker. The organization took an active part in the movement for better wages, but it showed a greater preference than the local German unions for a conciliatory approach toward employers. Class cooperation rather than class conflict characterized its tactics. Indeed, it looked for financial assistance from the wealthier elements of Polish society. Above all, it sought to organize Polish workers to protect them from Germanization in German trade unions rather than from exploitation by Polish or even German employers.[18]

Although the PZZ reacted positively to the call of the *Dziennik Śląski* for a fusion of the three Polish unions, it began actively to pursue an agreement when in 1905 it faced increasing competition from the ZZP in what it considered its regional domain.[19] At first, it found the ZZP largely unresponsive and then the ZZP laid down its own terms, which amounted to absorption of the PZZ by the ZZP rather than fusion on equal terms. Final agreement only came at a meeting in Bochum of the ZZP central directorate and board of supervisors along with the three members of the PZZ's directorate on 14 September 1908, nearly four years after the first suggestion of a fusion. According to the agreement, the PZZ would dissolve in 1909, with its members becoming members of the ZZP and one member of its directorate joining that of the ZZP. While the PZZ organ *Siła* (Strength) would cease publication with the new year, the ZZP agreed to adopt its name for its union organ as a relic of the former organization.

---

16. *Ibid.*, pp. 96–97; Tadeusz Filipiak, *Dzieje związków zawodowych w Wielkopolsce do roku 1919: Studium porównawcze z historii gospodarczo-społecznej* (Poznań: Wydawnictwo Poznańskie, 1965), pp. 195–196.

17. Jerzy Marczewski, *Narodowa Demokracja w Poznańskiem 1900–1914* (Warsaw: Państwowe Wydawnictwo Naukowe, 1967), pp. 143–144.

18. Chełmikowski, *Związki*, pp. 52–63, 244–249.

19. Adam Piotrowski, *Powstanie i rozwój polskich związków zawodowych pod zaborem pruskim* (Poznań: Nakładem i drukiem "Pracy" Sp. z ogr. p., 1910), pp. 114–131, provides the PZZ version of the negotiations leading to the fusion; the author served as general secretary of the PZZ directorate 1903–1908, *Wielkopolski słownik biograficzny*, p. 571.

The complete capitulation of the PZZ and particularly the decision not to move the union's headquarters to Poznań led to some criticism in the Polish press outside the Ruhr.[20] At the meeting in Bochum, the PZZ chairman Stanisław Nowicki explained his willingness to accept fusion on such uneven terms by invoking the Polish national cause and claiming that dissension among Polish trade unions led Polish workers to join German unions.[21] As Nowicki himself suggested, PZZ activists in the homeland felt this threat more keenly than their counterparts in the Ruhr. Indeed, throughout the discussion of consolidation of these organizations, ZZP activists gave priority to guarding their union's working-class character and their own interests as union leaders rather than to furthering the national cause.

Many migrants to the Ruhr who had worked as agricultural laborers for Polish landowners in the homeland were antagonistic to the Polish upper classes, whom they bitterly blamed for the economic necessity of their peregrinations far from home. ZZP leaders were also well aware of the domination of Polish society and its institutions in Prussian Poland by the professional intelligentsia and propertied elements. ZZP activists saw the PZZ in the same light. As a ZZP delegate for the Gdańsk region put it at a meeting in Pelplin in 1906, "There are those who are angry at the *Zjednoczenie Zawodowe Polskie* because it does not want to unite with people who are neither workers nor artisans. But the very idea of an organization of workers and artisans is not to succumb to the influence of capitalists."[22] Moreover, ZZP activists, as leaders of the far stronger of the two organizations, saw no advantage in subordinating their authority to Polish nationalist leaders in Poznań.

Still, the ZZP felt compelled not to reject entirely the possibility of fusion. In 1906 workers meeting in Gdańsk and Pelplin passed resolutions demanding unification of the two organizations, and this type of public pressure continued. The PZZ also had sufficient influence in some places to impede ZZP efforts at expansion. In addition, the economic downturn and an intensification of the anti-Polish policies of the Prussian authorities may have further influenced the ZZP.[23] Nevertheless, the ZZP only accepted the offer of a marriage when its suitor agreed to vanish leaving hardly a trace.

20. Chełmikowski, *Związki*, p. 108.

21. Mańkowski, "Historja," p. 78.

22. Chełmikowski, *Związki*, p. 104, citing *Gazeta Toruńska*.

23. *Ibid.*, pp. 99–101, 104; Piotrowski, *Powstanie*, pp. 123–126, 129; Filipiak, *Dzieje*, p. 218.

The third entity involved in the fusion of Polish worker organizations in 1909 did not originally have the character of a trade union. The *Związek Wzajemnej Pomocy Chrześcijańskiej Robotników Górnośląskich* (Union of Upper Silesian Workers for Christian Mutual Aid) or ZWP dated from 1889 and owed its existence to the initiative of clergymen and Adam Napieralski, long the leading Polish political leader in Upper Silesia and an advocate of cooperation with the German Catholic *Zentrum*. As its name suggests, the organization above all promoted mutual financial assistance among its members, particularly in case of death. In wage struggles, it played an essentially passive role, preferring to maintain good relations with employers. Only near the end of its separate existence did it develop in a more militant direction, as if in preparation for unification with the ZZP, which took a more aggressive stance in defense of the interests of its members.[24]

From the very beginning, talk of fusion always included the ZWP despite its different character. By 1907 the ZZP and the ZWP had already agreed to waive the initiation fee for each other's members if they moved between the Ruhr and Upper Silesia. Thus, at least temporarily, the ZZP accepted a regional partition with the ZWP, which it did not with the PZZ. No threat of domination emanated from Upper Silesia as it did from Poznań. Thus, once the ZZP absorbed the PZZ, it moved to bring in the ZWP as well. This time objections of a social character came not from the ZZP but from the other side, from some ZWP staff members with academic backgrounds who feared the changes that the working-class autodidacts of the ZZP might introduce. Nevertheless, the ZWP general assembly approved the fusion.[25]

Restructuring the ZZP

Meanwhile, the ZZP directorate and board of supervisors began work on restructuring the union in ways that significantly affected its relations with miners in the Ruhr. At Mańkowski's suggestion, the ZZP took up an earlier proposal to reorganize the union by trade, creating a separate section for miners as well as sections for other workers. Under the proposal the union's central directorate would retain control of a common treasury as a means of maintaining its authority.[26]

24. Chełmikowski, *Związki*, pp. 249–254; Piotrowski, *Powstanie*, pp. 97–98.
25. Mańkowski, "Historja," pp. 70, 82.
26. *Ibid.*, pp. 81, 83.

Final approval of the ZZP's revised statute came at a general assembly of representatives of the three organizations in Bochum held from 2 to 6 May 1909. Meeting in the Ruhr rather than in Poznań as PZZ activists desired, the assembly also marked the triumph of the ZZP by retaining its name for the consolidated union rather than that of the much older ZWP as activists from Upper Silesia proposed. But regional and organizational loyalties did not entirely disappear. Followers of Jan Brejski, whose influence the fusion was bound to diminish, attacked the ZZP chairman Sosiński for his growing political ties to Upper Silesia, which they saw as harmful to the interests of the union in the Ruhr. Only a threat on the part of the Upper Silesian delegates to walk out cut short the dispute. In the end, the assembly chose Sosiński to continue to head the ZZP as chairman; he together with another Ruhr miner, Józef Rymer, as secretary and the ZWP chairman Wojciech Wieczorek as treasurer constituted the union's central directorate. This central directorate not only controlled the union's assets but also had the right to appoint officials nominated for the union's sections and to audit their administration. After a long discussion, a slight majority voted to keep the central headquarters in Bochum; a large minority preferred Upper Silesia, while few chose Poznań, apparently out of a fear that non-workers would fill its offices.[27]

Regional particularism also haunted the discussion of the organization of the union's sections. The Upper Silesian delegates demanded that the Miners' Section have its headquarters in their region. They wanted to preserve the ZWP in some form, even proposing a cartel directed by the ZZP with Upper Silesia retaining the ZWP's separate treasury, but the Ruhr's delegates prevailed. For the directorate of the Miners' Section with its headquarters in Bochum, the assembly chose Mańkowski as chairman and three other ZZP activists from the Ruhr region, Franciszek Kołpacki, Józef Trzebniak, and Jan Jankowiak, as deputy chairman, secretary, and treasurer, respectively. The other sections built on the regional traditions of the predecessor unions, with the headquarters of the Metalworkers' Section in Upper Silesia and that of the Artisan-Workers' Section in

27. Murzynowska, *Polskie wychodźstwo*, p. 208–212; Mańkowski, "Historja," pp. 88–90; from time to time articles appeared in the Polish press demanding that people with academic training take over the leadership of the consolidated union, Wachowiak, *Polacy*, p. 128. With regard to a split within the ZZP, see STAM, OP 5365, RPA, 28 April 1909, which reports a conflict between Jan Brejski, who supposedly opposed unification with the ZWP out of personal and business reasons, and Sosiński, who had the backing of deputies Korfanty and Kulerski; Polizei-Präsident, Bochum, 8 Aug. 1909, who calls the May general assembly a defeat for Brejski and claims that wide circles in the Ruhr blamed the Brejski brothers and *Wiarus Polski* for the government's charges that the ZZP had been used for Polish national political goals.

Poznań. Each section would also publish its own biweekly union organ, with the Miners' Section issuing *Głos Górnika* (Voice of the Miner).[28] As their role in the leadership of the newly consolidated union indicates, Polish workers in the Ruhr, particularly coal miners, continued to dominate the ZZP. The old ZZP outweighed the two organizations it absorbed. Even though ZZP membership had apparently declined drastically in the months prior to unification, it probably still had twice the number of members of the other two organizations combined. Furthermore, 356,893.73 marks or 76 percent of the combined union assets came from the old ZZP. The newly formed Miners' Section of the ZZP, nearly 80 percent of whose members (17,772 out of 22,243) worked in the mines of the Ruhr, accounted for two thirds of the consolidated union's membership.[29]

This center of gravity in the Ruhr is of course what enabled the ZZP, an organization that had its origin among emigrants, to absorb the labor organizations in the homeland and dictate the form and even the character of the consolidated Polish labor organization in Germany. Thus, the ZZP played an important role not only in the labor movement in the Ruhr but in Prussian Poland as well. This role is perhaps unique in Polish history: is there another example of an organization formed in emigration that absorbed and dominated organizations that affected such a significant aspect of public life in the homeland? Writing about it years later, Mańkowski expressed justifiable pride in what workers in the Ruhr had accomplished, "without the help and efforts of higher circles."[30]

As part of its transformation following the 1905 strike, the ZZP also developed its internal administration. In January 1906, the ZZP directorate and board of supervisors voted to make the office of treasurer,

28. Murzynowska, *Polskie wychodźstwo*, p. 212; Mańkowski, "Historja," pp. 89–90.

29. There is little agreement on statistics regrading union membership at the time of consolidation. RPA, 15 Oct. 1908, to MdI, cites the claimed membership of the ZZP before consolidation as 45,000, that of the PZZ as 5,000, and of the ZWP as 10,000, copy, APP, Polizeipräsidium 2692, pp. 124–125. Other sources agree on the round figure of 5,000 for the PZZ: Chełmikowski, *Związki*, p. 53. But Kazimierz Popiołek, ed., *Dzieje górniczego ruchu zawodowego w Polsce (do 1918 R.)*, Vol. I (Warsaw: Wydawnictwo Związkowe CRZZ, 1971), p. 94, gave the membership of the ZWP as about 3,800 at the end of 1908; this is too low since the new miners' section alone had 3,798 members in Upper Silesia, and the new metalworkers' section had 5,749 members, presumably most of them in Upper Silesia, Mańkowski, "Historja," pp. 99–100. Murzynowska, *Polskie wychodźstwo*, p. 213, discusses discrepancies in the sources concerning membership, yet her estimate of 48,000 in the ZZP seems far too high since the new miners' section had only 17,772 members in the Ruhr after consolidation. On the assets of each of the unions, see Wachowiak, *Polacy*, p. 133.

30. Mańkowski, "Historja," pp. 84–85.

who served in the union's central directorate, a paid position, only the third such position in the union. By 1907 the ZZP headquarters in Bochum had five paid officials, by 1908 seven. Fusion of the unions and continued growth brought a further increase in the number of union officials, which reached a total of twenty-nine in 1911, seven of whom worked in the office of the Miners' Section.

The Polish workers' suspicion of non-workers kept the salaries of union officials low: although salaries were raised in 1907, even the ZZP chairman received only 180 marks per month. With the reorganization accompanying consolidation, the members of the central directorate were to receive a maximum of 210 marks. A decision in 1907 to grant district delegates attending conferences a meal allowance of 1 mark plus the cost of third-class travel led Mańkowski to grouse that, even five years after the start of the union, one worked for it almost for nothing. It offered no easy sinecures. Stanisław Wachowiak, himself the son of a Ruhr miner and an employee of the union, blamed the low union wages on workers' lack of appreciation for the difficulty of the union official's task.[31] The ZZP was to remain an organization both for and of the Polish working class. Bureaucratization did not remove union officials far from their working-class origins, nor did it greatly increase the union's administrative costs. In 1907, for example, they scarcely amounted to a remarkably low 8 percent and rose to about 11 percent by 1911.[32]

The union also safeguarded its character by choosing its officials almost exclusively from the working class. Nevertheless, it sought to increase the professionalism of its activists. In December 1905, the ZZP directorate and board of supervisors voted in favor of a course in bookkeeping for the treasurers of union locals. In July 1906 the union organized a course for union delegates on the union's internal administration and in recruitment methods. In addition, the ZZP decided to offer courses in economics to raise the level of speakers at union meetings. By 1911, the ZZP was running courses for the union's

---

31. *Ibid.*, pp. 66, 71, 73, 87, 90, 118–119; Chełmikowski, *Związki*, p. 133; Wachowiak, *Polacy*, pp. 161–163.

32. Herbert Fulde, *Die polnische Arbeitergewerkschaftsbewegung* (Weinfelden: A.-G. Neuenschwander'sche Verlagsbuchhandlung, 1931), p. 92; Chełmikowski, *Związki*, p. 171. Schönhoven, "Gewerkschaften," p. 231, notes the trend toward bureaucratization among German unions in the decade and a half before World War I and connects it with an attempt to achieve stability in the face of the large turnover in membership.

candidates for election as pension fund elders and other elective positions in the mines.[33]

Union Membership after the Fusion

The economic downturn of 1908 adversely affected the membership of the ZZP. Like other unions it suffered from a high turnover rate even at the best of times.[34] In 1906, when the economy was expanding, 9 percent of the ZZP's members either quit or were removed from its rolls.[35] Layoffs during an economic downturn forced miners to migrate in search of work, and they often lost contact with the union. This decline in the membership of the ZZP became apparent with the reorganization of the newly consolidated ZZP in 1909. The Miners' Section began with a membership of 17,772 in the Ruhr, which seems to be the smallest number of Ruhr miners to belong to the ZZP since the 1905 strike.[36]

The ZZP, however, was not unique in this regard: in 1909 the membership of the *Alter Verband* in the Ruhr also declined to its lowest point since the 1905 strike.[37] Apparently, the state of the economy played a decisive role here. Furthermore, it had a greater impact on migrants from the East than on other miners. While the size of the work force in the Ruhr's mines in 1909 exceeded that of 1908 by 1.5 percent, the number of those born in eastern Prussia actually declined in 1909 by 3.5 percent, the first decline since 1902, during the Ruhr's previous recession.[38] But the disputes connected with the fusion of the Polish trade unions within the ZZP and a preoccupation with the process probably also contributed to a membership decline. In the spring of 1909, some ZZP activists in

---

33. Wachowiak, *Polacy*, p. 160; Mańkowski, "Historja," pp. 66, 68; Chełmikowski, *Związki*, p. 133.

34. Schönhoven, "Gewerkschaften," p. 229, notes the high turnover rate among German unions.

35. Mańkowski, "Historja," pp. 69, 87.

36. *Ibid.*, p. 99.

37. Christoph Klessmann, "Klassensolidarität und nationales Bewusstsein. Das Verhältnis zwischen der Polnischen Berufsvereinigung (ZZP) und den deutschen Bergarbeiter-Gewerkschaften im Ruhrgebiet 1902–1923," *Internationale Wissenschaftliche Korrespondenz zur Geschichte der deutschen Arbeiterbewegung*, X (1974), 154; Schönhoven, "Gewerkschaften," p. 226, notes that, after a rapid growth in membership among German unions during the economic boom of 1902–1906, the recession of 1907–1908 brought a drastic shrinkage in their growth rates and, as the economic crisis reached its high point in 1908, even a decline in their membership.

38. Klessmann, *Polnische Bergarbeiter*, p. 265.

Westphalia attributed the loss in membership to the ability of other unions to recruit Polish workers by exploiting the split between Sosiński and Brejski.[39] In the Düsseldorf district, Polish membership in the other unions increased by just over 10 percent between 1908 and 1910, according to the estimates of the Prussian authorities.[40]

Membership in the Miners' Section of the ZZP in the Ruhr grew in the following years, to 26,309 by the end of 1910 and 30,164 by the end of 1911.[41] Statistics on union membership for 1910 indicate that from 19 percent to 22 percent of all organized miners in the Ruhr belonged to the ZZP.[42] Yet, according to statistics compiled by Prussian officials, in 1910 Poles constituted only 18 percent of the work force in the Ruhr's mines.[43] Moreover, based on these same official statistics on the number of Polish miners, the ZZP encompassed 38 to 43 percent of them in 1910, when 35 to 41 percent of the Ruhr's miners belonged to unions.[44]

In addition, some Polish miners joined unions other than the ZZP: according to the data gathered by Prussian officials, in 1910, while only 30 percent of the Polish miners in the Münster and Düsseldorf administrative districts belonged to the ZZP, an additional 26 percent belonged to the other unions—15 percent to the *Alter Verband* and 10 percent to the *Gewerkverein*.[45] In the Münster district, for which more detailed data on union membership is available, 70 percent of the Polish

39. STAM, OP 5365, RPA, 28 April 1909.

40. STAM, OP 6351, 26 March 1909, 15 April 1911.

41. Wachowiak, *Polacy*, p. 133.

42. Klessmann, "Klassensolidarität," p. 154, cites the following membership totals for the Ruhr in 1910: *Alter Verband* 80,378; *Gewerkverein* 32,616; and ZZP Miners' Section 26,309; STAM, OP 6351, cites the following for 1910: *Alter Verband* 60,193; *Gewerkverein* 32,616; Hirsch-Duncker 2,100; and ZZP c. 23,000; the differences account for the range in the percentage of the unionized miners encompassed by the ZZP.

43. STAM, OP 6351, RPM, 17 Feb. 1911, 15 April 1911. According to these statistics, Masurians made up another 9 percent of the work force. One official estimated that on 1 Jan. 1911 20 percent of Ruhr miners were Polish-speaking, reprinted in Gerhard Adelmann, ed., *Quellensammlung zur Geschichte der sozialen Betriebsverfassung. Ruhrindustrie unter besonderer Berücksichtigung des Industrie- und Handelskammerbezirks Essen*, Vol. I: *Überbetriebliche Einwirkung auf die soziale Betriebsverfassung der Ruhrindustrie* (Bonn: Peter Hanstein, 1960), pp. 300–301. In 1910 migrants from the Prussian East formed fully 36.7 percent of the work force, Klessmann, *Polnische Bergarbeiter*, p. 265.

44. Klessmann, "Klassensolidarität," p. 154; STAM, OP 6351, 15 April 1911, gives the total number of miners.

45. STAM, OP 6351, RPM, 17 Feb. 1911; 15 April 1911: the *Alter Verband* had 3,970 Polish members in the RM and 972 in the RD; the *Gewerkverein* had 2,520 and 949 respectively; the ZZP 6,772 and 3,126; and the Hirsch-Dunker had 113 in RD; STAM, OP 5758, f. 130, breaks the number of Polish coal miners down by county, and its figures differ from the above source only insignificantly.

miners belonged to a union (36 percent to the ZZP) compared with 45 percent of the remaining miners.[46] (In the Düsseldorf district only 36 percent of the Polish miners belonged to unions, 22 percent to the ZZP, but no data is available on the other unions in the district.) Union membership among Polish miners reached its peak in the Arnsberg district, where 60 percent of them belonged to the ZZP alone.[47] No figures exist on how many Poles in this district belonged to other unions, but, even without them, these statistics would indicate that 52 to 57 percent of Polish miners in the Ruhr belonged to a trade union in 1910, about 17 percent more than among all the Ruhr's miners.[48]

These calculations of union membership among Polish miners rest on official reports, which often underestimated the number of Polish-speaking miners and thereby contribute to an overestimation of their level of unionization. Nevertheless, it appears that the ZZP was extraordinarily successful in organizing those that it targeted for membership, dispelling the myth of the unorganizability of the Polish migrant. Scholars who attribute the weakness of the unions in the Ruhr to the presence of migrants from the East must look elsewhere for an explanation.[49]

Although the ZZP's center of gravity remained in the Ruhr, the importance of the homeland inevitably increased following consolidation. Even among coal miners, the group most closely identified with the origins of the ZZP, growth came faster in Upper Silesia than in the Ruhr, in part because of the strength of the ZZP in the Ruhr prior to consolidation and the weakness of the ZWP. Thus, the Ruhr's portion of the Section's total membership declined from 80 percent in 1909 to 64

46. STAM, OP 6351, RPM, 17 Feb. 1911: 23.8 percent belonged to the *Alter Verband*, 21.4 percent to the *Gewerkverein*, and .2 percent to the Hirsch-Duncker union.

47. This figure is reached by subtracting the ZZP's membership in the Münster and Düsseldorf regencies from the total for the Ruhr as a whole. STAM, OP 6351, estimated the ZZP's membership at 23,000 rather than 26,309, in which case the percentage would be 47.6.

48. Again, the range depends on whether the ZZP's membership is taken at its officially stated total or the lower figure cited by the Prussian authorities. These estimates find confirmation in the statistics in STAM, OP 5758, ff. 138–139, which suggest that 53.9 percent of Polish miners belonged to unions compared with 37 percent of other miners, but here the definition of miners' organizations encompasses religious-affiliated associations and others that took no direct part in the labor movement for higher pay and better working conditions: see the list of organizations in STAM, OP 6351, RPM, 17 Feb. 1911.

49. See, for example, Klaus Tenfelde, "Linksradikale Strömungen in der Ruhrbergarbeiterschaft 1905 bis 1919," in *Glück auf, Kameraden! Die Bergarbeiter und ihre Organisationen in Deutschland*, ed. by Hans Mommsen and Ulrich Borsdorf (Cologne: Bund-Verlag, 1979), p. 208, and Franz-Josef Brüggemeier, *Leben vor Ort. Ruhrbergleute und Ruhrbergbau 1889–1919* (Munich: C.H. Beck, 1983), pp. 233–234.

percent at the end of 1911.[50] A reassertion of regional particularism at the general assembly of the Miners' Section in Dortmund in late March 1911 reflected this shift in balance. The 41 delegates from Upper Silesia challenged the views of the other delegates, who included 105 from the Ruhr. Nevertheless, in the end, the delegates accepted the decisions of the majority, which reelected the Section's central directorate, including its chairman Mańkowski.[51]

Thanks to the continued growth in membership among miners following consolidation, their section even enhanced its importance in the ZZP. Whereas at the end of 1910 miners constituted 62 percent of the ZZP's membership, a year later they constituted almost 67 percent.[52] More importantly, in 1910 the Miners' Section accounted for 80 percent of the total funds that remained after subtracting each section's expenses from its income.[53] In these circumstances, the leadership of the Miners' Section chafed under the subordination of the interests of miners to those of other Polish workers. Friction arose among the three sections of the ZZP in the competition for the union's financial resources. The festering conflict came to a head at the first general assembly of the ZZP following consolidation, in Poznań on 25 May 1911. Delegates raised questions about the union's expenses, including those of the central directorate and those stemming from strikes and legal assistance. Miners in particular complained that, while their section saved money, other sections, which went on strike more often, did not manage to cover their own administrative costs.[54]

To remedy the situation, the Miners' Section made sixteen motions proposing changes in the union's operations to give its sections significantly greater independence. According to these motions, instead of a single board of supervisors for the entire union, each section would create its own. Each section would also have its own treasury, with which it would cover its administrative costs and obligations to its members, and send to the central directorate only a certain percentage of the remaining

---

50. Wachowiak, *Polacy*, p. 133. STAM, OP 5365, Polizei-Präsident, Bochum, 7 April 1911, dated the membership of 17,772 from 1 Oct. 1909, but, together with STAM, OP 6396, Polizeirat Goehrke, Bochum, 1 April 1911, f. 95, confirms these figures.

51. Wachowiak, *Polacy*, pp. 159–160; Mańkowski, "Historja," pp. 98–99, 101. See p. 96 concerning the growth in Upper Silesia and the greater attention it required of the ZZP leadership.

52. Wachowiak, *Polacy*, pp. 132–133.

53. Chełmikowski, *Związki*, pp. 174–175.

54. Wachowiak, *Polacy*, pp. 158–159; Chełmikowski, *Związki*, pp. 135–136; Mańkowski, "Historja," pp. 100–101, makes no mention of conflict at the meeting.

funds. Another motion ominously provided that, if the union excluded any section from its ranks, the union return the funds contributed by that section. Further, a motion proposed that each section, rather than the central directorate, have the right to appoint its own officials. In addition, the miners demanded that each section have its own printing press and organize its own permanent educational courses for its members. These motions provoked such an outcry that Mańkowski himself withdrew them in the name of the Miners' Section. Instead, the general assembly accepted more moderate proposals substituted by the section's delegates, including the requirement that the central directorate chose officials for the sections from among the candidates put forward by the sections. The assembly also recognized the need for organizing educational courses for union members and voted funds for this purpose, but none of these proposals changed the essential structure of the union.[55]

The general assembly did, however, seek to restrict the influence of outsiders by requiring five years of membership in the ZZP for election to the board of supervisors and as delegates to the general assembly (except from areas where the ZZP previously did not exist). At the same time the Upper Silesians won a victory when the general assembly voted to transfer the headquarters of the union's central directorate from Bochum in the Ruhr to Katowice (Kattowitz) in Upper Silesia. This was also a victory for Sosiński, who, after losing in a by-election for a seat in the Reichstag in Poznań to the PZZ and ZZP activist Nowicki in 1910, focused his political ambitions on Upper Silesia.[56]

Masurians

One group with whom the ZZP had little success in recruiting were the Masurians, who spoke an archaic form of Polish and were generally Protestant rather than Catholic. As early as 1905, the ZZP printed appeals in the Gothic script used by Masurians. The union also organized meetings for them with Masurians as speakers.[57] Still, according to the statistics of the Prussian authorities, there were only twelve Masurians among 3,138 members of the ZZP in the Düsseldorf district in 1910. But

55. Chełmikowski, *Związki*, pp. 136, 157.

56. Murzynowska, *Polskie wychodźstwo*, pp. 216–217.

57. Mańkowski, "Historja," p. 67; Hans Jürgen Brandt, ed., *Die Polen und die Kirche im Ruhrgebiet 1871–1919: Ausgewählte Dokumente zur pastoral und kirchlichen Integration sprachlicher Minderheiten im deutschen Kaiserreich*, (Münster: Aschendorff, 1987), p. 283.

the *Alter Verband* and the *Gewerkverein* did not have much success in organizing them either. According to these same statistics, only 25 percent of the Masurian miners (compared with 55 percent of Polish miners) in the Münster and Düsseldorf districts belonged to any union.[58] It is suggestive that the percentage of Masurians (25 percent) belonging to unions, none of which was Masurian, nearly equals the percentage of Poles (26 percent) who belonged to non-Polish unions. The Masurians lacked what the Poles had: a union led by people from their own class and culture with which they could identify.

Starting in 1910, the ZZP Miners' Section made a serious effort to persuade Masurians that it was such a union. Its organ announced a campaign in its issue of 3 February 1910: "the Masurians are of course our brothers!"[59] Within three weeks the German press reported that Poles were going house to house in districts densely populated by Masurian miners and trying to recruit them for the ZZP. To facilitate the process, Sosiński even went so far as to deny the Catholic and national Polish character of the ZZP, though in December 1910 the union's board of supervisors disavowed his comments.[60] But, according to a Polish newspaper founded in the Ruhr in 1909, the *Narodowiec* (Nationalist), in May 1911 the ZZP general assembly greeted with enthusiastic applause an appeal from someone who identified himself as a Masurian, who called on organized Polish workers and the whole Polish community, to whom many Masurians were supposedly looking as brothers, to save them from drowning in the sea of Germandom.[61]

In July 1911 the first issue of a ZZP journal for Masurians appeared. Under the name *Miesięcznik Górniczy* (Miners' Monthly) it was later published in runs of 400–500 copies distributed by ZZP union locals. According to an official report, the journal, printed in Gothic script,

---

58. STAM, OP 6351, 15 April 1911, RPM, 17 Feb. 1911, 15 April 1911. On union membership among Masurians, see also Valentina-Maria Stefanski, "Tożsamość i integracja. Polskie wychodźstwo zarobkowe w Zagłębiu Ruhry," in *Organizacje polonijne w Europie Zachodniej—Współczesność i tradycje. Materiały z konferencji naukowej w dniach 2 i 3 kwietnia 1987 r. w Poznaniu*, ed. by Barbara Szydłowska-Ceglowa and Jerzy Kozłowski (Poznań: Uniwersytet im. Adama Mickiewicza, 1991), p. 104.

59. Brandt, *Polen*, p. 284.

60. According to a report of a Prussian official, 13 March 1914, reprinted in *ibid.*, p. 284.

61. *Ibid.*, pp. 284–285; the Prussian official reporting on this speech regarded it as a sham for outside consumption.

deliberately avoided using the term "Masurian" and spoke instead of "brothers from East Prussia" allied with the Poles against the Germans.[62] Still, late in 1913 the ZZP had only several hundred Masurian members, according to a source close to the trade union. He attributed this to the linguistic and religious prejudices of the union's members.[63] An article surveying the history of the ZZP on its twenty-fifth anniversary pointed to the ZZP's success with Kaszubians, with their separate language but Catholic religion, as evidence that primarily the religious difference inhibited Masurian membership in the ZZP.[64] The ZZP itself did not see the religious difference as an obstacle. Nor did the condemnation of nondenominational trade unions in the papal encyclical "Singulari Quadam" issued in September 1912 cause the ZZP to fear, as the *Gewerkverein* did, the specter of church control over the union.[65] In fact, the statute of the ZZP Miners' Section adapted in 1909 and amended for the last time before the war at a general assembly in May 1913 made no reference to "Christian teaching" or to a prohibition of "agitation in the spirit of Social Democracy," as in original statute of the union, and stated only that the union "honors the convictions of its members and excludes in principle religious controversies and political matters."[66] In 1914 the ZZP renewed a campaign to recruit the predominantly Protestant Masurians in their homeland in East Prussia.[67]

Ties between the ZZP and Its Members

To its rank and file members, the ZZP from the beginning promised financial assistance in time of need. Following the 1905 strike, the union defined more exactly the situations in which members and their families could look to the union for support. Whereas provisions in case of the

---

62. *Ibid.*, pp. 285–286. See also, Wachowiak, *Polacy*, pp. 20, 132, who claims that this effort had little effect.

63. Brandt, *Polen*, pp. 285–286, citing Andrzej Wachowiak's *Przewodnik po Westfalii i Nadrenii. Podręcznik dla osób prywatnych i towarzystw* (Oberhausen: Drukiem J. Kawalera i Sp., 1913).

64. *Naród*, No. 239, 16 Oct. 1927, AAN, ARPB 2196, f. 128.

65. Brose, *Christian Labor*, pp. 274–279, 318.

66. Reprinted in *Arbeitsmaterialien des XIX. Betriebsräteseminars an der Ruhr-Universität Bochum zum Thema: "Ausländer, Gastarbeiter: Integrationsprobleme und ihre Lösungsansätze in historischer und Aktueller Perspektive"* (Bochum: Ruhr-Universität Bochum and Industriegewerkschaft Metall 1985), pp. 24–28; see also Klessmann, *Polnische Bergarbeiter*, pp. 112, 207.

67. Mańkowski, "Historja," p. 124.

death of a member remained unchanged, others expanded the assistance members could expect. In addition to the already noted pay during strikes, the union provided compensation in cases of illness and unemployment, including a travel subsidy of 2 Pfennige per kilometer to look for work. From the point of view of cost, the most expensive of these provisions proved to be the assistance given in case of illness, though in some years strike pay could impose a greater burden on the union treasury. In 1907 the union had to address abuses by members who "got sick" as soon as they belonged to the union long enough to receive assistance and then quit the union after collecting the maximum amount.[68]

The role of the ZZP in the life of its members, however, went far beyond that of providing a measure of financial security when fate turned against them. Rather, the ZZP, as the largest and strongest Polish organization in the Ruhr, took on features of a social movement, anticipating the character of another Polish trade union three quarters of a century later, Solidarity: both developed in an environment hostile to the Polish worker under a government that he regarded as alien. With one or more ZZP union locals in practically every community in the Ruhr with Polish migrants, the leaders of these locals were, as Mańkowski put it:

> everything for their fellow countrymen living in a given place. Poles turned to them in every need, such as in matters of insurance, taxes, disability payments, housing, last wills, real estate, etc., so that they took the place of government offices, in which Polish workers had no confidence and to which they had no access, not knowing sufficiently the language of these offices.[69]

According to Mańkowski, the officers of union locals even wrote letters for their members to their families in the homeland and took care of sending their money to their wives and to Polish banks.

Formally, the task of assisting union members in these areas fell to the legal aid service that the union provided from its earliest days. ZZP leaders even claimed that, by weaving a web of ties between the organization and its members, legal assistance constituted the most important function of the union.[70] In a brief account of the union in the Ruhr written in 1913, Mańkowski spoke of its role in educating migrants about the miners' pension fund, work contracts, and health and safety regulations in the mines. For example, after paying into the pension fund for years, migrants returning to the homeland forfeited the money they

---

68. Chełmikowski, *Związki*, pp. 181–187; Mańkowski, "Historja," p. 72.
69. Mańkowski, "Historja," pp. 94–95.
70. Chełmikowski, *Związki*, p. 188.

had paid into the fund if they did not know their rights. In these matters union members could readily turn to the ZZP legal aid bureaus for free advice from people who shared their working-class background. The union even appointed its own permanent representative in Berlin to plead the cases of union members before the highest court for insurance claims.[71] But the legal assistance offered by the ZZP went well beyond what one might expect from a trade union. A listing of matters handled by eight legal aid bureaus of the Miners' Section in 1911 and 1912 indicates that, while more inquiries dealt with injuries on the job than anything else, a significant portion dealt with matters totally unrelated to employment, such as the military, schools, taxes, and civil and criminal proceedings. According to a report at the ZZP's general assembly in 1911, members were even demanding that the union represent them in purely private legal matters.[72]

Over the years, the volume of legal assistance furnished by the union increased. In July 1906 the ZZP decided to open additional legal aid bureaus in several communities of the Ruhr with large numbers of Polish migrants. According to the annual reports, in 1906 the union legal aid service handled 2,482 written matters and gave oral advice in 2,118 cases; the totals for the eight bureaus of the Miners' Section for 1911 and 1912 were 17,359 written and 9,073 oral cases. The union necessarily devoted increasing resources to providing these legal services, 5,093 marks in 1907 rising to 39,592 marks in 1911, when they amounted to nearly 7 percent of the union's expenses.[73]

In addition to the legal aid bureaus, the union forged other links with its members. Stewards from the union locals visited individual members every two weeks to collect dues and distribute the union organ *Zjednoczenie*. Originally published monthly, the union newspaper itself served as another point of contact and source of information valuable to its members. News about the union, the labor movement, and social legislation predominated.[74] ZZP leaders also saw the union organ as an important instrument in its effort to recruit and retain members. In October 1905, they voted to make it a semimonthly after specifically noting that the German unions were now publishing Polish-language

71. Franciszek Mańkowski, "Związki zawodowe na wychództwie," *Pamiętnik wystawy przemysłowej w Bochum od 19–27 lipca 1913 roku* (Oberhausen: Nakładem Komitetu Wystawowego, n.d. [1913]), pp. 31–34; Mańkowski, "Historja," p. 98.

72. Chełmikowski, *Związki*, pp. 188–192.

73. Mańkowski, "Historja," pp. 68, 70; Chełmikowski, *Związki*, pp. 171, 189.

74. Chełmikowski, *Związki*, p. 197.

versions of their journals. In December 1905, the ZZP decided to register the union organ with the post office so that nonmembers could receive it by mail. By the end of 1907, consideration was being given to issuing the ZZP's organ in an expanded format and a year later to banning advertisements.[75] In 1908 *Zjednoczenie* had a circulation of about 46,000.[76] Following consolidation of the Polish unions, journals of each of the three sections replaced the union organ, which meant that the *Głos Górnika* could focus on news and information of direct relevance to the lives of the Ruhr's Polish coal miners. It began with a circulation of about 45,000 in 1909 and then grew to 60,000 by 1912.[77]

ZZP union locals, of which the Miners' Section had 142 in the Ruhr in 1909, 160 in 1910, and 171 in 1911, held monthly meetings, which provided personal contact between union activists and the rank and file.[78] ZZP leaders also saw these meetings as an opportunity to educate their members. Someone from the union directorate, the board of supervisors, or from among the officials elected in the mines, such as a pension fund elder, usually attended these meetings as the featured speaker.[79]

The Politics of the ZZP and the Prussian Authorities

Speakers at meetings organized by the ZZP did not confine themselves to purely trade union matters, nor was attendance at public meetings limited to members. With the approach of elections to the Reichstag, the ZZP organized a meeting in Oberhausen on 16 September 1906 attended by some 400 people at which the Reichstag Deputy and publisher of the *Gazeta Grudziądzka* Wiktor Kulerski spoke about the efforts of Polish deputies on behalf of workers and called for their support. When the electoral committee held an open meeting in Essen in late December 1906 to decide on candidates, Sosiński was one of the main speakers.[80] Then on 15 January 1907 the union journal *Zjednoczenie* asserted that "genuine

75. Mańkowski, "Historja," pp. 66, 73, 81, 126.

76. Klessmann, *Polnische Bergarbeiter*, p. 231.

77. Murzynowska, *Polskie wychodźstwo*, p. 233; Wachowiak, *Polacy*, p. 132; a police report in 1911 listed the circulation as 30,000, Klessmann, *Polnische Bergarbeiter*, Table 27, following p. 280.

78. Wachowiak, *Polacy*, p. 133; STAM, OP, 5365, Polizei-Präsident, Bochum, 7 April 1911.

79. Mańkowski, "Historja," pp. 94, 126–127.

80. HSTAD, RD Präs 877, ff. 24–29, 92–95, Königl. Polizei Kommissar, Essen, 19 Sept. 1906, Polizei-Verwaltung, Essen, 27 Dec. 1906.

Poles" cannot vote for any German candidates "since they are all obstinate Hakatists and the most dangerous Polish enemies.... *If one wants to fulfill his national obligation, so must every Pole give his vote to those candidates nominated by the Polish electoral committees.* Our national solidarity commands us to do so in the current Reichstag election."[81]

This involvement of the Polish Trade Union in political matters in 1907 led to a complaint by Jan Wilkowski, one of the founders of the ZZP and then a leader of the Union of Poles (ZPwN), which acted as the umbrella political organization of the Poles in emigration. Since its birth, however, the ZZP had gradually been displacing the ZPwN as the leading organization of the Poles of the Ruhr. Wilkowski now sought to halt this development by forbidding the ZZP to call so-called social-political meetings, a stricture that ZZP leaders rejected.[82]

But soon thereafter the Prussian authorities received the means by which they could effectively limit the ZZP's ability to use public meetings to spread its influence. Prussian officials had long sought to prevent trade unions from organizing public meetings. In 1906 the secretary of the ZZP reported to the union's general assembly that officials had successfully pressured some hall owners not to let Poles use their facilities. In 1907, the police refused to allow a trade unionist from Cracow, in the Polish part of Austria, to speak at the union's general assembly.[83] Although the *Wiarus Polski* noted later that the police allowed an editor from Austria to speak at a meeting of the *Alter Verband*, it suffered similar harassment.[84] But the Associations Act proposed by the German government and then passed by the Reichstag threatened no union more than the ZZP.

Passed in April 1908 and effective from 15 May 1908, the Associations Act for the first time legalized the rights of association and of assembly for all of Germany but at the same time imposed restrictions on those rights. Political associations and political meetings had to exclude all persons under the age of eighteen and register with the police, which in the case of an association meant submitting its statutes and

---

81. Emphasis in quote in Heinrich Imbusch, *Arbeitsverhältnisse und Arbeiterorganisationen im deutschen Bergbau* (Essen: Verlag des Gewerkvereins christlicher Bergarbeiter, 1908), p. 512; "Hakatist" was a contemporary neologism created from the first initials of the surnames of the founders of the *Ostmarkenverein* that stood for anti-Polish and Germanizing fervency.

82. Mańkowski, "Historja," p. 72.

83. *Ibid.*, pp. 67, 69–70.

84. *Uebersetzungen aus dem "Wiarus Polski,"* No. 104, 7 May 1907, p. 72, STAM, RM VII, Nr. 36c.

membership lists. The objections of labor leaders led to assurances by government officials that trade unions did not fall in this category. In fact, the Reichstag added a provision to the draft legislation that meetings of workers to discuss pay and working conditions did not need to register with the police. But the provision that most affected the Polish-speaking population of the Ruhr required that public meetings be held in German. The legislation exempted international congresses and meetings held in conjunction with parliamentary elections from this language requirement and temporarily suspended it for twenty years in districts where 60 percent or more of the population spoke a language other than German as their mother tongue, a condition fulfilled for the use of Polish by forty-seven counties in the homeland but by none in the Ruhr.[85]

The Prussian authorities wanted to require Polish organizations to use exclusively the German language in their public meetings, as a means of both facilitating surveillance and fostering Germanization.[86] Yet German socialists and trade unionists underrated the anti-Polish point of the legislation. Instead, they attacked the government's proposal to require the use of German as instigated by "industrial magnates, especially in the Rhineland and Westphalia," and as supposedly directed above all against German workers because it would prevent the trade unions from organizing "foreign-language" workers whom the industrialists could then use as wage-cutters and strikebreakers.[87]

In the Reichstag, the SPD deputy and *Alter Verband* leader Hue invoked a specter that haunted the Prussian authorities and German nationalists by warning that approval of the language restrictions would lead to a repeat of the riot of 1899, when "workers' blood flowed in the

---

85. The law is reprinted from *Reichs-Gesetzblatt*, No. 18, pp. 151–157, in *Arbeitsmaterialien*, pp. 53–56; see also, Józef Buzek, *Historya polityki narodowościowej rządu pruskiego wobec Polaków od traktatów wiedeńskich do ustaw wyjątkowych z r. 1908* (Lwów: Nakład H. Altenberga, 1909), p. 447. Zygmunt Hemmerling, *Posłowie polscy w parlamencie Rzeszy niemieckiej i sejmie pruskim (1907–1914)* (Warsaw: Ludowa Spółdzielnia Wydawnicza, 1968), pp. 216–230, discusses the passage of this legislation.

86. Klessmann, *Polnische Bergarbeiter*, p. 90; John J. Kulczycki, "The Prussian Authorities and the Poles of the Ruhr," *The International History Review*, VIII, No. 4 (1986), pp. 601–602.

87. See SPD deputies Carl Legien and Otto Hue, *Stenographische Berichte über die Verhandlungen des Reichstags*, Bd. 232, XII. Legislaturperiode, I. Session 1908, 140. Sitzung, 4 April 1908, pp. 4653–4657, 4684–4687; Otto Hue, "Die Väter des Sprachenparagraphen," *Die Neue Zeit*, XXVI (1908), pp. 445–453; Hans-Ulrich Wehler, *Sozialdemokratie und Nationalstaat: Die deutsche Sozialdemokratie und die Nationalitätenfragen in Deutschland von Karl Marx bis zum Ausbruch des Ersten Weltkrieges* (Würzburg: Holzner-Verlag, 1962), pp. 178–182; Brose, *Christian Labor*, p. 229; Chełmikowski, *Związki*, p. 116.

streets of Herne," although in that instance German workers and their union leaders, including Hue, had played the role of strikebreakers.[88] The Christian-Social deputy Franz Behrens, secretary general of the *Gewerkverein* since 1904, even voted for the bill's language provision in return for a statement from State Secretary for Internal Affairs Theobald von Bethmann Hollweg that it would not apply to trade unions, which, however, led the *Bergknappe* to call for Behrens's resignation from the leadership of the union for so naively trusting Bethmann Hollweg's interpretation of the law.[89]

Because the legislation did not precisely define political associations, the fears of labor leaders of abuse by the police proved justified. German trade unions suffered along with the ZZP, whose central directorate and locals came under a shower of fines for admitting persons under eighteen and for not furnishing a list of members to the police, who considered them political organizations, which resulted in 180 trials before World War I.[90] During a debate over the budget in the Reichstag in December 1908, in reply to questions raised about the treatment of trade unions, stated,

all trade unions without exception should be guaranteed the freedom to pursue their economic interests. If the so-called Polish trade unions...have been excluded from this assurance, this has happened because, and in so far as, they make the pursuit of Polish national goals the basis of their economic endeavors.[91]

Both the Polish Circle (as the Polish parliamentary party was known) in the Reichstag and the SPD interpellated the government concerning the administration of the Associations Act. On 21 January 1909, Brejski

88. *Stenographische Berichte über die Verhandlungen des Reichstags*, Bd. 232, XII. Legislaturperiode, I. Session 1908, 140. Sitzung, 4 April 1908, p. 4686.

89. Michael Schneider, *Die Christlichen Gewerkschaften 1894–1933* (Bonn: Verlag Neue Gesellschaft, 1982), p. 340; Brose, *Christian Labor*, p. 230. See *Stenographische Berichte über die Verhandlungen des Reichstags*, Bd. 232, XII. Legislaturperiode, I. Session 1908, 140. Sitzung, 4 April 1908, pp. 4666–4667, 4694, for Bethmann Hollweg's statement and Behrens's vote.

90. Antoni Banaszak, "Z.Z.P. a policja pruska i sądy w ostatnich latach przed wojną światową," in *Ćwierć wieku pracy dla Narodu i Robotnika* (Poznań: Nakładem Zarządu Centralnego Zjedn. Zawod. Polskiego, 1927), p. 542; Ullrich Feige, *Bergarbeiterschaft zwischen Tradition und Emanzipation: Das Verhältnis von Bergleuten und Gewerkschaften zu Unternehmern und Staat im westlichen Ruhrgebiet um 1900* (Düsseldorf: Schwann, 1986), pp. 108–109, cites a case of a local of the *Gewerkverein* being classified as a political organization.

91. *Stenographische Berichte über die Verhandlungen des Reichstags*, Bd. 233, XII. Legislaturperiode, I. Session 1908, 181. Sitzung, 11 Dec. 1908, pp. 6177–6178.

substantiated the Polish interpellation by claiming that the Prussian police, especially in the Ruhr, treated all associations formed by Poles as political. In reply, Bethmann Hollweg reiterated his view that the Polish Trade Union was in fact involved in political matters.[92]

The Associations Act provided for exemptions from its requirements to be granted by provincial officials. Accordingly, the ZZP applied to the authorities in the Ruhr for permission to hold meetings in Polish but was refused. The union also filed a complaint with Bethmann Hollweg and sent petitions to the Prussian diet and the German parliament, all in vain. Although Prussian officials granted exemptions to other national minorities in particular counties, neither in the Ruhr nor in the homeland did Poles ever receive any.[93]

Meetings held in Polish after the Associations Act came into effect exposed the ZZP to fines and court trials. Because the Prussian authorities would impose fines on each member of the directorate of a union local charged with a violation, the ZZP reduced the membership of the local directorates from seven to three to minimize the damage. The ZZP also sought to bypass what came to be known as the "gag law." At some meetings, a phonograph played a recording of a speech in Polish, which did not prevent officials from dissolving the meeting. In other instances, the union organized so-called "silent meetings," at which not a word was spoken: duplicated speeches were handed out and resolutions on a blackboard were voted on in silence. For example, the ZZP held two silent meetings in the Ruhr in October 1908: one in Bruckhausen drew about 1,000 participants and one in Essen about 1,500.[94]

Despite the popularity of such acts of defiance, they could not replace the public meetings as a means of educating and recruiting members. An immediate response of the ZZP was to rely more on closed meetings of members instead of meetings open to the general public. Thus, the number of public meetings called by the ZZP declined from 391 in 1907 to 192 in 1908 while the number of meetings of members rose from 1,872 to 2,113.[95] But meetings closed to all but members could not recruit migrants newly arrived in the Ruhr who knew nothing of the ZZP and its activities. Thus, the Associations Act must have greatly contributed to the

92. *Ibid.*, Bd. 234, XII. Legislaturperiode, I. Session 1909, 190. Sitzung, pp. 6437, 6453.

93. Otto Hue, "Väter," p. 445; Klessmann, *Polnische Bergarbeiter*, p. 223; Chełmikowski, *Związki*, pp. 117–118, 234–235; Wehler, *Sozialdemokratie*, p. 181.

94. Chełmikowski, *Związki*, p. 117; Mańkowski, "Historja," pp. 94, 109; Filipiak, *Dzieje*, p. 194, notes a third meeting in Witten in Dec. 1908.

95. Mańkowski, "Historja," pp. 88, 110.

heavy losses in membership that the ZZP suffered between the early months of 1908 and late 1909 after the fusion of the Polish trade unions.[96] Even closed membership meetings suffered from police intervention. In one instance a ZZP member filed a complaint against the police in Erkenschwick, near Recklinghausen, in October 1908. When he tried to call a meeting of the union local, the hall owner insisted that the meeting be registered with the police. The police in turn told him that, because it was to be a closed meeting for members only, it did not have to be registered; but at his request the police were willing to register it as long as it did not deal with political matters. On the day of the meeting, the police commissar came to observe it as if it were a public meeting. He ignored claims that it was a closed meeting for members and dissolved it when speakers used Polish rather than German.[97]

Nevertheless, in 1910, the ZZP Miners' Section organized 1,804 closed meetings for its members in 160 places in the Ruhr. In 1911 union locals of the Miners' Section held 1,444 regular meetings in the Ruhr and 102 extraordinary meetings. That same year the *Polizeipräsident* of Bochum referred to the Associations Act as "a blunt instrument" that actually encumbered the police's ability to report on "Polish national agitation":

> The meetings are designated for association members, but the acquisition of membership is mostly so facilitated and the introduction of guests is common to such a great extent that the sign with the notice 'closed gathering' which is usually attached to the entry door of the meeting room holds good only for police officers.[98]

In addition, the ZZP increasingly relied on sending its union organizers from "house to house."[99] This meant involving more local activists and demanding more of them, but it presumably established stronger and more durable ties between the union and its members than more impersonal public meetings could. In 1909 a socialist expressed envy at the success with which Poles developed this technique for evading the "gag law."[100] Thus, the union overcame the obstacles placed in its way by the Prussian

96. Wachowiak, *Polacy*, p. 130.

97. Biblioteka Raczyńskich, Poznań, Manuscript Division, MS. 785, Martin Tomczak, Rappen, 8 Oct. 1908, copy.

98. STAM, OP 6396, ff. 81, 95, Polizeirat Goehrke, Polizei-Präsident, Bochum, 1 April 1911; Chełmikowski, *Związki*, p. 154; Klessmann, *Polnische Bergarbeiter*, p. 90; Hemmerling, *Posłowie*, pp. 229, 259.

99. Mańkowski, "Historja," p. 110; Chełmikowski, *Związki*, p. 118.

100. J. Adamek, "Die Kampfesweise der polnischen Reichsfraktion," *Die Neue Zeit*, XXVII, No. 2 (1909), 781.

authorities at least to the extent that it continued to grow in size. Furthermore, Prussian officials may have intensified the solidarity among ZZP members by enhancing their feeling of sharing the fate of a persecuted minority.

The ZZP and the Interests of the Working Class

Besides acting in concert with other trade unions in the labor movement, the ZZP on its own also advocated proposals to enhance the position of workers, particularly in resolutions passed by its general assemblies. In Essen in April 1906, the ZZP's general assembly protested against changes made by a commission of the Prussian diet in a government bill for reform of the miners' pension fund and called on the government to reject the commission's version and on the Polish Circle in the diet to demand that the bill take into account the proposals put forward by a conference of delegates of Prussia's miners in February 1906. Although the ZZP noted that proposals such as an examination of the knowledge of German of pension fund elders and the abolition of the secret ballot seemed directed against Polish miners, the union also specifically opposed provisions that gave a privileged position to mine officials and mine owners, to the disadvantage of workers. The resolution also called for regulation of the mines through legislation of the German Reich, "since we have no confidence whatsoever in the Prussian diet."[101]

Another resolution of the ZZP general assembly in 1906 addressed the position of workers more generally, calling on the government of the Reich to submit a legislative project to parliament for the protection of workers covering thirteen areas, from limiting the working day to eight to ten hours and improving the protection of working women and youths, to proposals that would grant trade unions corporate rights, repeal legislation for the protection of strikebreakers, and give workers a voice alongside employers in wage commissions.[102] The proposals contained in this resolution were far-reaching, advocating more government

---

101. Chełmikowski, *Związki*, pp. 232–233, quotes the resolution. Note that none of the resolutions put forward by the ZZP alone, though reflective of the miners' traditions, are included among those in Klaus Tenfelde and Helmuth Trischler, eds., *Bis vor die Stufen des Throns: Bittschriften und Beschwerden von Bergleuten im Zeitalter der Industrialisierung* (Munich: Verlag C.H. Beck, 1986).

102. Chełmikowski, *Związki*, pp. 233–234, quotes the resolution as does Klessmann, *Polnische Bergarbeiter*, p. 115; note, however, that the German translation is not entirely reliable, for example translating "unemployment" as "strikes" in point 10.

intervention and regulation of industry in the interest of workers than seemed possible in 1906. But the proposals illustrated that the ZZP leadership concerned itself with the interests of the working class, not just the Polish nation, and that it shared the goals of other sections of the labor movement. At the very least, it saw the necessity of endorsing these working-class goals to legitimize its claim to represent Polish workers in Germany.[103] Whatever the motivation, such resolutions served to foster a consciousness of working-class interests among the Poles of the Ruhr.

In 1907 the general assembly meeting in Oberhausen formulated additional proposals, including demands for the right to a full pension after twenty-five years of work as a miner and an end to the prohibition against receiving a state pension along with the miners' pension.[104] Late in 1908, in addition to petitions to the Prussian diet and German parliament concerning the Associations Act, the ZZP directorate sent a petition to parliament demanding legislation that would clearly guarantee workers the right to organize and would apply to employers an article used in the past to protect strikebreakers by threatening employers with three months' imprisonment if they seek to discourage workers from making use of their right to organize by blacklisting or firing workers.[105]

In 1909, following the absorption of Polish worker organizations within the ZZP, it submitted a comprehensive memorandum to the Polish Circle in parliament encompassing an extensive list of proposals in three sections that together constitute the union's social vision at that time. The first section of the memorandum contained twenty-four demands on behalf of all male and female employees. They ranged from the general demand for the protection of life, health, and morality to specific demands for radical changes in labor relations, such as the consent of workers for any cuts in pay, equal pay for women and men doing the same work, and the obligatory participation of employers and employees in arbitration arrangements. The memorandum included agricultural workers among those to be protected, specifically demanding for them the right to organize, which could hardly appeal to the large landowners among the members of the Polish Circle. Although the demands included one for

---

103. Chełmikowski, *Związki*, pp. 258–259, refers to competition with other unions influencing the positions taken by the ZZP.

104. *Uebersetzungen aus dem "Wiarus Polski,"* No. 101, 3 May 1907, STAM, RM VII, Nr. 36c.

105. Chełmikowski, *Związki*, pp. 234–235.

amendment of the Associations Act, especially its language provision, the memorandum in no way put national interests above those of workers.[106] The memorandum's two remaining sections addressed issues of concern primarily to miners, in a section with ten demands, and to those who worked at home, in a section with five demands. The former section included demands that the ZZP had voiced previously as well as new ones, such as a demand for a refund of pension fund contributions to miners fired from their jobs who did not succeed in finding work at another mine and a demand for the regulation of a minimum wage on the basis of a wage agreement. As for those who worked in the home, the ZZP maintained that most industrialists used laborers in the home solely as a way of exploiting them to the highest degree by evading laws for the protection of workers. Therefore, the union's proposals sought to limit labor in the home and place it under the protection of existing laws.

These proposals and resolutions showed the ZZP to be a militant union that saw the mine owners as well as other employers as the adversaries of the working class. Although not endorsing the concept of class struggle, the union saw it as part of the workers' world, the reason for which the union organized workers. As Sosiński proudly put it in a speech to the union's general assembly in 1907, "We have understood how to protect ourselves against exploitation by capitalism without outside assistance."[107] Yet the ZZP saw this struggle as unequal and therefore sought government intervention to protect workers and to strengthen the position of the unions so that they might face their opponents on a level playing field.

National Solidarity versus Working-Class Interests

In April 1907, when the annual general assembly of the ZZP passed resolutions expressing appreciation for the "strong defense of workers' interests" by the parliamentary Polish Circle, it simultaneously deplored the lack of support for the union and even opposition to it on the part of many Polish newspapers in the homeland and urged them to take an interest finally in the material well-being of the worker.[108] Considerations

---

106. Quoted in *ibid.*, pp. 235–238.

107. *Uebersetzungen aus dem "Wiarus Polski," Aus anderen Blättern, Zjednoczenie*, No. 9, 1 May 1907, p. 73, STAM, RM VII, Nr. 36c.

108. WP, No. 101, 3 May 1907, *ibid.*, p. 71. These resolutions mirrored Sosiński's report to the meeting, *Zjednoczenie*, No. 9, 1 May 1907, *ibid.*, p. 73.

of national solidarity did not cause the ZZP to shrink from defending working-class interests, which at times brought the union into direct conflict with the intelligentsia and middle-class elements that led the Polish national movement centered in Poznań.

Thus, when in 1907 the ZZP and the *Wiarus Polski* undertook to promote the creation of consumer cooperatives, the objections of Polish merchants in the Ruhr received support from the Polish press in the homeland. The aggressively nationalist *Goniec Wielkopolski* (Great Poland Messenger) charged that the union and the *Wiarus Polski* were pursuing a "socialist" policy, that is, a policy hostile to Polish nationalism that took solely the interests of workers into account.[109] In response, the union emphasized its working-class character by denying active membership (with the right to vote or stand for election to union offices) to those who no longer made their living as workers but had become independent merchants.[110]

This emphasis on the ZZP as a trade union rather than a national organization also came to the fore during discussions of the unification of the ZZP with other Polish worker organizations.[111] The difference between the PZZ and the ZZP apparently led the organ of a workers' organization sponsored by the Catholic Church in Poznania to complain in February 1910 that "workers organized in the ZZP just don't want to admit to their group those who do not belong to their estate. This deepens ...class divisions harmful to society."[112] The class character of the ZZP continued to arouse the suspicions of Polish clerical circles. When the union's general assembly met in Poznań in May 1911, Bishop Edward Likowski ignored an invitation to participate, neither excusing himself nor sending a representative, and some speakers complained that the Polish clergy in Poznania and Upper Silesia opposed the union and obstructed its expansion.[113] But Rev. Arkadjusz Lisiecki, secretary general of the Union of Polish-Catholic Workers' Associations (*Związek Katolickich Towarzystw Robotników Polskich*) of the archdiocese of Gniezno-Poznań, who was present at the general assembly, denied any conflict of interest

---

109. Murzynowska, *Polskie wychodźstwo*, p. 177.

110. Mańkowski, "Historja," pp. 75–77.

111. Thus, in Aug. 1908, the ZZP put off consideration of a proposed fusion with an organization of emigrant women in the area of Bremen and Hamburg because the latter was a purely educational organization, not a trade union, but it apparently fused with the ZZP in 1909, Mańkowski, "Historja," pp. 77, 88.

112. Quoted in Filipiak, *Dzieje*, p. 295.

113. STAM, OP 5365, Polizei-Präsident, Bochum, 31 May 1911.

between his organization and the ZZP and argued that they should complement each other in their work.[114] An intensification of anti-Polish policies by the Prussian authorities and even the passage of the "gag law" by the Reichstag did not obliterate the differences between the Polish communities in the Ruhr and in the homeland nor did it dull the edge of ZZP's advocacy of the Ruhr coal miners' class interests within the Polish milieu. In 1909 a controversy arose that again pitted the economic interests of workers against the principle of national solidarity, and again the ZZP favored the former over the latter. This occurred when the Polish Circle in the Reichstag provided the margin of victory for the opposition, composed primarily of the *Zentrum* and German Conservatives, in rejecting a tax proposal of the Bülow government, which ultimately led to Bülow's resignation in July 1909.[115] But Bülow's proposal would have imposed an inheritance tax that affected only the wealthy. Furthermore, the Polish deputies then voted for the opposition's tax package, which included an increase in indirect taxes on items of necessity and thereby raised the cost of living for the working classes.

In defense of their decisions, Polish deputies touted their contribution to the overthrow of Bülow's government, whose anti-Polish policies had exceeded in severity and extent those of any previous government. Nevertheless, the tax increase set off a storm of protest and provided Polish socialists with an opportunity to denounce the policies of the Polish Circle as favoring the interests of the wealthy over those of workers.[116] Initially, the *Wiarus Polski* and other Polish newspapers actually attacked the social democrats in parliament for supporting Bülow's tax proposal, claiming that they favored a tax increase while demagogically ignoring that the tax in question was an inheritance tax on the wealthy.

The ZZP joined in the criticism of socialists for supporting Bülow, even accusing them of hoping he would "pass still more laws discriminating against Polish unions."[117] But the ZZP also opposed the position taken by the Polish Circle on the tax increase, and did not let the matter rest even after other Polish critics of the Polish Circle rose to its defense in the name of national solidarity. At a conference in November 1909, the ZZP passed a resolution calling for the participation of a

114. Chełmikowski, *Związki*, p. 136.

115. Hemmerling, *Posłowie*, pp. 230–245.

116. Adamek, "Kampfesweise," pp. 772–782; Julian Marchlewski, "Gorzałka a patriotyzm Koła Polskiego w Berlinie," in Julian Marchlewski, *Pisma wybrane*, Vol. II (Warsaw: Książka i Wiedza, 1956), pp. 401–409.

117. Adamek, "Kampfesweise," pp. 773–776.

representative of the working class in the Polish parliamentary delegations. Moreover, it demanded that, "in matters relating to workers, the Polish Circle consult with representatives of workers before taking a final decision."[118] Nearly two years later, the wound was still festering. In seeming contradiction to its earlier demand, a meeting of the ZZP central directorate and executive committee of the board of supervisors on 29 October 1911 decided that a paid union official elected as a deputy would have to resign his union office because as a member of the Polish Circle he would be bound by its rule of unanimity, and some of its decisions harmed the working class and thereby hindered the ZZP's organizational efforts. In December 1911 in Berlin a meeting with the full board of supervisors at first confirmed this decision, but the personal intervention of the Polish deputy Korfanty persuaded them to reconsider the matter and reverse the decision by a margin of a single vote.[119]

The relentlessness with which ZZP leaders maintained their opposition to the tax policies of the Polish Circle and the bitterness stemming from the difference of opinion with the Polish nationalist movement in the homeland even led to a court case. Among the staunchest defenders of the Polish Circle in this matter was the Polish deputy Kulerski, publisher of the *Gazeta Grudziądzka*, the most widely circulated and rabidly nationalist Polish newspaper in Germany and the homeland's most popular paper in the Ruhr.[120] After Mańkowski criticized the Polish Circle and the defenders of its tax policy in 1911, Kulerski used his newspaper to launch a personal attack on the leader of the ZZP Miners' Section. Accusing Mańkowski of profiting personally by supplying workers to agents of French mines, where working conditions were worse than in the Ruhr, Kulerski hoped to prevent Mańkowski's reelection as head of the Section. Kulerski also criticized the ZZP's cooperation with the socialist-

118. Marian Orzechowski, *Narodowa demokracja na Górnym Śląsku (do 1918 roku)* (Wrocław: Zakład Narodowy im. Ossolińskich, 1965), pp. 240-242.

119. Mańkowski, "Historja," pp. 102-103.

120. Marczewski, *Narodowa Demokracja*, pp. 295-297; on the *Gazeta Grudziądzka*, see Tadeusz Cieślak, "'Gazeta Grudziądzka' 1894-1918. Fenomen wydawniczy," *Studia i materiały do dziejów Wielkopolski i Pomorza*, III, No. 2 (1957), pp. 175-188; according to Klessmann, *Polnische Bergarbeiter*, p. 282, this newspaper accounted for over half the Polish newspapers received in the Oberpostamtsbezirk Dortmund in 1909 and 1911; Johannes Altkemper, *Deutschtum und Polentum in politisch-konfessioneller Bedeutung* (Leipzig: Duncker & Humblot, 1910), p. 233, refers to it as one of the most widely read Polish newspapers in the Ruhr, "which at least equals the *Wiarus Polski* in radicalism and in malicious tone." A German socialist opponent of the Polish national movement also acknowledged the influence of the newspaper in the Ruhr, Julius Bruhns, "Polenfrage und Sozialdemokratie," *Die Neue Zeit*, XXVI (1908), 762.

oriented *Alter Verband* in the labor movement in the Ruhr. He printed thousands of fliers critical of Mańkowski for the general assembly of the Miners' Section in Dortmund in March 1911. Kulerski's charges made for a stormy session of the general assembly. While the deputies Brejski and Nowicki took part as guests, the distributor of the *Gazeta Grudziadzka* in the Ruhr, Stanisław Kunz, was denied admittance. Nor did the criticism have the effect Kulerski sought: the assembly reelected Mańkowski by a nearly unanimous vote and passed a resolution sharply critical of the *Gazeta Grudziądzka*. For his part, Mańkowski denied that he would tolerate a recruitment business in the union's bureau and sued Kulerski and Kunz for libel, which kept the dispute alive until the court ruled in Mańkowski's favor in June 1912.[121]

Prussian officials classified the ZZP as a Polish nationalist organization.[122] Yet, within the Polish national movement in the years 1905–1912, the ZZP clearly stood for working-class interests and emphasized its class character. By absorbing labor organizations in the homeland and thus extending its aegis over all areas of Germany with significant concentrations of Polish-speaking workers, the ZZP took on the trappings of a national organization of the first rank. But its division into sections by trade and the continuing importance within the organization of coal miners of the Ruhr helped to ensure that it acted as a trade union. If it played a role in the Polish community in the Ruhr that went beyond that of a trade union and if it promoted itself as a Polish organization, this stemmed above all from the minority status of the Poles in the Ruhr and the discrimination that they suffered in their relations with the Prussian authorities and, to a lesser degree, with German trade unions. To be sure, the Polish character of the ZZP enabled it to compete successfully against the predominantly German unions in organizing the Polish-speaking miners of the Ruhr. But its role in the labor movement in the Ruhr also made it a viable alternative to the other unions and confirmed its working-class character.

121. STAM, OP 5365, Polizei-Präsident, Bochum, 7 April 1911; APP, Polizeipräsidium 6639, ff. 30, 32, 39–40, 42, press clippings; Murzynowska, *Polskie wychodźstwo*, p. 251; Mańkowski, "Historja," pp. 99, 107.

122. In their reports on local developments, Prussian officials regularly noted the activities of the ZZP under the rubric for Polish organizations rather than under the one for trade unions.

4
Integration of the ZZP in the Labor Movement, 1905-1914

Union Solidarity

The success of the Commission of Seven in leading the 1905 strike boded well for the future cooperation of the unions. At the conference in Essen on 9 February that decided to suspend the strike, the delegates passed a resolution proposed by Hue of the *Alter Verband* endorsing the continued leadership of the Commission in the pursuit of the miners' demands.[1] Then, at the end of March 1905, the Commission held a conference in Berlin of representatives of all of Prussia's miners. The ZZP had only eight delegates out of 117 at the conference, but Józef Regulski from the union's directorate served on the executive board of the conference and gave one of the major reports at the meeting. Also, although the delegates focused on the mining bill then before the Landtag, they acceded to a request of the Poles to resolve that mines be required to issue rules and regulations in the miners' mother tongue.[2] But the *Alter Verband*'s suggestion of fostering greater cooperation among the unions by forming a cartel ran into the objections of the *Gewerkverein*, illustrating the tensions within the labor movement and foreshadowing the separate road that the *Gewerkverein* would take.[3]

In early November 1905 the Commission of Seven sent letters to the Prussian Minister of Trade and Industry and to Chancellor Bülow

1. Hans Mommsen *et al.*, *Bergarbeiter. Ausstellung zur Geschichte der organisierten Bergarbeiterbewegung in Deutschland* (Bochum: Berg-Verlag GmbH, 1969) (unpaged), illustration 122, reproduces the resolution; also reprinted in Gerhard Adelmann, ed., *Quellensammlung zur Geschichte der sozialen Betriebsverfassung. Ruhrindustrie unter besonderer Berücksichtigung des Industrie- und Handelskammerbezirks Essen*, Vol. I: *Überbetriebliche Einwirkung auf die soziale Betriebsverfassung der Ruhrindustrie* (Bonn: Peter Hanstein, 1960), pp. 267–268.

2. Marjan Chełmikowski, *Związki zawodowe robotników polskich w Królestwie Pruskim (1889-1918)* (Poznań: Fiszer i Majewski, 1925), pp. 221–222; Krystyna Murzynowska, *Polskie wychodźstwo zarobkowe w Zagłębiu Ruhry w latach 1880-1914* (Wrocław: Ossolineum, 1972), pp. 162–163. The ZWP also had representatives at conferences of Prussian miners.

3. Stanisław Wachowiak, *Polacy w Nadrenii i Westfalii* (Poznań: Nakładem Zjednoczenia Zawodowego Polskiego, 1917), p. 140; Max Jürgen Koch, *Die Bergarbeiterbewegung im Ruhrgebiet zur Zeit Wilhelms II. (1889-1914)* (Düsseldorf: Droste, 1954), p. 130.

complaining of measures taken by mine owners to institute work rules that violated the 1905 mining law and restricted the freedom of miners to seek employment.[4] The issue came before a district conference of the Commission attended by twenty-three delegates from the ZZP along with 158 delegates from the other three unions. Although the Poles took little part in the discussion, one told of how he had difficulty getting a job at one mine after quitting at another, and Sosiński, who served as one of two secretaries at the meeting, denounced the view in the press that advocated locking out Polish miners.[5]

With the cost of living rising, a pay increase as well as reform of the miners' pension fund became the main topics of the second conference of delegates of Prussia's miners in Essen in mid-February 1906, with seventeen ZZP delegates among the 157 in attendance. Sosiński supported the view that the ongoing economic boom justified a demand for a pay increase. At the same time, he criticized priests who told ZZP members to quit the union and to join craft associations under the Church's patronage and prevented those who refused from bringing their association banners into church on feast days. The ZZP considered such craft associations yellow-dog unions.[6]

The *Alter Verband* leader Sachse, however, put Sosiński on the defensive by proposing that the ZZP cede one of its seats in the Commission of Seven to the ZWP, the Polish workers' organization in Upper Silesia with which the ZZP would later merge, so that the Commission could represent all the miners of Prussia. Sosiński demurred and at the end of the conference plaintively asserted that the Poles had behaved properly and that he favored the promotion of unity and therefore asked the other unions to stop attacking the *Wiarus Polski* in their journals.[7] But the conference did pass a resolution offered by the ZZP that the new miners' pension fund statute be published for Polish miners and for the Moravian miners of Upper Silesia in their native tongues.[8]

---

4. Reprinted in Klaus Tenfelde and Helmuth Trischler, eds., *Bis vor die Stufen des Throns: Bittschriften und Beschwerden von Bergleuten im Zeitalter der Industrialisierung* (Munich: Verlag C.H. Beck, 1986), pp. 424–426.

5. HSTAD, RD 15933, ff. 147–162, Polizei-Verwaltung, report.

6. Wachowiak, *Polacy*, p. 145.

7. HSTAD, RD 15933, f. 200, report, pp. 1–111; see especially pp. 20, 57–59, 81–82, 109–111.

8. WP, No. 34, 13 Feb. 1906, clipping, Biblioteka Raczyńskich, Poznań, Manuscript Division, MS. 800, f. 17.

The Split in the Commission of Seven

The unity of the Commission of Seven broke down not over any national difference but over how best to respond to the rejection by the Mine Owners Association of the Commission's demand for a pay raise. Whereas the *Gewerkverein* favored a more conciliatory approach, the ZZP along with the *Alter Verband* took the view that the owners needed to be pressured into making concessions.[9] In October 1906 the *Wiarus Polski* attacked the *Gewerkverein* for allegedly going back on its promise to support a demand for higher pay by the Commission of Seven. Citing the example of the ZZP, whose support of coke workers at the Graf Schwerin mine in Castrop supposedly led to a pay raise, the article suggested that only by taking a firm stand in support of demands for higher pay could success be achieved.[10]

Increasingly, the *Gewerkverein* went its own way. After a series of public assemblies in March 1907 advocating the institutionalization of cooperation between mine owners and workers, represented by trade unions, the *Gewerkverein* held exploratory talks with mine owners in the Ruhr. But the union's optimism that conciliation would achieve more than confrontation proved unwarranted. The majority of mine owners remained firmly antilabor, and in 1908 their newly formed Mine Association (*Zechenverband*) proceeded to blacklist union leaders and harden management's hostile stance toward organized labor.[11]

Not even a disaster in the mines could bridge the growing split within the labor movement. On 12 November 1908 an explosion at the Radbod mine resulted in the death of 344 miners (including about twenty Poles).[12]

9. WP, No. 269, 23 Nov. 1906, clipping, in *ibid.*, f. 23; HSTAD, RD 15934, ff. 101–102, 104, Bezirks-Polizeikommissar, Essen, 21 Nov. 1906.

10. WP, No. 226, 2 Oct. 1906, clipping, Biblioteka Raczyńskich, Poznań, Manuscript Division, MS. 800, f. 20.

11. Eric Dorn Brose, *Christian Labor and the Politics of Frustration in Imperial Germany* (Washington, D.C.: The Catholic University of America Press, 1985), pp. 232–233. The account of the *Gewerkverein* here is based primarily on this work.

12. Franciszek Mańkowski, "Historja Z.Z.P.," in *Ćwierć wieku pracy dla Narodu i Robotnika* (Poznań: Nakładem Zarządu Centralnego Zjedn. Zawod. Polskiego, 1927), p. 80; Hans Georg Kirchhoff, *Die staatliche Sozialpolitik im Ruhrbergbau 1871-1914* (Cologne: Westdeutscher Verlag, 1958), pp. 170–171, blames the rise in accidents above all on the increase of unskilled workers from outside the region, especially foreigners and Poles; for a counter argument, see John J. Kulczycki, "Scapegoating the Foreign Worker: Job Turnover, Accidents, and Diseases among Polish Coal Miners in the German Ruhr, 1871-1914," in *The Politics of Immigrant Workers: Labor Activism and Migration in the World Economy Since 1830*, ed. by Camille Guerin-Gonzales and Carl Strikwerda (New York: Holmes & Meier, 1993), pp. 133–152.

During the debate that followed in the Reichstag, Brejski repeated the demand for a mining law for all of Germany and the introduction of safety inspectors elected by miners. Along with the *Zentrum*, he called the language restrictions of the Associations Act one of the causes of the tragedy.[13] But when the *Alter Verband* issued an invitation to the other three unions to meet on 23 December 1908 in Essen to push for measures to protect workers, the *Gewerkverein* refused to attend, citing attacks on the *Gewerkverein* by the *Alter Verband*.[14] Nor did the *Gewerkverein* attend the miners' congress in Berlin at the beginning of February 1909, at which the ZZP had seventeen delegates out of the 136 in attendance and its leader Sosiński served as co-chairman and reported on blacklisting by mine owners, one of three main topics on the agenda.[15]

Whereas the ZZP stood together with the *Alter Verband* and the Hirsch-Duncker union in demanding workers' safety inspectors independent of the mines, the *Gewerkverein* did not.[16] Thus, when the Prussian Landtag passed a mining law in 1909 that provided for the election of safety inspectors, who, however would remain in the employ of the mine, the *Gewerkverein* regarded it as progress while the other three unions rejected the law as unsatisfactory.[17]

The *Gewerkverein* only joined with the other three unions when in October 1909 the Mine Association voted to create its own labor exchange through which all Association members would hire their workers based on certificates issued by their previous employer indicating their dates of employment and thus provide management with a better

13. Zygmunt Hemmerling, *Posłowie polscy w parlamencie Rzeszy niemieckiej i sejmie pruskim (1907–1914)* (Warsaw: Ludowa Spółdzielnia Wydawnicza, 1968), p. 252, citing *Stenographische Berichte über die Verhandlungen des Reichstags*, CCLVIII, 684.

14. *Der Verrat des schwarz-gelben Gewerkvereins der Bergarbeiter: Eine Darstellung der Bergarbeiterbewegung und -kämpfe in der Zeit nach dem Ruhrbergarbeiterstreik im Jahre 1905 bis einschliesslich des Streiks im Jahre 1912* (2nd rev. ed.; Bochum: Vorstand des Verbandes der Bergarbeiter Deutschlands, 1912), pp. 8–13; this anti-*Gewerkverein* source cited the incident as part of the union's betrayal of the miner, the final act occurring during the 1912 strike.

15. *Dziennik Poznański*, No. 26, 2 Feb. 1909, *Kurjer Poznański*, No. 27, 4 Feb. 1909, clippings, Biblioteka Raczyńskich, Poznań, Manuscript Division, MS. 800, f. 31; Chełmikowski, *Związki*, p. 222; Christoph Klessmann, *Polnische Bergarbeiter im Ruhrgebiet 1870–1945: Soziale Integration und nationale Subkultur einer Minderheit in der deutschen Industriegesellschaft* (Göttingen: Vandenhoeck & Ruprecht, 1978), p. 234, gives a different total of nineteen ZZP delegates among 138.

16. This was one of the demands that the ZZP presented to the Polish Circle, Chełmikowski, *Związki*, p. 237.

17. Hans Jürgen Teuteberg, *Geschichte der industriellen Mitbestimmung in Deutschland. Ursprung und Entwicklung ihrer Vorläufer in Denken und in der Wirklichkeit des 19. Jahrhunderts* (Tübingen: J.C.B. Mohr [Paul Siebeck], 1961), p. 460.

means of combating labor turnover. At the first meeting of representatives of the four unions on 18 October, disagreements arose over the form their cooperation should take, with the *Gewerkverein* rejecting decisions by majority vote and the other three unions rejecting the *Gewerkverein* proposal for a revival of the Commission of Seven with the *Gewerkverein* leader Behrens as its chairman.[18]

At a conference at the end of 1909, the four unions jointly protested against the labor exchange and threatened to strike when the demand for coal rose.[19] But this show of unity masked the deep division in the labor movement. Indeed, by emphasizing cooperation as opposed to confrontation and class conflict, German Christian labor leaders were at this time again trying to convince the more important entrepreneurs that Christian trade unions made safe, reliable partners.[20]

This difference of approach between the *Gewerkverein* and the other unions also manifested itself in the international forum. Although the *Gewerkverein* sent representatives to the international miners' congresses in 1906 and 1907, a resolution passed at the 1907 congress that each state be represented by one united delegation prompted the *Gewerkverein* not to attend any further congresses, supposedly because of its fundamental differences with the social democratic tendencies of the *Alter Verband* but also out of a fear of being overwhelmed and deprived of an independent voice by the stronger union.[21]

For its part, the ZZP participated in the international miners' congresses regularly, beginning in 1907. In 1909, when the congress was held in Berlin, Józef Rymer, chosen as secretary of the congress, used the occasion to refer to the Associations Act or "gag law" passed by the German Reichstag in 1908; by speaking at the congress in Polish, he took

---

18. *Dzieje Zjednoczenia Zawodowego Polskiego 1889–1939* (Chorzów: Nakładem Kartelu Zjednoczenia Zawodowego Polskiego na Śląsku, 1939) (hereafter cited as *Dzieje ZZP*), p. 174; *Verrat*, p. 15; HSTAD, RD 15934, ff. 237–238, Polizei-Präsident, Essen, 20 Oct. 1909, claimed that the *Gewerkverein* would be outvoted in any majority decision "since as a result of their participation in the international miners' congress the Hirsch-Duncker union and the Polish Trade Union are committed to the sense of the endeavors of the German Miner Union [*Alter Verband*], and the Polish Trade Union already on its own gladly follows the orders of the latter."

19. HSTAD, RD 15935, ff. 2–3, Polizei-Präsident, Essen, 28 Dec. 1909.

20. Brose, *Christian Labor*, pp. 240–241.

21. Heinrich Imbusch, *Arbeitsverhältnisse und Arbeiterorganisationen im deutschen Bergbau* (Essen: Verlag des Gewerkvereins christlicher Bergarbeiter, 1908), p. 660; on the fears of the *Gewerkverein*, see Michael Schneider, *Die Christlichen Gewerkschaften 1894–1933* (Bonn: Verlag Neue Gesellschaft, 1982), p. 296; Koch, *Bergarbeiterbewegung*, p. 131, puts the final congress attended by the *Gewerkverein* in 1906, apparently erroneously.

advantage of a provision in the law that allowed languages other than German at international meetings. The ZZP further distinguished itself at these congresses by opposing, often alone, resolutions calling for the nationalization of mines by the state. Its preference for private ownership derived in part from the anti-Polish policies of the Prussian government. At the congress in London in 1911, the ZZP argued, "if in the German state all mines came into the hands of the government, then the government would also use its influence for anti-Polish purposes."[22]

As a constituent member of the International Federation of Miners, the ZZP's members could join the Federation's other unions without paying an initiation fee, which Polish miners who migrated to the United States could take advantage of. These international contacts took on such importance for the ZZP that following the congress in Paris in 1908, at which the ZZP's delegates claimed the workers from around the world learned about the situation faced by Polish workers in Germany, the union considered having one or two of its officials learn French and English. Unlike the *Gewerkverein*, the ZZP did not see a threat in cooperating with the *Alter Verband*; rather, the ZZP saw its participation as a confirmation of the need for a Polish trade union.[23]

A Christian Union

The Catholic Church's increasing criticism of Christian trade unions from about 1907 contributed to the tempering of the tactics of the *Gewerkverein* and other German Christian trade unions as they came to fear a papal condemnation if they participated in any new wave of strikes. In 1907 Pope Pius X issued an encyclical that condemned "modernism," and in the following years controversy arose over whether the Christian trade unions represented an example of this heresy. The Vatican's undersecretary of state Umberto Benigni, who interpreted Pope Leo XIII's 1891 encyclical, "Rerum Novarum," as denying Catholic workers the right to participate in independent, nondenominational trade unions, sought to convince his superiors that Christian trade unions represented "modernism in practice." The papal nuncio in Munich regarded strikes as a violation of moral law. Conservative German Catholics, including members of the

22. Chełmikowski, *Związki*, pp. 222–224; Wachowiak, *Polacy*, p. 156; Murzynowska, *Polskie wychodźstwo*, p. 215. Klessmann, *Polnische Bergarbeiter*, p. 115, reads a greater antisocialist significance into this opposition to nationalization.

23. Mańkowski, "Historja," pp. 74, 76.

German episcopate, shared these views. Some bishops insisted on the right of supervision over the predominantly Catholic Christian trade unions, which threatened them with a loss of Protestant members if they agreed and of Catholic members if they resisted. To appease these circles by demonstrating its independence of social democratic influences, in October 1908 the *Gewerkverein* severed ties with the Commission of Seven and in December decided to boycott a miners' congress convened by the *Alter Verband*.[24]

Thus, not only faith in conciliation of capital and in cooperation with the German government separated the *Gewerkverein* from the other unions. Despite the avowedly Christian character of the ZZP and its overwhelmingly Catholic membership, the Polish Trade Union did not exhibit any of the fear of offending the Catholic hierarchy that affected the *Gewerkverein* and other German Christian trade unions. The Christian character of the ZZP lay above all in the close tie between Catholicism and Polishness rather than Christian teaching on the social role of a trade union. At a meeting in June 1908, the ZZP's leadership discussed sending an official to Mönchen-Gladbach, the headquarters of the Christian-social wing of the Center Party, "for the purpose of learning about Christian social matters," but there is no evidence that contact was made or that anything specific came of it, which is hardly surprising given Mönchen-Gladbach's ties with the *Gewerkverein*.[25] Nor did the ZZP send representatives to the International Congress of Christian Trade Unions, first held in Zurich in 1908 and attended by leaders of the German Christian trade unions.[26]

In 1911 the report of the ZZP's central directorate to the general assembly invoked "Rerum Novarum" as sharply condemning the injustice suffered by workers and as recognizing their right to organize.[27] But, in "Rerum Novarum," Leo XIII expressed a preference for exclusively Catholic associations that included both workers and employers. Although the document did not categorically reject strikes, it advocated eliminating their causes and making them unnecessary.[28] None of this inhibited the ZZP in its anticapitalism the way that it did the *Gewerkverein*, which

24. Brose, *Christian Labor*, pp. 242, 257–259, 261–263, 266–268.

25. Mańkowski, "Historja," p. 76.

26. Brose, *Christian Labor*, p. 260.

27. Christoph Klessmann, "Klassensolidarität und nationales Bewusstsein. Das Verhältnis zwischen der Polnischen Berufsvereinigung (ZZP) und den deutschen Bergarbeiter-Gewerkschaften im Ruhrgebiet 1902–1923," *Internationale Wissenschaftliche Korrespondenz zur Geschichte der deutschen Arbeiterbewegung*, X (1974), 162–163.

28. Brose, *Christian Labor*, pp. 73–75.

unlike the ZZP could not entirely rid itself of clerical interference. The Christian label served above all as a legitimization of the ZZP in the eyes of its predominantly Catholic audience as well as a justification of its condemnation of the abuses of the capitalist system.

The "Socialist" Union

Identification of the *Alter Verband* as socialist placed it out of bounds for Christians and thereby provided the *Gewerkverein* with its very *raison d'être*. In opposing the *Alter Verband*, the ZZP could have used the words of a 1907 *Gewerkverein* appeal:

> The Free Trade Unions [of which the *Alter Verband* was one] are the mortal enemies of Christianity and of every national sentiment. They are based on the materialist philosophy and have thereby created an unbridgeable gulf between themselves and the Christian and nationally-minded workers.[29]

In combating the *Alter Verband*, the ZZP also referred to its supposedly socialist revolutionary goals, for which Polish workers would serve merely as pawns. In 1906 the police commissar of Essen reported that Sosiński had stated at a public meeting that the social democrats needed the miners for a mass strike, and the Polish workers were supposed to lend a hand.[30] In 1911 the report of the ZZP central directorate returned to this argument, denying the social democratic view that only through international unity could complete victory over capital be attained and better pay and shorter hours be achieved; indeed, it accused the social democrats of only wanting the Poles to strengthen their unions.[31]

Such arguments ignored the criticism that some socialists heaped on the *Alter Verband* for being insufficiently revolutionary.[32] In fact, the Free

29. Quoted in S.H.F. Hickey, *Workers in Imperial Germany: The Miners of the Ruhr* (Oxford: Clarendon Press, 1985), p. 237. "Therefore, no true Christian could be expected to join this trade union," according to Koch, *Bergarbeiterbewegung*, p. 130.

30. HSTAD, RD 15934, f. 12, 26 Sept. 1906; the commissar noted, however, that this argument was made in a rather unconvincing way.

31. Klessmann, "Klassensolidarität," p. 162.

32. Otto Hue, "Über den Generalstreik im Ruhrgebiet," *Sozialistische Monatshefte*, Feb. 1905, pp. 201–221; Klaus Tenfelde, "Linksradikale Strömungen in der Ruhrbergarbeiterschaft 1905 bis 1919," in *Glück auf, Kameraden! Die Bergarbeiter und ihre Organisationen in Deutschland*, ed. by Hans Mommsen and Ulrich Borsdorf (Cologne: Bund-Verlag, 1979), pp. 212–215.

Trade Unions, which included the *Alter Verband*, overwhelmingly rejected the tactic of a mass political strike at their congress in May 1905.[33] The reformist approach of the *Alter Verband*, in which the union saw the primary interests of workers not in class conflict but in improvement of economic and social conditions, provided the very basis of cooperation between the *Alter Verband* and the ZZP.[34] Other attacks by the ZZP on the socialists appealed to ludicrous but popular misconceptions. In 1906 at a local recruitment meeting, Jan Korpus, a member of the ZZP's central directorate, warned against being influenced by social democrats because they themselves little practiced what they preached, citing as proof of this that the socialist leader August Bebel kept for himself property that he had inherited instead of sharing it with his colleagues.[35] Such attacks on the *Alter Verband* led a Polish socialist and *Alter Verband* official Józef Adamek to accuse the ZZP of being more concerned with winning over Polish members of the Free Trade Unions than with recruiting unorganized workers.[36]

Adamek, however, also chided German socialists for not doing more to promote the establishment of Polish social-democratic associations in the Ruhr, with the result that the SPD and the socialist-oriented Free Trade Unions like the *Alter Verband* were losing Polish-speaking members to the Polish national movement. In his view, "the Polish comrade" was initially so isolated from the rest of the Polish population,

> that he has not at all noticed that in the city—where he has worked and lived for years—several church, trade union, political, and sport associations have been founded, which at every opportunity snatch one member after another from his trade union and from his party. He notices it finally first when they approach him to say "that he is a traitor to his people," when he resists joining their trade union, which "naturally is much better." If he is by chance loyal to the party, is convinced enough and doesn't give in to pressure, then *his wife* is filled with enthusiasm for the sounds of her homeland during house to house recruitment—which now under the language articles [of the Associations Act] is especially pursued by the Poles better than by us—and incited against her

33. Klaus Schönhoven, "Die Gewerkschaften als Massenbewegung im Wilhelmischen Kaiserreich 1890 bis 1918," in *Geschichte der deutschen Gewerkschaften von den Anfängen bis 1945*, ed. by Ulrich Borsdorf (Cologne: Bund-Verlag, 1987), p. 240.

34. On the reformism of the free trade unions, see Stefan Goch, *Sozialdemokratische Arbeiterbewegung und Arbeiterkultur im Ruhrgebiet: Eine Untersuchung am Beispiel Gelsenkirchen 1848–1975* (Düsseldorf: Droste Verlag, 1990), p. 132.

35. HSTAD, LR Moers 788, f. 488, Polizei-Verwaltung, Hochemmerich, 17 Dec. 1906.

36. J. Adamek, "Die Kampfesweise der polnischen Reichsfraktion," *Die Neue Zeit*, XXVII, No. 2 (1909), 777.

"god-less red" husband. For the sake of peace in the house, he lets himself be persuaded to accept an invitation to the founder's day celebration of the Polish association. There he hears the sounds of his homeland, there he hears a chauvinistic prologue, there perhaps he sees his first Polish theatrical performance, there perhaps he finds a fellow countryman from his hometown and his wife likewise a girl friend, and so on. His wife is still more enthused than he, and he joins the Polish association because he feels at home there and does not know to what purpose he will be misused there.—This is how life runs its course and not otherwise.[37]

In a resolution passed by its general assembly in 1907, the ZZP declared, "The Polish Trade Union has as its goal the organization of all Polish workers and craftsmen on the basis of Christian and national principles."[38] The ZZP's existence made membership in a German trade union equivalent to national betrayal. As the ZZP's organ *Zjednoczenie* stated in 1906,

> The German trade unions combat each other, but when it comes to a battle against the Polish Trade Union, then all the organizations are in agreement.... Apparently, the socialists as well as the *Zentrum*-ites and Hirsch-ites have forgotten that, as long as the world is no other, a German will never be a Pole's brother! Polish workers will never submit to foreign control, even if all Germans became red Hakatists.[39]

Whereas its avowed Christian character enabled the ZZP to compete successfully against the *Gewerkverein*, the national argument stood against Polish membership in any German trade union, even an officially "internationalist" union like the *Alter Verband*.

Miners' Elections

Miners' elections provided the workers with an opportunity to choose their own representatives. Such directly chosen representatives could subvert the claim of the trade unions to represent workers; unions attempted to prevent this by running their own candidates, and in this they

---

37. *Ibid.*, p. 781, emphasis in original.

38. Chełmikowski, *Związki*, p. 256; *Uebersetzungen aus dem "Wiarus Polski,"* No. 101, 3 May 1907, STAM, RM VII, Nr. 36c. At the general assembly held in 1911, Sosiński invoked these same principles when he asserted that "the worker organized in the Polish Trade Union is loyal to the Church and society," Chełmikowski, *Związki*, p. 265.

39. Chełmikowski, *Związki*, p. 208.

were quite successful.[40] But, while the victory of a union candidate would confirm the union's status as the workers' representative, the election campaign naturally brought the unions into conflict with each other, hardly contributing to harmony within the labor movement.

The first election following the 1905 strike illustrated this divisive effect. Ironically, although the strike had resulted in the passage of the mining law of 1905, its provisions for workers' committees allowed the mines to disqualify the strike's participants from being chosen in the first election because the mines could regard them as newly hired after the strike and therefore lacking the required minimum term of employment at the same mine. To protest this anomaly and the possibility of the election solely of strikebreakers, the *Alter Verband* called for a boycott. Characteristically, the *Gewerkverein* decided to participate in the elections, thereby demonstrating its willingness to cooperate with mine owners.[41]

The ZZP attached much importance to the election of Poles in miners' elections. A dispute in 1898 between Polish community leaders in the Ruhr and the *Gewerkverein* over Polish candidates in the pension fund elders' election of that year contributed to the decision to establish a Polish trade union. According to an early historian of the Polish community in the Ruhr who worked for the ZZP in these years, the effort to support Polish candidates in Reichstag elections that they had no chance of winning derived its justification from the political education it provided the community so that it would support Polish candidates for offices they could win, such as in the miners' elections.[42] The rapid growth of the ZZP during the 1905 strike made the victory of a substantial number of Polish candidates a real possibility. Thus, although the ZZP initially supported the stance taken by the *Alter Verband*, it later decided

---

40. For a discussion of the competition between the two forms of leadership among miners, see Tenfelde, "Linksradikale Strömungen," pp. 201–202; Hue insisted that elected workers' committees serve as organs of the trade unions, supplementing them and not supplanting them, quoted in Adelmann, *Quellensammlung*, Vol. I, p. 361; at the mines of the Gutehoffnungshütte Company, 124 out of 127 safety inspectors elected prior to World War I were union men, Donald P. Panzera, "Organization, Authority, and Conflict in the Ruhr Coal Mining Industry: A Case Study of the Gutehoffungshütte, 1853–1914" (Unpublished Ph.D. Dissertation, Northwestern University, 1980), pp. 479–480.

41. Koch, *Bergarbeiterbewegung*, pp. 111–112; Irmgard Steinisch, "Der Gewerkverein Christlicher Bergarbeiter," in *Glück auf, Kameraden! Die Bergarbeiter und ihre Organisationen in Deutschland*, ed. by Hans Mommsen and Ulrich Borsdorf (Cologne: Bund-Verlag, 1979), p. 279.

42. Wachowiak, *Polacy*, p. 170.

to take part in the first elections of workers' committees in 1905.[43] Even though the relatively few mines that disallowed candidates who had participated in the strike included ones with large contingents of migrants from the East, some Poles won election to the workers' committees along with *Gewerkverein* members and unorganized miners.[44]

Polish candidates won five seats as pension fund elders in 1904 and, in the years after the 1905 strike, the ZZP made every effort to increase that number. In the 1908 election of pension fund elders, the ZZP put up candidates in all districts with large numbers of Poles but emerged with only six seats. The *Wiarus Polski* accused the other unions of filling the second spot on their slates of candidates with the Polish names of "Germanized Polacks" to confuse and attract less enlightened Polish voters.[45] In 1909 the ZZP resorted to a demagogic ploy of its own to discredit the *Alter Verband*'s candidate in the election of a pension fund elder in Obermarxloh in the Rhineland by charging the social democrats in the Reichstag with voting for an increase in taxes, though the increase would have come in inheritance taxes that did not touch the working class.[46] In these years Poles also won election as assessors to the mining courts (*Berggewerbegerichte*): they held two seats in 1905, twelve in 1906, and nine in 1909.[47]

Due to the already existing differences among the trade unions, particularly between the *Gewerkverein* and the other three unions, the

43. Mańkowski, "Historja," p. 65; Gerhard Adelmann, *Die soziale Betriebsverfassung des Ruhrbergbaus vom Anfang des 19. Jahrhunderts bis zum Ersten Weltkrieg unter besonderer Berücksichtigung des Industrie- und Handelskammerbezirks Essen* (Bonn: Ludwig Röhrscheid Verlag, 1962), p. 138; Koch, *Bergarbeiterbewegung*, p. 112, reports that at the conference on 18 Nov. 1905 the *Gewerkverein* favored participating in elections while the other three unions were opposed; according to Bezirks-Polizeikommissar, Essen, 12 March 1906, report to RPD, reprinted in Adelmann, *Quellensammlung*, Vol. I, p. 370, the ZZP and the Hirsch-Duncker union took part in the election along with the *Gewerkverein*.

44. HSTAD, RD 15933, Bezirks-Polizeikommissar, Düsseldorf, 21 March 1906; Koch, *Bergarbeiterbewegung*, p. 112; the Mine Owners Association notified its members on 27 Oct. 1905 of their obligation to exclude from participation in the election any worker notified of his dismissal during the strike; the mines could also exclude workers for other reasons: the Gutehoffnungshütte Company claimed to have allowed strikers to vote but nevertheless disenfranchised 46 percent of the eligible work force, Panzera, "Organization," pp. 471–472; OBAD, report to MfHuG, 31 Dec. 1905, listed some mines where strikers were disenfranchised, Adelmann, *Quellensammlung*, Vol. I, pp. 363–364; Adelmann, *Soziale Betriebsverfassung*, p. 139.

45. WP, No. 117, 27 May 1908, clipping, Biblioteka Raczyńskich, Poznań, Manuscript Division, MS. 800, f. 28; Mańkowski, "Historja," p. 88.

46. Adamek, "Kampfesweise," p. 772.

47. Mańkowski, "Historja," pp. 67, 70, 88; Chełmikowski, *Związki*, p. 203; Klessmann, *Polnische Bergarbeiter*, p. 284, gives totals for some years.

miners' elections in 1910 had broader repercussions than in the past. The unions fought them with such vehemence that a report to the ZZP general assembly in 1911 commented that "elections to parliament scarcely arouse greater passion."[48] As provided for in the 1909 mining law, safety inspectors elected in 1910 also acted as electors of the workers' committees established under the 1905 mining law.[49] Thus, by participating in this election, the *Alter Verband* could redeem the loss of influence on the workers' committees that it suffered through its boycott of the previous election in 1905. In the election the ZZP won 105 seats (7 percent of the total) compared with 1,040 for the *Alter Verband* and 311 for the *Gewerkverein*. The safety inspectors in turn elected 62 of the ZZP's candidates to workers' committees.[50] (One Pole won a safety inspector election decided by lot, but the *Alter Verband* challenged it, and the Superior Mining Office nullified it on the grounds that the Pole was insufficiently literate.[51])

In spite of its relatively small number of victories, the ZZP gained influence at some individual mines. For example, at the Vondern shaft of the Oberhausen mine, where migrants from the East formed 41 percent of the work force in 1905 and 49 percent in 1912, six of the eleven safety inspectors elected belonged to the ZZP.[52] Because one of them won by only a small margin, the management used its power to gerrymander the election by merging his department with another that had a strong majority for the *Gewerkverein* but to no avail: the Polish candidate was nevertheless reelected.[53] The Polish majority apparently made some difference because following the election in 1910 the workers' committee of the Vondern shaft alone among all the workers' committees of the

---

48. Quoted in Chełmikowski, *Związki*, p. 203.

49. Kirchhoff, *Staatliche Sozialpolitik*, p. 172.

50. OBAD, report to MfHuG, 12 Jan. 1911, reprinted in Adelmann, *Quellensammlung*, Vol. I, p. 407; Klessmann, *Polnische Bergarbeiter*, p. 284; Hickey, *Workers*, p. 244. According to Koch, *Bergarbeiterbewegung*, p. 128, ZZP candidates for safety inspector won sixty-three out of 935 mandates or 6.7 percent; according to Schneider, *Christlichen Gewerkschaften*, p. 297, they won 115 out of 1,621 mandates or 7.1 percent; Chełmikowski, *Związki*, pp. 202–203, notes that the report at the ZZP general assembly in 1911 claimed that 118 ZZP candidates for safety inspector won.

51. Bergrevierbeamter des Bergreviers Oberhausen, report to OBAD, 10 Dec. 1910, reprinted in Adelmann, *Quellensammlung*, Vol. I, p. 406.

52. Adelmann, *Quellensammlung*, Vol. II: *Soziale Betriebsverfassung einzelner Unternehmen der Ruhrindustrie* (Bonn: Pub. der Gesellschaft für Rheinische Geschichtskunde, 1965), p. 228; on the composition in 1905, see Franz Schulze, *Die polnische Zuwanderung im Ruhrrevier und ihre Wirkung* (Munich: Josefs Druckerei, Bigge, 1909), p. 102; in 1912, Panzera, "Organization," p. 341.

53. Panzera, "Organization," pp. 477–478.

Gutehoffnungshütte Company insisted on the firm's matching a contribution to the mine welfare fund by its miners.[54]

In the election of pension fund elders in 1910, the ZZP increased its percentage of the votes more than any other union. Despite the language restrictions imposed on public meetings by the Associations Act, ZZP candidates garnered 13 percent of the votes compared with 54 percent for the candidates of the *Alter Verband* and 29 percent for those of the *Gewerkverein*. This gave the ZZP only twenty-nine seats or 7 percent of the total compared with 299 for the *Alter Verband* and 83 for the *Gewerkverein*.[55] Still, the results made a socialist newspaper in Bochum sit up and take notice:

> To the detriment of the movement as a whole, in the Ruhr region a third miners' organization developed that we must take into account. It continues to grow more than ever, and years will pass before it meets the fate of the Christian *Gewerkverein*. For this reason our comrades and trade unionists should pay more careful attention than they have so far to this Polish organization, learn its methods of combat in order to oppose it successfully.[56]

The comment about "the fate of the Christian *Gewerkverein*" suggests that the *Alter Verband* and its allies viewed the election results as proof that it could crush its chief rival. The election victories stirred the ambitions of the ZZP. According to the report of the general assembly in 1911, "The task of the Polish Trade Union must be to manage the pension fund elections in such a way that neither the socialists nor the Gewerkvereinites have a majority in the pension fund. In this case, the Polish Trade

54. Evelyn Kroker, "Arbeiterausschüsse im Ruhrbergbau zwischen 1906 und 1914," *Der Anschnitt*, XXX, No. 6 (1978), 207–208; p. 207 notes an increased activity of the workers' committees from 1910 and connects this with the election of members of the *Alter Verband*, but no mention is made of the role apparently played here by the ZZP. At the Gutehoffnungshütte Company, a traditional stronghold of the *Gewerkverein*, the ZZP won altogether twelve seats on the workers' committees to the Christian trade union's seventeen, with twenty-seven going to the *Alter Verband* and three to the Hirsch-Duncker union, Panzera, "Organization," p. 507.

55. Chełmikowski, *Związki*, pp. 134, 203; Ullrich Feige, *Bergarbeiterschaft zwischen Tradition und Emanzipation: Das Verhältnis von Bergleuten und Gewerkschaften zu Unternehmern und Staat im westlichen Ruhrgebiet um 1900* (Düsseldorf: Schwann, 1986), p. 53; Hickey, *Workers*, p. 244. Klessmann, *Polnische Bergarbeiter*, p. 284, gives a different total for the *Alter Verband*. These election results illustrate the fallacy of measuring the strength of the ZZP by its percentage of victorious candidates, as done by Richard Charles Murphy, *Guestworkers in the German Reich: A Polish Community in Wilhelmian Germany* (Boulder, Colorado: East European Monographs, 1983), p. 73, rather than by its percentage of the total votes.

56. Quoted in Chełmikowski, *Związki*, p. 209.

Union will hold the balance."[57] In elections of assessors to the mining courts in December 1911, the ZZP again showed it could not be ignored. Its candidates won 11 percent of the vote (compared with 52 percent for the *Alter Verband* and 29 percent for the *Gewerkverein*) and twenty-seven seats—14 percent of the total.[58]

The Triple Alliance

An economic recovery in 1910 provided the opportunity for the labor movement to renew pressure on mine owners. Faithful to its chosen tactics, the *Gewerkverein* refused to join with the other unions in this effort. Nevertheless, at a conference in Bochum on 30 November 1910, the remaining three unions, which came to be called the Triple Alliance (*Dreibund*), decided to send their demands to the Mine Association.[59]

The leadership of the ZZP saw the danger in the division in union ranks but could not hold back. As the *Wiarus Polski* put it, "The Polish Trade Union, slandered and boycotted by the German unions, Christian as well as social-democratic, therefore demonstrates greater concern for the interests of the worker when despite all it does not refuse its cooperation as often as this cooperation is sought by the German organizations." But the *Wiarus Polski* cautiously expressed the hope that "the Poles will not pull any chestnuts out of the fire for the Germans and, in view of the division in the workers' camp—brought about by the brutality of the social democrats and the treason of the *Gewerkverein*—will remain calm." The article closed with a plea addressed to

> those numerous Poles...who are still lost in German organizations and must contribute to the pointless conflict between these organizations. It is obvious that only the [Polish] Trade Union honestly defends the workers' interests....A Pole who pays dues to an alien organization harms himself and his family.[60]

When the Mine Association rejected its demands, the Triple Alliance turned to the individual mine managements and organized miners'

57. Quoted in *ibid.*, p. 134.

58. *Uebersetzungen aus dem "Wiarus Polski,"* No. 7, 16 Feb. 1912, p. 96, *Narodowiec*, No. 36, 14 Feb. 1912, STAM, OBAD 887.

59. HSTAD, RD Präs 846, ff. 57, 59–60, Polizei-Präsident, Essen, 2 Dec. 1910; reprinted in Tenfelde and Trischler, *Bis vor die Stufen*, pp. 448–452.

60. WP, 10 Dec. 1910, No. 282, in German translation, HSTAD, RD Präs 846, f. 47.

meetings in January 1911 to rally grass-roots support.[61] A bilingual German-Polish flier announced such a meeting in Laar for workers of the Westende mine. The ZZP leader Regulski was one of two main speakers, although the *Polizei-Präsident* of Essen later claimed in a report concerning these meetings that ZZP representatives spoke only briefly to agree with the extensive explanations of speakers from the *Alter Verband*. The same report asserted that the attendance at the meetings only amounted to 10–18 percent of the work force of the mine in question, but the *Landrat* of Dinslaken noted that the meeting in Bruckhausen of the work force of the Neumühl mine drew about 4,000 or 80 percent of the work force, mainly members of the *Alter Verband* and the ZZP.[62]

Nevertheless, the split in union ranks led a majority of delegates of the Triple Alliance to vote against a strike when they met on 12 February 1911. A bilingual German-Polish flier put out by the unions of the Triple Alliance after the conference asserted that miners were getting poorer while producing riches for "a handful of exploiters of the treasures of the earth." It, however, accused the *Gewerkverein* and the *Zentrum* of saying that the "poor" mine magnates cannot afford a 15 percent pay raise. The flier acknowledged that some mines had granted raises, but argued that the unions would have achieved more if the *Gewerkverein* had not stood in the way. Urging members of the *Gewerkverein* to put pressure on their leaders, the Triple Alliance claimed that the battle was not over, only postponed to give mine owners a chance to fulfill their promises. Ominously, the flier predicted that in the future the *Gewerkverein* would face the choice of fighting in the interest of the workers or joining with the strikebreaker yellow organizations. Finally, calling for support of the three unions ready to fight for improved conditions, it exhorted the unorganized to join one of the three unions so as not to undermine the solidarity that alone could bring victory.[63]

The plans of English miners for a strike in the spring of 1912, which would increase the demand for coal from the Ruhr, gave new life to the suggestion of a strike among the Ruhr's miners. But, at meetings of representatives of all four of the miners' unions on 12 October 1911 and on 5 February 1912, the *Gewerkverein* continued to refuse to go along with the other unions in demanding a pay increase from mine owners.

61. *Arbeiter-Zeitung*, 29 Dec. 1910, clipping, HSTAD, RD Präs, 846, f. 62; *Verrat*, pp. 19–20; *Dzieje ZZP*, p. 175.

62. HSTAD, RD Präs 846, ff. 69, 71–72, 75–77, Polizei-Verwaltung, Duisburg, 10 Jan. 1911, LR Dinslaken, 17 Jan. 1911, Polizei-Präsident, Essen, 31 Jan. 1911.

63. *Ibid.*, Polizei-Präsident, Essen, 25 Feb. 1911.

Although in the fall of 1911 the ZZP still hesitated because of doubts about the success of any strike over which the unions were divided, at the February meeting the ZZP joined with the *Alter Verband* and the Hirsch-Duncker union in reactivating the Triple Alliance and in issuing mine owners a demand for a pay raise.[64]

The Polish press in the Ruhr endorsed the demand and regarded it as just in light of the cost of living and company profits, even though a strike might be the result. In an article under the headline "Miners' Strike in View in the Rhineland and Westphalia," the *Wiarus Polski* explicitly warned miners that only those who belonged to a union would receive strike pay and therefore those who wished to protect their families from hunger should join the ZZP without delay. The *Wiarus Polski* suggested that the tactics of the *Gewerkverein* approached those of the yellow unions. The *Narodowiec* went even further with an article entitled, "The Treason of the Christian *Gewerkverein*," in which it linked the union's dissent to the electoral agreement between the *Zentrum* and the National Liberals, the mine owners' party, in the Reichstag elections in early 1912.[65]

Following the mine owners' rejection of the demands of the Triple Alliance, the chairmen of ZZP locals in the Ruhr meeting on 18 February declared their support for a strike. Yet the continued opposition of the *Gewerkverein* raised doubts in some minds. At the end of February, the *Wiarus Polski*, noting the positions taken by the German trade unions, commented with foreboding, "the conflict will be sad. If only Polish workers would harvest good fruit from this. If only they would understand that their place is in a Polish organization....If only they would see the true picture, that Polish workers are not at fault, only Germans, because they allow such a swindle with regard to the general question."[66]

When representatives of the Triple Alliance met on 7 March and proposed that the strike begin on 11 March, the delegates of the ZZP were among those in favor of an immediate strike. At this point, however, the ZZP chairman Sosiński intervened. Recently elected as a deputy to the Reichstag from Upper Silesia with the support of the *Zentrum* Party, he

---

64. For a more detailed account of the decision to strike, see John J. Kulczycki, *The Foreign Worker and the German Labor Movement: Xenophobia and Solidarity in the Coal Fields of the Ruhr, 1871–1914* (Oxford, Providence, USA: Berg Publishers, 1994), pp. 222–229.

65. WP, No. 31, 7 Feb. 1912, in German translation, *Übersetzungen der westfälischen und anderen polnischen Zeitungen*, No. 6, 9 Feb. 1912, pp. 78–79; *Narodowiec*, No. 31, 8 Feb. 1912, in *ibid.*, No. 7, 16 Feb. 1912, p. 86, STAM, OBAD 887.

66. Murzynowska, *Polskie wychodźstwo*, p. 244.

apparently persuaded the ZZP Miners' Section chairman Mańkowski to seek a delay.[67] But, at a conference of the Triple Alliance on 10 March, Mańkowski's proposal to postpone the strike until 1 April, which would allow miners to give notice and thus avoid fines for breach of contract, met with denunciations from German delegates, forcing him to retreat and endorse the strike.[68] Pressure from its own rank and file together with fear of being branded as a traitor to the workers' cause along with the *Gewerkverein* left the ZZP no other choice.

The ZZP, however, confined its support of the strike to the Ruhr and did not advocate its spread to Upper Silesia. There the opposition of the *Zentrum* loomed larger than in the Ruhr region. Moreover, although over half of the organized miners of Upper Silesia belonged to the ZZP, it encompassed barely 12 percent of the region's work force.[69]

A Divided Labor Movement

The adamant opposition of the *Gewerkverein* doomed the strike from the start. Hopes that most of the union's members would desert their leaders and join the strike proved vain. The opposition of the Christian union to a strike led by the socialist-oriented *Alter Verband* also meant that the predominantly Catholic Poles came under particular pressure from at least some of the German clergy who ministered to them. A priest in Neumühl sympathetic to the aim of the strike doubted a claim of a Polish reporter from Warsaw that a cleric had ordered a Christian baker not to sell bread to strikers; furthermore, he believed that only clergymen who served as patrons of German associations that opposed the strike were agitating against it.[70] But a number of Catholic miners' and workers' associations published appeals denouncing the strike.[71] A contemporary ZZP activist

---

67. Wachowiak, *Polacy*, pp. 150–151; *Dziennik Poznański*, No. 92, 23 April 1912, *Gesammtüberblick*, No. 18, 7 May 1912, p. 423; Murzynowska, *Polskie wychodźstwo*, pp. 243, 245. On Sosiński's election, see Marian Orzechowski, *Narodowa demokracja na Górnym Śląsku (do 1918 roku)* (Wrocław: Zakład Narodowy im. Ossolińskich, 1965), p. 277.

68. Mańkowski, "Historja," p. 105; Chełmikowski, *Związki*, p. 228.

69. Kazimierz Popiołek, ed., *Dzieje górniczego ruchu zawodowego w Polsce (do 1918 R.)*, Vol. I (Warsaw: Wydawnictwo Związkowe CRZZ, 1971), p. 96; Murzynowska, *Polskie wychodźstwo*, pp. 250–251, makes much of this dichotomy in the ZZP's support of the strike without noting the weakness of the union in Upper Silesia.

70. *Kurjer Warszawski*, No. 81, 21 March 1912, in German translation, *Uebersetzungen aus westfälischen und anderen polnischen Zeitungen*, No. 17, 26 April 1912, p. 182.

71. *Bergknappe*, No. 11, 16 March 1912.

claimed that in some places the clergy visited homes of strikers and encouraged them to return to work.[72] According to one report, the priest in Werne ordered the removal of a Polish religious banner from the local church because Poles were taking part in the strike.[73] Such incidents led Poles to protest against the intervention of the clergy in the strike.[74] Impending defeat also split the ranks of the Triple Alliance. The Polish press in the Ruhr later charged that a large number of *Alter Verband* members abandoned the strike with the union's approval on its sixth day, 16 March, because of a threat by mine owners that those miners who did not report to work that day would forfeit the pay from six shifts; the Polish press also asserted that eight days after the Triple Alliance announced the strike half of the *Alter Verband*'s members had already resumed work.[75] Although the strike suffered its first significant decline on 16 March, only anecdotal evidence supports the claim that members of the *Alter Verband* were responsible.[76]

At the conference on 19 March called to consider whether to continue the strike, the leadership of the ZZP joined that of the *Alter Verband* in advocating a return to work.[77] But this decision went against the sentiment of most strikers, who did not want to admit that their sacrifices had achieved nothing. To avoid the resentment that now turned against the unions, the Poles falsely claimed that they had wanted to continue the strike but that the German delegates had outvoted them.[78] In its proclamation of the end of the strike dated 19 March 1912, the ZZP Miners' Section alleged that German workers abandoned the strike "in droves" and thereby forced their representatives at the conference in Bochum to end the strike despite the resistance of the ZZP. "In the face of this decision, we cannot ask you to continue to strike but rather are forced

---

72. Wachowiak, *Polacy*, p. 142.

73. *Verrat*, p. 75.

74. Murzynowska, *Polskie wychodźstwo*, p. 246.

75. The charges, which will be considered below, originally appeared in *Narodowiec*, No. 71, 27 March 1912, WP, No. 72, 27 March 1912, *Uebersetzungen aus westfälischen und anderen polnischen Zeitungen*, No. 13, 29 March 1912, p. 158, STAM, OBAD, 887.

76. One observer reported that by 18 March "many members of the *Alter Verband*" were returning to work at the Carolinenglück mine, David F. Crew, *Town in the Ruhr: A Social History of Bochum, 1860–1914* (New York: Columbia University Press, 1979), p. 204.

77. HSTAD, RD 15939, ff. 270–271, 20 March 1912; Murzynowska, *Polskie wychodźstwo*, p. 248.

78. *Narodowiec*, No. 71, 27 March 1912, *Uebersetzungen aus westfälischen und anderen polnischen Zeitungen*, No. 13, 29 March 1912, p. 159, STAM, OBAD 887; *Jubileuszowy Kalendarz Wychodźczy "Wiarusa Polskiego" 1890–1940 na r. 1940* (Lille, France: "Wiarus Polski," 1940), p. 144.

with a heavy heart to recommend that you return to work. Thanks to the betrayal of some Germans and the deficient perseverance of other Germans, we have not reached the goal we strove for."[79] Yet the ZZP urged its members not to be discouraged. Instead, they should work on building up their organization so that in a future movement for higher wages they would not need to look to German organizations.

"After every lost war the people ask: 'Who is responsible for our defeat?'" So began an article entitled "Who's Guilty?" which the *Wiarus Polski* carried on 22 March 1912. In the first place, the *Wiarus Polski* defended the decision of the ZZP to support the strike to avoid being branded as a union of strikebreakers. "The material damage, which the Poles suffered because of the strike, is great, but it was unavoidable, as unavoidable as our national uprisings, which inflicted great material damage on the nation, but protected the Poles from moral ruin." That the strike was unavoidable, the *Wiarus Polski* blamed on the *Gewerkverein*: if the *Gewerkverein*, it argued, had joined with the other unions in making demands on the mine owners, they would have conceded raises of 10–15 percent because the time was favorable for a strike, but the betrayal of the *Gewerkverein* also made victory impossible. A second circumstance making victory impossible the *Wiarus Polski* saw in the agitation against the strike by the "patrons of the Christian *Gewerkverein*," particularly the clergy and the German middle classes, with bakers and butchers even refusing to sell strikers their wares. According to the *Wiarus Polski*, the participation of the clergy in the agitation against the strike irreparably damaged the Church in the eyes of Polish men and women.[80]

The early end to the strike, however, the *Wiarus Polski* attributed to "the respect of the German Michael for the uniform and the fear of the spiked helmet," referring to the military forces brought into the Ruhr that others have cited as hastening the end of the strike.[81]

> In the view of the German, only the gendarme and the noncommissioned officer direct the fate of mankind; they regarded the strike as lost when they saw the noncommissioned officer and the sergeant-major standing on the side of the strikebreaker. At the sight of the gendarme and the military, the red Michaels took off their red ties and rushed to the mine office as if on

79. *Uebersetzungen aus westfälischen und anderen polnischen Zeitungen*, No. 12, 22 March 1912, p. 151, STAM, OBAD 887.

80. WP, No. 69, 22 March 1912, in *ibid.*, No. 13, 29 March 1912, p. 155.

81. For example, Franz-Josef Brüggemeier, *Leben vor Ort. Ruhrbergleute und Ruhrbergbau 1889–1919* (Munich: C.H. Beck, 1983), p. 231.

command, stood at attention and meekly declared that they are "at the service" of the mine.

In conclusion the *Wiarus Polski* wondered,

> Now, should the Poles join with the Germans in a common struggle if even the reddest German does not even dare to sneeze without the consent of high officials? Were all Poles to read Polish newspapers and belong to the Polish Trade Union, then they would have won at least there where they form a majority of the workers.[82]

Less than a week later the *Wiarus Polski* followed this anti-German appeal to Polish solidarity with an attack on both of the major German unions. In an article whose title paraphrased a biblical warning (Ecclesiastes 10:8), "Whoso diggeth a pit shall fall into it," the *Wiarus Polski* accused the "social democrats" of organizing the strike mainly for the purpose of destroying the other unions, an argument used earlier by the *Gewerkverein*.[83] The article alleged that, although the ZZP had greater financial resources per capita than the *Alter Verband*, the latter expected foreign union assistance to enable it to provide strike pay longer than the ZZP and thus draw away the Polish union's members en masse.

As for the *Gewerkverein*, the *Wiarus Polski* claimed that it believed the ZZP "would not dare to join the strike without the *Gewerkverein*" and thus would draw "the hate and persecution of the social democrats," diverting attention from the betrayal of the *Gewerkverein*: "It is well known that the social democrats charge the Poles with the greatest crime for something that among Germans counts as a simple misdemeanor." But the *Wiarus Polski* cautioned against letting the anger against the *Gewerkverein* and the "clerical Germanizers" and others who supported the strikebreakers turn against the Catholic Church "because the Poles were always loyal to the holy Church."[84]

To deflect criticism from the ZZP, Polish leaders in the Ruhr continued their attacks on the *Alter Verband*, making their most serious specific accusation within a week of the end of the strike. On 27 March the *Narodowiec* published a copy of a "work card" (*Arbeitskarte*) issued by the *Alter Verband* to members exempted from participating in a strike.

82. WP, No. 69, 22 March 1912, *Uebersetzungen aus westfälischen und anderen polnischen Zeitungen*, No. 13, 29 March 1912, p. 155, STAM, OBAD 887.

83. WP, No. 73, 28 March 1912, in *ibid.*, No. 14, 6 April 1912, pp. 161–162, STAM, OBAD 888. I wish to thank Richard S. Levy for bringing the biblical reference to my attention.

84. *Ibid.*, p. 162.

Such a permit might be granted, for example, to invalid miners who would lose their benefits if they did not report for work and had no possibility of obtaining work elsewhere. But the article, entitled "Scandalous Betrayal of the Polish Trade Union and the Polish Miner by the '*Verband*,'" charged that on 16 March the *Alter Verband* distributed these cards to "a large number of known social democrats and *Verband* members."[85] Following a strategy of "the worse, the better," the social democrats supposedly expected to reap the anger of the population over the defeat of the strike by winning more votes in the next election, enabling Hue to regain the seat in the Reichstag that he lost in 1912.

Illustrating the seriousness of this charge, the *Gewerkverein* reprinted the entire *Narodowiec* article in its union journal.[86] The *Gewerkverein* activist Imbusch also cited the Polish accusation and reprinted the work card in defense of his union's stance in 1912.[87] Although he declined to choose between the Polish version that "thousands" of such cards were distributed and the *Alter Verband*'s claim that only a small number were, Imbusch emphasized that the *Alter Verband* did this secretly while trying to force older men in the *Gewerkverein* to work.

The *Alter Verband* itself reprinted the *Narodowiec* article in its account of the strike and accused the ZZP of giving in to outside influences. The *Alter Verband* argued that similar cards had been used during the strike in 1905 and other strikes and that it had distributed scarcely a hundred such cards and none to workers actually engaged in digging coal. Moreover, it maintained that the union leaders of the Triple Alliance had agreed upon the work cards at their meeting on 8 March and therefore the executive directorate of the ZZP should not only not have contributed to the spread of this false charge but should also have contradicted it. In addition, the ZZP's leaders should protest against being portrayed as puppets: they agreed with the decisions as they were made, and it is unseemly after the failure of the strike for these leaders to seek to push the responsibility onto the *Alter Verband*.[88] The dispute continued, with the *Alter Verband* taking the *Narodowiec* to court for giving offense to the

85. *Narodowiec*, No. 71, 27 March 1912, in *ibid.*, No. 13, 29 March 1912, STAM, OBAD 887, pp. 158–159.

86. *Bergknappe*, No. 14, 6 April 1912.

87. Heinrich Imbusch, *Bergarbeiterstreik im Ruhrgebiet im Fruhjahr 1912* (3rd ed.; Cologne: Christl. Gewerkschaftsverlag, n.d. [1912]), pp. 44–45.

88. *Verrat*, pp. 80–83.

leaders of the union and winning a court decision in March 1913 that resulted in a 20 mark fine for the Polish newspaper.[89]

Disaffection with the Unions

The police in Hamborn believed that whether miners remained in the unions would depend on the strike pay they received: if they got less than they paid in dues, then they were inclined not to pay any more and were stricken from the membership rolls.[90] In addition, the decision of the Triple Alliance to break off the strike provoked anger among some miners. Miners blamed union leaders for deciding on a strike that ended in defeat. At a meeting announcing the end of the strike in Radbod, some of the miners tore up their union membership booklets.[91] On 22 March the Münster district *Präsident* reported that many miners had quit the *Alter Verband*.[92]

The ZZP was not immune to this disaffection. A police report one month after the strike noted, "also in members' circles [of the ZZP] voices of dissatisfaction are stirring; because the strike ended with a defeat of the worker's organization, the view that membership in the organization is pointless gets a hearing among the Poles as well."[93] A history of the ZZP admitted a decline in the membership of the Miners' Section in the Ruhr in the first two months following the strike.[94] But, alone among the miners' unions of the Ruhr, the ZZP Miners' Section finished the year with more members than before the strike: 30,354 compared with 30,164 members at the start of 1912.[95] When combined with the decline in the

89. When in 1912 the Polish socialist and *Alter Verband* activist Adamek charged the central executive board of the ZZP with falsifying its financial reports, the ZZP in turn instituted a suit for calumny, Antoni Banaszak, "Z.Z.P. a policja pruska i sądy w ostatnich latach przed wojną światową," in *Ćwierć wieku pracy dla Narodu i Robotnika* (Poznań: Nakładem Zarządu Centralnego Zjedn. Zawod. Polskiego, 1927), p. 545.

90. HSTAD, RD 15945, f. 38, Polizei-Verwaltung, Hamborn, 25 March 1912.

91. HSTAD, RD Präs 851, f. 97, RPM to MfHuG, 20 March 1912, copy. Polizei-Verwaltung, Hamborn, reported on 23 March 1912 that miners at the Deutscher Kaiser mine were rather indifferent to the mine management's decision not to rehire thirty-eight miners regarded as ringleaders of the strike: miners now had no great sympathy for those who had advocated the strike, HSTAD, RD 15939, f. 313.

92. HSTAD, RD Präs 851, f. 109, to MdI, 22 March 1912, copy.

93. STAM, RM VII, Nr. 31, f. 29, Polizei-Präsident, Bochum, 22 April 1912.

94. *Dzieje ZZP*, p. 178.

95. Chełmikowski, *Związki*, p. 162; Klessmann, *Polnische Bergarbeiter*, p. 283; STAM, OP 5758, f. 388, Polizei-Präsident, Bochum, 3 May 1913, put the membership in the Ruhr at about 28,000 in 181 locals and noted that participation in the unsuccessful strike had cost

other unions, this slight increase meant that the ZZP's share of the unionized miners of the Ruhr rose from 19 percent in 1910 to 22 percent at the end of 1912.[96] No less than the unions of the Triple Alliance, the *Gewerkverein* suffered disappointment and therefore eventually changed course and leadership as it tried to wash away the stigma of a "strikebreaker" and responsibility for both the intervention of the military and the defeat of the strike. Although the *Gewerkverein* concentrated its attacks on the *Alter Verband* and the social democrats, virtually ignoring the ZZP and the Poles, its emphasis on its loyalty to the German nation-state in opposition to the internationalist social democrats could hardly attract any nationally conscious Poles. A *Gewerkverein*-sponsored meeting in Duisburg-Laar immediately following the strike even featured a local secretary of the National Liberal Party as a speaker alongside the prominent *Gewerkverein* activist Imbusch.[97]

The defeat of the strike also affected the attitudes of miners toward the divisions among the unions. The district leader of the *Alter Verband* in Gelsenkirchen reported that, after the strike, a number of members began discussing the fusion of the unions, particularly those in the Triple Alliance.[98] These members met with local leaders of the other unions and even drew up a statute for a single united trade union. A survey conducted in Hamborn following the strike found that many miners quit unions out of discouragement over the defeat of the strike in the belief that the labor movement would only succeed when the unions merged into one big union.[99]

This apparent increase in class consciousness among German workers in the Ruhr as a result of the strike encompassed Polish-speaking migrants

the ZZP a number of members.

96. Klessmann, "Klassensolidarität," p. 154; no comparison to 1911 is possible since the *Gewerkverein* membership in the Ruhr is unknown. The proportion of miners born in the East remained virtually unchanged, rising from 36.7 percent of the work force in 1910 to 36.8 percent in 1912, Klessmann, *Polnische Bergarbeiter*, p. 265.

97. HSTAD, RD 15921, ff. 427–429, meeting, 24 March 1912. The speakers made no mention of the Poles; the *Gewerkverein* journal *Bergknappe* also virtually ignored them in its criticism of the strike.

98. Murzynowska, *Polskie wychodźstwo*, p. 249; see also Tenfelde, "Linksradikale Strömungen," p. 209.

99. Klessmann, *Polnische Bergarbeiter*, p. 235, citing Li Fischer-Eckert, *Die wirtschaftliche und soziale Lage der Frauen in dem modernen Industrieort Hamborn im Rheinland* (Hagen: Karl Stracke, 1913), p. 132.

as well.[100] At a local Polish electoral association meeting in Düsseldorf-Gerresheim, a Polish nationalist critic of the ZZP alliance with the *Alter Verband* during the strike learned that an appeal just to national sentiments no longer sufficed. After a speech in which he criticized social democracy for advocating class conflict and praised the ZZP for not supporting wildcat strikes, the audience ran him out of the meeting.[101] In August 1912 an article in the Polish press in the homeland bemoaned the mutual aversion between the Polish entrepreneurial-merchant class and the Polish working class in the Ruhr.[102] Signaling how little the differences among the unions mattered to some, a Polish miner wrote in his memoirs how, after serving on a strike committee as a member of the *Alter Verband* in the Ruhr in 1912, he lost his job and returned to Upper Silesia, where he worked with the ZZP in support of the strike that broke out there in 1913.[103]

But union leaders rejected efforts on behalf of a fusion. The chairman of a ZZP union local, in Westenfeld near Wattenscheid, spurned an invitation from members of the *Alter Verband* to attend a meeting to discuss the matter.[104] At a meeting of the *Alter Verband* union local in Gelsenkirchen in December 1912, a speaker also opposed the idea, arguing that both the *Gewerkverein* and the ZZP were linked to political parties. Instead, he advocated working for the growth of the *Alter Verband* and thereby achieving victory.[105] The ZZP pursued the same goal, competing against the other unions by emphasizing both its class and its national character to recruit and keep new members. Thus, one cannot take seriously Mańkowski's claim that German workers, seeing that the ZZP followed the right course in the strike, began to apply for membership.[106] Indeed, the ZZP's strategy depended above all on setting up a wall between German and Polish workers.

100. On the increase in class consciousness among German workers, see Klaus Saul, *Staat, Industrie, Arbeiterbewegung im Kaiserreich: Zur Innen- und Aussenpolitik des Wilhelminischen Deutschland 1903-1914* (Düsseldorf: Bertelsmann Universitätsverlag, 1974), pp. 281-282.

101. GR, No. 45, 18 April 1912, *Uebersetzungen aus westfälischen und anderen polnischen Zeitungen*, No. 17, 26 April 1912, p. 182, STAM, OBAD 888.

102. *Dziennik Bydgoski*, No. 178, 8 Aug. 1912, *Gesammtüberblick*, No. 32, 13 Aug. 1912, p. 715.

103. Związek Zawodowy Górników, *Życiorysy górników* (Katowice: Wydawnictwo Związku Zawodowego Górników w Polsce, 1949), p. 179.

104. WP, No. 98, 29 April 1912, *Uebersetzungen aus westfälischen und anderen polnischen Zeitungen*, No. 18, 3 May 1912, p. 190, STAM, OBAD 888.

105. STAM, RA I, Nr. 1476, report, 16 Dec. 1912, copy.

106. Mańkowski, "Historja," p. 107.

Divisions in the Polish National Movement

The participation of the ZZP in the 1912 miners' strike alongside the socialist-oriented *Alter Verband* in opposition to the Christian *Gewerkverein* fueled the criticism that conservatives in the Polish national movement in the homeland had earlier made of the ZZP and its leadership. On 24 March 1912, the *Dziennik Poznański* (Poznań Daily), which represented the so-called conciliatory faction in the Polish national movement in Poznań, printed an article by "a worker" from Bochum. After listing the losses suffered by the strikers, he criticized Mańkowski for supposedly having been a greater enthusiast of the strike than the "socialists." Above all, he assailed the allegedly pro-socialist tendency of the ZZP: "these men, like Mańkowski, at meetings revile not only the capitalists, the German nobility, and the Polish lords but even our clergy." He called for a change in the ZZP. "Class conflict, which we today pursue against our will, is especially to be eliminated from the scene. Then the leadership of the miner organization should be assumed by better educated people, who do not let themselves be steered by the socialists but manage their affairs themselves." He blamed the leadership for allegedly promoting a strike as the sole weapon of the workers and saw the fatal mistake in the decision at the conference on 10 March to order the strike for the next day, instead of postponing it for at least a week or until 1 April—the very thing the *Alter Verband* later criticized the ZZP leadership for trying to do.[107]

Postęp (Progress), another Polish newspaper in Poznania but one linked to the aggressively Polish nationalist faction, dismissed such criticism and suggested that class interests linked the Polish conciliators with German industrialists: "they do not throw themselves into large speculative mining ventures, but they wish the wages of the agricultural workers would be as low as possible so that they can gamble away their profits playing cards at the town casino or in Monte Carlo."[108] More convincingly, the *Narodowiec* later attributed the attacks on Mańkowski, in which the *Dziennik Poznański* was joined by the *Katolik* of Upper Silesia and the *Gazeta Grudziądzka* of West Prussia, to the conciliators'

107. *Dziennik Poznański*, No. 69, 24 March 1912, *Gesammtüberblick*, No. 16, 23 April 1912, pp. 355–356.

108. *Postęp*, No. 71, 28 March 1912, *Gesammtüberblick*, No. 14/15, 16 April 1912, pp. 338–339.

desire for revenge for his opposition to their support in parliament for the government's financial reform.[109] In a long article on 13 April, the *Dziennik Poznański* attempted to refute point by point the defense put forward by ZZP leaders for their decision to support the strike. The article criticized Mańkowski in particular for supposedly supporting the strike even before the "socialists," and it rejected his argument that joining the strike prevented the "socialists" from destroying the ZZP because it did not prevent them from declaring a war on the Polish trade union after the strike. A quote from the ZZP's journal *Głos Górnika* formed the basis for an accusation that Mańkowski and the other ZZP leaders accepted that the average Pole viewed socialism as the "saviour of mankind."

> From this same source pour those attacks on the Polish nobility and the Polish clergy, that incitement of class conflict in the meetings of locals of the union in the West...The tendency fomented in the union in the West poses a serious danger not only for our emigrants, but also for the homeland. The emigrants return to the homeland from abroad and bring with them the conviction that socialism is the savior of mankind.[110]

The next day the *Dziennik Poznański* printed a note from the editor of the *Głos Górnika* with a correction of a supposed misprint in the quoted article that altered its meaning, but the *Dziennik Poznański* did not retract its charges.[111] The ZZP took such criticism seriously. On 5 April a local of the ZZP Artisans' Section meeting in Düsseldorf expressed its confidence in the leadership and members of the Miners' Section and its regret over the attacks against Mańkowski by some newspapers in the homeland.[112] Then on 14 April 1912, the ZZP convoked a joint meeting in Berlin of its central executive board, its board of supervisors, the boards of the union's sections, and the district secretaries. At this meeting the ZZP formally concluded that the leadership of the Miners' Section had acted properly

109. *Narodowiec*, No. 90, 20 April 1912, *Uebersetzungen aus westfälischen und anderen polnischen Zeitungen*, No. 17, 26 April 1912, p. 184, STAM, OBAD 888. It should be recalled that Mańkowski's suit for libel against the *Gazeta Grudziądzka* was before the courts at this time, with a hearing on 18 April 1912, WP, No. 90, 19 April 1912, in *ibid.*

110. *Dziennik Poznański*, No. 84, 13 April 1912, *Gesammtüberblick*, No. 16, 23 April 1912, pp. 353–355.

111. *Dziennik Poznański*, No. 85, 14 April 1912, in *ibid.*, p. 356; Wachowiak, *Polacy*, p. 143, claims authorship of the article in *Głos Górnika*, saying that it was misunderstood.

112. WP, No. 89, 18 April 1912, *Uebersetzungen aus westfälischen und anderen polnischen Zeitungen*, No. 17, 26 April 1912, p. 182, STAM, OBAD 888.

and not under the influence of any German trade union—a counter to those who saw it as acting at the behest of the *Alter Verband*. The communiqué signed by the thirteen top leaders of the ZZP argued that the *Gewerkverein* could risk opposing the strike "because it had influential protectors," but the ZZP would have dug its own grave "solely to the benefit of social democracy" if it had followed the same course. To this affirmation of the defense of their actions by the leaders of the Miners' Section and its supporters, the communiqué added a new accusation against the *Gewerkverein* by charging that the union had deliberately kept silent about what it knew of the plans of the social democrats to destroy the other unions, hoping to benefit as well from the collapse of the ZZP.[113]

The communiqué specifically rejected the "reproaches of some newspapers" that Polish workers gravitate toward social democracy, pointing out that in a movement for better wages it is normal for the unions to form a common front. Furthermore, it asserted,

> For years Germans for easily explained reasons have charged the Polish worker in the emigration with competing with the German worker and with working for lower wages. If Polish workers had now followed the example of the Christian *Gewerkverein*, by their behavior they would have confirmed that fairy tale, and the already sad situation of the emigration would only have worsened.[114]

As for the attacks on the leadership of the Miners' Section and especially on Mańkowski, the communiqué attributed them more to personal animosity than to concern for the interests of the Polish worker and his union. At the same time, it again corrected the alleged misprint in the article in the *Głos Górnika* cited by the union's Polish critics.

The *Dziennik Poznański* printed Mańkowski's own response to the accusations made against him on 23 April 1912.[115] He naturally denied the role attributed to him in promoting the strike before the Triple Alliance decided on it and, on the contrary, claimed that he had advocated delaying it. At the same time, however, he claimed that the leaders of the ZZP had

---

113. *Kurjer Poznański*, No. 89, 19 April 1912, *Gesammtüberblick*, No. 17, 30 April 1912, p. 397; WP, No. 90, 19 April 1912, *Uebersetzungen aus westfälischen und anderen polnischen Zeitungen*, No. 17, 26 April 1912, pp. 183–184, STAM, OBAD 888; see also a summary in Mańkowski, "Historja," pp. 107–108.

114. WP, No. 90, 19 April 1912, *Uebersetzungen aus westfälischen und anderen polnischen Zeitungen*, No. 17, 26 April 1912, p. 184, STAM, OBAD 888; *Kurjer Poznański*, No. 89, 19 April 1912, *Gesammtüberblick*, No. 17, 30 April 1912, p. 397.

115. *Dziennik Poznański*, No. 92, 23 April 1912, *Gesammtüberblick*, No. 18, 7 May 1912, p. 423.

not expected the "betrayal by the German unions." Mańkowski also denied that he or other speakers at meetings of ZZP union locals "criticize the Polish nobility or the clergy."

The ZZP and Ethnic Solidarity

If the strike tested and found wanting the ties of union solidarity and if the ZZP faced the criticism of conservative elements in the Polish national movement, the ZZP continued to look for support based both on its ethnic and its class character. Even before the strike ended and penalties rained down on the strikers, a ZZP union local in Duisburg-Laar appealed to "dear fellow-countrymen in the homeland" asking for contributions because "we are suffering much want and hunger, especially the Polish miners who are married and have several children."[116] The appeal specifically asked estate owners and farmers to send potatoes so that people would not starve. Hardly had the strike ended when the executive board of the ZZP Miners' Section addressed its own appeal for contributions to the Polish community, arguing that the union's effort to improve the lot of the Polish miners would also benefit the community as a whole. Moreover, the union claimed to have recruited many Poles who took part in the strike but belonged to no union, which supposedly also served the interests of the community, and contributions would assist in this endeavor.[117]

Like the other unions, the ZZP provided strike pay. Depending on the level of dues paid weekly, the ZZP paid 9–13 marks plus half a mark per child in strike pay weekly; this compared with the 6–14 marks depending on the length of membership in the union plus 1 mark per child paid by the *Alter Verband*.[118] According to one report, altogether the ZZP paid out 195,000 marks.[119] After the strike, the ZZP undertook a lawsuit costing several thousand marks in a vain attempt to prevent mine owners from penalizing strikers by deducting pay for six shifts.[120]

116. *Siła*, No. 6, 25 March 1912, in *ibid.*, No. 13, 2 April 1912.

117. WP, No. 69, 22 March 1912, *Uebersetzungen aus westfälischen und anderen polnischen Zeitungen*, No. 13, 29 March 1912, pp. 155–156, STAM, OBAD 887.

118. HSTAD, RD 15939, f. 428, Polizei-Präsident, Essen, 29 April 1912.

119. STAM, RM VII, Nr. 31, f. 29, Polizei-Präsident, Bochum, 22 April 1912, to RPA, copy; also, HSTAD, RD 15939, f. 437, Polizei-Präsident, Essen, 18 July 1912; see, however, f. 509 for a copy of the ZZP report for 1912/13, which listed 14,220.01 marks paid out in strike pay.

120. Mańkowski, "Historja," p. 106.

Once the dimensions of the cost of the strike became clear, the ZZP Miners' Section made another appeal, this time "to the Polish worker in the homeland and in German areas." Citing the many Polish men and women imprisoned following the strike, the appeal insisted that "we must at least provide bread for those children whose mothers are in jail." The union asserted that it was a question not of its members but of those who have been left to their fate without any protection. In addition, the appeal noted that many who struck were blacklisted, and therefore workers should resist the recruitment efforts of mine agents sent to the homeland. "Polish brother, worker! Remember that the fate of the Polish miner here, your brother, is dependent on you alone. We have seen during the last strike that we cannot count on the German worker, all the same whether he is organized or not."[121]

This emphasis on ethnic solidarity as opposed to class solidarity also marked an appeal shortly after the strike of the ZZP Miners' Section to its members and "to all other Polish miners who approve of the program of this union." In view of the way in which the Associations Act condemned Polish miners to silence during the strike while Germans discussed as they wished, the appeal urged the following watchword: "attend no German meetings and also restrain others from doing so." The appeal argued that the ZZP could no longer speak as freely at meetings of union locals, which few members attended anyway.

> Others, on the contrary, are doing everything they can to incite Polish workers to attend German meetings. There other nourishment will be provided them, there other convictions will be implanted in them, and there all that we have laboriously achieved at meetings of union locals is rooted out.[122]

The appeal also called on the Polish press not to divide the ranks of the union but rather to promote the watchword that Polish workers avoid German meetings.

At the same time, the union announced that it was organizing courses to augment the number of speakers for union locals and to bind them closely to the union's program. Beginning in May the Miners' Section offered socio-political courses for its activists in various places, a total of fifty such courses in 1912 alone. By 1913 the lecturers included editors of the Polish press and the more educated members of the emigration like

121. WP, No. 95, 25 April 1912, *Uebersetzungen aus westfälischen und anderen polnischen Zeitungen*, No. 18, 3 May 1912, p. 189, STAM, OBAD 888.
122. WP, No. 84, 12 April 1912, in *ibid.*, No. 16, 19 April 1912, p. 178; also, *Siła*, No. 8, 25 April 1912, *Gesammtüberblick*, No. 18, 7 May 1912, p. 430.

Stanisław Wachowiak, the son of a miner and recipient of support from the Polish St. Josaphat Educational Aid Society. The free courses covered both general educational topics and professional matters, such as economic and social developments, civil and criminal law, and hygiene. In addition, the Miners' Section decided to broaden its courses concerning the miner's insurance and pension fund.[123]

In August 1912 the ZZP central directorate addressed an appeal to all its branches to celebrate the tenth anniversary of the founding of the union and issued a special commemorative stamp for its members. In the appeal the central directorate claimed that, although the recent strike did not result in any immediate gains, the situation in the Ruhr had already improved.[124] The *Głos Górnika* marked the occasion of the tenth anniversary of the ZZP with an article published on 10 November 1912. The article began with a reference to the skepticism that greeted the union a decade earlier.

The Germans, who treated us in a stepmother-like fashion in their trade unions, did not want to believe that the Polish worker, who in their opinion was only a work-animal, who in their view did not have the slightest understanding for the idea of a trade union, could be capable of erecting a solid structure based on a strong foundation for the defense of his class interests [*Standesinteressen*] and ideas.

The article took particular pride in the ZZP being "the work of the people, the simple people of the hammer and pickax."[125]

As the union's greatest moral achievement, the article saw "the enlightenment of the Polish worker." Popular education forms the basis for material prosperity and ensures solidarity.

How widely disseminated in our trade union is the conviction of solidarity was shown by the movement for better wages. Our trade union and its members have never betrayed the worker's cause. The solidarity of our organized worker came into play best in the last strike: we were almost the only ones who did not abandon the picket line until the last minute.

123. Klessmann, *Polnische Bergarbeiter*, p. 113; Mańkowski, "Historja," p. 121; Wachowiak, *Polacy*, p. 131; Krystyna Murzynowska, "Ruch zawodowy robotników polskich w Zagłębiu Ruhry," in *Ruch zawodowy w Polsce: Zarys dziejów*, ed. by Stanisław Kalabiński, Vol. I (Warsaw: Instytut Wydawniczy CRZZ, 1974), p. 504.

124. Mańkowski, "Historja," p. 111.

125. *Głos Górnika*, No. 20, 10 Nov. 1912, *Gesammtüberblick*, No. 47, 26 Nov. 1912, pp. 1037–1038.

Recounting the benefits that the ZZP provided for its members, the article admitted that other unions did the same. "But has the Pole found in alien trade unions the same fraternal, honest, unselfish assistance as in his own? No, never! We can be proud of the possession of our own trade union. In our social-economic life it is the primary factor."[126]

In an article on "Trade Unions in Emigration" written for a commemorative book for a Polish industrial exhibit in Bochum in July 1913, Mańkowski himself admitted that

> the Polish emigrants were formerly charged with working more cheaply than other workers, with begging for work cap in hand, and so forth. In a word, Polish emigrants were showered with abuse; because of their lack of understanding of workers' affairs, German workers were much harmed in their earnings.[127]

In Mańkowski's view this was no longer the case, thanks to the educational work of the ZZP.

While the ZZP thus tried to maintain a balance between its class and its ethnic character, an escalation of the anti-Polish policies of the Prussian authorities late in 1912 pressured the Polish trade union to put a greater emphasis on Polish ethnic solidarity. Although the government's announcement in October 1912 of its decision to expropriate four Polish estates posed no direct threat to the working-class Poles in the Ruhr, the "struggle over the soil" in the East made it more difficult for the migrant to realize the dream of saving enough money to buy a farm in the homeland. According to an SPD deputy during the debate that followed in the Reichstag, the average price for one hectare of land in the East rose from 570 marks in 1886 to 1,395 marks in 1911.[128]

The Poles in the Ruhr also felt the heavy hand of the Prussian authorities directly. Although the Main Polish Electoral Committee directed Polish voters to boycott the election held in May 1913 for the Prussian Landtag, the Polish community in the Ruhr used the occasion to organize public meetings in Polish, as permitted in connection with

---

126. *Ibid.*

127. Franciszek Mańkowski, "Związki zawodowe na wychództwie," *Pamiętnik wystawy przemysłowej w Bochum od 19–27 lipca 1913 roku* (Oberhausen: Nakładem Komitetu Wystawowego, n.d. [1913]), pp. 32–33.

128. An excerpt from this speech is reprinted in Hans Jürgen Brandt, ed., *Die Polen und die Kirche im Ruhrgebiet 1871–1919: Ausgewählte Dokumente zur pastoral und kirchlichen Integration sprachlicher Minderheiten im deutschen Kaiserreich*, (Münster: Aschendorff, 1987), p. 263.

elections under the Associations Act of 1908.[129] In his annual report for 1913, the Prussian police official charged with surveillance of the Poles in the Ruhr complained that the meetings did not serve the purpose of the elections, "rather the general agitation for the Polish-national endeavors."[130] Along with other subjects, the speakers at these meetings called for strengthening of organizational activity, especially within the ZZP. The police tried to stop this end run around the "gag law." Shortly after the election they instituted some eighty suits against speakers at these meetings, including Jan Brejski and Mańkowski, arguing that they had no right to speak in Polish since the meetings had nothing to do with the election. But the courts found the Poles not guilty.[131]

In addition, the Prussian police in a number of cases in 1913 tried to use the law against ZZP union locals, which the police claimed were political organizations and therefore obligated to register with the police both their statutes and a list of officers. But again the courts found the union leaders not guilty.[132]

At the beginning of November 1913, the leaders of the Polish community in the Ruhr organized a two-day conference in Winterswijk, Holland, beyond the reach of the Prussian authorities. Some 1,200 heard Jan Brejski give the main speech, in which he surveyed the tasks of the various Polish organizations in defense of their members' Polish nationality. A miner also spoke about the German clergy's efforts at Germanization of the Polish migrants. The first resolution passed at Winterswijk created an Executive Committee (*Komitet Wykonawczy*), of which Mańkowski became a member, and mandated it to work for the unity of Polish organizations in cooperation with the National Council (*Rada Narodowa*) formally inaugurated a month earlier in Poznań and whose membership included Jan Brejski. The second resolution recommended the formation of committees in each community to regulate and direct the activities of local Polish associations. It also opposed the membership of Germans in Polish associations since experience has shown that they only promote the interests of various German parties. Every Pole over eighteen had the duty to join at least one Polish national

129. Jerzy Kozłowski, *Rozwój organizacji społeczno-narodowych wychodźstwa polskiego w Niemczech w latach 1870–1914* (Wrocław: Ossolineum, 1987), p. 231.

130. Quoted in Murzynowska, *Polskie wychodźstwo*, p. 187.

131. Kozłowski, *Rozwój*, p. 232; Banaszak, "Z.Z.P.," pp. 548–549.

132. Banaszak, "Z.Z.P.," p. 551.

association that recognized the authority of the National Council and to belong to the ZZP.[133]

The ZZP on the Eve of the War

The atmosphere of German-Polish national confrontation and polarization also reinforced the ZZP's attempts to distance itself from the *Alter Verband*. After the ZZP organized a miners' strike in Upper Silesia that lasted for three weeks in April and May 1913, which had no more success than the strike in the Ruhr the previous year, the ZZP retorted to criticism emanating from the *Alter Verband* with the cry, "Do we not here have enough proof that the social democrats are the most malicious haters of Poles [*Polenfresser*] and worse than all the Hakatist parties? Riffraff and nothing more!"[134]

Mańkowski carried his campaign against the *Alter Verband* to the stage by writing a two-act play about Polish migrant coal miners in the Ruhr. Published by the Miners' Section of the ZZP shortly before the war, it portrayed Poles who joined the *Alter Verband* as demoralized individuals who, denying their nationality, become Germanized and forget their parents in the homeland.[135]

Following its second defeat in a major strike in little over a year, the Miners' Section of the ZZP held its last biannual general assembly before the war, in Upper Silesia in late May 1913. It refused to allow a representative of the *Alter Verband* to take part in the meeting.[136] Furthermore, in reference to the 1912 strike, the report of the Miners' Section for 1911/12 said of its members, "They saved their honor, they were not strikebreakers or cowards as the Germans showed themselves to be."[137]

Despite the strike defeats, the miners reelected the same leaders with Mańkowski at the head, although delegates from Upper Silesia raised some objections, allegedly inspired by Korfanty, an echo of the criticism

---

133. Brandt, *Polen*, pp. 275–281, 292; Klessmann, *Polnische Bergarbeiter*, pp. 103–104; Witold Jakóbczyk, *Studia nad dziejami Wielkopolski*, Vol. III: *1890–1914* (Poznań: Państwowe Wydawnictwo Naukowe, 1967), pp. 215–217, 219. The chairman of the ZZP was also a member of the National Council's socio-economic section.

134. Klessmann, "Klassensolidarität," p. 163.

135. Franciszek Mańkowski, *Za chlebem w świat* (Bochum: Oddział Górnikow Zjednoczenia Zawodowego Polskiego, n.d. [ca. 1913]).

136. STAM, RM VII, Nr. 36c, Polizei-Präsident, Bochum, 28 June 1913.

137. Quoted in Chełmikowski, *Związki*, p. 227.

Mańkowski faced from some Polish leaders in the homeland two years earlier. Meanwhile, the Miners' Section, with its headquarters in Bochum in the Ruhr, established a branch office in Upper Silesia following the strike there. Under the vice-chairman of the Miners' Section, the office functioned in Upper Silesia in the name of the Section's executive committee with a certain amount of autonomy.[138]

At the beginning of June 1913, the ZZP as a whole held its general assembly in Berlin. In light of the strike defeats of 1912 and 1913, the union's executive committee faced considerable criticism, though delegates voted a resolution approving the position taken by the leadership. Nevertheless, Sosiński did not win reelection as chairman of the ZZP. In his place the delegates chose Józef Rymer, formerly a coal miner in the Ruhr. Miners also dominated the newly elected board of supervisors, taking twenty-five out of forty-two seats. At the same time, the delegates rejected proposals of the executive committee that would have increased its control over the union's sections. For its part, the Miners' Section no longer pushed for more independence after the recent strikes had demonstrated that it could not survive financially on its own.[139]

In not reelecting Sosiński, a deputy in the Reichstag since 1912, the ZZP seemed to manifest its rejection of the Polish Circle, which symbolized the upper-class dominance of Polish society in Prussia, but went against the union's earlier demand for a workers' representative in parliament. In fact, in 1913 Sosiński showed that he could represent them when he broke the solidarity of the Polish Circle to vote in favor of a law permitting the lowering of duty on cattle and meat, which favored the interests of urban workers even as it went against those of Polish estate owners.

In the course of 1913 membership in the ZZP Miners' Section in the Ruhr declined by 5 percent to 28,936.[140] Membership in the other miners' unions, however, declined by even more. Thus, on eve of the war, the ZZP saw no reason to move away from its new emphasis on the national character of the union and its conflict with the predominantly German unions, though the conflict among the unions probably contributed to the decline that all of them suffered.

The ZZP also showed signs of vitality at this time. The Miners' Section encompassed workers at coking plants and associated chemical plants. Because Poles formed a high proportion of these workers, the ZZP had

---

138. Mańkowski, "Historja," pp. 114–115, 120.
139. Chełmikowski, *Związki*, pp. 142–143, 174; Mańkowski, "Historja," pp. 117–118.
140. Chełmikowski, *Związki*, p. 162; Klessmann, "Klassensolidarität," p. 154.

earlier taken an interest in their cause, particularly in favor of limiting their workday to eight hours.[141] In 1914 it created a separate section for them within the ZZP, and it soon organized eleven union locals. Then, in May 1914, in the name of standardizing the work of the ZZP, the central executive board called a three-day meeting in Poznań of all the union's officers. Mańkowski, the head of a section that once sought to widen its independence from the union's central authority, gave one of the three main speeches. At the meeting the union endorsed harmonious cooperation with all Polish organizations that stood for Polish and Christian ideals while condemning international Marxism as opposed to these ideals. At the same time, the ZZP declared its intention to fight the German trade unions and take from them every Pole who still belonged to them, although it stated it would work with the German unions in moments of need when the good of workers was at stake. As the worst anti-Polish element, the ZZP singled out Polish socialists, who supposedly served as translators for German unions and the Prussian authorities and spied on the Polish movement in general and on the ZZP in particular.[142]

The ZZP emerged from the 1905 strike as a partner of the German-led unions in the Ruhr, and in the years that followed it participated fully in the region's labor movement. Its militant stand during the 1905 strike won it recognition, and it continued in this vein. When the labor movement split over tactics in relation to mine owners, the ZZP sided with the more aggressive approach of the *Alter Verband* rather than with the conciliatory efforts of the *Gewerkverein*. Although an avowedly Christian union, the ZZP did not let the label limit its militancy in the way that the *Gewerkverein* did. At the same time, the ZZP sharply differentiated itself from the international socialist image promoted by the *Alter Verband*. These features of the ZZP enabled it to back candidates in the miners' elections with some success.

When conditions seemed to favor a confrontation with mine owners, the ZZP joined with the *Alter Verband* and the much smaller Hirsch-Duncker union in the creation of the Triple Alliance, which ultimately called for a strike in the spring of 1912. Despite the opposition of the *Gewerkverein*, which doomed the strike from the start, the militant image in defense of workers' interests cultivated by the ZZP prevented it from following any other course. When defeat of the strike led to mutual recriminations among the allied unions, the ZZP continued to project

141. *Naród*, No. 245, 23 Oct. 1927, AAN, ARPB 2196, f. 129.
142. Mańkowski, "Historja," pp. 124, 128–129.

itself as the more militant defender of the miner and accused the *Alter Verband* of flagging in the midst of the struggle.

The fragmentation of the labor movement that followed the defeat of the 1912 strike led to disaffection with the unions among the miners of the Ruhr. Membership in all the unions declined following the strike. Although the ZZP suffered fewer losses than the other unions, it too faced a decline, which became apparent at the end of 1913. The disarray in the labor movement combined with an intensification of the anti-Polish policies of the Prussian authorities led the ZZP to reemphasize its ethnic ties with the Polish national movement. Still, it never abandoned its defense of working-class interests. Its conflict with the German-led unions did not preclude future cooperation. With the coming of the Great War in the summer of 1914, the ZZP faced a renewed threat to its existence both as a part of the Polish national movement in Prussia and as part of the labor movement in the Ruhr. A similar threat to the other unions and an opportunity to seek the achievement of long-term goals led to a resumption of cooperation within the labor movement.

PART II
National Solidarity in the Interest of the Polish Nation-State

5

The World War and the Reorientation of the ZZP

Since its formation in 1902, the ZZP put national solidarity at the service of the working-class interests of its members, which meant integrating the Polish Trade Union within the labor movement in the Ruhr region. When the defense of working-class interests conflicted with the interests of the leadership of the Polish national movement in the homeland, the ZZP did not hesitate to challenge that leadership. This stemmed from a conviction that equated the interests of the Polish nation with those of the Polish working class. But the world war transformed the situation of Polish workers and led the ZZP to redefine their interests and therefore give the union's efforts a new direction.

The Immediate Impact of the War

The workers of Germany generally greeted the outbreak of the war in 1914 with enthusiasm. According to an official in Dortmund, the excitement was especially high among the miners of the Ruhr.[1] The Poles of the region did not share this patriotic zeal, and many fled to Holland to avoid military service.[2] According to Mańkowski, as members of the ZZP Miners' Section received their draft notices, they came in the hundreds to union headquarters in Bochum to seek advice, turn in their union booklets, and say goodbye, crying, "For what reason and purpose am I supposed to die, for this oppression and misery, for the fact that we Poles were treated like dogs?"[3]

---

1. Jürgen Reulecke, "Der Erste Weltkrieg und die Arbeiterbewegung im rheinisch-westfälischen Industriegebiet," in *Arbeiterbewegung an Rhein und Ruhr: Beiträge zur Geschichte der Arbeiterbewegung in Rheinland-Westfalen,* ed. by Jürgen Reulecke (Wuppertal: Hammer, 1974), p. 211; see also Hans Mommsen *et al., Bergarbeiter. Ausstellung zur Geschichte der organisierten Bergarbeiterbewegung in Deutschland* (Bochum: Berg-Verlag GmbH, 1969) (unpaged), section 13.

2. HSTAD, RD 16021, f. 328, Polizeirat Augustini, Bochum, 31 Aug. 1920.

3. Franciszek Mańkowski, "Historja Z.Z.P.," in *Ćwierć wieku pracy dla Narodu i Robotnika* (Poznań: Nakładem Zarządu Centralnego Zjedn. Zawod. Polskiego, 1927), p. 130.

Publicly, however, the Polish community maintained a loyal stance toward the government, whose arsenal of repressive weapons increased with the war. In a state of war, the Prussian Law of Siege of 1851 empowered the commanding officers of the military regions into which the state was divided to take over virtually all police functions and to dissolve and ban all meetings deemed harmful to the war effort.[4] One of the rare overt signs of opposition came in Gerthe, a community with a high concentration of Poles, where manifestations of anti-German feelings led to the arrest of a Pole.[5]

Patriotism and fear of repression stood behind the decision of the General Commission of Trade Unions, to which the *Alter Verband* and other Free Trade Unions belonged, to proclaim a policy of civic truce (*Burgfrieden*) on 2 August 1914. In promising an end to all strikes, the union leadership received assurances from the government not to suppress its organizations or seize their assets as long as they maintained their loyalty. But the union leadership also expected that cooperation with the authorities would bring the unions the official recognition that they had sought for so long as well as democratic reforms and an improved legal and social status for the working class.[6] These goals, shared by all the unions, including the ZZP, provided a basis for their cooperation during the war, which brought more unity to the labor movement in the Ruhr than it had seen since the 1905 strike.

Nothing, however, could protect the unions from the immediate impact of the war with its call-up to arms of the young men that made up the overwhelming bulk of their membership. By 1915 the total work force in the Ruhr's mines declined from its pre-war peak in 1913 by 30 percent.[7] The unions, especially the ZZP, suffered even greater losses. Between 1913 and 1915, the membership in the *Alter Verband* in the Ruhr fell by 53 percent, while the ZZP Miners' Section in the Ruhr lost just over two

4. Christoph Klessmann, *Polnische Bergarbeiter im Ruhrgebiet 1870–1945: Soziale Integration und nationale Subkultur einer Minderheit in der deutschen Industriegesellschaft* (Göttingen: Vandenhoeck & Ruprecht, 1978), p. 146; John A. Moses, *Trade Unionism in Germany from Bismarck to Hitler 1869–1933*, Vol. I: *1869–1918* (Totowa, New Jersey: Barnes & Noble, 1982), pp. 180, 182. HSTAD, RD 16021, f. 328, Polizeirat Augustini, Bochum, 31 Aug. 1920, attributed the lack of "Polish agitation" to the efforts of the district's military commander.

5. S.H.F. Hickey, *Workers in Imperial Germany: The Miners of the Ruhr* (Oxford: Clarendon Press, 1985), pp. 34, 297.

6. Moses, *Trade Unionism*, Vol. I, pp. xvii, 175, 180, 188–190, 211.

7. Klessmann, *Polnische Bergarbeiter*, p. 265; Franz-Josef Brüggemeier, *Leben vor Ort. Ruhrbergleute und Ruhrbergbau 1889–1919* (Munich: C.H. Beck, 1983), p. 240, cites a decline from 425,600 before the war to 305,000 at the end of 1914 and to 280,000 in Aug. 1915, a decrease of 34 percent.

thirds of its members, declining from 28,936 in 1913, to 16,137 in 1914, to 9,130 in 1915.[8] In April 1915, the union treasury was running a deficit of 86.20 marks. As the union's leader in the Ruhr region put it in 1927, "At the start of the war to the end of 1914 and the beginning of 1915, it seemed that the last hour of our organization had struck."[9] The *Burgfrieden*, which limited union activity in defense of workers, probably induced some to quit and save money on dues. Uncertainty about the future had the same effect, as did the hope of some Poles that the war would result in the resurrection of Poland, where the working classes would rule and therefore have no need of a union.[10] At a meeting of the ZZP Miners' Section local in Hochlar in September 1915, the ten people present listened to the speaker lament that many members were not coming to meetings and saying, "I won't pay my dues during the war but as soon as it is over, I'll start paying them again." At the end of the meeting, the organizer announced that the next one would probably be held in three months.[11] At a meeting of the ZZP union local in Disteln in August 1915, attended by twelve members, the speaker made the same complaint and noted that several locals could not even collect enough dues to forward any money to the union treasurer in Bochum.[12]

Mańkowski claimed that the government had targeted the leadership of the ZZP. The steady stream of members coming to the union offices in Bochum aroused suspicion and resulted in Mańkowski's temporary detention. Doubts about Polish loyalties might well have influenced the military call-up, which Mańkowski maintained did not touch many younger officials of the German unions: though forty-four years old he had to report for military service along with two other leaders of the Miners' Section, leaving only the treasurer and his deputy, men in their 60s; other sections of the ZZP and its central directorate suffered comparable losses. This bred passivity and a siege mentality among the remaining union officials, who often did not even try to collect dues from members for fear that they would quit.[13] Income from membership dues in the Miners' Section dropped by 47 percent from 1914 to 1915;

---

8. Klessmann, *Polnische Bergarbeiter*, p. 283.

9. Franciszek Kołpacki, "Zjednoczenie Zawodowe Polskie we Westfalji (w Niemczech)," in *Ćwierć wieku pracy dla Narodu i Robotnika* (Poznań: Nakładem Zarządu Centralnego Zjedn. Zawod. Polskiego, 1927), p. 487.

10. Mańkowski, "Historja," p. 134.

11. STAM, RM VII, Nr. 36c, police report, Amt Recklinghausen, Hochlar, 12 Sept. 1915.

12. *Ibid.*, Polizei Amt, Recklinghausen, 29 Aug. 1915.

13. Mańkowski, "Historja," pp. 130, 132–133.

indicative of the threat of the union's collapse, income from initiation fees from new members declined in the same period by 84 percent![14] The loss of staff and decline in resources also inhibited union activity. At first publication of the union press ceased altogether, and later it came out less frequently and in smaller editions than before the war. Eventually, in 1916, the leadership of the ZZP decided that the organ of the Miners' Section *Głos Górnika* would replace those of the other sections.[15]

Union Cooperation

Weakness, the threat of repression, and shared goals inclined the ZZP to work with the German-led unions in seeking an accommodation with the authorities. Moreover, the war created new hardships for workers that the unions had to address. In late December 1914 the ZZP together with numerous German unions formed the Committee for Consumer Interests during the War, which acted as a pressure group at the local and national level to protect the ordinary citizen from the spiraling inflation of food prices.[16] In January 1915 the ZZP Miners' Section signed an agreement of cooperation with the other three miners' unions in the Ruhr, and thereafter acted with them in representing miners' interests before the authorities.[17] On 6 February 1915 the four miners' unions submitted a petition to the Ministry of Trade and Industry complaining about miners being fired or threatened with being sent to the trenches for refusing to work overtime and about pay cuts that made it impossible to cover the rising cost of living. Because mine owners refused to negotiate wages with workers' committees, the unions requested the ministry's support for the creation of conciliation bureaus in the mines.[18] Throughout the war

14. Stanisław Wachowiak, *Polacy w Nadrenii i Westfalii* (Poznań: Nakładem Zjednoczenia Zawodowego Polskiego, 1917), tables following p. 136.

15. Marjan Chełmikowski, *Związki zawodowe robotników polskich w Królestwie Pruskim (1889–1918)* (Poznań: Fiszer i Majewski, 1925), p. 145; Mańkowski, "Historja," p. 139.

16. Eric Dorn Brose, *Christian Labor and the Politics of Frustration in Imperial Germany* (Washington, D.C.: The Catholic University of America Press, 1985), p. 333.

17. Krystyna Murzynowska, "Związki polskiego wychodźstwa zamieszkałego w Zagłębiu Ruhry z krajem w latach 1870–1918," in *Polska klasa robotnicza: Studia historyczne*, ed. by Elżbieta Kaczyńska, Vol. X (Warsaw: Państwowe Wydawnictwo Naukowe, 1983), p. 123. STAM, OP 6617, Polizei-Präsident, Gelsenkirchen, 25 Jan. 1915, copy, reported to RPA on a meeting of representatives of the four miners' unions on 20 Jan. 1915, which considered workers' complaints concerning demands for increased productivity.

18. STAM, OP 6617, copy.

there followed a series of joint petitions and complaints of the four unions to mine owners and government officials concerning conditions in the mines and in the Ruhr in general.[19] Union cooperation went beyond joint declarations. In anticipation of the election of mine safety inspectors at the end of August 1915, the four unions agreed to nominate and support common candidates in opposition to those nominated by yellow or company unions.[20] At a meeting held to discuss the matter, when the representative of the *Alter Verband* proposed a fusion of the four unions into a single miners' union as the only way to triumph over the workers' enemies, the ZZP delegate agreed, but the *Gewerkverein* representative opposed the idea as premature.[21]

The ZZP also continued its own initiatives. In a statement dated 22 February 1915, the Polish union complained of mistreatment of Polish miners at the Teutoburgia mine because of their nationality.[22] Nor did the ZZP representatives assume a passive role in relation to the other unions. When in May 1915 the four miners' unions met to discuss a joint proposal to mine owners for a wage increase, Mańkowski criticized as offensive to the dignity of workers the justification in the proposal that a pay raise would better enable workers to fulfill their obligations. When his German colleagues rejected his complaint by saying that as a Pole he did not understand the situation because he did not care what happened to Germany, he replied that the demand for higher pay was justified because workers in all their dignity constituted a powerful section of the state and therefore should earn more so that the working class could achieve an appropriate standard of living, which was the highest good of the state. Every peasant cleaned and oiled his machines and fed his horse well before the harvest to improve their performance, and he accused his

---

19. Walter Neumann, *Die Gewerkschaften im Ruhrgebiet. Voraussetzungen, Entwicklung und Wirksamkeit* (Cologne: Bund Verlag, 1951), p. 171. See the examples in STAM, OP 6617; HSTAD, RD 9081, I; and Klaus Tenfelde and Helmuth Trischler, eds., *Bis vor die Stufen des Throns: Bittschriften und Beschwerden von Bergleuten im Zeitalter der Industrialisierung* (Munich: Verlag C.H. Beck, 1986), pp. 477–482, 484–487. In 1919 the *Alter Verband* published a collection of over 350 pages of complaints and petitions that it issued during the war either on its own or together with the other three unions, Christoph Klessmann, "Klassensolidarität und nationales Bewusstsein. Das Verhältnis zwischen der Polnischen Berufsvereinigung (ZZP) und den deutschen Bergarbeiter-Gewerkschaften im Ruhrgebiet 1902–1923," *Internationale Wissenschaftliche Korrespondenz zur Geschichte der deutschen Arbeiterbewegung*, X (1974), 170.

20. HSTAD, RD 9081, I, ff. 53, 62, Polizei-Präsident, Essen, 20 Aug. 1915, and joint proclamation.

21. HSTAD, RD 15935, f. 62, Polizei-Präsident, Essen, 23 Sept. 1915.

22. STAM, OP 6617.

German colleagues of treating workers similarly by demanding higher pay for miners so that they could produce more.[23]

POW's and Forced Labor in the Mines

The military conscription of thousands of laborers created a manpower shortage for the German wartime economy. Responding to this need, the authorities lifted strictures on the employment of workers of foreign citizenship in industry in the Ruhr, and in 1915 the recruitment of workers in German-occupied Russian Poland gradually took the form of forced labor. The growing number of prisoners of war captured by the German army, including Russian Poles, provided another potential labor pool, and from April 1915 the mines began to use an increasing number of prisoners of war: by December 1916 they made up 14 percent of the work force in the mines.[24]

The regional military commands enforced strict discipline among these foreign workers. The command in Münster, which encompassed mines in the Ruhr, warned in November 1915 that "unruly Poles who have not been induced to work quietly and behave properly even by the otherwise proven means (intensified incarceration and the like)" would be placed "in military protective custody." Later, the command recommended that "the conditions of arrest be made more stringent, by partial denial of food, light, or bed, until those under arrest promise to be obedient."[25] Such measures rendered the foreign workers defenseless before their employers and led to a marked deterioration in pay and working conditions. Even the regional military command in Münster later recognized that employers often maltreated the foreign workers, particularly the Poles.[26]

23. Mańkowski, "Historja," p. 135.

24. Ulrich Herbert, *A History of Foreign Labor in Germany, 1880–1980: Seasonal Workers/Forced Laborers/Guest Workers* (Ann Arbor: The University of Michigan Press, 1990), pp. 89–90, 94, 97.

25. *Ibid.*, p. 96.

26. *Ibid.*, pp. 94, 97, 113, 115–116. For a personal account of a POW who deliberately injured himself to escape from work in the mines, see Władysław Habrowski, "Do was się zwracam, młodzi górnicy . . . ," in *Pamiętniki Górników*, ed. by Bronisław Gołębiowski (Katowice: Wydawnictwo "Śląsk," 1973), pp. 99–100. See also the account in Mańkowski, "Historja," pp. 136–139. The *Alter Verband* filed a complaint with the *Oberbergamt* Dortmund over the treatment of prisoners of war at one mine in June 1916, Tenfelde and Trischler, pp. 483–484. According to Lothar Elsner, "Foreign Workers and Forced Labor in Germany during the First World War," in *Labor Migration in the Atlantic Economies: The European and North American Working Classes During the Period of Industrialization*, ed. by Dirk Hoerder (Westport, Connecticut: Greenwood Press, 1985),

In their petition to the Ministry of Trade and Industry on 6 February 1915, the four miners' unions opposed the use of prisoners of war in the mines.[27] At a conference later that year with the minister, the unions raised the issue of maltreatment of foreigners working in the mines of Upper Silesia.[28] The ZZP, of course, had a special interest in these foreign workers. Its central board charged the directorates of its sections to observe how management treated the workers and to come to their defense and recruit them for the union. But in April 1916 the regional command in Münster blamed dissatisfaction and insubordination among Russian Poles on the influence of the ZZP Miners' Section and prohibited, under threat of up to a year in prison or a 1500 mark fine, any further contact with the foreign workers concerning their working conditions.[29] In his history of the ZZP, Mańkowski complained bitterly that German Jews could come to the defense of Jewish workers from Russian Poland but Polish trade unionists could not do the same for their brothers. Citing Imbusch of the *Gewerkverein*, he accused the other unions of approving the use of corporal punishment of workers from Russian Poland as supposedly the only thing they understood.[30]

The Revival of the Labor Movement

When the German government realized that the war would not end in a quick victory and that a decline in the productivity of the mines hurt the war effort, the authorities began to release many skilled miners from military service so that they could return to the mines. This together with the foreign workers resulted in a slight increase in the size of the work force in 1916, for the first time since the war began.[31] That same year the membership in the German-led unions in the Ruhr slowly began to rise. Weaker than the others, the ZZP Miners' Section in the Ruhr in 1916 could manage no more than to limit a further loss in membership to 1

---

p. 210, Polish workers from German-occupied Russian Poland "suffered the most brutal treatment of all" foreign workers during the war.

27. STAM, OP 6617, copy.

28. Chełmikowski, *Związki*, p. 147.

29. HSTAD, RD 9081, I, f. 114, to RPA, 18 April 1916, copy. A memo of the Minister of War, 18 Nov. 1917, justified the refusal to allow the ZZP to accept members from outside of Germany on the basis that it was suspected of "pan-Polish agitation" and therefore "anti-German tendencies," Murzynowska, "Związki," pp. 121–122.

30. Mańkowski, "Historja," pp. 136–138.

31. Klessmann, *Polnische Bergarbeiter*, p. 264, indicates an increase of 7 percent.

percent. But in September 1916 the ZZP launched a campaign to recruit the unorganized worker, and in fact initiation fees collected in 1916 increased nearly fivefold over the previous year, which indicates that the ZZP had also begun its comeback. Late in 1916 many of the experienced ZZP activists and some union officials returned home from the front, so that the Miners' Section achieved a significant growth in membership in the Ruhr to 12,746 in 1917, a rise of 41 percent over 1916, and then to 20,834 in 1918, an increase of 63 percent.[32]

Part of this revival stemmed from the increase in hardship experienced by the miners of the Ruhr along with the general population on the home front, which gave the unions a renewed importance at the same time as they gained leverage with the authorities. For example, discussions of the four unions with the government during the debate over the Auxiliary War Service Bill passed by the Reichstag in December 1916 resulted in the unions winning substantial if temporary rights of codetermination with management.[33] Within ten days of the bill's passage, the ZZP Miners' Section published an appeal that used the bill as a basis for recruiting the unorganized.[34] In a report in May 1917, the Recklinghausen Landrat attributed the increase in organized workers to the government's frequent consultations with the four miners' unions, which gave them a legitimacy that they had previously not enjoyed.[35]

An amendment of the Associations Act of 1908 in the spring of 1916 also benefited the unions, particularly the ZZP. The change meant that the authorities could no longer classify trade unions as political organizations, a tactic widely exploited to harass the ZZP. Furthermore, this made it legal for youths, who during the war became part of the underground work force in the mines, to join unions.[36] In addition, once Germany and Austria-Hungary created a Kingdom of Poland in the territory of the old Polish-Lithuanian Commonwealth formerly occupied by Russia, the

---

32. *Ibid.*, p. 283; Mańkowski, "Historja," p. 140; Chełmikowski, *Związki*, pp. 148, 162–163; *Dzieje Zjednoczenia Zawodowego Polskiego 1889–1939* (Chorzów: Nakładem Kartelu Zjednoczenia Zawodowego Polskiego na Śląsku, 1939), p. 76. Kołpacki, "Zjednoczenie," p. 488, gives a somewhat lower membership figure of 11,380 for 1917 but a higher figure of 38,759 for 1918.

33. Moses, *Trade Unionism*, Vol. I, pp. 204–206; Chełmikowski, *Związki*, pp. 146–147; Brose, *Christian Labor*, p. 348.

34. Klessmann, *Polnische Bergarbeiter*, p. 114.

35. STAM, RM VII, Nr. 17, Bd. 1, 13 May 1917.

36. Brose, *Christian Labor*, p. 344.

Minister of Internal Affairs in February 1917 urged police officials to use caution in handling Polish "national-political" matters.[37] Yet the revival of the unions and their progress in achieving official recognition did not strengthen them enough to preserve the civic truce that began with the war. From mid-1916 wildcat strikes flared up in the Ruhr. Although the authorities recognized the hardships, particularly food shortages, imposed by a war with no end in sight as part of the combustible material that inflamed the workers, officials blamed the trade unions, including the ZZP, despite their weakness at the time. During strikes in August 1916, officials in Recklinghausen and Datteln found the representatives of the *Alter Verband*, the *Gewerkverein*, and the ZZP suspiciously knowledgeable about the local wildcat miners' strikes. Officials also saw an unfavorable influence in the contact between Polish-speaking miners and the Russian Poles working in the mines.[38] In addition, the regional military command in Münster regarded the *Wiarus Polski* as a source of agitation and therefore imposed prior censorship on it.[39] When, in their call for an end to the strike, the four miners' unions blamed it on unorganized workers, officials interpreted the appeal as an attempt by the unions to recruit those workers.[40]

Following strikes in early 1917, local officials reported observing little difference in the behavior of organized and unorganized miners.[41] Where 100 Russian Poles had joined a strike, the police blamed it on the influence over them of the local miners.[42] Nevertheless, in a joint memorandum to the head of the War Office in Berlin asking for a meeting to discuss the situation, the four miners' unions of the Ruhr put the onus for the strikes on management. The unions claimed that by its actions management compounded the effects of the Belgian and Russian Polish prisoners of war, who "do not have the same interest in our fatherland and our industry and express this forcefully in part through their behavior."[43] Furthermore, the unions warned that, if the interests of workers were

---

37. Klessmann, "Klassensolidarität," p. 170.

38. STAM, RM VII, Nr. 17, Bd. 1, Landrat Recklinghausen, 16 and 18 Aug. 1916; Amtmann, Datteln, 15 Aug. 1916, copy; ff. 71–72, report of a conference of RPM officials.

39. *Ibid.*, VII. Armeekorps, Stellvertr. Generalkommando, Münster, 28 Aug. 1916, copy.

40. *Ibid.*, f. 72, the report of a conference of RPM officials; the appeal was published in the *Bergarbeiter-Zeitung*, No. 35, 26 Aug. 1916.

41. *Ibid.*, Landrat Lüdinghausen, 22 May 1917; Landrat Recklinghausen, 13 May 1917; Oberbürgermeister, Buer, 18 May 1917; Oberbürgermeister, Recklinghausen, 14 May 1917.

42. *Ibid.*, f. 140, Buer, 20 Jan. 1917.

43. *Ibid.*, 13 March 1917, copy.

ignored, the mass of unorganized workers would provide the impetus for further strikes. Differences could arise among the unions, as when in January 1918 the Christian, Polish, and Hirsch-Duncker unions suspected the *Alter Verband* of maneuvering to curry the favor of the unorganized.[44] Still, when another wave of strikes swept over the Ruhr region in August 1918, the *Alter Verband*, the *Gewerkverein*, and the ZZP Miners' Section issued a joint appeal to their members not to take part in the strikes and at the same time called on workers' committees at the mines to propose pay raises.[45]

Since their inception, the unions had sought the recognition of management as the representatives of and bargaining agents for its employees. With the outbreak of revolution in Germany and the country's defeat in the war, the miners' unions of the Ruhr finally achieved their longstanding goal of recognition by the mine owners on 14 November 1918.[46] A joint declaration of the Mine Association and the four miners' unions on 15 November 1918 announced the recognition of the unions along with a moderate pay raise and general implementation of the eight-hour workday. But the spirit of German patriotism also colored the preamble, which stated that "the enemies intend to take from us one of our granaries in the East," a clear reference to the lands claimed by the new Polish state. The declaration also spoke of the danger threatening "our people" and closed with a call for miners to help "your fellow nationals [*Volksgenossen*] through your labor!"[47] By signing the declaration, the ZZP demonstrated its formal loyalty to the German people and their state, though the sympathies of the Polish trade union lay elsewhere.

44. *Ibid.*, Bd. 2, Polizei-Präsident, Gelsenkirchen, 31 Jan. 1918.

45. Hans Spethmann, *Zwölf Jahre Ruhrbergbau*, Vols. I-IV (Berlin: Verlag von Reimar Hobbing, 1928–1930), Vol. I, p. 71.

46. Klaus Tenfelde, "Gewalt und Konfliktregelung in den Arbeitskämpfen der Ruhrbergleute bis 1918," in *Gewalt und Gewaltlosigkeit: Probleme des 20. Jahrhunderts*, ed. by Friedrich Engel-Janosi *et al.* (Munich: R. Oldenbourg Verlag, 1977), p. 235; Martin Martiny, "Arbeiterbewegung an Rhein und Ruhr vom Scheitern der Räte- und Sozialisierungsbewegung bis zum Ende der letzten parlamentarischen Regierung der Weimarer Republik (1920–1930)," in *Arbeiterbewegung an Rhein und Ruhr: Beiträge zur Geschichte der Arbeiterbewegung in Rheinland-Westfalen*, ed. by Jürgen Reulecke (Wuppertal: Peter Hammer, 1974), pp. 243–244; Hans Mommsen, "Die Bergarbeiterbewegung an der Ruhr 1918–1933," in *Arbeiterbewegung an Rhein und Ruhr: Beiträge zur Geschichte der Arbeiterbewegung in Rheinland-Westfalen*, ed. by Jürgen Reulecke (Wuppertal: Peter Hammer, 1974), pp. 282–284; Gerald D. Feldman, "German Business Betwen [*sic*] War and Revolution: The Origins of the Stinnes-Legien Agreement," in *Entstehung und Wandel der modernen Gesellschaft*, ed. by Gerhard A. Ritter (Berlin: Walter de Gruyter & Co., 1970), p. 335.

47. Spethmann, *Zwölf Jahre*, Vol. I, pp. 360–361.

The triumph of the unions did not satisfy all workers, some of whom soon put the unions on the defensive. To consolidate their achievements and to avert political and economic chaos, the recognized unions, including the ZZP, now became defenders of the new social and political order in Germany, which opened their leadership to attack. The unions got a taste of things to come when a strike broke out in the region around Hamborn in December 1918. In the negotiations with the Mine Association to end the strike, two leaders of the ZZP Miners' Section took part along with those of the other unions.[48] Thus, the ZZP became involved in a double game, one to maintain its status in Germany as a recognized representative of Polish miners and the other to establish itself in the new Polish state.

The Changing Geopolitical Situation

During the war, the ZZP cooperated with the other unions in the efforts to win concessions for workers from management and the government, but by 1916 international developments increasingly distracted its primary attention to other concerns. All of the Russian-ruled former Kingdom of Poland came under the occupation of the Central Powers in 1915, and its future increasingly became a subject of speculation and manipulation. On 5 November 1916 the German and Austrian authorities announced the creation of a self-governing Kingdom of Poland. Then with the collapse of the tsarist government in March 1917, the Russian Provisional Government followed the Petrograd Soviet in recognizing the right of the Poles to national self-determination. The entry of the United States into the war in April 1917 would eventually assure an Allied victory, though the Bolshevik revolution in November 1917 and the withdrawal of Russia from the war temporarily relieved the pressure on the Central Powers.[49]

Before the end of 1916, in an unguarded moment, Mańkowski's deputy Stanisław Piecha let slip to representatives of the other unions that Poles would prefer to see the Central Powers lose because that would be better for Poland. Although Piecha claimed he was referring to the attitude among Russian Poles, the other unions forced the executive board of the

---

48. *Ibid.*, p. 137.

49. For a succinct account of the events during the war that led to the creation of a Polish state, see Piotr S. Wandycz, *The Lands of Partitioned Poland, 1795–1918* (Seattle and London: University of Washington Press, 1974), pp. 331–370.

Miners' Section to disavow the statement.[50] In fact, the Polish community in the Ruhr showed little enthusiasm for Polish cooperation in the creation of a state in Russian Poland under the domination of the Central Powers.[51] Rather, at the end of 1916 Jan Brejski used the lessening of repression to resume the work begun before the war by activating the Executive Committee called for at the conference in Winterswijk, Holland, in November 1913. Mańkowski served on the committee, and the ZZP joined as a constituent member of what was intended to be the central umbrella organization for the entire Polish community of the Ruhr: in 1920 the Executive Committee encompassed 246 ZZP union locals among its 1,451 associations, more than any other type of organization. Although the Committee initially concerned itself with social issues, the changed circumstances following the war led a general assembly in Herne on 22 December 1918 to declare the Executive Committee the highest representative organ of the Poles in western Germany, and it effectively functioned as the community's political directorate.[52]

Meanwhile, at a meeting of the board of supervisors and central and sectional officials of the ZZP on 30 July 1917, discussion generally assumed the certainty of the creation of an independent Poland and considered the preparatory work needed for rooting the union in Prussian Poland. At a session on 26 August they discussed the return of the migrants to the homeland. When ZZP officials met in Berlin on 18 December 1917, they unanimously agreed that the war would end with Germany's defeat and considered the necessity of moving the directorate of the Miners' Section or creating separate directorates for Upper Silesia and the mining region in Russian Poland.[53]

Even earlier in 1917 the ZZP Miners' Section joined in an initiative to facilitate the return of the migrants to their homeland with the founding of a cooperative Workers' Bank (*Bank Robotników*) in Bochum in May 1917. Deposits grew rapidly, which enabled the bank to donate substantial sums to the Executive Committee and to educational and charitable causes in the Polish community of the region. In 1920 the bank had over seven

50. Mańkowski, "Historja," pp. 139–140.

51. See the comments in WP, No. 186, 14 Aug. 1915, *Gesammtüberblick*, 24 Jg., No. 30, 31 Aug. 1915; WP, No. 49, 29 Feb. 1916, *Gesammtüberblick*, 25 Jg., No. 10, 14 March 1916; APP, Polizeipräsidium 4939, pp. 370–372, Polizeipräsident, 4 Aug. 1917, copy, and APP, Polizeipräsidium 27256, p. 65, Polizeipräsident report to RPA, 16 Feb. 1918, copy. See Klessmann, *Polnische Bergarbeiter*, p. 147, on the friendlier reaction of the *Narodowiec*, the press rival of the *Wiarus Polski*.

52. HSTAD, RD 16021, f. 341, Polizeirat, Bochum, 31 Aug. 1920; Klessmann, *Polnische Bergarbeiter*, pp. 103–105.

53. Mańkowski, "Historja," pp. 141, 143, 145.

offices in the Ruhr and branches in Toruń and Katowice.[54] The bank managed to survive into the 1930s, and the chairman of the ZZP in Bochum then still served in its directorate.[55]

In 1917 Mańkowski himself took several initiatives with an eye to preparing the return of the migrants to an independent Poland. Thus, the head of the ZZP Miners' Section advocated organizing agricultural workers. In the face of resistance from part of the Polish national leadership in Poznań, Mańkowski argued that working conditions on the landed estates in the homeland must improve if the migrants from the Ruhr were to return and not emigrate again. The directorate of the ZZP Miners' Section on its own printed 4,000 questionnaires concerning working conditions on estates in the homeland for distribution to union members and their friends and relatives returning to the homeland. The Miners' Section received over 400 completed questionnaires and reported the results in its publications.[56]

The issue of agricultural workers, first raised by the ZZP in 1909, now came to the fore. The publication of various contracts for rural workers, in which the hours of work and the compensation varied widely, resulted in controversy in the press and confusion among employers. Information printed in the union's press spread to others in the homeland, much to the embarrassment of some estate-owners known as Polish "patriots."[57] In September 1918 the *Wiarus Polski* carried a long article on the conditions endured by rural workers entitled, "The Greatest Social Wound," and a few days later a correspondent from Castrop complained in another long article that the leaders of the ZZP gave the matter of the low pay of rural workers no attention.[58] But, at a meeting in Bochum on 22 September 1918, the leadership of the ZZP with the backing in particular of the Miners' Section voted to create the first permanent secretariat for agricultural workers in Poznań.[59]

As independence for Poland increasingly became a certainty, educational activity rapidly increased in the Ruhr to prepare for the

---

54. STAM, OP 5758, f. 483, Polizeirat, Bochum, 31 Aug. 1920; Klessmann, *Polnische Bergarbeiter*, p. 114.

55. Anna Poniatowska, "Działalność społeczno-polityczna," in *Związek Polaków w Niemczech w latach 1922–1982*, ed. by Jerzy Marczewski (Warsaw: Wydawnictwo Polonia, 1987), p. 92.

56. Mańkowski, "Historja," p. 142.

57. *Ibid.*, pp. 143–144.

58. In translation, No. 212, 13 Sept. 1918; No. 217, 10 Sept. [*sic*] 1918, clippings, APP, Polizeipräsidium 27256, pp. 87, 91–92.

59. Mańkowski, "Historja," p. 147.

eventuality of a return migration. The ZZP organized numerous circles for the teaching of Polish grammar. Later the directorate of the Miners' Section organized a kind of higher school with lectures twice a week on economics, particularly agricultural economics, in preparation for the situation in the new Poland. These lectures had a political edge in that they condemned the large estates in the hands of a few individuals and prepared agitators for the organization of agricultural workers. The courses continued in Bochum until 1919.[60]

A Socio-Political Program for the ZZP

The changed situation of the unions in 1917 and the revival of the ZZP gave it the confidence to set forth a formal program for the union for the first time in its history. In his memoirs, Andrzej Wachowiak, who worked closely with Mańkowski, argued that such a program had not been possible earlier, when the union had to concentrate on defending itself against the anti-Polish policies of the Prussian authorities.[61] However, a belief in the imminent creation of a Polish state as a new field of operation for the ZZP made the elaboration of a program a necessity.

When at a conference in Poznań on 27 October 1917 the chairmen of the sections of the ZZP voted to adopt a program for the union and issue a wide-ranging list of demands for the working class, their actions also reflected a phenomenon common to the rest of the labor movement in Germany. In the winter of 1915–1916, the Christian trade unions prepared a new program that included an impressive list of social and democratic reforms.[62] Similarly, from February through April 1916, the journal of the Free Trade Unions published a twelve-part series entitled "Social Policy toward the Worker and the Trade Unions." In fact, the Free Trade Unions published an eighteen-point socio-political program in January 1918, a few months later than the ZZP.[63]

The program and demands set forth by the ZZP in 1917 shared elements with those of both the Christian unions and the socialist-oriented

60. *Ibid.*, pp. 146–147; Kołpacki, "Zjednoczenie," p. 487.

61. Andrzej Wachowiak, "Wspomnienia z polskiej, robotniczej emigracji do Westfalii i Nadrenii oraz do Francji z konca XIX i początku XX wieku" (Typed manuscript, 1965), p. 81, Wspomnienie No. 839, Zakład Historii i Teorii Ruchu Zawodowego, Centrum Studiów Związków Zawodowych, Ogólnopolskie Porozumienie Związków Zawodowych, Warsaw.

62. Brose, *Christian Labor*, pp. 334–335.

63. Moses, *Trade Unionism*, Vol. I, pp. 207–210.

Free Trade Unions and resulted from a compromise among the leaders of the ZZP.[64] Together, the program and demands of the ZZP sought a far-reaching democratization of German politics and society and the creation of a system of social welfare that would improve the lives of the working classes of Germany. Its programs and demands defined the ZZP as a reformist union, which while accepting a capitalist system based on private property called for government regulation of the system and protection of workers from its abuses. In opposing the nationalization of the mines, the ZZP reiterated a position that it had consistently taken from its birth and derived from its distrust of the state in which it lived. Yet the union called for increased intervention by that same state.[65]

The demands and program of the ZZP did not, in the main, set it apart from the other unions of Germany. The program did of course deviate from the norm when it declared that the union "aspires to a close link with Polish society."[66] The same section hinted at the union's expectation of imminent change in its geopolitical situation:

> As long as the Polish nation in whole or in part is included in a state structure alien to it, the ZZP bases its activity on the constitution and laws of that state and urges the Polish working class within the framework of the labor movement to fulfill the obligations and take advantage of the rights deriving from belonging to the state.[67]

At the same time, the union pledged cooperation with the alien state and its nation "if the state will not block the cultural and economic development of the Polish nation." Thus, the program prepared the union for whatever political situation it would face after the war.

The National Workers' Party

Mańkowski also advocated another initiative that would deeply involve the ZZP in Polish political life, the creation of a workers' party. By arguing that workers must be prepared politically for life in independent Poland, he tried to counter fears that the Polish press would brand the party's organizers as socialists. In his view, the ZZP had to remain

---

64. Chełmikowski, *Związki*, lists the demands on pp. 240–242 and reprints the program on pp. 273–275; see Appendix 2.

65. Chełmikowski, *Związki*, pp. 275–276, makes the same point.

66. *Ibid.*, p. 273.

67. *Ibid.*, p. 274.

politically neutral and therefore needed a party to play the role it could not.[68] Perhaps the pre-war experience of harassment by the Prussian authorities as an allegedly political organization inspired the insistence on the union's apolitical stance.[69] Moreover, during the war, the leadership of the ZZP, particularly Mańkowski, began to chafe under the political dependence on the leadership of the Polish national movement in Poznań and at the same time feared the growth of socialist influence among the increasingly restless workers of the Ruhr region. A simultaneous relaxation of the government's anti-Polish policy towards the end of the war offered an opportunity that did not exist earlier for the establishment of a Polish workers' party.[70]

Discussions in the summer of 1917 resulted in the unofficial founding of the National Workers' Party (*Narodowe Stronnictwo Robotników* or NSR) in Wanne on 17 October 1917 under the leadership of activists from the ZZP Miners' Section. Then, on 20 January 1918, with numerous representatives from all over the region, another meeting officially called the party into existence. Its program resembled that of the ZZP adopted the previous year and included a rejection of class struggle and an endorsement of the social teachings of Pope Leo XIII.[71]

The party expanded to Prussian Poland at a meeting in Poznań on 7 April 1918, and the Ruhr region became one of the party's four districts. The *Wiarus Polski*, however, criticized the composition of the seven-member central directorate chosen at the meeting. According to the *Wiarus*, the directorate, made up primarily of leaders from Poznań, should consist mainly of workers, not "lawyers, pharmacists, or capitalists."[72] Mańkowski took up the same point at an extraordinary party meeting later that month in Berlin and argued against opening the party to one and all, for which Korfanty denounced him as "national vermin" and a "pure-blooded demagogue."[73]

Nevertheless, the ZZP continued its support of the NSR, and the party in the Ruhr district, where membership grew rapidly, simply went its own way. A meeting of the full leadership of the ZZP in Berlin on 9 May 1918 voted that union officials should work for the NSR as part of their civic

---

68. Mańkowski, "Historja," p. 142.

69. Antoni Banaszak, "Z.Z.P. a policja pruska i sądy w ostatnich latach przed wojną światową," in *Ćwierć wieku pracy dla Narodu i Robotnika* (Poznań: Nakładem Zarządu Centralnego Zjedn. Zawod. Polskiego, 1927), p. 552.

70. Klessmann, *Polnische Bergarbeiter*, p. 129.

71. *Ibid.*, pp. 129–130; Mańkowski, "Historja," p. 146.

72. Klessmann, *Polnische Bergarbeiter*, p. 130.

73. *Ibid.*

duty. Then, at a meeting on 9 February 1919, the ZZP leadership decided to take part in an NSR congress in Bochum. In addition to Jan Brejski, three leading members of the ZZP, including Mańkowski, gave speeches at the congress held on 6 April 1919.[74] The congress elaborated the party's program, which now included an explanation of the party's name: "It is wrong to assume that we call ourselves a 'Workers' Party' because we intend to organize only workers; that is what the trade union (ZZP) is for. We so call ourselves because we wish to espouse especially the cause of the propertyless stratum."[75] The ZZP directorate returned the compliment in the *Głos Górnika* on 10 September 1919: "The National Workers' Party is the vanguard of the trade union (ZZP), it paves the way and removes the obstacles."[76] In essence, the relationship between the ZZP and the NSR reflected the relationship between the *Gewerkverein* and the *Zentrum* and between the *Alter Verband* and the SPD.

As the ZZP expanded in the new Poland and sought to absorb other unions, it encountered charges from the political right that the union was not sufficiently "Christian" and patriotic and that it was waging class warfare. These charges seemed to find confirmation in the union's ties to the NSR, which in February 1920 added a passage to its program blaming capitalism for class conflict.[77] This led to the resignation from the party of those who saw the NSR as flirting with socialism, which facilitated a merger with the Warsaw-based National Workers' Union (*Narodowe Związek Robotników*) in May 1920, creating the National Workers' Party (*Narodowa Partja Robotnicza* or NPR) with Jan Brejski as chairman and three ZZP activists from the Ruhr in the party's directorate. The united party's program voted at a meeting in Cracow in September 1921 confirmed the existence of class conflict in the nation but denied that the party sees such conflict as universal or that it sought to intensify the conflict. At the same time, the program omitted all references to Catholic social teaching and instead endorsed religious toleration and opposed abuse of the pulpit for political purposes.[78]

The program approved at Cracow also emphasized the party's ties to all Poles in Germany, in particular, to the organizations united in the Executive Committee of Bochum. Also, the new central directorate

74. *Ibid.*, pp. 130, 131; Mańkowski, "Historja," pp. 152–153.

75. Klessmann, *Polnische Bergarbeiter*, p. 131.

76. Cited by *ibid.*

77. Mańkowski, "Historja," pp. 163–164, 176, 179; Klessmann, *Polnische Bergarbeiter*, p. 132.

78. Klessmann, *Polnische Bergarbeiter*, p. 132.

included two representatives from the Ruhr region. The party's organ for its members in the Ruhr characterized the program as having found a middle road between "narrow-minded, self-seeking clericalism" and the "ideas of Marxist socialists, who deliver the worker to Jewish-Bolshevik ranks and impatiently await his destruction."[79] For the ZZP, the claim of political neutrality served as a basis for rejecting cooperation with socialist and Christian-democratic unions, which it regarded as merely creatures of political parties. For its part, however, the ZZP looked to the NPR as a party which, it claimed, understood the union's needs and stood precisely for the union's program, which the union characterized as "Christian-national."[80]

Transformation of the ZZP

With the creation of an independent Poland and the union's political involvement there as well as its continued existence in Germany, the union had to undergo a transformation to adapt to the new political realities. At the beginning of December 1918 the ZZP board of supervisors of the central directorate and the chairmen of the various sections of the union met in Poznań. In addition to approving the creation of a new section for agricultural and forestry workers, they decided that Mańkowski should temporarily replace the chairman Rymer at the union headquarters in Upper Silesia because of Rymer's increasing involvement in the new Polish political leadership in the former Prussian Poland. In the absence of Mańkowski, Michał Sołtysiak was to lead the miners in the Ruhr region.[81]

One of the problems that the union faced was the loss of many of its leaders who took positions within the new Polish administration. Only in Austrian Poland did any large number of Poles have the opportunity to gain administrative experience in the civil service under the foreign occupation before 1918. Thus, the experienced activists of the ZZP provided a ready cadre for the new Polish state. The Miners' Section in

---

79. *Ibid.* "In a good part of the world after World War I, the myth of Judeo-Bolshevism enjoyed wide currency, counterevidence not withstanding," Richard S. Levy, "Introduction: The Political Career of the *Protocols of the Elders of Zion*," in Binjamin W. Segel, *A Lie and a Libel: The History of the* Protocols of the Elders of Zion, trans. and ed. by Richard S. Levy (Lincoln, Nebraska, and London: University of Nebraska Press, 1995), p. 20; for a discussion of the counterevidence, see pp. 16–19.

80. Mańkowski, "Historja," p. 212.

81. *Ibid.*, pp. 149–151.

the Ruhr suffered particularly heavy losses as its officials took positions that enabled them to return to the homeland. The union's extension of its activities into the new Poland also drew officials from the Ruhr to the homeland. In the course of 1919, the Miners' Section in the Ruhr lost three leading officials, including its treasurer, and three other activists, all of whom assumed union offices in the homeland.[82]

Turnover and the consequent instability plagued the Miners' Section in the Ruhr at the very top of its hierarchy. Mańkowski took Rymer's place in Upper Silesia while officially still heading the Miners' Section in Bochum. A meeting of the full board of supervisors and officials of the ZZP in Berlin on 22–24 September 1919 sought to settle this and other questions of leadership by naming Mańkowski to a new seven-member central directorate of the union and moving its headquarters from Upper Silesia to Poznań. The board of supervisors now also appointed Sołtysiak as Mańkowski's successor, a role that he had been playing on a temporary basis. Sołtysiak, however, turned down this appointment, so that, at a meeting on 22 December 1919, the board named Józef Jakubowicz, who earlier in the year had taken over as treasurer, to head the section. But at the end of February 1920 the board called upon Jakubowicz to fill a vacancy in the central directorate and appointed Franciszek Kołpacki as the fourth chairman of the Miners' Section in the Ruhr in less than half a year.[83] The loss of activists and the turnover in leadership weakened the union and hindered its growth, according to Jan Brejski.[84]

At the beginning of 1919, the Miners' Section still dominated the ZZP, but the section's future now seemed uncertain. Union leaders expected Polish miners to leave the Ruhr region, but did not yet know if Upper Silesia would be part of Poland. Therefore the directorate of the Miners' Section requested that the central directorate divide the funds of the Section in two and also publish separate union organs for miners in Bochum and in Katowice for Upper Silesia. With the rapid growth of the union in Poland and the conflict over the future of Upper Silesia hampering communication between Bochum and Katowice, a division of labor became all the more imperative. Thus, at the request of the Miners'

---

82. *Ibid.*, pp. 151–153, 160.

83. *Ibid.*, pp. 154, 158–159, 163.

84. Jan Brejski, "Dlaczego powstało 'Zjednoczenie Zawodowe Polskie?'—Bo chciał tego lud polski," in *Ćwierć wieku pracy dla Narodu i Robotnika* (Poznań: Nakładem Zarządu Centralnego Zjedn. Zawod. Polskiego, 1927), p. 515.

Section the central directorate of the ZZP effectively divided the Section in two as of 1 March 1919.[85]

In addition, the union's growth, both in members and in the number of sections representing various occupations, prompted the ZZP leadership to consider reforming the union's structure to give the sections responsibility for their own financing and greater autonomy. The project came before a meeting of the full board of supervisors, the central directorate, and representatives of the various sections on 6–10 June 1920. As a result, the union's sections gained their independence, both administratively and financially.[86] This transformation of the structure of the union together with the earlier division of the Miners' Section laid the basis for the Miners' Section in the Ruhr region to function in practice as a separate trade union, which the post-war circumstances that it faced required. Henceforth, in ZZP parlance it was known as the Miners' Union in Bochum.

Because of the conflict over Upper Silesia, the ZZP did not hold its first congress in independent Poland until the end of October 1921, in Poznań. The congress confirmed the autonomous self-governing status of the individual unions that belonged to the ZZP. As officials of the Miners' Union of Bochum, Kołpacki and Sołtysiak played a role in the commissions of the congress, and Kołpacki was elected to the ZZP council. But the representation allotted to the union, only five delegates out of 130, demonstrated the marginalization of the source—in a real sense—from which the ZZP originally flowed and drew its strength. Moreover, although Sołtysiak represented the ZZP Miners' Section of Bochum at future congresses in 1923 and 1926 and they reelected Kołpacki to the ZZP council, this proved to be a mere formality, for Kołpacki evidently never attended any of the council's meetings or took part in any of its decisions.[87] Thus, the Polish Miners' Union of Bochum came to create its own history, separate from that of ZZP in Poland.

The final step in the reorganization of the ZZP in response to the geopolitical changes following the war came in 1922 with the creation of a separate central directorate for the ZZP in Germany: the Miners' Section, including the miners of the Ruhr and of that part of Upper Silesia that remained in Germany after its partition, and the Metalworkers' Section. Headquartered in Bochum, the central directorate of the ZZP in

85. Mańkowski, "Historja," pp. 150–151, 155–156. *Dzieje ZZP*, p. 76, gives 1 Oct. 1919 as the date of the division.

86. Mańkowski, "Historja," pp. 166–167.

87. *Ibid.*, pp. 186–190, 201, 218, 246–247, 252.

Germany served primarily to present a united front in relation to the German authorities, trade unions, and employers and to enable the Polish trade union organizations in Germany to lay claim to the rights that the ZZP had previously enjoyed. Differences between Germany and Poland in pay and currency also dictated the creation of a separate central directorate for the ZZP in Germany. It consisted of three representatives of its two sections, who received no additional compensation as members of the directorate. As its chairman, Kołpacki assumed the role of leader of the ZZP in Germany. Nevertheless, the Miners' Section and the Metalworkers' Section, each with its own statutes, functioned as independent union organizations.[88]

True to its origins as an organization of migrant workers abroad, the ZZP in Poland did not entirely abandon them to their fate. The central directorate discussed their protection at a meeting on 30 April 1922. On 14 April 1923, during a visit of the Polish premier Władysław Sikorski to Poznań, the ZZP gave him a memorandum concerning the Polish migrants in Germany. In particular, the memorandum blamed the lack of sufficient construction of housing in western Poland for preventing those in Germany who opted for Polish citizenship from returning to Poland and for forcing those who did return to emigrate to France. It further claimed that the government gave more assistance to migrants from the East and therefore asked for more funds to help settle migrants from Germany. The ZZP leadership regarded the migrants in Germany as "better" than the migrants from Russia "of uncertain origin, such as Jews, Rusins [*sic*], etc." and sought to assist them. A Committee for Re-emigrants was formed in Poznań, which, however, succeeded in building only twenty-four homes.[89] A credit association to assist re-emigrants also lacked sufficient funding to have an impact.[90]

Furthermore, the ZZP did not succeed in getting the central Polish authorities to undertake the measures the union felt necessary to receive the returning migrants. At the meeting of the union's council and central directorate on 25 July 1925, at which the migrants again came up for discussion, Mańkowski reported one reason why assistance from the Polish government had been difficult to obtain: in a conversation with Mańkowski, Polish Foreign Minister Marian Seyda, originally from

88. AAN, ARPB 2019, ff. 11–14, consul, Essen, report, 15 July 1924, copy; ARPB 2196, ff. 14–16, 67–68, consulate, Essen, Cultural-Educational Report, No. 6, 21 May 1927, copy, vice-consul, Essen, 3 Oct. 1927.

89. Mańkowski, "Historja," pp. 195, 197–200.

90. Stefan Hulanicki, "Reemigracja Polaków z Niemiec i Ameryki," *Strażnica Zachodnia*, I, Nos. 5–6 (1922), 75–76.

Poznań, charged that the migrants in Germany had socialist convictions.[91] The validity of this claim can be tested against the post-war history of the Polish migrants in the Ruhr region.

The shared wartime experience enabled the miners' unions to overcome the bitterness that divided them following the defeat of the 1912 strike. Moreover, Germany's collapse in the war provided the opportunity for them to emerge triumphant as recognized representatives of the workers. The ZZP fully participated in these developments in the labor movement of the Ruhr region.

Nevertheless, the creation of the long-dreamt-of independent Polish state would prove of greater significance for the future of the ZZP in Germany. Before the war ended, the ZZP turned its primary attention to developments in the new Polish state and took several initiatives to ensure that it would have a role in that state. The new geopolitical realities necessitated yet another reorganization of the ZZP so that the Miners' Section in the Ruhr could continue its cooperation with the other recognized trade unions in Germany. But this would prove to be a mere shadow play, with the real action directed by other concerns, foreign to the labor movement in the Ruhr region.

91. Mańkowski, "Historja," p. 239.

6

Polish Disengagement from the German Labor Movement, 1918–1924

The November revolution initiated a period of turmoil in the Ruhr region. Mass movements, large-scale strikes, violent unrest, and foreign occupation marked the labor movement in the Ruhr in the first phase of the movement's history under the Weimar Republic until the mid-1920s, when the situation stabilized and social protests lost their momentum.[1] Polish miners played a marginal role in these events and therefore receive little or no attention in the accounts of this period. Nevertheless, an examination of their role and that of the Polish trade union illuminates their relationship to the labor movement in the Ruhr region after the world war.

The Post-War Turmoil in Germany and the ZZP

Germany's defeat in the war and the collapse of the German Empire aroused expectations among wide sections of the working class of continued revolutionary change that would fundamentally alter the worker's situation. The traditional trade unions, however, contented themselves with the long-sought-after recognition that they achieved in the agreement reached with employers in mid-November 1918 and therefore became defenders of the newly established order. Thus, although a movement of councils of workers and soldiers had carried out the revolution in Germany, the trade unions opposed them as potential rivals for the leadership of the working class and as obstacles to economic recovery. The unions also rejected demands for the immediate socialization of industry, which led to bitterness against the unions in some circles. Opposition to the trade unions and the new order crystallized in the Spartacist movement, which tried to use the councils to carry the revolution forward in the name of international socialism and

1. Stefan Goch, "Radical Left-Wing Miners' Organizations in the Ruhr Area 1917 to 1925," paper presented at the Third International Mining History Conference, Golden, Colorado, 6–10 June 1994, p. 1; see also Karin Hartewig, *Das unberechenbare Jahrzehnt: Bergarbeiter und ihre Familien im Ruhrgebiet 1914–1924* (Munich: Verlag C.H. Beck, 1993).

world revolution. When the Spartacists founded the Communist Party of Germany (KPD) at the end of 1918, the party virtually declared war on the trade unions.[2] The revolutionary events in Germany that followed its defeat in the war placed the ZZP in a difficult situation. The union did not see quarrels among German socialists and with the Spartacists as the affair of a Polish trade union, nor could its leaders foresee who would emerge victorious from these conflicts.[3] Therefore, as the strike movement in early 1919, took on massive proportions, the ZZP sought to protect its recent achievement of official recognition by continuing its cooperation with the three other recognized miners' unions. Together with them, it reached an agreement with the Mine Association on 9 January 1919 in the vain hope of ending the strikes. In February 1919 the four unions spoke out against the strikes and demanded that the government protect strikebreakers from the "heavily-armed Spartacist bands." Again, in March 1919 the ZZP joined the other unions in condemning a commission set up for the socialization of the mines, which the unions saw as displacing them from their role as the workers' representatives.[4]

The unions came under greater pressure in April 1919 when, after they had negotiated a seven-and-a-half-hour day, strikers demanded a six-hour day, which the unions believed the country could not afford.[5] But an appeal published in the *Wiarus Polski* suggests how little the Poles in Germany concerned themselves with these matters:

Duty commands that we warn against meddling in these affairs. The German press, which opposed the rectification of our position, exploits the unrest to make the Poles responsible for the bloodshed. Stay away from this quarrel... Our solution should be: We don't stick our nose in the stinking brew of the German worker parties. We are and remain neutral. Whoever is not, whoever

2. John A. Moses, *Trade Unionism in Germany from Bismarck to Hitler 1869–1933*, Vol. I: *1869–1918* (Totowa, New Jersey: Barnes & Noble, 1982), pp. 213–241; Goch, "Radical Left-Wing Miners' Organizations," pp. 4–5.

3. Franciszek Kołpacki, "Zjednoczenie Zawodowe Polskie we Westfalji (w Niemczech)," in *Ćwierć wieku pracy dla Narodu i Robotnika* (Poznań: Nakładem Zarządu Centralnego Zjedn. Zawod. Polskiego, 1927), p. 488.

4. Hans Spethmann, *Zwölf Jahre Ruhrbergbau*, Vols. I–IV (Berlin: Verlag von Reimar Hobbing, 1928–1930), Vol. I, pp. 241, 374, 386–387; quote on p. 241.

5. Hartewig, *Unberechenbare Jahrzehnt*, pp. 252–253; Spethmann, *Zwölf Jahre*, Vol. I, p. 274.

meddles in the quarrels of others, he has broken with us, and the organization cannot be responsible for him.[6]

Apparently, many of the members of the ZZP shared this same sense of indifference to the conflicts in Germany. Although the *Alter Verband* lost more than a fifth of its membership following the strike, the ZZP suffered no such consequences.[7] Also, the ZZP seems to have grown more than the other unions after union representatives, including one from the ZZP, and the Mine Association reached the first overall wage agreement in the mining industry on 25 October 1919 and the Minister of Labor suggested that the agreement applied only to those miners who belonged to one of the four labor unions.[8]

In 1920 a near civil war resulting from the Kapp Putsch brought the Ruhr region its most severe political crisis. In a joint declaration on 16 March 1920, the miners' unions, including the ZZP, and three employee unions condemned the attempt to overthrow the government.[9] Although the ZZP did not want to become involved in the internal conflicts in Germany, it thus confirmed and defended its status as a recognized trade union.

At the end of August 1920, the police counselor charged with overseeing the activities of the Poles came to the following conclusion about the ZZP:

> In the great wage conflicts of the miner in the West in recent years, in order to bring its power and influence more to bear, the local Polish Miners' Section

6. Christoph Klessmann, "Klassensolidarität und nationales Bewusstsein. Das Verhältnis zwischen der Polnischen Berufsvereinigung (ZZP) und den deutschen Bergarbeiter-Gewerkschaften im Ruhrgebiet 1902–1923," *Internationale Wissenschaftliche Korrespondenz zur Geschichte der deutschen Arbeiterbewegung*, X (1974), 174.

7. Manfred Dörnemann, *Die Politik des Verbandes der Bergarbeiter Deutschlands von der Novemberrevolution 1918 bis zum Osterputsch 1921 unter besonderer Berücksichtigung der Verhältnisse im rheinisch-westfälischen Industriegebiet* (Bochum: Berg-Verlag, n.d. [1966]), pp. 99, 269.

8. Hans Mommsen, "Die Bergarbeiterbewegung an der Ruhr 1918–1933," in *Arbeiterbewegung an Rhein und Ruhr: Beiträge zur Geschichte der Arbeiterbewegung in Rheinland-Westfalen*, ed. by Jürgen Reulecke (Wuppertal: Peter Hammer, 1974), p. 287; Hartewig, *Unberechenbare Jahrzehnt*, p. 254. See Spethmann, *Zwölf Jahre*, Vol. II, p. 31, for an example of a ZZP union local cooperating with the other miners' unions in preventing wage agreements from applying to the unorganized in Sept. 1919.

9. Carl Severing, *1919/1920 im Wetter- und Watterwinkel* (Bielefeld: Buchhandlung Volkswacht, 1927), pp. 160–161; reprinted in Spethmann, *Zwölf Jahre*, Vol. II, pp. 343–344. Initially, the four miners' unions had urged calm above all, Klaus Tenfelde, "Die Bergarbeiter, ihre Gewerkschaften und der Kapp-Putsch," in *Ruhrkampf 1920*, ed. by Johannes Gorlas and Detlev J.K. Peukert (Essen: Klartext, 1987), p. 52.

(of the ZZP) sought contact with similar German worker organizations, the Free, Christian, and Hirsch-Duncker trade unions. This contact followed solely from the most particular interests of the Polish worker. Otherwise, the Polish Trade Union, as in previous years, so also now at every opportunity has shown itself to be hostile to all things German [*deutschfeindlich*]. In this respect the revolution and the democratization and radicalization connected with it have in no way brought the masses to an approach of the Polish worker to the German in western Germany.[10]

Although this assessment missed the role that the union played in integrating its members in the labor movement in the Ruhr, it accurately reflected the duality in the union's approach. To protect the interests of its members in the Ruhr, the ZZP followed the lead of the other recognized trade unions. But the primary attention of the union was focused elsewhere, on developments in Poland. Some members may well have seen such a response to the revolutionary events in Germany as a betrayal of the workers' cause. Before the war, the ZZP had played a leading role in the labor movement in the Ruhr; now it became a follower of the other unions and a defender of the established order.[11] This stance contributed to the marginalization of the ZZP in the labor movement in the Ruhr region. In rejecting the spontaneous expressions of the miners' dissatisfaction and attributing the strikes to radical leftists, all four recognized unions relinquished their leadership role in the forging of the workers' will and abandoned much of their potential membership to the radical forces they opposed.[12]

Polish Participation in the Revolutionary Movement in the Ruhr

It is difficult to establish the extent of Polish participation in the revolutionary events, the wildcat strikes, and disorders that occurred in Germany in the years immediately following the war. The Prussian

10. HSTAD, RD 16021, f. 380, Polizeirat, Bochum, 31 Aug. 1920. Klessmann, "Klassensolidarität," p. 176, questions the accuracy of the assessment, particularly with regard to the integration of the Polish worker.

11. Klessmann, "Klassensolidarität," p. 175, on the contrary sees "a certain radicalization" of the ZZP in comparison with the pre-war period; at the same time, he portrays the Polish worker in the Ruhr as basically conservative, Christoph Klessmann, *Polnische Bergarbeiter im Ruhrgebiet 1870–1945: Soziale Integration und nationale Subkultur einer Minderheit in der deutschen Industriegesellschaft* (Göttingen: Vandenhoeck & Ruprecht, 1978), p. 148.

12. With regard to the *Alter Verband*, see Mommsen, "Bergarbeiterbewegung," pp. 290, 299.

authorities, who focused on the role that the Polish migrants played in strikes before 1914, seem either to have been overwhelmed by the extent of mass participation in the strikes and disorders or to have concluded that other elements posed a greater threat. In any case, the archives have not yielded the kinds of reports that allowed a delineation of Polish participation in pre-war strikes. Yet the matter is significant as an indication of the relationship between the ZZP and its putative constituency. Did the leadership of the union accurately reflect the views and mood of its members? Was the leadership more or less radical than the rank and file? Although the evidence available does not allow a clear-cut answer to these questions, we must examine that which is to hand.

Even without documentary evidence, one can reasonably assume that the Poles of the Ruhr region greeted with enthusiasm the November revolution overthrowing the government of the Kaiser.[13] But the defeat of Germany and the revolution not only brought an end to a government often hostile to workers; it also made possible the recreation of a Polish state, and this is what drew the attention of most of the Polish migrants of the Ruhr.[14] For them, as for the leadership of the ZZP, the conflicts that ensued among various German political factions did not concern them as much as the question of the future of Poland and their return migration to the homeland. The very lack of documentary evidence on the role of the Poles in the conflicts in Germany suggests that overall it was not large.

Still, certain issues involved in these conflicts concerned Polish miners as well, and at least in some places they became involved. Within days of the overthrow of the monarchy in November 1918, strikes broke out in Bottrop and Gladbeck at three mines with large contingents of Polish-speaking migrants in their work forces. The executive of the Münster administrative district blamed "bands of Polish and radical leftist elements" for preventing others from working and for provoking an exchange of gunfire at one of the mines that killed one person and wounded seven others.[15] When in December 1918 these same mines as

13. Klessmann, *Polnische Bergarbeiter*, p. 243; Antoni Czubiński, "Rewolucja 1918–1919 w Niemczech wobec kwestii polskiej w listopadzie i grudniu 1918 roku," in *Powstanie wielkopolskie 1918–1919*, ed. by Zdzisław Grot (Poznań: Wydawnictwo Poznańskie, 1968), p. 85.

14. At a meeting on 24 Jan. 1919 of officials of Westphalia, the Münster *Regierungs-Präsident* stated, "The Poles no longer consider themselves Germans," STAM, OP 6350, f. 67, VII. Armeekorps, Generalkommando, Münster, 26 Jan. 1919, report.

15. STAM, OP 5844, 20 Nov. 1918, telegram; two of the mines, Rheinbabenschacht and Möllerschächte, appear in a list of mines that employed over 1,000 Poles, Stanisław Wachowiak, "Wychodźtwo polskie westfalsko-nadreńskie," in *Ćwierć wieku pracy dla Narodu i Robotnika* (Poznań: Nakładem Zarządu Centralnego Zjedn. Zawod. Polskiego,

well as two others experienced sporadic strikes, the Recklinghausen county executive took it for granted that "Polish nationalist elements" as well as Spartacists were responsible.[16]

Although the Spartacists came in for most of the blame for the strikes at a meeting of officials of the province of Westphalia and representatives of the regional military command in Münster in late January 1919, the executive of the Münster administrative district noted the prominence of Poles in Bottrop, which still had 3,000–4,000 laborers imported from Russian Poland during the war, and claimed that Poles, especially Polish youths, took part in all manner of disorders.[17] In a report in mid-April 1919, however, this same official linked the Spartacists with the lawlessness that continued in January and February and connected the Poles only with the strikes for higher wages that occurred in December.[18] When strikes broke out in Recklinghausen in April, the regional military command relayed reports that most of the agitators and pickets were Poles.[19] Nevertheless, when in September 1919 the executive of the Münster administrative district wrote a report to the Minister of Internal Affairs in Berlin concerning the strikes and tumults that had occurred since November 1918, he did not even mention the Poles and instead laid the primary responsibility on "foreign agitators" with Spartacist views and political, not local economic, goals.[20]

In the Arnsberg administrative district, where in 1910 nearly half of the Polish-speaking population of the Ruhr region resided, Poles proved less suspect in the strikes and disorders immediately following the war.[21] At the meeting of provincial officials in January 1919, the district executive observed only, "The Poles are quiet but remain unreliable."[22] When in October 1919 he filed an extensive report on the violence that swept over parts of his district in the first three months of 1919, including communities with significant Polish-speaking minorities, he referred to

1927), p. 23.

16. STAM, RM VII, Nr. 17, Bd. 2, f. 164, 23 Dec. 1918. See also, STAM, OP 6007, f. 271, RPM, report, 14 April 1919.

17. STAM, OP 6350, f. 67, VII. Armeekorps, Generalkommando, Münster, 26 Jan. 1919, report.

18. STAM, OP 6007, f. 271, 14 April 1919, report.

19. STAM, OP 6523, Münster, 17 April 1919.

20. *Ibid.*, 20 Sept. 1919, copy of report.

21. For population figures, see Klessmann, *Polnische Bergarbeiter*, p. 261.

22. STAM, OP 6350, f. 67, VII. Armeekorps, Generalkommando, Münster, 26 Jan. 1919, report.

the Poles not at all and blamed "radical leftist elements" and Spartacists.[23] Similarly, no evidence seems to link the Poles with the wave of strikes in the Düsseldorf administrative district, not even in Hamborn, the scene of violent clashes between Polish miners and security forces during the strike of 1912.[24] In mid-December 1918 at a meeting of a work force in Obermarxloh, where one of the tumults occurred in 1912, two miners with Polish surnames argued for a strike, but the local leaders of all four recognized trade unions seem to have favored a strike at this time.[25]

In sum, besides repeating old stereotypes about the Polish miners, officials reported that in some places they participated in strikes that sought higher wages but that Spartacists with their political goals bore most of the responsibility for the strikes and disorders of 1918 and 1919. This sharp dichotomy drawn by officials between the purely economic strikes and those supported by the Spartacists does not stand up to closer examination. Moreover, the question remains as to the participation of Polish miners in the Spartacist and allied movements.

Polish Miners and Left-Wing Radicalism

The goals that Spartacists, the KPD, and syndicalist unions clamored for—a government of workers' councils instead of a parliament and direct action by decentralized unions instead of agreements negotiated between management and nationally recognized unions—had no particular appeal for Polish miners who focused on an early return to the homeland.[26] In the first months of 1919, the Polish communist Julian Marchlewski-Karski

23. STAM, OP 6523, 18 Oct. 1919.

24. Peter von Oertzen, "Die grossen Streiks der Ruhrbergarbeiterschaft im Frühjahr 1919. Ein Beitrag zur Diskussion über die revolutionäre Entstehungsphase der Weimarer Republik," *Vierteljahrshefte für Zeitgeschichte*, 6. Jg. (1958), 231–262, makes no mention of Poles; see p. 241 concerning Hamborn; Hans Mommsen, "Soziale Kämpfe im Ruhrbergbau nach der Jahrhundertwende," in *Glück auf, Kameraden! Die Bergarbeiter und ihre Organisationen in Deutschland*, ed. by Hans Mommsen and Ulrich Borsdorf (Cologne: Bund-Verlag, 1979), p. 263, links the presence of "the considerable percent of socially unincorporated Polish miners" with the strength of the syndicalist movement in the region without presenting any evidence or examining their incorporation into the Polish community. On the violence in 1912, see John J. Kulczycki, *The Foreign Worker and the German Labor Movement: Xenophobia and Solidarity in the Coal Fields of the Ruhr, 1871–1914* (Oxford, Providence, USA: Berg Publishers, 1994), pp. 236–247.

25. HSTAD, RD 15032, ff. 12–14, 20–22. A search of the archive resulted in no additional evidence of Polish participation in the strikes of 1918–1919 in the Düsseldorf administrative district.

26. See Goch, "Radical Left-Wing Miners' Organizations," p. 2, for the use of the term "left-wing radicalism" in reference to these diverse groups.

spoke at a number of Polish meetings in the Ruhr region for socialization of the mines and against the government in ways that the authorities feared would further agitate the already aroused miners. But, even though the authorities saw him as one of the spiritual leaders of the Spartacist movement and as a link between local communists and Russian Bolsheviks, no evidence indicates that he had much of an impact on Polish miners.[27]

Nevertheless, strikes led by Spartacists could draw support from both Polish and German miners by taking up their economic grievances along with the broader political issues. One historian finds the demands put forward during the general miners' strike of 1 April 1919 "astonishingly unpolitical."[28] In addition to the removal of the government, Spartacists at a meeting in Buer, which had a large Polish minority, made the following demands: the introduction of a six-hour workday, the reimbursement with interest for the loss of pay for six shifts for those penalized following the strike of 1912, and immediate one-time bonuses for miners with families.[29]

Thus, even in the ranks of the ZZP some voices cried out in support of the Spartacists as the only group that would assist workers.[30] German officials also linked a number of Poles to the strikes and disorders that they attributed to the Spartacists. In Bochum in April 1919, a Polish miner spoke in favor of continuing the strike at a meeting attended by 600–700, who called for the removal from office of union leaders who did not support the miners' demands. Also in April, the authorities found three machine guns, grenades, and other weapons in the possession of a Polish worker in Essen. A list of twelve people arrested in Bochum in mid-April as leaders of the communist and Spartacist movements included two with Polish surnames.[31] A three-month prison term for agitating for a violent strike did not deter a Pole from remaining "the soul of radical society" in Datteln.[32] In Gelsenkirchen the leadership of the KPD included a Pole,

27. STAM, OP 6007, f. 263, Polizeipräsident, Bochum, 15 March 1919, copy.

28. Hans Manfred Bock, *Syndikalismus und Linkskommunismus von 1918-1920: Zur Geschichte und Soziologie der Freien Arbeiter-Union Deutschlands (Syndikalisten), der Allgemeinen Arbeiter-Union Deutschlands und der Kommunistischen Arbeiter-Partei Deutschlands* (Meisenheim am Glan: Verlag Anton Hain, 1969), p. 111.

29. STAM, OP 5844, f. 76.

30. Kołpacki, "Zjednoczenie," p. 488.

31. STAM, OP 6007, ff. 174, 238, VII. Armeekorps, Generalkommando, Münster, 10 April, 15 April 1919, reports.

32. STAM, Büro Kölpin 230, VII. Armeekorps, Generalkommando, Münster, 2 Aug. 1919, report XXX.

and a miner active in the Spartacist movement in Westphalia later became a founder of the first communist organizations in Poznań.[33] Following the November revolution, the Münster regional military command directed a former police agent and wartime spy to set up an office to gather information, even by illegal means, on the political parties in the Ruhr, particularly those of the radical left, and this bureau's lists of agitators on behalf of the Spartacists, the KPD, and the syndicalist unions include a number of Polish surnames.[34] The reports on individual Polish communities, however, convey a mixed and changing picture. According to this source, the Poles in most places showed increased activity from late May 1919. At the Gutehoffnungshütte mine, in Horst, and in Oberhausen, where the ZZP local had some 315 members, Poles aligned themselves with radical leftists and the Independent Social Democratic Party (USPD).[35]

But in other communities there seems to have been a division of loyalties or a volatile combination that pulled the Poles in different directions. In Karnap, the Poles split between Christian and communist orientations, the latter led by a Pole whom a report characterized as "a vexatious agitator." In Buer-Westerholt, a Polish miner served as secretary of the USPD, which supposedly indicated the adherence of the Poles to the independent socialist faction, but in the same community the Polish *Sokół* gymnastic association, regarded by the authorities as a militant Polish nationalist organization, had renewed its activity after a long dormancy.[36] Similarly, a report identified the leader of the *Sokół* in Bottrop as a radical member of the USPD, and another report found the Poles of Boy–Bottrop to be thoroughly on the side of the independent socialists at the same time as they were "outspokenly anti-German."[37] At the end of June 1919 an agent noted increased activity among Polish associations, including the ZZP, and the open display of Polish insignia previously worn covertly—signs of rising Polish national consciousness—and at the same time asserted, "The Poles want to go

---

33. Czubiński, "Rewolucja," p. 87.

34. STAM, Büro Kölpin 230. On this source, see STAM, Findbuch B 138, p. II.

35. STAM, Büro Kölpin 230, VII. Armeekorps, Generalkommando, Münster, 10 June 1919, report XVIII, pp. 9–10; 25 July 1919, report XXIX, p. 6; 22 Sept. 1919, report XXXXIII [*sic*]. The USPD was formed during the war when a minority within the Social Democratic Party split off from the SPD because of the majority's continued support of the government.

36. *Ibid.*, 10 June 1919, report XVIII, pp. 9–10; quote on p. 9.

37. *Ibid.*, 25 June 1919, report XXII, p. 5; 10 June 1919, report XVIII.

forward with the communists simultaneously in the East as well as in the [Ruhr] industrial region."[38]

At the Osterfeld mine the Poles showed less interest in German political conflicts than in national goals, such as obtaining a schoolroom for the teaching of Polish.[39] Elsewhere, the renewed activity of Polish associations contributed to a change over the summer of 1919 among Poles involved in the radical leftist movement. Thus, the ZZP held a meeting in Lünen on 15 June at which speakers argued against Poles shedding their blood for others and leaving their families to starve. They also urged Poles not to give a single vote in the next election to the USPD or the KPD and asserted that an honorable Pole can never be a Spartacist.[40] At the mines around Dorsten, Polish miners who belonged to the ZZP were reported to be "calm and restrained" since the signing of the Versailles peace treaty at the end of June, though mine officials continued to distrust them.[41] According to a report in late July, the Poles in Hamborn were leaving a syndicalist association and the KPD to rejoin the ZZP.[42] A Pole who chaired the workers' committee at the Christian Levin mine and who earlier had supported the syndicalist movement attacked the communists at a work force meeting on 21 September 1919 and argued that in the future only members of the four recognized unions should be admitted to the meetings.[43]

In mid-November 1919, the chief of staff of the sixth army corps command area in the Ruhr reported the following:

> The Polish workers almost without exception have no sympathy for communism and the USPD but for the most part hold the view of the left wing of the majority socialists. In the cases in which Poles have taken part in the disorders, one must look for the causes more in anti-German than in Spartacist agitation. It is not excluded that in possible disorders in the future, the agitation will result in Polish participation.[44]

At about the same time, the military command in Kassel claimed, "The sympathy among the Polish workers for the KPD and the syndicalists

38. *Ibid.*, 30 June 1919, report XXIII, p. 4.
39. *Ibid.*, 10 June 1919, report XVIII, pp. 9–10.
40. *Ibid.*, 30 June 1919, report XXIII, p. 3.
41. *Ibid.*, 5 July 1919, report XXIV, p. 7.
42. *Ibid.*, 25 July 1919, report XXIX, p. 6.
43. STAM, Büro Kölpin 327, ff. 184–185, n.d., report.
44. STAM, Büro Kölpin 19, f. 247, Wehrkreis-Kommando VI, Münster, 14 Nov. 1919, draft; Czubiński, "Rewolucja," p. 84, cites this report from a source misdated Nov. 1918.

continues to fade. In general they seek to join the Christian trade unions."[45] On 19 February 1920, the executive of the Münster administrative district reported that in his district,

> the overwhelming majority of Polish workers are members of the Polish Trade Union. . . . A large part of the Poles also became members of the [syndicalist] Miners-Union, which swims entirely in the communist channel. A great many of its members seem though to be still treated as members in the locals of the [Polish] Trade Union, whereas in reality they belong to the [syndicalist] Union."[46]

What can one make of such contradictory reports? At best they present snapshots and partial views of a volatile situation. At worst they employed party labels that meant little during this revolutionary period.[47] Nevertheless, one can surmise that Polish miners took part in the strikes and disorders of 1918–1919 but not as a prominent element and not for the same reasons as the German left-wing radicals who led the revolutionary movement. Poles shared the economic grievances of other members of the working class in Germany, and these grievances drew them as well as others into the movement. (According to one report, Polish women, some of them carrying large baskets and sacks, predominated in the food riots in Bottrop in 1919.[48]) With the failure of the revolutionary movement and a realization that their immediate future lay in the Ruhr region, not in Poland, many Polish miners returned to the recognized unions and Polish associations to better their lot through the formation of consumer cooperatives and other self-help efforts.[49] At the same time, some may have continued to believe that they could best defend their interests through the "direct action" advocated by the syndicalists.

45. STAM, OP 5435, p. 8, Reichsgruppenkommando II, 23 Nov. 1919, report.

46. STAM, OP 5760.

47. See Dick Geary, "The Ruhr: From Social Peace to Social Revolution," *European Studies Review*, X (1980), 504, on party labels.

48. STAM, Büro Kölpin 230, VII. Armeekorps, Generalkommando, Münster, 25 July 1919, report XXIX, p. 6.

49. STAM, Büro Kölpin 19, f. 247, Wehrkreis-Kommando VI, 14 Nov. 1919, draft. Studies of this period typically pass over the role of the Poles in silence. Inge Marssolek, "Sozialdemokratie und Revolution im östlichen Ruhrgebiet. Dortmund unter der Herrschaft des Arbeiter- und Soldatenrates," in *Arbeiter- und Soldatenräte im rheinisch-westfälischen Industriegebiet: Studien zur Geschichte der Revolution 1918/19*, ed. by Reinhard Rürup (Wuppertal: Peter Hammer Verlag, 1975), pp. 241, 243, notes the presence of Poles in Dortmund and the existence of the ZZP, but makes no further reference to the Poles or their union.

Polish Miners and the Kapp Putsch

On 13 March 1920 the monarchist Wolfgang Kapp and General Walther von Lüttwitz attempted to overthrow the government by means of a coup. Because German military leaders at first chose to remain neutral, SPD ministers in the cabinet called for a general strike. Union leaders, who earlier had opposed a general strike when it was directed against the government, now supported one in defense of the republic. Initially, they also sought the cooperation of the USPD and the KPD, which, however, formed their own strike committees. The success of the strike and the decision of the military not to intervene in support of the coup brought a swift end to the Kapp Putsch on 17 March. When, however, the government called for a halt to the strike, union leaders used the success of the strike to put forward a list of mostly political demands, including democratization of the state. On 20 March the government and the unions reached a compromise agreement, and union leaders called off the general strike. The USPD finally joined the call for an end to the strike on 23 March.[50]

The reaction in the Ruhr to the Kapp Putsch took an independent direction. Bitterness toward the military for the role it had played in brutally crushing strikes and demonstrations in 1919 plus the ambiguity or even sympathy toward the coup of the local military authorities led to the formation of a Red Army of workers, which then proceeded to take control of much of the Ruhr region. With the defeat of the coup and the end of the general strike, representatives of the government and the SPD, USPD, and part of the KPD of the Ruhr region reached an agreement on 24 March to disarm the workers. But a considerable portion of the Red Army refused to accept the agreement and also ignored the government's ultimatum on 30 March. Nevertheless, plagued by internal conflicts and insufficient organization, the Red Army fell apart and the German military crushed its scattered forces in the first days of April. Once in control of the region, the military then repaid the workers in kind for their violence.[51]

50. Gerard Braunthal, *Socialist Labor and Politics in Weimar Germany: The General Federation of German Trade Unions* (Hamden, Connecticut: Archon Books, 1978), pp. 43–44.

51. Bock, *Syndikalismus*, pp. 288–289. The head of the local Polish committee in Henrichenburg reported that organized German workers supported the revolutionary movement because of the brutality of the military in dealing with workers accused of participating in the uprising, AAN, KGRPB 2, f. 62, to MSZ, 14 May 1920, copy.

According to a report on developments in Bochum in the first days following the Putsch, "The workers' defense force consists of all strata of the worker population. Every worker enters the conflict with great enthusiasm and also does not fear the discomforts of a long watch and patrol."[52] But the rapid formation of the Red Army and its early success led to suspicions of a planned and organized "Bolshevist" uprising rather than a spontaneous, disorganized reaction to the apparent sympathy of the German military for the Kapp Putsch.[53] Thus, on 7 April 1920, the day after the last stronghold of the Red Army was taken, the executive of the Düsseldorf administrative district issued a circular to officials asking for reports on the events, including "the participation of foreign Bolsheviks, especially Russian Jews."[54] This marked a change in official preoccupations in connection with disorders: before the war such circulars customarily inquired after Polish participation. Perhaps officials shared a journalist's view reported by the head of the provincial security police on April 3: "The Poles are said to be unanimously against the general strike, with the exception of at most 10 percent. The participation of Poles in the battle at the front cannot be great; they explain that a victory of the Bolsheviks would be their downfall."[55]

Nevertheless, besides a report from the Lord Mayor of Hamborn that "many persons with Mongolian features" were seen in the streets, the circular elicited information that in rural Essen county non-German-speaking Poles—presumably from Russia—served in the Red Army and that in Oberhausen its leading ranks included "numerous" Poles.[56] In the eastern Ruhr region, reports from Lünen and Dortmund indicated extensive participation by Poles in the uprising.[57] On 4 April 1920 the army corps command in Münster observed,

To what degree the Poles took part in the movement is not yet entirely apparent. The Polish trade unions seem faithful to their old tendency to have stayed out of the last general strike as well as out of the radical political leadership. It is certain that in any case numerous Polish elements were active

52. STAM, OP 6201, report, Münster, 20 April 1920.

53. Bock, *Syndikalismus*, p. 290.

54. HSTAD, RD 15980, f. 5.

55. STAM, OP 6201, OP Kommando der Sicherheitspolizei, 3 April 1920, daily report, no. 13.

56. HSTAD, RD 15980, f. 93, Oberbürgermeister, Hamborn, 13 April 1920; f. 75, Landrat Landkreis Essen, 13 April 1920; f. 108, Oberbürgermeister, Oberhausen, 10 April 1920.

57. STAM, Büro Kölpin 179, ff. 102, 107, Nachrichtenblatt, Münster, 31 March 1920, copy; Joseph Greis, report, 31 March 1920, copy.

as leaders and agitators behind the front and in the conflict. The names of the personages taking part in the action committees and in leadership of the conflict also attest to this.[58]

Lists of people later charged in connection with the uprising in the Ruhr region do indeed include a number of Polish surnames.[59] In Bochum, however, those arrested included several Russian Poles who worked at local mines and coke ovens, and therefore surnames alone could mislead the authorities about the role played by the pre-war Polish migrants who formed the bulk of the Polish community.[60]

Some two months after the uprising in the Ruhr, though not in direct reference to it, an official in Dortmund commented that "the Poles above all almost always take part in all uprisings and riots, and the most radical districts are directly occupied by Poles, such as Hamborn and Oberhausen."[61] This reflected the decades-old stereotype of the Polish migrant in the Ruhr more than his role in the movement in the region, though Poles apparently took a more active part in Dortmund than in most other places. In the last months of 1920, various officials remained convinced of the old stereotype. At the end of October in a report on the "Polish movement" in the Ruhr, the military claimed, "It is also ascertained that mainly Polish elements had a hand in the recent strikes against overtime. Strikes also occurred almost exclusively at mines lying in Polish districts, while the especially radical region around Hamborn remained rather calm."[62] German official views of the role of the Poles apparently did not depend on whether places with a high concentration of Poles, such as Hamborn, remained calm or not.

The Official Polish View

From January 1920 there was another office, new to the Ruhr region, that gave primary attention to the participation of Poles in these revolutionary movements: a Polish vice-consulate (from October 1920, consulate) in

58. *Ibid.*, f. 132, Wehrkreis-Kommando VI, Münster, 4 April, 1920, copy.

59. STAM, Generalstaatsanwaltschaft Hamm 3573.

60. STAM, Büro Kölpin 179, f. 189, Bochum, 10 April 1920.

61. HSTAD, RD 16021, f. 25, Reichszentrale für Heimatdienst—Berlin, Abteilung Dortmund, 17 June 1920; Klessmann, "Klassensolidarität," p. 171, dismisses the validity of the statement.

62. STAM, Büro Kölpin 147, pp. 2–3, Münster, 29 Oct. 1920. Strikes against overtime occurred in Feb. 1920, Hartewig, *Unberechenbare Jahrzehnt*, p. 257.

Essen.[63] Prior to the Kapp Putsch, the authorities of the new Polish state had expressed their concern over reports of increasing "Bolshevik" agitation among Polish workers in the Ruhr region, who might bring the contagion to the homeland.[64] This concern prompted an inquiry addressed to Jan Brejski, now a deputy secretary of state, who responded to the Polish ministry in charge of the formerly Prussian territory:

> The fear that a cadre of native Bolshevism is being organized in Westphalia is groundless. Today the Polish worker in Westphalia is the most conservative worker in the world. For he stands steadfastly on a Catholic foundation and is nationally conscious.[65]

Not all Polish diplomats, however, shared Brejski's tolerance for working-class demands. In a report to the Ministry of Foreign Affairs in Warsaw, the vice-consul in Essen expressed his satisfaction that in February 1920 the unions reached an agreement with the government on a longer workday for miners than the six-hour day that they demanded: he hoped that this patriotic gesture on the part of the unions in Germany would set an example for Polish workers and expressed relief that the Polish miners in the Ruhr, the overwhelming majority of whom he expected to return to the homeland, would not get used to a six-hour workday.[66]

According to the Polish vice-consul in Essen in early April 1920, the first phase of the response in the Ruhr to the Kapp Putsch was a model of discipline and order as all workers, without difference of politics or even citizenship, rallied round the banner of defense of the gains of the revolution. But, with the collapse of the coup, the movement split, and those in favor of continuing the strike resorted to violence to prevent others from working. In general, however, the "communists" treated the Poles properly, in the view of the vice-consul. "In several individual cases darker elements pressed a weapon into the hands of a Pole by force and placed him at the most visible guard post to show thereby that the Poles ally themselves with the communists. These sporadic instances, however, in general do not count." As for the Poles themselves, he asserted that they

63. Klessmann, *Polnische Bergarbeiter*, p. 151.

64. AAN, ARPB 268, f. 43, MSZ, 10 March 1920. See Valentina-Maria Stefanski, *Zum Prozess der Emanzipation und Integration von Aussenseitern: Polnische Arbeitsmigranten im Ruhrgebiet* (Dortmund: Forschungsstelle Ostmitteleuropa an der Universität Dortmund, 1984), p. 187, for examples of the Polish press with the same view of the Poles in the Ruhr.

65. AAN, ARPB 1835, April 1920, ff. 3–5, copy submitted by MSZ, 21 April 1920, written in response to an inquiry of 12 March 1920, before the Kapp Putsch.

66. AAN, KGRPB 2, ff. 10–11, 3 March 1920, copy.

generally behaved correctly. "There were cases, not numerous, where unbalanced Poles eagerly took up arms and even fell [in battle]. Most of these ill-advised were completely Bolshevized Russian Poles [*królewiacy*]."[67]

In another report about a week later, the vice-consul again asserted that the Poles of the Ruhr in general stood aside from the whole "revolutionary movement," but he promised a more thorough investigation.[68] In many locations in the Ruhr region where Polish migrants lived in larger numbers, their associations formed local umbrella organizations or committees of Polish associations. The Polish vice-consulate in Essen had 174 such committees in its region and named their chairmen its agents. It now sent them questionnaires to fill out and also requested general remarks about Polish participation in the disorders in the Ruhr. Their reports provide a unique insight into attitudes within the Polish community toward the revolutionary movement in the Ruhr, and therefore we refer to them extensively below.[69]

Both the vice-consulate and its agents in the Polish community were at least as eager as the German authorities to identify Poles involved in the excesses that occurred in the Ruhr after the Kapp Putsch. According to the vice-consul, Polish associations on their own immediately excluded members who actively took part in the revolutionary movement. Based on the reports from its agents, the vice-consulate compiled a "black book" listing 826 individuals supposedly involved, whom therefore the vice-consulate declared ineligible to receive Polish citizenship or even a visa to visit the homeland.[70] Thus, participation in a spontaneous working-class movement that in large part reacted to the use of excessive force by the military could result in actions alienating from the Polish community some of its potential members.

The vice-consul compared the number of individuals in his "black book" with the hundreds of thousands of Poles in the Ruhr and concluded that in general the Poles had not participated in the revolutionary movement stemming from the Kapp Putsch. One could argue that these 826 merely comprised the most active individuals, deeply involved in the

67. *Ibid.*, ff. 13–15, to MSZ, 3 April 1920, copy.

68. *Ibid.*, ff. 16–18, 12 April 1920, copy.

69. *Ibid.*, f. 32, to MSZ, 14 May 1920, copy; copy of the questionnaire sent to local Polish committees and excerpts from their responses, ff. 40, 42–65. Except for Marian Orzechowski, "Z dziejów polskiego ruchu robotniczego w Nadrenii-Westfalii w latach 1918–1933," mimeographed (Poznań: Instytut Zachodni, 1969), no studies have previously examined these reports in detail.

70. AAN, KGRPB 2, f. 33.

revolutionary movement, and therefore functioned as the "bearers of its ideology in the concentrations of Polish population."[71] Yet, in fact, only 195 of these individuals belonged to any Polish associations, so that one cannot regard the remaining 631 as leaders in the Polish community. Nevertheless, the total probably understates Polish support for the revolutionary movement, particularly among those less identifiable Polish-speaking miners who did not belong to Polish organizations. Wide groups of miners in the Ruhr sympathized with the protest movement, but relatively few played a prominent role in the uprising that occurred there.[72]

Part of the difference between Polish and German perceptions of Polish participation in the revolutionary events lies in their nearly diametrically opposite stereotypes of the Poles in the Ruhr, and each saw what they wanted and expected to see. There were also differences in judgment over who were Poles and what were excesses. The chairman of the local committee in Westerholt claimed that even Germans agreed that "true Poles by no means meddled [in the movement], those were only individuals who are not connected with our associations or with us anywhere."[73]

As we saw, the vice-consulate identified Russian Poles as more numerous among those involved, and local Polish associations may have seen them as transient elements who did not really count. The vice-consul himself seems to have excluded another group when he reported that some 500–600 people assisted the Red Army in Bottrop, but noted that the thousands of Polish-speaking Upper Silesians there did not belong to Polish organizations. The local committee in Meiderich referred to participants in the movement as "people from under a black star, who did not want to work and, even worse, several Russian Poles but mostly Jewry from [Russian] Poland and Galicia." In Dortmund-Huckarde, Rotthausen, and Gelsenkirchen, the vice-consulate's agents blamed Masurians, whose Slavic surnames and speech the German authorities did not always distinguish from those of Poles.[74]

The Polish consulate in Cologne as well as the vice-consulate in Essen noted that in several cases Polish workers were forced to take an active part in the movement, and these were probably not included in the "black

---

71. Orzechowski, "Z dziejów," p. 21.
72. Tenfelde, "Bergarbeiter," p. 42.
73. AAN, KGRPB 2, f. 60, to MSZ, 14 May 1920, copy.
74. *Ibid.*, ff. 34, 44, 45, 56, 58; quote on f. 58.

book."[75] Among the seventy-eight excerpts compiled by the vice-consulate in Essen from the reports it received, we find mention of Poles being forced to participate in Oberhausen-Vondern, Holthausen, and Duisburg-Beeck. The Polish committee in Katernberg also observed,

> The local Polonia behaved in an exemplary fashion during the revolutionary disorders, listening to the watchwords issued by the local organization. In the general strike all workers took part, at first with enthusiasm because of dissatisfaction with the lack of food. Later 40 percent struck out of communist-socialist convictions, and 60 percent had to strike because of communist terror.[76]

Evidently, some of the local Polish activists, upon whom the vice-consulate depended for information, sympathized with the revolutionary movement, or at least with the grievances that motivated it, and therefore were less likely to blame those involved and report them. In Brambauer, "Christian workers and Poles remained neutral; nevertheless, with regard to the general strike, all took part."[77] The chairman of the local committee in Wanheim argued,

> Hunger and the worker's misfortune are the true communist. Communism will disappear without a trace if only the worker would earn enough so that a person could live. I am thinking of fathers with several children, where in these times he becomes desperate, does not know how to help himself, and therefore in the end also loses patience. And so he also grabs a weapon and takes part in the disorders thinking that maybe in this way he will overcome his misfortune.[78]

Similarly, the committee chairman in Westerfilde observed, "we have good, religious hard-working countrymen here abroad, but, because of these disturbances, the aggravation of hunger, and the very high cost of living, they are weakening spiritually and physically, which is harmful for our dear fatherland."[79]

---

75. *Ibid.*, f. 37; ARPB 1835, ff. 1, 7, to MSZ, 18 May 1920, draft, consul to embassy, Cologne, 11 May 1920.

76. AAN, KGRPB 2, ff. 42, 47, 51–52, 54, to MSZ, 14 May 1920, copy; quote on ff. 51–52.

77. *Ibid.*, f. 42.

78. *Ibid.*, ff. 60–61.

79. *Ibid.*, f. 59.

Some of the local Polish activists distinguished between the revolutionary movement itself and the disorders that broke out in its wake. As the committee chairman in Marten put it,

we can condemn their program in so far as it is a question of robbery, trickery, thievery, accosting innocent people, women, and so forth, as well as encroaching on and appropriating the property of others; in part their program is ridiculous, and there is no answer for it. But, where it is a question of the life of the worker, this we cannot condemn, if it is a question of better pay and work as well as of a general strike in the trade, then we can only find an improvement in our existence.[80]

The chairman of the local committee in Kley said the same more succinctly: "I believe it is good if workers defend their rights, but condemn theft and plundering because that leaves a blot on workers."[81] According to the committee in Freisenbruch, "Many communists had good intentions with regard to the working class to improve its existence. Because they were joined by people of poor character and criminals, offenses occurred."[82]

These disreputable elements included Poles, as some of the reports admitted. The chairman of the committee in Elberfeld wrote,

My opinion of the communist movement is that taking part in it are elements that scorn honest work and reach out without scruples for the property of others...that the ignorant masses stirred up by Jewish agitators, by promises of every kind, harm themselves and their new fatherland. Whereas the demands put forward by a second group of enlightened workers cannot be rejected without consideration and assurance of a better existence.[83]

The chairman of the local committee in Hamborn-Marxloh regretfully reported,

Unfortunately, we also have among our countrymen some unworthy that the Polish earth gave birth to them, and mainly all those who already returned to

80. *Ibid.*, f. 45.
81. *Ibid.*, f. 46.
82. *Ibid.*, f. 62.
83. *Ibid.*, f. 52. Note again the reflection of the widespread myth of Judeo-Bolshevism, Richard S. Levy, "Introduction: The Political Career of the *Protocols of the Elders of Zion*," in Binjamin W. Segel, *A Lie and a Libel: The History of the* Protocols of the Elders of Zion, trans. and ed. by Richard S. Levy (Lincoln, Nebraska, and London: University of Nebraska Press, 1995), p. 20.

Poland and came back, and also Russian Poles not worth anything, because, although they may be in the Polish trade union, it is for the reason that now everyone must be in a union; it may only be by coercion, because, whereas I know also strongly radical Poles, who are organized and are even chairmen of [union] locals, they did not praise these disorders.[84]

In Essen the local committee observed:

Those Poles who fought with a weapon in hand, that is not from awareness, because now they are already convinced. In my locality, however, we disclaim them and do not recognize them as Poles, and they are excluded from all Polish associations.[85]

Nevertheless, even these reports suggest that those who became involved in the movement represented at most a small minority of the Polish-speaking population of the Ruhr region.

Despite some sympathy for the goals of the revolutionary movement in the Ruhr region in the spring of 1920, many Poles simply regarded it as not their affair. The chairman of the Polish people's parish council in Hamborn-Neumühl called it "German political theater." He further explained, "Having longer contact here abroad, in recent times we have become so accustomed to this German theater that we look at it all with sang-froid and we make nothing of it, convinced of the false work of Germans."[86]

Thus, many local committees, like the one in Leithe near Wattenscheid, reported that the Poles in their communities did not become involved in the movement: "Because our countrymen are organized in the trade union and politically abide by the appeals of their unions and the highest authority of the Executive Committee in Bochum, which gave out the watchword not to meddle in any disturbances. We are completely indifferent to what the Germans are doing in their fatherland."[87] After explaining that organized German workers supported the revolutionary movement because of the military's brutality in dealing with workers accused of taking part in the uprising, the chairman of the local Polish committee in Henrichenburg added, "but we Poles are indifferent to these matters."[88] As the committee in Gelsenkirchen reported, "The local Poles

---

84. AAN, KGRPB 2, f. 54.
85. *Ibid.*, f. 63.
86. *Ibid.*, f. 43.
87. *Ibid.*, f. 45.
88. *Ibid.*, f. 62.

are contemplating the idea of getting to the fatherland as quickly as possible."[89]

The Polish committee for Welper and Hattingen even won the approval of Germans for Polish neutrality:

> The chairmen of workers' organizations were called together, and here in this district a general strike was also voted unanimously, since Poles abstained from voting and I also gave them a written declaration that this is a purely German affair, and as such Poles have nothing in common with it, to which also the Germans of all shades truly agreed, and we even stipulated that arms by chance not be thrust into the hands of Poles by force, for which, in case of counter reaction, Poles would suffer, and in this way Poles stayed quietly at home.[90]

Elsewhere, Poles rejected the revolutionary movement and what it stood for. In Gladbeck the chairman of the local Polish committee admitted, "The communists behaved rather well during the whole time of their rule." But he added,

> I noticed that a large number of insurrectionists had ideal thoughts and were guided by them, but most did not have the slightest notion of communist ideas. Their government was to steal, murder, and so forth. The third goal was to unite as quickly as possible with the Bolsheviks and dismember Poland; they even wanted to go with the military against France and so forth.
> I condemn this kind of communism; the communist idea has completely atrophied. Every worker desires freedom and self-government and sometimes gladly gets rid of supervision, but only Christian love of neighbor can bring us this, never communism.[91]

The chairman of the committee of Polish associations in Brauck-Buttendorf elaborated on the international implications of the movement in the Ruhr:

> My opinion is that the Germans are trying by all means to invalidate the peace treaty and not bear the burdens of the war. The right as well as the most extreme left have one goal, that is, the return of the borders to 1914. The people at the head of this movement here were certain that they would succeed in linking up with the Russian Bolsheviks, and after that, they wanted to settle

89. *Ibid.*, f. 57.
90. *Ibid.*, f. 49.
91. *Ibid.*, f. 48.

with Poland, and if they succeeded in that, then they wanted to move on France.[92]

Several other local Polish committees similarly connected the movement in the Ruhr region to the Polish-Soviet war and to opposition to provisions of the Treaty of Versailles. Rumors circulated in the Ruhr that the Soviet Red Army had already taken Warsaw, though the Soviet advance into Poland would not come until the summer of 1920.[93] The committee in Altenbochum reported that many of those in the recognized unions believe "that only Bolshevism can free Germany from the burdens placed on it by the Allies."[94] But the chairman of the local committee in Recklinghausen saw in the uprising in the Ruhr a plot by "capitalists" to convince the Allied powers to allow the stationing of a strong military force in the demilitarized zone of the Ruhr to impose discipline on the workers because strikes and agitation disrupted the coal deliveries imposed on Germany as part of its war reparations.[95]

Nationally conscious Poles who saw the movement in the Ruhr in this light could not have found it attractive. As the local committee in Düsseldorf put it, "Organized Poles . . . are becoming disgusted with the whole movement."[96] In addition, the movement in some places took on specifically anti-Polish accents. From Buer it was reported,

> Polish workers, mostly persons at the head of Polish associations, especially the chair of the committee of associations, are put under great pressure by the revolutionary side. Revolutionary agitators in a deceitful way make Poles [appear] abominable and suspect by asserting that they allow themselves to be used as tools of the capitalists and thereby harm German workers.[97]

The local committee chairman in Dortmund claimed, "Almost every German is an inflexible enemy of Poles and Polishness."[98]

These views of the revolutionary movement that arose following the Kapp Putsch, voiced by local leaders of the Polish community, strongly suggest that, at least among those who identified with that community,

---

92. *Ibid.*, f. 55.
93. *Ibid.*, ff. 44, 47, 60.
94. *Ibid.*, f. 50.
95. *Ibid.*, f. 53; the committee in Wanne-West took a similar view, f. 52.
96. *Ibid.*, f. 64.
97. *Ibid.*, f. 57; the report from Duisburg-Beeck also mentioned speeches attacking Poland well received by workers at communist meetings, f. 53.
98. *Ibid.*, f. 51; the report from Wanne also speaks of growing hatred towards Poles, f. 55.

relatively few took part in the movement, particularly in its later phases. If, however, the Polish vice-consulate in Essen underestimated Polish participation in the general strike that arose in opposition to the Kapp Putsch, it recognized the working-class radicalism of the Polish community in the Ruhr and even exaggerated the threat it posed. Based on his investigation of the events in the Ruhr, the vice-consul in Essen came to the following conclusion about the character of the Polish migrant in the Ruhr:

> In general the people here are very good, modest, meek, and hard-working and possess all the attributes of the former hireling of Great Poland [the region of Poznania]. But the radical disposition of their political leaders pushed them too far to the left. The resolutions voted at meetings and announced in the press are mostly the product of a handful of individuals, who often by means of demagogic slogans carry the assembled with them and feel no responsibility for their activities in relation to society.

Yet, the vice-consul concluded,

> the soul of our Rhineland-Westphalian worker is preparing itself involuntarily for the easy acceptance of the principles of political freedom. Here he defends himself hand and foot against communism as a foreign influence, originating with Germans, the enemies of Poland, which he loves. He does not have a factual appreciation of communism. If, however, this communism is propagated in the homeland by "his Polish brother workers," then there is not the slightest doubt that, his soul tossed about by various radical demands of his political leaders on one hand, and by the exploration of sprouts of freedom by the German worker on the other, he will be incomparably more inclined to accept the principles of communism than his colleague who always lived and worked only in his fatherland.[99]

The Polish consul in Cologne came to a similarly worrisome view based on the participation of Poles in the revolutionary movement in the area of his jurisdiction, which included part of the Düsseldorf administrative district. From the reports of his local agents, he concluded that there was an unreliable element among the Poles, which earlier had allied with the German Catholic *Zentrum* and now in part came under the influence of the communists: although not hard-core communists, some Poles, especially easily influenced younger ones, were agitating on behalf

99. *Ibid.*, ff. 35–36.

of the communist cause, whether because of the general mood or because of the threat of force.[100]

German-Polish Antagonism, 1920–1922

More than just Polish participation in strikes concerned the German authorities. They also focused on the growing Polish-German conflict in the Ruhr, which had international implications. In December 1920 after touring the Ruhr for a week, a German journalist from Poznań claimed that many worker circles mistrusted the Polish worker and demonstrated "a certain antipathy" toward him that had not existed some nine months earlier. The journalist also reported that tales of mistreatment told by Polish refugees from the Ruhr and their demand for retaliatory measures had aroused the population in Poland against the German minority living there.[101]

The hostility towards Poles manifested by some elements of the revolutionary movement following the Kapp Putsch spread to other sections of the German working classes in the next few months. As the Soviet Red Army advanced into ethnically Polish territory in the summer of 1920 in its war with the new Polish state, enthusiasm rose among workers in the Ruhr to the point that the German authorities feared the outbreak of another uprising.[102] Polish communists had no success in winning support among Polish workers in the Ruhr region "despite zealous agitation."[103] German workers were a different matter. The USPD in particular tried to rally them to prepare for a general strike to prevent arms from being sent to aid the Polish side in the war.[104] The party also sought to exploit the frustration among the high number of unemployed. A USPD meeting held in Dortmund on 22 August 1920 passed a

100. AAN, ARPP 51, ff. 11–12, consul, Cologne, 6 June 1921, copy.

101. *Essener Allgemeine Zeitung*, No. 316, 18 Dec. 1920, AAN, ARPB 1836, f. 46, clipping.

102. STAM, Büro Kölpin 128, ff. 75, 75a, report, Dortmund, 23 July 1920, copy; Büro Kölpin 192, report, Münster, 27 June 1920; Büro Kölpin 294, report, Dortmund, 14 July 1920.

103. STAM, Büro Kölpin 210, report, Lünen, 13 July 1920; RM VII, Nr. 31, report, 15 Sept. 1921.

104. STAM, Büro Kölpin 193, report, Essen, 27 July 1920, copy; Büro Kölpin 192, report on a USPD meeting in Herne, 1 Sept. 1920; see also the report of wall posters in Hamborn, Büro Kölpin 193, Wesel, 4 Sept. 1920.

resolution in favor of a general strike until all Poles were fired.[105] Thus, hostility toward "reactionary Poland" found a scapegoat in Polish workers in the Ruhr region.[106] Although strikes at some individual factories actually did force the owners to let their Polish workers go, the Mine Association at least initially resisted the pressure with the argument that the mines could hardly do without Polish miners.[107]

Hatred of all things Polish, which according to the Polish vice-consulate in Essen reached unprecedented heights at this time, found additional fuel in the second Polish uprising in Upper Silesia, which began on 19 August 1920.[108] On 20 August an organization of Upper Silesians loyal to Germany [*Heimattreuer Oberschlesier*] held an open meeting in Gelsenkirchen—a Pole at the meeting later charged that the crowd nearly killed him as a suspected spy.[109] Thus began a series of meetings at which speakers denounced Poland and called for punitive actions against Poles and Polish organizations in the Ruhr, including the expulsion of Polish "agitators" and those who returned to Poland after the war and subsequently came back to the Ruhr.[110] According to the Polish vice-consul in Essen, no one could guarantee the personal safety of Poles as attacks occurred on Polish associations, breaking up their meetings and destroying their property. In his view, only the fear of a French occupation of the industrial region restrained the Germans in dealing with the Poles.[111]

The explosiveness of the situation led the four recognized miners' trade unions to meet on 27 August 1920 and publish a joint appeal in the Polish and German press. In it the unions blamed "reactionary elements" for attempting to "kindle the nationality conflict within the working class." It warned that organized workers must always and everywhere oppose nationalist incitement to avoid the bloodshed among workers that unfortunately occurred in Upper Silesia. Finally, it called on the workers to "stand, faithful to the decision of the international miners' congress in

---

105. AAN, KGRPB 2, f. 103, Komitet Towarzystw Rada Ludowa, Dortmund, to vice-consul, Essen, 23 Aug. 1920, copy.

106. *Ibid.*, f. 93, to MSZ, 20 Aug. 1920, copy; see also STAM, Büro Kölpin 296, report, 2 Aug. 1920.

107. AAN, KGRPB 2, f. 97, to MSZ, 26 Aug. 1920, copy.

108. *Ibid.*, ff. 93, 96, to MSZ, 20 Aug., 26 Aug. 1920, copies.

109. *Ibid.*, f. 101, Józef Witecki, Gelsenkirchen, to consulate, Essen, 20 Aug. 1920, copy.

110. See the somewhat different versions of the resolutions passed at a meeting in Herne, 22 Aug. 1920: *ibid.*, f. 100, to MSZ, copy; HSTAD, RD 16021, f. 99.

111. AAN, KGRPB 2, ff. 96, 107, to MSZ, 26 Aug., 29 Aug. 1920, copies.

Geneva, for the fraternization of peoples."[112] Even though the appeal voiced some sentiments contrary to the Polish patriotism of the ZZP, the Polish trade union prudently signed the appeal along with the other recognized unions.

The appeal did not prevent an anti-Polish demonstration in support of Soviet Russia in Essen on Sunday 29 August. Although the demonstration itself passed peacefully enough, several hundred participants broke off from it, headed toward the working-class district, and there attacked a Polish library and reading room, seriously maltreating some Poles in the process. That evening, the same group armed with clubs sought to disrupt a meeting of Polish Upper Silesians in Dellwig-Essen, but forewarned they dispersed before the mob arrived, so that it could only take revenge on the association's property. Damage in both places amounted to 36,000 marks according to the Poles, 2,000 marks in the view of the German authorities. Although the group carried communist signs and sang communist songs and communist agitation supposedly inspired the incidents, the German authorities concluded that the participants were youths from a camp for refugees and expellees from Upper Silesia and the lands lost to independent Poland. According to the *Polizei-Präsident* in Essen, the violence of Poles against Germans in those territories caused great bitterness among German workers and created the atmosphere in which the incidents in Essen occurred.[113]

Following these incidents, the Polish vice-consul in Essen reported that the mood among Germans had calmed, and another Polish diplomat even found cause for optimism in the high value that mine owners placed on Polish miners and the weakness of German nationalism in the Ruhr that he saw in the low attendance of German workers at the meetings organized on behalf of German Upper Silesians, the opposition of the socialist and labor leaders to the anti-Polish resolutions voted at these meetings, and the cooperation of the German miners' unions with the ZZP. Nevertheless, the incidents in Essen together with the threats of individual German workers greatly agitated the Polish population of the Ruhr region. Foreseeing more trouble, the vice-consul advised Polish associations to suspend their activities, including a gathering of Polish

---

112. *Ibid.*, ff. 105–106, *Essener-Arbeiter-Zeitung*, 28 Aug. 1920; on the meeting on Aug. 27, see f. 107, to MSZ, 29 Aug. 1920, copy.

113. *Ibid.*, ff. 108, 111–112, to MSZ, 29 Aug., 31 Aug. 1920, copies; ARPB 1836, ff. 27–31, Auswärtiges Amt, *aide-mémoire*, 19 Jan. 1921; HSTAD, RD 16021, f. 118, Polizei-Präsident, Essen, 29 Oct. 1920.

gymnasts from all over Germany planned for Dortmund in September.[114] The German Foreign Office, however, later claimed that Polish associations did need to suspend their activities, "so long as they did not openly pursue and work to incite anti-German agitation."[115]

Yet even the highest German government circles considered punitive actions against the Poles of the Ruhr along the lines demanded by German Upper Silesians at their meetings. On 9 September the Prussian Minister of Internal Affairs sent a memo to the governor of Westphalia:

> For some time now a lively Polish agitation is noticeable in the Rhineland-Westphalian industrial district, which in the main is connected with Polish preparations for the Upper Silesian plebiscite. According to a series of reports submitted here, the Polish movement in the industrial district meanwhile seems to continue to develop and also to pursue wider-ranging goals. The suspicion has been raised that efforts are being made to cause new uprisings on the part of the Poles in the industrial district and thereby play into the hands of the French plans to march into the Ruhr region. A spirited alarm has taken possession of the German population in view of the, in part openly very provocative, behavior of the Poles. In this connection a role is played by the fact that in the Ruhr region there are significant numbers of unemployed, who feel severely wronged by the numerous workers of Polish nationality employed, especially at the mines there.

The minister went on to note that the German population had expressed its anger at numerous meetings with excessive demands that violate the constitution, but which nevertheless "amount to a discussion of all of the Polish policies to follow in the future."[116]

Government officials themselves took up this discussion of policies toward the Poles at a meeting in Berlin in mid-September 1920. Echoing the demands of German Upper Silesians at their protest meetings, the executive of the Münster administrative district raised the possibility of a mass expulsion of the Poles, though he recognized this was impossible because of the effect it would have on both foreign policy and coal production. He saw the "Polish peril" in the Ruhr region as extraordinarily great with the creation there of a kind of Polish state that was thoroughly anti-German and sympathetically inclined to France. But the only feasible measure he could suggest was the eviction from miner housing of families

---

114. AAN, KGRPB 2, ff. 113, to MSZ, 3 Sept. 1920, copy; ARPB 268, ff. 72–73, report, 23 Sept. 1920.

115. AAN, ARPB 1836, f. 30, *aide-mémoire*, Auswärtiges Amt, 19 Jan. 1921.

116. STAM, OP 5760, 9 Sept. 1920.

of Polish miners who went to Poland to investigate the possibility of re-emigrating. The representative of the Minister of Trade endorsed this suggestion, but he also reported that officials at state mines were endeavoring as far as possible to replace Polish miners with Germans and urged the executives of administrative districts to persuade the management of privately owned mines to do the same.[117]

The March 1921 plebiscite in Upper Silesia to decide the disputed German and Polish claims to the region provided migrants born there with the right to return and participate in the voting. The campaign to recruit voters in the Ruhr region, which added to the antagonism between the nationalities, began later on the Polish side than the German. In early March 1920 the Polish vice-consul in Essen reported that agitation for Upper Silesia remaining part of Germany had assumed an especially bitter tone. He claimed that the mines were putting together lists of Upper Silesians and trying to influence them to support Germany while making life difficult for those who were overtly Polish. At the same time, he lamented that a lack of funds prevented the Poles from doing anything.[118]

Finally, in April 1920, an agent of the Polish Plebiscite Commission in Upper Silesia opened a bureau of the Re-Emigration Committee for Upper Silesians in Moers, and in mid-June it moved to Krefeld.[119] At that time a number of "agitators" arrived in the Ruhr from Upper Silesia to promote a vote in the plebiscite for Poland, according to an office of the Münster regional military command.[120] The bureau in Krefeld set up subcommittees in a number of communities throughout the Ruhr and recruited the assistance of local activists, including leading members of the ZZP Miners' Section and other Polish organizations.[121] Beginning in July 1920 they initiated meetings and established local associations for Polish Upper Silesians. The police arrested some of those advocating a vote for Poland in the plebiscite and accused some of offering bribes to win over supporters, but the laws of the Weimar Republic did not sanction such anti-Polish measures, and the courts released those arrested.[122]

---

117. *Ibid.*, report on meeting, 15 Sept. 1920.

118. AAN, KGRPB 2, f. 10, to MSZ, 3 March 1920, copy.

119. Marian Orzechowski, "Akcja plebiscytowa na rzecz Górnego Śląska w Nadrenii i Westfalii," *Zaranie Śląskie*, XXVIII, No. 2 (1965), 475–476.

120. STAM, Büro Kölpin 192, report, Bochum, 18 June 1920.

121. See the list of names in STAM, Büro Kölpin 147, pp. 7–8, and Orzechowski, "Akcja," pp. 476–477.

122. AAN, ARPB 3688, ff. 22, 24–25, consul general, Berlin, 18 Nov. 1920, Auswärtiges Amt, 17 March 1921; STAM, Büro Kölpin 147, pp. 3, 6, Münster, 29 Oct. 1920; Orzechowski, "Akcja," pp. 488–489.

Without the help of the police and employers, the Poles had difficulty in identifying those eligible to vote in the plebiscite. Thus, the speaker at a meeting of a Polish association in East Recklinghausen in December 1920 asked for assistance in collecting the addresses of Upper Silesians. Earlier, an attempt to obtain a list of Upper Silesians by penetrating the central office of the umbrella organization of the associations of Upper Silesians loyal to Germany failed. But in December 1920 someone posing as a criminal investigator confiscated from an association member about 400 applications of Upper Silesians requesting registration in the rolls of those qualified to vote in the plebiscite, and the authorities strongly suspected that the perpetrator worked for the Polish bureau in Krefeld. As the date for the plebiscite approached, the German authorities claimed that Polish agitation increased and that almost all German Upper Silesians daily received various newspapers and fliers in German and Polish urging them to vote for Poland.[123]

The conflict over Upper Silesia affected relations between German and Polish workers. Demands continued for the expulsion of the Poles, which would have the added benefit of creating job opportunities for unemployed Germans.[124] In Radbod near Hamm a large part of the German work force refused to work with Poles or Jews. Because of attacks on their meeting halls, Poles kept their expensive association banners at home and considered sending them to Poland for safekeeping.[125] Although the German Foreign Office later maintained that no further acts of violence occurred after the incidents in Essen on 29 August 1920, the Polish consulate reported a similar incident that took place in Essen on 2 December 1920. Again, German refugees from the East, some thirty to forty in number, armed with clubs and firearms allegedly attacked a meeting of the National Workers' Party (NPR) attended by some 600–700 people, a third of them women and children. According to the Polish consul, some forty people were injured in the attack, several of them seriously.[126]

Following the plebiscite in Upper Silesia in March 1921, Polish Upper Silesians returning to the Ruhr region inundated the Polish consulate in Essen with complaints of mistreatment at the hands of *"Heimattreuer"*

---

123. STAM, OP 5370, Nachrichtenblatt, No. 20, 7 Jan. 1921; HSTAD, RD 15379, Nachrichtenblatt, No. 23, 7 March 1921; Orzechowski, "Akcja," p. 477.

124. STAM, Büro Kölpin 193, Report 82, 21 Oct. 1920.

125. STAM, Büro Kölpin 147, Münster, 9 Oct. 1920, 27 Nov. 1920.

126. AAN, ARPB 1836, ff. 17–19, 29, consul, Essen, 2 Dec. 1920, Auswärtiges Amt, 19 Jan. 1921.

Upper Silesians.[127] They also encountered accusations of treason when they returned to work. For example, when Franciszek Bluszcz showed up for work at the Rheinpreussen mine in Moers his supervisor laughed derisively, "You Poles, we don't need you at all, go back to Poland because you are worse than the communists."[128] In his memoirs a Polish Upper Silesian miner who helped organize voters on behalf of Poland in the plebiscite related how he had found the post-plebiscite atmosphere at the Prosper III mine so hate-filled that he quit and moved back to Upper Silesia at the end of April 1921.[129] The antagonism extended to all areas of the life of the Polish community. In April 1921 German Catholics in Bochum-Riemke held a meeting to protest the creation of Polish schools and the use of the Polish language in religious services.[130]

At the beginning of May 1921 a third Polish uprising in Silesia, the most serious of them all, further embittered relations between German and Polish workers. In Essen more than a dozen people again invaded a meeting hall and tore down signs of the ZZP and other Polish organizations and attacked people in the streets. Before a Polish miner could reply to the question, "Are you also one of the Polacks?" he was punched in the face and had a tooth knocked out.[131] In Wanne German miners reportedly demolished the home furnishings of Polish miners.[132] The police there proved so tolerant of the anti-Polish activities of a well-known "*Heimattreuer*" that ZZP leader Kołpacki met with the police director and warned him that these activities were driving the Poles to emigrate to France.[133] The main council of the ZZP and representatives of its constituent sections took up the matter of German "terror" directed against Polish workers in Germany for the first time at a meeting in Poznań on 3 June 1921.[134] In response to reports in the Polish press of large numbers of organized Polish workers being fired, the ZZP in

---

127. *Ibid.*, ff. 168–180, reports on individual incidents, consul, Essen, 4 April 1921.

128. HSTAD, RD 16022, f. 15; other incidents are also described in this file.

129. Związek Zawodowy Górników, *Życiorysy górników* (Katowice: Wydawnictwo Związku Zawodowego Górników w Polsce, 1949), p. 278.

130. STAM, OP 5370, Nachrichtenblatt, No. 26, 24 May 1921, pp. 11–12.

131. AAN, ARPB 1836, f. 244, protocol, consulate, Essen, 7 June 1921.

132. HSTAD, RD 15740, f. 21, Polizei, Sterkrade, 1 June 1921, copy.

133. AAN, ARPB 1836, ff. 296–297, report, Cezary Kreczy, consular secretary, n.d., received 18 July 1921.

134. Franciszek Mańkowski, "Historja Z.Z.P.," in *Ćwierć wieku pracy dla Narodu i Robotnika* (Poznań: Nakładem Zarządu Centralnego Zjedn. Zawod. Polskiego, 1927), p. 181.

Germany sharply attacked those responsible and called on all those affected to notify the union.[135]

The descriptions of such incidents in the Polish press led the German Minister of Internal Affairs to order that they be investigated as a way of combating Polish agitation and charges of inadequate protection of the Polish minority.[136] The reports of attacks on Poles in Germany also prompted acts of revenge against German workers in Poland. In an effort to calm the situation, a commission composed of three representatives each from the ZZP and a German worker organization in Poland arrived in the Ruhr region to investigate, and a German commission was to make a corresponding visit to Poland.[137] A Polish diplomat also met in Essen and Bochum with representatives of the Polish community to hear their complaints.[138]

Queried by the governor of Westphalia, local officials denied that organized Polish workers were being fired in their districts, though the *Polizei-Präsident* in Essen regarded reports that such was the case in the districts of Dortmund and Bochum as reliable. The Lord Mayor of Hamborn even claimed that firms were rehiring Poles who re-emigrated to Poland and then, disappointed with conditions in the homeland, returned to the Ruhr.[139] In mid-September 1921 the police counselor in Bochum who oversaw the Polish movement in the Ruhr also claimed in his annual report that very few Poles had been fired because of their nationality and only at the request of the works council.[140] Opposed to massive re-emigration to the homeland, Polish diplomats privately agreed with German officials that representatives of Polish workers, for their own political purposes, exaggerated the extent of Poles losing their jobs.[141] But this was only true of the Ruhr region. At the lignite mines of central Germany, hundreds of Poles were let go at this time on the demand of their fellow German workers, in some cases, according to one report, just

135. STAM, RM VII, Nr. 31, f. 52, Polizeirat, Bochum, 15 Sept. 1921; HSTAD, RD 15740, f. 1, OP, Münster, 13 June 1921.

136. HSTAD, RD 16022, f. 1, 3 July 1921.

137. AAN, ARPB 1627, f. 209, report, Berlin, 30 June 1921; Mańkowski, "Historja," pp. 182–183.

138. AAN, ARPB 1836, ff. 286–289, report, to MSZ, 30 June 1921, copy.

139. HSTAD, RD 15740, ff. 5, 10, 12, Polizei-Präsident, Essen, 30 June 1921, Oberbürgermeister, Hamborn, 13 July 1921, RD Nebenmeldestelle, Essen, 25 July 1921, draft.

140. STAM, RM VII, Nr. 31, Polizeirat Augustini, Bochum, 15 Sept. 1921.

141. AAN, ARPB 1836, ff. 286–288, report, to MSZ, 30 June 1921, copy.

for belonging to the ZZP.[142] That this would alarm Polish miners in the Ruhr and their trade union leaders is hardly surprising.

Nevertheless, the main reason why the Poles in the Ruhr could no longer bear to remain in Germany, according to their representatives who met with a Polish diplomat investigating the situation, concerned not their employers or the German authorities but "the daily harassment of German workers and their organizations abetted by outside provocateurs coming mainly from Upper Silesia."[143] But, even after he met five Polish workers who had been beaten, the Polish diplomat agreed with the official German view that hostile attacks on Poles were being exaggerated. He also feared the negative conclusions of the commission of Polish and German worker representatives when they compared the situation of Poles in the Ruhr with that of Germans in Poznania.[144]

Although the police counselor in Bochum denied in his annual report in September 1921 that any serious or noteworthy clashes between Germans and Poles had occurred, for which he credited "solely the prudent behavior of the German population," he admitted that Germans had committed some "excesses" in isolated instances against those Poles and Polish associations who had, in his view, distinguished themselves by their anti-German activity, particularly before and during the plebiscite. In general he blamed the "extremely tense relations" between Germans and Poles on "Polish subversive activity" and on the violence and cruelty of the Poles in Upper Silesia during the uprising.[145] Whereas a Polish diplomat reporting on the situation also cited the plebiscite and the uprisings as causes, he in addition blamed the chauvinistic tone of the German press for having aroused the nationalistic tendencies of the broad masses. He saw German workers as exploiting the situation to get rid of "unpleasant competitors" in the job market.[146] Furthermore, even if isolated, the "excesses" perpetrated against Poles in the Ruhr continued into 1922, feeding Polish fears and consequently the desire to leave Germany.[147]

Despite the German-Polish conflicts, the ZZP Miners' Section continued to cooperate with the other recognized trade unions, mine

142. HSTAD, RD 15740, f. 21, Polizei, Sterkrade, 1 June 1921; AAN, ARPB 1836, ff. 222–223, 376–378, 374–376, consulate general, attaché for emigrant affairs, 14 May 1921, MSZ, Wydział Północny, Warsaw, 23 June 1921, to MSZ, 4 July 1921, copy.

143. AAN, ARPB 1836, ff. 286–288, report, to MSZ, 30 June 1921, copy.

144. *Ibid.*

145. STAM, RM VII, Nr. 31, Polizeirat Augustini, Bochum, 15 Sept. 1921.

146. AAN, ARPB 1836, f. 374, to MSZ, 4 July 1921, copy.

147. AAN, ARPB 1839, ff. 1–16, materials dating from Feb. through April 1922.

owners, and the German authorities as a way of maintaining its status. In doing so, the ZZP followed the dual path noted earlier: although developments in Poland drew its primary attention, the Polish union ostensibly placed German national interests ahead of those of the workers. Thus, in March 1921 the ZZP endorsed a decision on overtime, which the German government advocated as a means of increasing production, and publicly declared that it agreed so that the Poles would not again be slurred as communists, rioters, and traitors: they did not seek to harm the state but rather to labor for its good.[148] When in August 1922 the recognized unions again accepted an agreement on overtime that led to considerable miner dissatisfaction and a strike, the ZZP issued an appeal attacking the communists, who supported the strike.[149] Just where the loyalty of the ZZP and Polish miners lay would be put to its greatest test a few months later when in 1923 the French occupied a major portion of the Ruhr region.

The French Occupation of the Ruhr

By the terms of the armistice that ended the war, the left bank of the Rhine, including part of the Ruhr industrial region, came under Allied military control. Although relatively few Polish miners lived in the occupied districts, reports spread that a significant portion of the Polish-speaking population welcomed the French and Belgian troops and assisted them by identifying German officials and the leading German patriots to be arrested.[150] Poles in one community supposedly put up a ceremonial

---

148. STAM, RM VII, Nr. 31, f. 52, Polizeirat, Bochum, 15 Sept. 1921; Hartewig, *Unberechenbare Jahrzehnt*, p. 257.

149. STAM, RM VII, Nr. 35, p. 77, report, Polizeirat, Bochum, 1 Oct. 1922; Hartewig, *Unberechenbare Jahrzehnt*, pp. 257–258; Spethmann, *Zwölf Jahre*, Vol. II, pp. 328, 349–350. See the copies of fliers distributed at the Herkeles mine in Sept. 1922 that attacked all four recognized unions for their support of the decision on overtime, HSTAD, RD 15554, ff. 65–66; reprinted in Spethmann, *Zwölf Jahre*, Vol. II, pp. 347–348. The issue of overtime initially led to the only split of the four recognized unions when in the summer of 1922 the Christian trade union opposed the strategy of the *Alter Verband* aimed at winning concessions from mine owners, and the ZZP sided with the *Alter Verband*, Mommsen, "Bergarbeiterbewegung," pp. 300–301; STAM, RM VII, Nr. 35, p. 77, report, Polizeirat, Bochum, 1 Oct. 1922. At this time Polish diplomats also saw a greater chance of Poland reaching an agreement with German socialists than with the *Zentrum*, AAN, ARPB 179, f. 97, to MSZ, 16 July 1922, copy.

150. AAN, ARPB 1842, f. 55, consulate, Essen, to MSZ, 25 April 1921, copy, suggests that these reports of Polish cooperation with the occupying Allied troops were accurate.

arch to welcome the troops.[151] In the rest of the Ruhr, warm relations between the Poles and the various French missions caused suspicion. In July 1919 a report circulated that an agent sought to recruit a Polish miner for employment with the Allies when they occupied the region.[152] Early in 1920 the German authorities arrested some eighty Poles and charged them with espionage. Though they were released for lack of evidence, the Polish vice-consul in Essen learned that many of them were indeed in the service of the French.[153] By the end of 1920 the conviction had taken root throughout the region that the Poles would serve the French if they occupied it.[154]

Whereas fear of occupation by the French could inhibit mistreatment of Polish workers in the Ruhr, it also inflamed German hostility toward them.[155] The perceived sympathy among the Poles for the French in case of their threatened occupation of the Ruhr aggravated the "extremely tense relations" between Germans and Poles in the Ruhr in 1921 reported by the police counselor in Bochum who oversaw Polish activities.[156] By the same token, the manifestations of German antagonism toward the Poles in the Ruhr inclined them to look to France as an ally. As a speaker put it at a meeting of a Polish association in East Recklinghausen in December 1920, "France is with Poland against Germany. The more France presses the Germans, the better it is for Poland. To promote this is the task of the Polish miners."[157] In conclusion he expressed the wish that France push the Germans still further to ruin and that Upper Silesia be taken from them.

In the spring of 1921 the inhabitants of the Ruhr commonly believed a French occupation was imminent, according to the Polish consul in Essen. He also reported that the Allied forces, especially the French, were seeking to recruit intelligence operatives among Polish activists in the Ruhr through Poles working with them in the already occupied districts.[158]

151. STAM, Büro Kölpin 230, f. 105, Report XXIII, VII. Armeekorps, Generalkommando, Münster, 30 June 1919.

152. HSTAD, RD 15975, f. 247, Polizei-Präsident, Essen, 3 July 1919.

153. AAN, KGRPB 2, ff. 4–5, 10, vice-consul, Essen, to MSZ, 6 Feb. 1920, 14 Feb. 1920.

154. *Essener Allgemeine Zeitung*, No. 316, 18 Dec. 1920, AAN, ARPB 1836, f. 46, clipping. The Polish embassy reported on 23 Sept. 1920 that the French occupation of the Ruhr was widely discussed there, AAN, ARPB 268, ff. 70–71.

155. AAN, KGRPB 2, f. 107, vice-consul, Essen, 29 Aug. 1920; *Essener Allgemeine Zeitung*, No. 316, 18 Dec. 1920, AAN, ARPB 1836, f. 46, clipping.

156. STAM, RM VII, Nr. 31, Polizeirat Augustini, Bochum, 15 Sept. 1921.

157. STAM, OP 5370, Nachrichtenblatt, No. 20, p. 5, 7 Jan. 1921.

158. AAN, ARPB 1842, f. 55, to MSZ, 25 April 1921, copy.

In June a German police official claimed that preparations were already under way for the Poles, with their knowledge of local conditions, to serve as guides in the ranks of the French military occupational forces.[159] French members of an Allied mission visited the Polish consulate in Essen in early July 1921 in search of information about Polish miners in the Ruhr, including their political views as well as their professional qualifications. To counter Great Britain's claims that Poland did not have enough qualified workers to exploit the riches of Upper Silesia, the French wanted to be able to argue that Polish miners in the Ruhr region could supply the needed skilled personnel. But the French visitors to the consulate also raised the possibility that France might need to occupy all of the Ruhr and wanted to know what the attitude of the Poles in the region would be toward the occupiers.[160]

According to the Polish consul in Essen, a French occupation force would have to make no great effort to gain the assistance of the less politically-minded Poles. In his view the best recruiters for the occupiers were the *"Heimattreuer,"* with their attacks on defenseless Poles, including women and children. In this the consul saw a great danger: by openly serving the occupier, the Poles would lose their claim to German citizenship and to rights based on citizenship. After all, the consul observed, the Poles would be here longer than the occupier. He therefore immediately contacted the leaders of Polish organizations and secretly instructed Polish activists that, while naturally sympathetic to the occupiers, the Poles should maintain the strictest possible neutrality.[161]

In taking this initiative, the consul recognized that care had to be taken not to arouse antipathy to the French or to let the French learn of his efforts. He seems not to have anticipated the reaction of his superiors in Warsaw, who sternly warned him that the Polish Ministry of Foreign Affairs did not approve of any activity whatsoever undertaken by the consul among the Polish population that hampered the work of the French in occupied territory. "For such an action, in connection with improving Polish-German relations, will always be of doubtful value, but easily discovered by French organs, it may directly cause the Polish state irreparable harm."[162] Not for the first time, the young Polish state put its

---

159. HSTAD, RD 15740, f. 22, Sterkrade, 20 June 1921, copy.

160. AAN, ARPP 50, f. 1, consul, Essen, 6 Aug. 1921, copy.

161. AAN, ARPB 1842, f. 56, to MSZ, 25 April 1921, copy.

162. *Ibid.*, f. 58, MSZ, Wydział Północny, Warsaw, to consul, Essen, 20 May 1921, copy.

conception of *raison d'état* above the welfare of the Poles in the Ruhr region.

The long anticipated occupation of the Ruhr region east of the Rhine began on 11 January 1923 as French and Belgian troops moved into the area after the Allied Reparation Commission declared Germany to be in default of its coal deliveries. Passive resistance grew out of the response of German unions and employer associations and received the sanction of the German government. The factories and mines taken over by the French stood idle as workers refused to cooperate. The French responded with additional repressive measures and isolated the Ruhr from the rest of the country, which had a disastrous effect on the German economy. To maintain the passive resistance in the Ruhr, the government had to subsidize it despite a lack of revenue, and as a result the inflation rate reached fantastic proportions. The pauperization of much of the middle and working classes was its inevitable effect.[163]

The recognized miners' unions, including the ZZP, aligned themselves with the call for passive resistance on 13 January.[164] Together with the other union leaders, Kołpacki and Sołtysiak met that same day with the Inter-Allied Control Commission (Mission Interalliée de Controle des Usines et des Mines) and took the same line as their colleagues.[165] After the occupying authorities resorted to arrests and the use of force, the four recognized unions warned miners not to allow themselves to be provoked: "Nothing would suit French-Belgian imperialism and militarism more than a general uprising of the population of the Ruhr."[166] At the same time, the unions issued an appeal to the workers of the world in which they asked for support in their struggle "against militarism and imperialism."[167]

In the formulation of these public protests, the ZZP Miners' Section was confronted with a *fait accompli*. According to the Polish consul in Essen, when the ZZP representative arrived for a meeting of the recognized unions, the other three unions simply presented the already

163. S. William Halperin, *Germany Tried Democracy: A Political History of the Reich from 1918 to 1933* (New York: W.W. Norton & Company, 1946), pp. 248–253; Braunthal, *Socialist Labor*, pp. 49–52; John A. Moses, *Trade Unionism in Germany from Bismarck to Hitler 1869–1933*, Vol. II: *1919–1933* (London: George Prior Publishers, 1982), pp. 337–353.

164. Hartewig, *Unberechenbare Jahrzehnt*, p. 308.

165. Spethmann, *Zwölf Jahre*, Vol. III, p. 69.

166. AAN, ARPB 1842, f. 21, excerpt, *Essener Arbeiter Zeitung*, 17 Feb. 1923. A joint declaration of the four miners' unions at the end of March 1923 also spoke of "French militarism and imperialism," Spethmann, *Zwölf Jahre*, Vol. IV, pp. 378–379.

167. AAN, ARPB 1842, f. 21, excerpt, *Dortmunder Zeitung*, 16 Feb. 1923.

prepared texts for his signature. A refusal to sign could be treated as a betrayal of the interests of the German worker and used to exclude the ZZP from the ranks of the recognized unions. The consul believed that this would mean the end of the ZZP as a viable union and pleaded that the Polish ambassador in Berlin explain to his French counterpart the situation that the Poles, as German citizens, found themselves in.[168]

Polish workers also indicated that their greatest concerns lay elsewhere than with the German authorities. Following the arrest of the industrialist Fritz Thyssen, his Polish workers and employees in Hamborn sent a protest to French headquarters in Düsseldorf in which they declared their loyalty to their employer and the German government but also called attention to "the extraordinary misery and distress" that the arrest brought upon them.[169] Thus, "An Appeal to the Poles of the Rhineland and Westphalia" printed in the *Wiarus Polski* on 16 January 1923 and endorsed by all Polish organizations more accurately reflected the sentiment of the Polish community in the Ruhr than did the trade union appeals signed by the ZZP. Without evincing any support for resistance to the occupation, the *Wiarus* simply called on Poles to do nothing that might harm the community. "Strive constantly to fulfill your duties to the state whose citizen you are. Do not meddle in matters that are none of your business."[170]

The line taken by the *Wiarus Polski* was in accord with that recommended by the Polish consul. Just as in 1921, the consul raised with his superiors the question of the fate of the Poles who remained in the Ruhr once the occupation ended: "*Is it permissible to expose ca. 400,000 Polish German citizens living here to unforeseen harassment and destitution out of consideration for the Polish-French friendship and alliance?*"[171] The consulate took the position that the Poles in the Ruhr should outwardly remain neutral but inwardly their friendliness to France should be maintained and deepened. Because a victory for the occupier indirectly meant a victory for Poland, those Poles who knew how to aid the occupier without harming general Polish interests in the Ruhr should do so. Polish worker organizations should avoid taking part in defensive actions or protests directed against the occupation, unless their very existence, which the consulate regarded as essential for Polish interests in

---

168. *Ibid.*, ff. 12–16, Political Report, No. 5, 18 Feb. 1923.

169. Spethmann, *Zwölf Jahre*, Vol. III, p. 90.

170. Klessmann, *Polnische Bergarbeiter*, pp. 162–163.

171. AAN, ARPB 1842, f. 15, Political Report, No. 5, 18 Feb. 1923, emphasis in original.

the Ruhr, was threatened by not acting in solidarity with German unions. In that case the consulate urged that the Polish organizations regard such actions as "a necessary evil." The consulate, however, cautiously recommended that Poles break with the German unions when the occupiers said that it was absolutely necessary and it served Polish interests to do so.[172]

The consulate explained the situation to the occupying authorities, with whom it secretly cooperated from the first days of their entry into the region. They, in turn, stated that they would gladly accept the covert assistance of the Polish population.[173] Either from the Polish consulate or from their own contacts with members of the Polish community in the Ruhr, the French authorities from the very beginning of the occupation had the names and addresses of all of the important Polish organizations.[174] The consulate later reported that leading members of the Polish community rendered an important service for the occupiers from the start of the occupation by providing complete local information.[175] The German authorities also cited individual instances of Poles openly sympathizing and cooperating with the occupier in the first months of 1923. According to one source, at the beginning of February Polish members of the works council in Horst declared their loyalty to the occupational authorities.[176]

The Polish consulate believed that the Poles of the Ruhr would "fall into the arms" of the French if they knew that the occupation were permanent.[177] The sole party in Poland to criticize the occupation was the Polish Socialist Party, and only because it feared a strengthening of revanchism in Germany.[178] In any case, Polish protests against the occupation, whether signed by the ZZP along with the German unions or, for example, by the Polish fraction of the Gelsenkirchen city council, were not taken at face value by the German authorities or the general

---

172. *Ibid.*, f. 54, 16 April 1923; this time the MSZ approved the consul's actions, f. 64, 25 May 1923.

173. *Ibid.*, f. 15, Political Report, No. 5, 18 Feb. 1923. The Polish consul was later awarded the French Legion of Honor, Klessmann, *Polnische Bergarbeiter*, p. 249.

174. Klessmann, *Polnische Bergarbeiter*, p. 163.

175. AAN, ARPB 2154, f. 120, *aide-mémoire*, consul, Essen, 19 Nov. 1923.

176. Klessmann, *Polnische Bergarbeiter*, pp. 163, 248.

177. AAN, ARPB 1842, f. 15, Political Report, No. 5, 18 Feb. 1923.

178. Andreas Lawaty, *Das Ende Preussens in polnischer Sicht: Zur Kontinuität negativer Wirkungen der preussichen Geschichte auf die deutsch-polnischen Beziehungen* (Berlin: de Gruyter, 1986), p. 78.

public.[179] In March the consulate noted that Polish-German relations in the Ruhr were worsening and anti-Polish agitation rising, with the German press printing false accusations against the Poles.[180] The German authorities also distrusted the Poles, for example, repeatedly arresting workers in transit from Poland to France on the suspicion that their ultimate goal was to work in the Ruhr for the occupying authorities.[181]

As the passive resistance continued, the occupiers found themselves in increasing difficulty. The French authorities made considerable efforts to persuade the leadership of the ZZP Miners' Section to approve work under their direction, promising that the French government would pay the workers' social insurance and surround the mines with French troops to provide protection. But the Polish union leaders feared retribution: because of underground connections between mines, a cordon of soldiers could not prevent sabotage that could mean a death sentence for Polish miners.[182]

Nevertheless, when the French began to mine coal on their own from mid-August 1923, Polish miners decided at meetings in Ickern, Rauxel, and Habinghorst—all around Castrop, which had a large concentration of Poles—to work in the French-run mines. In November 1923 the consulate reported that 1,000 Polish miners were working at these mines, in addition to 500 Polish workers at several coke ovens. The consulate claimed that this willingness of Polish miners to work for the French greatly weakened the position of the German government, which called off the passive resistance on 26 September 1923.[183] In the eyes of the Polish embassy in Berlin, the decisive role that Polish workers supposedly played in the French tactical victory in the Ruhr entitled Poland to have a voice in decisions concerning the future of the Ruhr.[184]

As early as April 1923, the economic consequences of the occupation and the failure of passive resistance to prevent the occupying powers from

179. On the protest in Gelsenkirchen, AAN, ARPB 1842, f. 16, Political Report, No. 5, 18 Feb. 1923.

180. *Ibid.*, 1842, f. 49, Synthetic Report Nr. II, 27 March 1923, press officer, consulate, Essen, 27 March 1923.

181. *Ibid.*, ff. 2, 57, chargé d'affaires, to MSZ, 5 May 1923, copy, Auswärtiges Amt, Berlin, 2 May 1923.

182. AAN, ARPB 182, f. 196, to MSZ, 15 Aug. 1923, copy.

183. AAN, ARPB 2154, f.120, *aide-mémoire*, consul, Essen, 19 Nov. 1923, which refers to "Hawinghorst," obviously, a typographical error; on the Polish population in these communities some 15 years later, see *Leksykon Polactwa w Niemczech* (Warsaw: Państwowe Wydawnictwo Naukowe, 1973), p. 102; on the end to passive resistance, Halperin, *Germany*, p. 264.

184. AAN, ARPB 183, f. 46, Wojtkowski, desk officer, to MSZ, 27 Sept. 1923.

exploiting the industrial capacity of the region prompted the miners' unions to call on the German government to propose a reparations plan to end the crisis. By the latter half of August German miners were increasingly ready to work under the French.[185] Thus, devotion to France and hatred of Germany alone did not motivate the Polish miners who broke with the passive resistance. According to the Polish consul, those who worked for the occupiers were not, at the current wages, the worst off, but those who did not faced hunger and adversity and therefore needed to be assisted in leaving the Ruhr.[186] In the massive layoffs that followed the end of passive resistance, Polish miners were often the first to lose their jobs and those who had chosen Polish citizenship found no work elsewhere. Moreover, some communal governments cut off unemployment compensation to Polish workers while continuing to pay it to German workers. In a dozen places communal governments offered to pay all transportation costs to the Polish-German border for those who decided to return to Poland.[187]

Perhaps in response to this situation, the Central Board of the Inter-Allied Control Commission directed that the mines taken over by the occupying authorities should first hire Polish workers recommended by the consulate in Essen. Also, the French military set up soup kitchens with free food for needy Poles with identity cards issued by the consulate through their agents in the Polish community.[188]

But the Polish consul saw the best solution in the migration of the Poles in the Ruhr to France. All those working for the Allies should stay in the Ruhr if the French government officially agreed that, with the end of the occupation or in case of a threat to their lives and property, these workers would be transported to and settled in France at the expense of the French government. As for Poles not working directly for the occupying authorities, the French government should intervene to facilitate their relocation to France as quickly as possible. "Poland desires with all its heart that this very valuable and highly socialized Polish material work to the advantage of the Allied states and not of the enemy,

---

185. Heinrich Potthoff, *Gewerkschaften und Politik zwischen Revolution und Inflation* (Düsseldorf: Droste Verlag, 1979), pp. 333–334; Spethmann, *Zwölf Jahre*, Vol. IV, pp. 150–155, 209–210.

186. AAN, ARPB 2154, f. 121, *aide-mémoire*, consul, Essen, 19 Nov. 1923

187. Klessmann, *Polnische Bergarbeiter*, p. 165; AAN, ARPB 2154, ff. 88–89, 91, Report No. II, consul, Essen, 26 Nov. 1923. German workers were also given moving expenses to leave the occupied zone.

188. AAN, ARPB 2154, ff. 88–89, 91, Report No. II, consul, Essen, 26 Nov. 1923.

at least as long as the homeland itself cannot utilize these forces for its own domestic economy."[189]

As the occupational authorities gradually decreased their direct control over the Ruhr in 1924, the Poles found that their situation worsened. In the mines the French had taken over, they retained control of only the management of the mine on the surface and returned the handling of the details of labor and production underground to German functionaries, who could then harass those who had cooperated with the occupier. In addition, a lessening of the French and Belgian military presence allowed the German police to mistreat Poles. The Polish consuls in Essen and Cologne both reported that intervention on behalf of Poles denied unemployment compensation had lost some of its previous effectiveness, and the consul in Cologne expected a worsening of all aspects of the situation of the Poles in the Ruhr as the withdrawal of the occupying forces continued.[190] Not only had a substantial section of the Polish community in the Ruhr cooperated with the occupying forces, but also the French and Belgian authorities had shown favoritism toward the Poles, in everything from commerce to the punishment of criminal offenses.[191] In these circumstances manifestations of German hostility toward the Poles could reasonably be anticipated.

A Resumption of the Battle over the Length of the Workday

The occupation had negative consequences for all miners in the Ruhr and their unions, which only added to the difficulties faced by Polish miners and the ZZP. Even before the occupation, German industrialists demanded a lengthening of the workday with no increase in wages as a solution to the growing inflation. Their views did not change as inflation skyrocketed during the occupation. At the same time, the collapse of the German currency together with an increase in unemployment depleted the resources of the unions. Moreover, in the negotiations with the Inter-

189. *Ibid.*, f. 121, *aide-mémoire*, consul, Essen, 19 Nov. 1923.

190. AAN, ARPP 50, ff. 37–38, Political Report No. 1, consul, Essen, 7 April 1924, copy; the consul general in Cologne blamed the central German government rather than communal authorities, who especially in the Rhineland were mostly not anti-Polish, ARPP 53, ff. 159–160, 25 July 1924.

191. AAN, ARPB 1842, f. 458, consul general, Cologne, to MSZ, 18 Oct. 1924, who complained, however, that the French and Belgian authorities did not adequately distinguish between Poles and Jews: "Unfortunately, this naturally leads to a certain confusion of the concepts of what is Poland and who are Poles."

Allied Control Commission to end the occupation, German industrialists assumed a policy-making role without the necessity of consulting organized labor, on whom they sought to shift much of the cost of any agreement reached. Once the government called off the passive resistance and ended its financial support at the end of September 1923, mine owners initiated a wave of dismissals and mine closings as a means of enforcing a longer workday. For example, in the mining district of West Recklinghausen, once a district with a high concentration of Polish miners, the number of employed miners declined by 30 percent in one week in December 1923. Owners claimed that the seven-hour workday together with the establishment of a minimum wage and the burden of reparations made the mines in question unprofitable.[192]

By a close vote on 1 December 1923, the *Alter Verband* accepted an agreement worked out in Berlin for a temporary lengthening of the workday by one hour underground. The Polish consul in Essen urged the ZZP Miners' Section to do the same even though the Christian *Gewerkverein* rejected the agreement. In a meeting with ZZP chairman Kołpacki, the consul passed on information from employers that a circular would be sent to all mine owners asking them to hire only members of the unions that accepted the Berlin agreement. The consul argued that, because the Polish government and Polish leaders in the Ruhr agreed that the Polish community there should either be liquidated or reduced to a minimum, the Polish union had no future in the Ruhr and therefore no interest in working conditions in Germany. The poverty existing among Poles in the Ruhr dictated that they take every opportunity to work. With one of the strongest labor organizations endorsing the Berlin agreement, the ZZP "should not be more Catholic than the pope" and should for the good of its members accept the longer workday. Although the consul regretted that the longer workday would aid an enemy state, the Polish worker needed to be able to support his family.[193]

The consul found Kołpacki in full agreement with these views, and a meeting of ZZP activists voted unanimously in favor of accepting the Berlin agreement. At a conference of the recognized unions and employers in Essen on 5 December 1923, Polish acceptance of the agreement supposedly surprised the employers, who regarded the Poles as hostile to all things German.[194]

192. Hartewig, *Unberechenbare Jahrzehnt*, pp. 276–282; Moses, *Trade Unionism*, Vol. II, pp. 338, 345–346, 348, 351–352.

193. AAN, ARPB 2154, f. 107, Political Report, No. 26, 6 Dec. 1923, copy.

194. *Ibid.*, ff. 106–109, Political Report, No. 26, Essen, 6 Dec. 1923, copy.

The question of the permanence of the eight-hour workday for underground workers became one of the main points of dispute in the negotiations between the recognized unions and the mine owners over a new contract. When negotiations broke down in April 1924, the unions announced that from 1 May the lack of a contract meant a reversion to the previous contract with its seven-hour day and directed their members to leave the shafts after seven hours. The owners responded by threatening to lock out any miners who refused to work eight hours starting 6 May. Thus began a lockout of over 90 percent of the work force of the mines of the Ruhr region that lasted until the end of May. Although the unions won recognition of the seven-hour day for underground workers in principle, they had to accept the eight-hour day in practice. Ultimately, the mandatory arbitration system that settled the conflict meant the undoing of the union's hard-won victory of recognition as a collective bargaining agent for the workers.[195]

Following the occupation of the Ruhr and the lockout of May 1924, neither the Polish coal miners nor their union played a role of any significance in the labor movement in the Ruhr region. The number of Polish coal miners had diminished greatly, and most of those who remained no longer belonged to the ZZP. Although the Polish trade union continued to act together with the other recognized miners' unions, its participation became as much a formality as was the collective bargaining itself. In part the recognized miners' unions, including the ZZP Miners' Section, brought this on themselves by failing to exploit their strength when it was at its height to achieve a better situation for the Ruhr coal miner.[196] The ZZP made the mistake of assuming that the situation of the Ruhr coal miner would ultimately not matter to its members as it pursued its own self-liquidation and that of the Polish community in the Ruhr. This gave the union an entirely different character after the world war than before. To understand the role that the ZZP Miners' Section played in the years after the war, we must examine this process of self-liquidation and the final decline of the union.

Although incomplete, sufficient evidence exists to invalidate claims of significant Polish involvement in the revolutionary events and protest

195. Hartewig, *Unberechenbare Jahrzehnt*, pp. 282–283; Mommsen, "Bergarbeiterbewegung," pp. 204–206; Gerald D. Feldman, "German Business Betwen [*sic*] War and Revolution: The Origins of the Stinnes-Legien Agreement," in *Entstehung und Wandel der modernen Gesellschaft*, ed. by Gerhard A. Ritter (Berlin: Walter de Gruyter & Co., 1970), p. 313.

196. Hartewig, *Unberechenbare Jahrzehnt*, p. 283.

movements that marked the early history of the Weimar Republic in the Ruhr region. Based more on decades-old stereotypes than on reality, official suspicions and accusations either exaggerated or distorted the instances of Polish participation. Poles joined strikes and movements most often when they expressed grievances widely shared by all miners, but Poles seem even then to have been followers rather than leaders. In part, the question of Polish involvement revolves around the matter of national identification. Those most closely associated with the Polish community almost by definition had their gaze fixed on their newly independent homeland. Widely-shared expectations of an early return migration diminished their interest in the long-term fate of the working class in Germany. Poles more deeply involved in the struggle for better working conditions in Germany probably thought less about leaving the Ruhr and thereby distanced themselves from the Polish community. In the eyes of the community and Polish officials, they ceased to have an unambiguous Polish identity.

The Miners' Section of the ZZP continued its involvement in the labor movement in the Ruhr, but as part of a double game. The Polish union regarded its cooperation with the other miners' unions as simply a rear-guard action to cover the retreat of the Polish community from the Ruhr. As one of four recognized miners' unions, it could offer a haven to Polish miners, providing them with representation in labor negotiations while protecting them from the influence of the German-led unions. The Polish union had precious little say in the decisions of the recognized unions, but it accepted a passive role to safeguard the status it had achieved. In the long run, which initially the union leadership thought it did not have to concern itself with, this marginalized the Polish trade union. It lost all significance among the recognized miners' unions, which themselves declined in importance and membership by the mid-1920s.

The occupation of a major portion of the Ruhr region by Allied military forces in January 1923 put the Polish community to the severest test of its loyalties. Caution forbade all overt and immediate cooperation with the occupier, but Poles gave covert assistance from the very beginning. Ultimately, a significant number of Polish miners broke with the passive resistance to work in the mines controlled by the French authorities. Although misery and hunger played a role, the decision suggests that these Polish miners identified their future with Poland and France rather than with Germany. The Polish trade union itself contributed greatly to this perception of where the interests of the Polish miner lay. An examination of the involvement of the ZZP Miners' Section in the migration of Polish miners from the Ruhr region during these same years will confirm this conclusion. Only after the 1924 lockout devastated all of the recognized unions did the Polish miners' union turn to efforts to preserve its presence in the Ruhr, ultimately in vain.

7

The Self-Liquidation of the Polish Miners' Union

The migration of Polish miners out of the Ruhr region after the world war would undermine the existence of their separate trade union just as the Polish migration into the region made possible its birth and growth. Thus, the decline and dissolution of the ZZP Miners' Section seems due to "natural causes," requiring no explanation. What is missing in this account, however, is the role that the ZZP Miners' Section itself played in promoting and facilitating the migration from the Ruhr, which in turn elucidates the post-war priorities of the Polish trade union in the Ruhr region.

The Return to the Homeland

According to the *Polizeipräsident* of Poznań, as early as the beginning of 1916, the issue of the return of Polish migrants in Germany came before the Polish Political Committee in Berlin, which originated in the 1890s.[1] The Committee favored the creation of one organization for all of Germany to deal with the matter in cooperation with the Executive Committee in the Ruhr and the Polish National Council in Poznań. A first step in that direction came at a meeting of representatives of the Polish communities of Berlin and the Ruhr in Berlin on 15 July 1917, including representatives of both of the Ruhr's Polish newspapers, the *Wiarus Polski* and *Narodowiec*. They agreed that Poles abroad should return after the war to lift the level of crafts and industry there and to do so without delay before other nationalities stole a march on the Poles in their own land. To expedite the return and gather funds for this purpose, an organization was to be established within three months by a committee, half of whose members were to be chosen in the Ruhr region.[2]

By the end of 1916 the prospect of a return to an independent Poland occupied the minds of many in the Polish community in the Ruhr. It

---

1. APP, Polizeipräsidium 6272, p. 55, to RP Allenstein, 25 Sept. 1918, copy. On the Polish Political Committee, see Anna Poniatowska, *Polacy w Berlinie 1918-1945* (Poznań: Wydawnictwo Poznańskie, 1986), pp. 32-33.
2. APP, Polizeipräsidium 6272, p. 16, Polizeipräsident, Berlin, 10 Aug. 1917.

provoked such lively interest that in August 1917 Jan Brejski felt it necessary to warn in the *Wiarus Polski* that it would not be possible to return immediately after the war, only after a year or two when Polish labor would no longer be needed in Germany and preparations for the return could be completed in Poland so that a new migration abroad would not be necessary. He urged the migrants to get ready for the return by working and saving their earnings and studying the Polish language, customs, and old Polish national and religious hymns.[3] Meanwhile, so many migrants in the Ruhr besieged the Parceling Bank of Poznań with requests to purchase farms in the homeland that in September 1917 the bank announced that it would give priority to those with deposits at the bank of at least 100 marks.[4]

In the summer of 1918, with the goal of strengthening the ethnically Polish elements in the Prussia's eastern provinces, the Polish National Council in Poznań and the Executive Committee, with the backing of Mańkowski and Jan Brejski, opened a Re-Emigration Bureau in Bochum. In July the office distributed 50,000 copies of a questionnaire through the locals of the ZZP Miners' Section and other Polish organizations to gather information about the extent of the potential re-emigration, the type of jobs the migrants sought, and the level of their skills and financial resources.[5]

The achievement of Polish independence long dreamt of by the Polish community in the Ruhr had a profound effect on many of its members. As the executive of the Münster administrative district reported, they ceased to consider themselves Germans and therefore in January 1919 followed the advice of their leaders not to vote in the elections to the German national constituent assembly.[6] The Polish leadership in the Ruhr promoted this orientation towards Poland. In mid-September 1921 the police counselor in Bochum who had responsibility for keeping track of

3. Krystyna Murzynowska, "Związki polskiego wychodźstwa zamieszkałego w Zagłębiu Ruhry z krajem w latach 1870–1918," in *Polska klasa robotnicza: Studia historyczne*, ed. by Elżbieta Kaczyńska, Vol. X (Warsaw: Państwowe Wydawnictwo Naukowe, 1983), pp. 130–131; WP, 18 Aug. 1917, in German translation, APP, Polizeipräsidium 6272, pp. 17–19.

4. WP, No. 219, 22 Sept. 1917, in German translation, APP, Polizeipräsidium 6272, p. 20, clipping.

5. *Ibid.*, pp. 34–44, 53–55, copy of original questionnaire, RPA, 13 July 1918, copy, RP Allenstein, 10 Sept. 1918, copy, Polizeipräsident, Poznań, to RP Allenstein, 25 Sept. 1918, copy.

6. STAM, OP 6350, f. 58, report on meeting, 24 Jan. 1919, VII. Armeekorps, Generalkommando, 26 Jan. 1919. Kołpacki also claimed that Poles followed orders to boycott the election, AAN, ARPB 3260, f. 12, report on meeting in Brussels, 8–9 May 1920.

the Polish community claimed that the Polish organizations in the Ruhr had the closest of contacts with Polish ministries and officials. Moreover, the heads of these organizations, though German citizens, were only interested in the good "of their fatherland Poland." In addition, he maintained that the Polish press in the Ruhr eagerly followed all events in Poland but remained cool toward those in Germany.[7]

At the same time, some members of the Polish community in the Ruhr became deeply involved in developments in the homeland. In the latter half of November 1918 the Poles in the Ruhr region, like those elsewhere in Germany, chose a representative, the National Workers' Party (NSR) activist Szczepan Piecha, for the Provincial Parliament called by the Main People's Council (*Naczelna Rada Ludowa* or NRL), which now claimed the leadership of Poles in Prussian Poland. When the parliament met in Poznań in early December 1918, it chose Piecha as one of its vice-marshals. The ZZP chairman Rymer, who represented Upper Silesia, was also named a vice-marshal as well as one of the five members of the Commissariat of the NRL, which served as its executive body.[8]

Under the influence of the NSR, allegedly some 6,000 migrants from the Ruhr returned to the homeland in late 1918 and early 1919 and took part in the Polish uprising that broke out in Poznania at that time. The first Polish insurrectionist to fall in battle was a miner from the Ruhr, Franciszek Ratajczak. In mid-January 1919 the NRL Commissariat reported that twenty to fifty people per day were arriving from the Ruhr to join the insurrectionary forces despite the efforts of the German authorities to intern anyone suspected of returning for this purpose. Many of these Poles remained in Poznania and later brought their families and thus formed part of the first post-war return migration from the Ruhr region.[9]

The NRL sought to bring this spontaneous return to the homeland under control. In mid-December its commission for emigrant affairs issued a statement assuring emigrants that it was doing everything to facilitate a speedy return to the homeland but at the same time asking

---

7. STAM, RM VII, Nr. 31, 15 Sept. 1921.

8. Antoni Czubiński, "Sytuacja polityczna w zaborze pruskim po rewolucji listopadowej w Niemczech (listopad-grudzień 1918 roku)," in *Powstanie wielkopolskie 1918–1919: Zarys dziejów*, ed. by Antoni Czubiński, Zdzisław Grot and Benon Miśkiewicz (3rd ed., rev.; Warsaw, Poznań: Państwowe Wydawnictwo Naukowe, 1988), pp. 145, 148, 153.

9. Antoni Czubiński, "Działalność polityczna władz powstańczych," in *Powstanie wielkopolskie 1918–1919: Zarys dziejów*, ed. by Antoni Czubiński, Zdzisław Grot and Benon Miśkiewicz (3rd ed., rev.; Warsaw-Poznań: Państwowe Wydawnictwo Naukowe, 1988), pp. 428, 434, 490, 492.

them to postpone their return until conditions were more favorable, particularly with regard to employment and housing. Meanwhile, it requested that prospective returnees fill out its questionnaire and directed those in the Ruhr to the NRL office in Bochum.[10] A month later the NRL again appealed to the migrants to delay their return, warning that there was no employment available in Poznania.[11] Still, the return migration from the Ruhr continued, particularly following the signing of the Treaty of Versailles at the end of June 1919.[12] The migrants in the Ruhr took it for granted that the entire community would soon return to the homeland, if not of its own volition, then as a result of expulsion by the German government. Thus, attempts to restrain the movement led to complaints against the Polish authorities, such as those voiced at an NSR meeting in Bochum in September 1919.[13]

Nevertheless, thanks to warnings issued at numerous public meetings, an awareness of Poland's economic weakness spread among the migrants, which according to a report of the German military in mid-November 1919 resulted in an almost complete halt in the return migration. By the spring of 1920 Jan Brejski reported to the Polish government that disappointed migrants were returning from the homeland to the Ruhr, cursing Poland and spreading negative views about conditions there.[14] That summer German officials confirmed a significant decline in the migration to Poland as well as the return to the Ruhr of a large number of those who did migrate. At that point the Polish-Soviet war and fear of being drafted to serve in it dampened the desire to return to the homeland. But the police counselor in Bochum claimed that, even before the Polish-Soviet war, the homeland did not meet the expectations of the migrants, with its lack of housing and employment, low pay, poor treatment of workers, disorder and insecurity everywhere, and the helplessness and inefficiency of the authorities. A later report of the Polish consulate in Cologne indicated that of those within its jurisdiction who returned to the

10. *Dziennik Śląski*, XXI, No. 289, 14 Dec. 1918.

11. Czubiński, "Działalność," p. 461.

12. HSTAD, RD 16021, f. 331, Polizeirat, Bochum, 31 Aug. 1920. See Halina Janowska, *Emigracja zarobkowa z Polski 1918–1939* (Warsaw: Państwowe Wydawnictwo Naukowe, 1981), p. 172, for further evidence of a large migration at this time.

13. Christoph Klessmann, *Polnische Bergarbeiter im Ruhrgebiet 1870–1945: Soziale Integration und nationale Subkultur einer Minderheit in der deutschen Industriegesellschaft* (Göttingen: Vandenhoeck & Ruprecht, 1978), p. 245; Poniatowska, *Polacy*, p. 68.

14. STAM, Büro Kölpin 19, f. 247, Wehrkreis-Kommando VI, 14 Nov. 1919; AAN, ARPB 1835, ff. 3–5.

homeland about 20 percent migrated back to the Ruhr region. Still others migrated from the homeland to a third country, in particular to France.[15] From January 1920 the Polish government had its own representative in the Ruhr in the person of a vice-consul in Essen. Although convinced that the vast majority of Polish miners in the Ruhr would eventually migrate to the homeland, he joined in the effort to regulate this movement. To return to the homeland, the migrants had to obtain a Polish visa for their German passports. In May 1920 the vice-consul reported issuing about 400 visas per day, but only to those who could prove that they had housing and employment or means of support in Poland and who obtained a certificate from their local Polish committee attesting to their political reliability. He recognized that giving preference to the wealthy would further embitter the majority in the Ruhr, where a lack of confidence in the Polish authorities was already growing. It seemed as if Poland refused to take in its "poorer brothers," but he believed their turn would come, and he strove to demonstrate the Polish government's concern for their fate and thereby win it their support.[16] For the present at least, Poland wanted only those elements less likely to become economic or political liabilities for the government.

The leadership of the ZZP Miners' Section remained directly involved in the migration from the Ruhr. Questions concerning the pensions of miners, which were normally not paid outside of Germany, naturally fell within the purview of the union, and late in 1919 the ZZP asked the Polish government to look into the matter. As its members returned to the homeland in the following years, the ZZP advised them to continue to pay their dues to the pension fund so as not to lose their rights.[17] But the ZZP leadership in the Ruhr also played a key role in deciding the fate of the Polish community in western Germany.

Kołpacki, the chairman of the ZZP Miners' Section in the Ruhr, took part in a meeting of Polish diplomats in Brussels on 8 and 9 May 1920 that discussed the community's future. There he admitted that to maintain political discipline among Polish miners their leadership had promised them an early return to the homeland without having foreseen the

15. STAM, Büro Kölpin 192, 18 June 1920; HSTAD, RD 16021, f. 331, Polizeirat, Bochum, 31 Aug. 1920; AAN, ARPB 1632, f. 40, consulate, Cologne, n.d., copy; Janine Ponty, *Polonais méconnus: Histoire des travailleurs immigrés en France dans l'entre-deux-guerres* (Paris: Publications de la Sorbonne, 1988), pp. 62, 68.

16. AAN, KGRPB 2, ff. 10–11, 26, 28, 30, 32, 36, to MSZ, 3 March 1920, copy, to consul in Berlin, 1 May 1920, to MSZ, 13 May 1920, copy, to MSZ, 14 May 1920, copy.

17. STAM, OP 5760, report, 26 Dec. 1919; RM VII, Nr. 31, f. 54, Polizeirat, Bochum, 15 Sept. 1921.

difficulties involved. Now these workers were beginning to lose patience and in large numbers were seeking to leave Germany, particularly as economic conditions deteriorated, making it impossible for them to save any money. According to Kołpacki, out of a round number of 100,000 Polish miners and metalworkers, some 8,000–9,000 returned to the homeland. He, however, favored finding a way to halt this migration and believed that the best way would be to find work for them in a country where they could earn well and not face national persecution, for example, in Belgium or France.[18]

At this meeting the Polish attaché for emigrant affairs in Berlin stated that the task for the time being was to halt the return migration to the homeland. The vice-consul in Essen reported that those who returned to the homeland consisted mainly of former workers—petty merchants, entrepreneurs with the money to buy property in Poland. The remaining elements had no resources. They understood, he maintained, that conditions were not ripe for a return to Poland. But their difficult situation in the Ruhr and the decline of their organizations prompted many to try to enter France illegally, which resulted in their expulsion and return to the Ruhr without a penny. Therefore he proposed that worker organizations assume control over this migration. They could send a delegation to check into working conditions and social insurance. If the delegation were satisfied, the vice-consul believed that it would be easy to arrange a mass migration. All agreed that France seemed the best candidate for such a migration.[19]

The increase in anti-Polish violence in connection with the Polish-Soviet war and the conflict over Upper Silesia heightened the desire among Poles to leave the Ruhr. Following the anti-Polish demonstration and violence in Essen at the end of August 1920, crowds of Polish workers overwhelmed the vice-consulate in Essen demanding advice and assistance in leaving Germany, to the point that consular officials had to call in the police to maintain order.[20] Yet the Polish authorities had difficulty in finding a suitable destination for a mass migration. In September 1920 the Polish embassy in Berlin doubted that a large number of Polish workers in the Ruhr would find the economic situation in France attractive enough to migrate there. Some ZZP leaders hoped that Upper Silesia might offer an alternative destination. The Polish embassy, however, recognized both the inability of Polish workers to replace

18. AAN, ARPB 3260, f. 12.

19. *Ibid.*, ff. 13–16; KGRPB 2, f. 29, vice-consul, Essen, to MSW, 13 May 1920, copy.

20. AAN, KGRPB 2, f. 113, to MSZ, 3 Sept. 1920, copy.

German technicians and the threat migration to Upper Silesia posed of provoking anti-Polish violence against those left behind in the Ruhr. Therefore the embassy concluded that in general Polish workers would remain in the Ruhr.[21]

In fact, in the second half of 1920 the return migration to Poland declined.[22] Nevertheless, interest remained high. For example, the German authorities reported that a meeting called to discuss the issue in Erkenschwick in Recklinghausen county on 4 December 1920 drew an extraordinarily large audience, which followed with great interest a two-hour-long speech by a Polish deputy from Poznań about the political and economic situation in Poland.[23]

Thus, when in the first months of 1921 peace was achieved with Soviet Russia and the Upper Silesian conflict seemed close to settlement while the anti-Polish atmosphere continued in the Ruhr, the tendency to plan a mass return to the homeland re-emerged with renewed force. The Polish consuls in Essen and Berlin tried to discourage this tendency by pointing out the difficulties. At a meeting in Bochum with representatives of the Polish community on 18 April 1921, the consul general in Berlin in particular tried to scotch the "fantastic hope" that the Polish government would provide financial aid for the return migration.[24] Some migrants were not to be put off. In early June 1921 the Polish Ministry of the Formerly Prussian Zone complained to the embassy in Berlin that lately an increasing number of migrants from Germany were arriving in Poland with their families and all their belongings without either employment or housing, much to their confusion and dissatisfaction.[25] Both the German Ministry of Internal Affairs and the Polish Ministry of Foreign Affairs noted a large number of Poles in Germany returning to the homeland at this time.[26]

The movement to return to the homeland, however, did meet some opposition. A Polish Christian Democratic Party, which unsuccessfully sought to challenge the dominance of the NSR among Poles in the Ruhr, organized a meeting in Herne on 5 March 1921, at which a speaker cast

21. AAN, ARPB 268, ff. 73–74, 23 Sept. 1920, copy.

22. *Ibid.*, f. 73, 23 Sept. 1920, copy; ARPB 1627, f. 146, consul general, Berlin, to Urząd Emigracyjny, Warsaw, 19 April 1921.

23. STAM, OP 5370, Nachrichtenblatt, No. 19, p. 4, 15 Dec. 1920.

24. AAN, ARPB 1627, ff. 146–150, consul general, Berlin, to Urząd Emigracyjny, Warsaw, 19 April 1921.

25. AAN, ARPB 3524, f. 256, 2 June 1921.

26. HSTAD, RD 15740, f. 13, MdI, to OPM, 10 June 1921, copy; AAN, ARPB 1836, ff. 367–368, MSZ, Wydział Północny, Warsaw, 23 June 1921.

doubt on the Polish government's willingness to protect the returning migrant from capitalist exploitation and even accused it of discriminating against residents of the former Prussian zone in favor of those from Russian Poland or Galicia.[27] In July 1921 the mayor of Hamborn reported that those who migrated to Poland and then, disappointed with conditions there, returned to the Ruhr were also warning their countrymen against going to Poland. In his annual report on the Poles in the Ruhr in mid-September 1921, the police counselor in Bochum claimed that the negative experiences of those who migrated to Poland had crippled the desire of others to return, although Polish miners still counted on a mass migration to Upper Silesia should it be handed over to Poland.[28]

Opting for Polish Citizenship

Article 91 of the Treaty of Versailles gave Poles living in Germany as well as Germans living in Poland the right until 10 January 1922 to opt for citizenship of either country. According to the Polish consul in Essen, few of the 400,000 Poles who resided in the Rhineland and Westphalia after the war understood the complicated procedures for making a choice and even fewer the possible consequences of doing so. To one and all it initially seemed certain that every true Pole living in Germany had the honor and duty to opt for Polish citizenship. As an awareness of the lack of economic opportunity in Poland spread, the realization grew that not everyone could return at the same time. Still, many remained convinced that they must reject citizenship of the former occupier of Poland and choose the citizenship offered by the fatherland.[29]

By the spring of 1921, with the approach of the deadline for exercising the option, the matter became a main focus of attention of the Polish community. Differences between Germany and Poland over the interpretation of the treaty provisions regulating the option delayed the process, but Polish organizations undertook preparations for a mass exodus, including negotiations with the Polish government concerning accommodations and employment and with the Polish consulate

---

27. STAM, OP 5370, Nachrichtenblatt, No. 26, p. 11, 24 May 1921.

28. HSTAD, RD 15740, f. 10, to RP reporting office, Essen, 13 July 1921; STAM, RM VII, Nr. 31, 15 Sept. 1921.

29. Leon Barciszewski, "Z życia emigracji polskiej w Niemczech i Francji," in *Ćwierć wieku pracy dla Narodu i Robotnika* (Poznań: Nakładem Zarządu Centralnego Zjedn. Zawod. Polskiego, 1927), pp. 518–519, 529–530.

concerning passport fees and transportation.[30] The police counselor in Bochum, however, estimated in his annual report on the Poles in mid-September 1921 that no more than a third to a half of them would opt for Polish citizenship. In his view, they would decide on a practical, not a sentimental, basis: overwhelmingly, only those who intended to return to Poland would opt for Polish citizenship. He believed that many long-term residents of the Ruhr and particularly those born there had no thought of migrating to Poland.[31]

Practical considerations did indeed come to the fore. Reports circulated that German officials were confiscating the property of those returning to the homeland and were even preventing their entry into Poland, contrary to the treaty provisions regarding the citizenship option. Out of fear of harassment by the German authorities, many migrants preferred to wait to choose Polish citizenship until just before returning to the homeland. The Polish consul in Essen also believed that opting for Poland would lead to massive dismissals from mines and factories, especially of the leaders of Polish organizations. He, too, concluded that the migrants saw opting for Poland solely as a means to return to the homeland, not just to obtain Polish citizenship.[32]

But, with the support of the leadership of the Polish community in the Ruhr, the Polish consul also sought to discourage anyone from exercising his right to opt for Polish citizenship who did not expect to find housing and employment in the homeland within a year of the option deadline, that is, by 10 January 1923. As the Polish consul in Essen, Leon Barciszewski, later explained, a citizen always has a better chance to defend his rights than a foreigner, and in Germany workers who were citizens had more rights than foreign workers. Should the economic situation worsen, the authorities could expel foreign workers. Furthermore, German social legislation favored citizens over foreigners. After giving their best years to German industry, retired Polish workers or those living on disability pensions might be forced to depend on the generosity of the Polish government. The Polish authorities tried above all to persuade the leaders of the Polish community and activists in its organizations not to opt for Polish citizenship. Their expulsion from

---

30. STAM, OP 5370, Nachrichtenblatt, No. 26, 24 May 1921; AAN, ARPB 1627, ff. 147–148, consul general, Berlin, to Urząd Emigracyjny, Warsaw, 19 April 1921, copy.

31. STAM, RM VII, Nr. 31, Polizeirat, Bochum, 15 Sept. 1921.

32. AAN, ARPB 3524, ff. 268, 271–272, 286–287, vice-consul, Berlin, to MSZ, Warsaw, 28 Oct. 21, consul general, Berlin, to MSZ, 4 Nov. 1921.

Germany as foreign citizens would leave the rest of the Polish migrants "like soldiers without officers."[33]

But *raison d'état*, pure and simple, also motivated official Polish opposition to the migrants opting for Polish citizenship: a large group of Polish citizens residing in the Ruhr would give the German government a hostage to use in relation to the Polish government and its policies toward the Germans living in Poland. Also, care for the retirees and the disabled would impose a financial burden on the young state. The Polish consul general in Berlin concluded that in Poland's current economic circumstances a massive return of migrants would be a catastrophe.[34]

For decades the leaders of the Polish national movement had held out the rebirth of Poland as its goal, as the fulfillment of a dream. Therefore they and the Polish consul faced considerable resistance and even anger and resentment in arguing, now that the dream had come true, that the Poles of the Ruhr should not opt for Polish citizenship. "When there was no Poland, you urged us to believe in it, but now that there is a Poland, you forbid Polish workers to return to it."[35]

As the consul and the leaders of the Polish community in the Ruhr propagated their views at public assemblies and meetings in the Ruhr, they encountered further objections. Polish workers saw the opting for citizenship as a right that they could exercise only once and within the given time frame. By not opting now for Polish citizenship, they would be at the mercy of the Polish authorities when they applied for it in the future—a concern whose validity even the consul recognized. When Polish leaders could not give assurances that the Polish government would grant citizenship to every Pole living in Germany who requested it after 10 January 1922, meetings ended in protests directed against Polish organizations and the consulate.[36]

Out of a fear of German retribution and on the advice of their own leaders, at first relatively few migrants in the Ruhr opted for Polish citizenship.[37] Then, following negotiations between Poland and Germany over procedures, on 3 December 1921 the German government published regulations requiring that Poles in Germany opting for Polish citizenship

33. *Ibid.*, ff. 259–260, Executive Committee, Bochum, to consulate, Essen 14 Dec. 1921; Barciszewski, "Z życia," pp. 520–521, 525; quote on p. 525.

34. Barciszewski, "Z życia," pp. 520–521, 525; AAN, ARPB 3524, ff. 286–287, consul general, Berlin, to MSZ, 4 Nov. 1921.

35. Barciszewski, "Z życia," p. 522.

36. *Ibid.*, pp. 522–523.

37. AAN, ARPB 3524, ff. 268, 271–272, vice-consul, Berlin, to MSZ, Warsaw, 28 Oct. 1921.

file with the German authorities as well as with the Polish consulate by the deadline of 10 January 1922. This caused considerable additional consternation in the Polish community. Those who had trusted assurances that their option would be kept secret until their departure now felt betrayed to German reprisals. But above all bitterness arose out disappointment of a hope that the deadline for declaring one's option would be extended. If the migrants were to secure housing and employment in the homeland within a year of opting for Polish citizenship, an extension of the deadline would have given them more time to gather the resources to meet these requirements.[38] Thus, one more route to realizing the dream of a return to the homeland seemed closed off with the consent of the Polish government.

In these circumstances, a significant portion of the Poles in the Ruhr came to believe that the Polish government wanted at any price to prevent their return to the homeland. Among the dissatisfied, the Polish consulate distinguished two groups. The first, less interested in returning, originally viewed opting for Poland as a necessary declaration of Polish patriotism. Members of this group now interpreted the Polish government's handling of the question as an attempt to abandon the Polish community in the Ruhr, and they threatened to break with the community. The second group similarly saw the Polish government as opposed to a return to the homeland. To defy the Polish government this group called for all Poles to opt for Polish citizenship and present themselves at the Polish border. Emotions were so inflamed that the consulate successfully persuaded the two Polish newspapers in the Ruhr not to print articles along these lines.[39]

On 14 December 1921 the directorates of the Executive Committee, the ZZP Miners' Section, and the National Workers' Party (NPR) met in Bochum and formulated a series of demands to present to the Polish consulate. In case of necessity, they selected a delegation, including Kołpacki, to convey their grievances to the Polish government in Warsaw. First of all, they demanded a guarantee of housing and employment for those who opted for Poland and were forced to leave Germany because of German "terror." Secondly, they demanded that the consulate arrange satisfactory railroad transportation in the spring for a mass return to the homeland. Finally, they demanded written assurances that the Polish government would not raise difficulties for Poles who apply for Polish citizenship after 10 January 1922. If the Polish leadership of the Ruhr did

38. *Ibid.*, ff. 259–260, 265–267, Executive Committee, Bochum, to consulate, Essen, 14 Dec. 1921, consulate, Essen, 18 Dec. 1921; Barciszewski, "Z życia," p. 523.

39. AAN, ARPB 3524, ff. 265–267, consulate, Essen, 18 Dec. 1921.

not receive a satisfactory response, it threatened to urge the whole community to opt for Polish citizenship, "because it is impossible that those who for decades have lived with the thought of return, and for this reason made great sacrifices, be required to become German citizens because of the consulate or the Polish government."[40] The consul immediately replied that he could not give a written guarantee concerning future applications for Polish citizenship but claimed that the Polish government never intended to raise difficulties.[41] In fact, as we have seen, the Polish authorities were eager to screen re-emigrants to keep out the most radical elements, particularly communists. To calm the fears of the migrants, the Polish authorities issued a declaration promising that those Poles who did not now exercise their right to opt for Polish citizenship would be able to obtain it by means of a streamlined procedure when they leave Germany, which would still allow the Polish authorities to check the applicant's "moral character."[42] Once again, Polish *raison d'état* triumphed over the national rights of Poles in the Ruhr. The question of their acceptability continued to be debated after the option deadline. In February 1922 in an article in the *Dziennik Berliński*, the NPR sought to reassure the Polish authorities on this point: "The Polish element in Germany is, to be sure, of a radical disposition, but that is mainly in relation to a foreign government and in a foreign environment. In its own land that radicalism will moderate and may concern only the defense of legitimate economic demands."[43]

At a conference with the leaders of the Polish community in the Ruhr, the Polish consul argued the impracticality of their demand that the Polish government arrange a mass return migration to the homeland. To their suggestion that the consulate provide one empty train a week for the migrants, he replied that that would allow only 500 people to return each week and the whole process would take 15 years![44] If a mass re-emigration was not feasible in the short run, the option deadline militated against a mass return also in the long run. The Polish authorities themselves initially thought that the agreement over procedures reached with Germany meant that those who migrated to Poland after 10 January 1923—one year following the option deadline—would effectively lose

40. *Ibid.*, ff. 258–260, Milczynski, secretary, Executive Committee, Bochum, 15 Dec. 1921, Executive Committee, Bochum, to consulate, 14 Dec. 1921, copies. Sołtysiak represented the ZZP at the meeting.

41. *Ibid.*, f. 261, to Executive Committee, 15 Dec. 1921, copy.

42. Barciszewski, "Z życia," pp. 522–523.

43. Quoted in Poniatowska, *Polacy*, p. 87.

44. Barciszewski, "Z życia," pp. 521–522.

their rights to collect pensions based on their years of work and contributions in Germany. This posed a painful dilemma, of which the migrants were not yet fully aware: either give up their rights to a pension or abandon their hope of returning to the homeland.[45] In theory a German-Polish agreement approved in July 1922 solved the problem, but in practice many faced difficulties in collecting their pensions until the German-Polish Social Insurance Treaty of July 1931 finally settled the matter.[46]

The passing of the deadline for opting for Polish citizenship under article 91 of the Treaty of Versailles did not end the demands for assistance from the Polish government or the protests against its policies. In March 1922 a group ready to return to the homeland charged that the Polish government had reneged on a promise to provide land to settle on.[47] When the Polish authorities raised consular fees, they encountered further complaints. A letter to the Polish Ministry of Foreign Affairs at the end of June 1922 protested that thousands had opted for Polish citizenship with the hope of obtaining assistance and rights, not just obligations. They felt wronged when they had to turn over their savings to cover the cost of a passport. They undertook the difficult and risky venture of returning to the homeland mainly because of the harassment they suffered after opting for Polish citizenship. Now "the Polish government demands to be paid by people who want to avoid the suffering borne precisely for the Polish state."[48]

Many of those who opted for Poland wished to return to the homeland as soon as possible, either because of German harassment or because of concessions granted those who moved before 10 January 1923 to the country whose citizenship they chose. In late July 1922 the *Wiarus Polski* commented bitterly that the Polish government was doing very little to assist them. As a consequence it feared that they would migrate further west instead of to the homeland or that they would develop a complete aversion to Polish organizations and associations, resulting an inevitable decline in the life of the Polish community in the Ruhr.[49]

In fact, German officials reported evidence that the controversies surrounding the citizenship option might have led some migrants to turn

---

45. AAN, ARPB 1627, ff. 216–223, Attaché for Emigrant Affairs, 22 Dec. 1921, copy; another copy is in ARPB 3524, ff. 303–310.

46. Klessmann, *Polnische Bergarbeiter*, pp. 166–167.

47. Poniatowska, *Polacy*, p. 70.

48. AAN, ARPB 2018, ff. 126–132, 30 June 1922, copy. See also Poniatowska, *Polacy*, p. 88.

49. Quoted in Klessmann, *Polnische Bergarbeiter*, pp. 159–160.

away from the Polish community just as the *Wiarus Polski* feared. In the spring of 1922 the officials noted "a perceptible stillness" in the Polish movement in the Ruhr: "Association activities have considerably slackened. The Polish population is completely indifferent."[50] In his annual report on the Polish community at the beginning of October 1922, the police counselor in Bochum reported a large number of changes of Polish-sounding names to German ones, not only among migrants from East Prussia, that is, primarily Masurians, but also among those from the other formerly Prussian parts of Poland.[51]

The deadlines connected with the citizenship option also forced migrants to make decisions that otherwise might have been postponed. The number of Polish migrants leaving Germany, either for the homeland or for other countries, particularly France, rose significantly in 1922, as did the number of Polish citizens working in the Ruhr region, mainly migrants who opted for Polish citizenship but did not leave the country.[52]

When German-Polish relations deteriorated, particularly during the occupation of the Ruhr in 1923, the Polish citizens still in the Ruhr bore the brunt of the antagonism. German officials denied them unemployment benefits as Ruhr industrialists took advantage of the Ruhr crisis to rationalize their firms. Thus, when the Stinnes concern laid off 100,000 miners, the consulate reported that they included 2,000 Polish citizens, which meant that, together with their families, 6,000 Poles lost all means of support. The situation of Polish citizens in the Ruhr deteriorated to such a point that, in early November 1923, the Polish consul in Essen sent a delegate to Poland to gather charitable contributions for their support. A month later a report of the Polish consulate in Essen spoke of actual starvation of infants in some places.[53]

A relatively large percentage of migrants who opted for Polish citizenship with the Polish consulate did not register their option with the German government as required by the regulations issued on 3 December 1921. Therefore in the eyes of German officials they retained German citizenship and received unemployment assistance during the Ruhr crisis.[54] Seeing a benefit in the revelation of who in Poland had opted for German citizenship, the Polish government again put *raison d'état* ahead

---

50. HSTAD, RD 15379, f. 233, Nachrichtenblatt, No. 54, 21 May 1922.

51. STAM, RM VII, Nr. 35, p. 77, Polizeirat, Bochum, 1 Oct. 1922.

52. *Ibid.*; RA I, Pa 94, 1 Nov. 1923, report on Polish movement, copy.

53. AAN, ARPB 2154, ff. 34–35, ff. 111–115, report, 7 Nov. 1923, Report No. III, Essen, 6 Dec. 1923, copy.

54. *Ibid.*, ff. 92–93, consul, Essen, 26 Nov. 1923.

of the welfare of the Polish community in the Ruhr region when it signed an agreement in Vienna with the German government at the end of August 1924. By recognizing the validity of the so-called silent option, the agreement exposed additional Poles in the Ruhr to the same threats, including expulsion, as those who had registered their option with the German authorities. Particularly tragic were the consequences for families of mixed Polish-German marriages in which one of the spouses refused to move to Poland. In one case a seventeen-year-old youth who did not want to be a "Polack" split his father's head with an axe when the father refused to renounce his option, which made his underage children Polish citizens.[55] Others, including a miner with a Polish surname who sent an appeal to German President Paul von Hindenburg, sought to regain German citizenship by claiming to be the victims of circumstances or ignorance.[56]

Within the jurisdiction of the Polish consul in Essen, about 12,000 individuals opted for Polish citizenship. These included some 11,000 heads of families, whose decision was binding for their wives and underage children, and about 1,000 others—single adults and widows. Based on these figures, the consul estimated that the option for Polish citizenship covered some 50,000–60,000 Poles residing in the Ruhr region, which amounted to only a small percentage of those eligible.[57] Incomplete official German statistics suggest an even lower total number of migrants who opted for Polish citizenship, but at least until the 1924 agreement the German government did not recognize those who registered their option only with the Polish consulate.[58]

In addition, the Polish government kept its promise to a further 11,000 who did not opt for Polish citizenship within the time limit set by the Treaty of Versailles but decided to leave Germany. The consulate in Essen, after an investigation of about a month's duration, granted them temporary certificates of Polish citizenship and confirmed Polish citizenship in some 4,000 other cases. Together with their dependents, these amounted to a further 25,000 individuals. (Evidently, more older

55. AAN, ARPB 3517, ff. 40, 51–52, emigration counselor, Berlin, to MSZ, 24 Sept. 1925, consul, Essen, to MSZ, 29 May 1925; Barciszewski, "Z życia," pp. 527–528.

56. Klessmann, *Polnische Bergarbeiter*, p. 161; AAN, ARPB 3517, ff. 52, 80, consul, Essen, to MSZ, 29 May 1925, to embassy, 15 Jan. 1926.

57. AAN, ARPB 2154, ff. 10, 117, *aide-mémoire*, consul, Essen, to ambassador, 6 Nov. 1923, 19 Nov. 1923, copy; Barciszewski, "Z życia," p. 525.

58. Klessmann, *Polnische Bergarbeiter*, pp. 158–159, estimates that the option for Polish citizenship covered only 30,000–40,000 individuals in the Ruhr region.

heads of families chose to exercise their option for Polish citizenship without delay, while younger ones continued to work.[59])

Obviously, the vast majority of Poles in the Ruhr did not exercise their option to choose Polish citizenship as provided for in the peace treaty. According to the Polish consul in Essen, these included the more prominent members of the Polish community, who acceded to the consulate's recommendation that they remain German citizens so as not to weaken the community.[60] The consul saw the mass of those eligible to opt for Polish citizenship as passive: they simply neglected to act and thereby retained their German citizenship.[61] This passivity did not necessarily indicate anything about their national loyalty. In the eyes of the Polish authorities, the distinction between Poles who opted for Polish citizenship and those who did not formally opt at all had no meaning. The consulate regarded German citizenship as a temporary expedient for Poles until conditions favoring migration ripened.[62] As far as the Polish authorities were concerned, if a Pole later requested Polish citizenship, he would receive it, as long as he produced the necessary documents, including a recommendation from the ZZP or other Polish organization.[63] In 1925 when the German government began to expel Poles in greater numbers, it also did not always distinguish between those who opted for Polish citizenship and those who did not.[64]

Counting only nationally conscious Poles, excluding "those who through a warped life nationally or politically placed themselves outside of Polish social life," the Polish consul in Essen estimated the number of Polish heads of families with German citizenship in the Ruhr at 18,000 in the fall of 1923. Far from dismissing them because of their German citizenship, he considered them sometimes more valuable than those who

---

59. Barciszewski, "Z życia," p. 526.

60. AAN, ARPB 3517, to MSZ, 29 May 1925. A German official report on the Polish movement, 1 Nov. 1923, on the contrary claimed that among those who opted for Polish citizenship and emigration from the Ruhr were the "radical" elements that organized almost all of the Polish associations, STAM, RA I, Pa 94.

61. AAN, ARPB 3517, f. 5, consul, Essen, to ambassador, Berlin, 16 Aug. 1924. Thus, Kazimierz Ożóg and Jadwiga Śrutek, "Komentarz historyczny," in Antoni Taront, *Wspomnienia emigranta polskiego z północnej Francji*, ed. by Daniel Beauvois, Kazimierz Ożóg, and Jadwiga Śrutek (Wrocław, Warsaw, Cracow: Zakład Narodowy im. Ossolińskich, 1994), p. 91, err in asserting that the majority of Polish workers in Germany opted for Polish citizenship.

62. AAN, ARPB 1632, f. 41, consulate, Cologne, n.d., copy.

63. AAN, ARPB 3517, f. 50, consul, Essen, to MSZ, 29 May 1925.

64. AAN, ARPB 1632, f. 12, governor of Poznania, to Ministry of Internal Affairs, 20 Aug. 1925.

opted for Polish citizenship because in following the advice of the consulate they had subordinated their interests to those of Poland.[65] But they could also run into problems once they decided to leave Germany. If the Polish consulate raised no difficulties in granting Polish citizenship, the German government did not necessarily recognize it in such cases and even confiscated the temporary Polish passports issued by the Polish consulate.[66]

Thus, the right to opt for Polish citizenship provided for in the Treaty of Versailles, although meant as a safeguard for the Polish national minority living in Germany, created painful problems and dilemmas for this minority. Those who yearned to return to their homeland or even just to stay loyal to their national identity often encountered difficulties no matter what choice they made. These difficulties may have prompted many to retain their German citizenship and remain in Germany. As before the war, the migrants could still delude themselves that they were simply postponing their return to the homeland until conditions improved. In 1924 the Polish embassy in Berlin, which saw in a return migration the advantage of an increase in the ethnically Polish percentage of the population of Poland, maintained that every patriotic Pole living in Germany still wanted to return to the homeland and that only the economic situation of Poland held them back.[67]

The embassy, however, complained to the Polish Ministry of Foreign Affairs that the policy toward the Poles in Germany lacked clarity and asked about plans for repatriating the broad masses of the migrants. "We know that it is not the intention of the Polish government to maintain these centers of Polishness in the future. Rather, the government inclines toward a project of liquidating these centers of Polishness."[68] The embassy reported that the unsuccessful attempts at remigration to the homeland due to insufficient assistance given to the migrants discouraged some, but it regarded this as temporary. Nevertheless, bitterness and disappointment over the policies of the Polish government toward the migrants could facilitate assimilation into German society even among those less than ambivalent about their Polish national identity. Others looked for a third way, or at least a third country, and most often chose France as their new home.

65. AAN, ARPB 2154, ff. 117–118, *aide-mémoire*, 19 Nov. 1923; quote on f. 117.
66. AAN, ARPB 3517, f. 51, consul, Essen, to MSZ, 29 May 1925.
67. AAN, ARPB 1842, ff. 86–87, chargé d'affaires, to MSZ, 24 April 1924, copy.
68. *Ibid.*

Migration to France

A migration of Polish miners to France began before World War I. Recruited by mines in northern France, the first large number of Polish miners from the Ruhr region arrived in 1909. Even earlier, Stefan Rejer, the first chairman of the ZZP, who resigned after being fired for his union activity, migrated to France and later became the first chairman of the Union of Polish Workers in France.[69]

After the war, Poles from both the Ruhr region and from Poland itself migrated to France in greater numbers than to any other country. Initially, the Polish migrants of the Ruhr wanted to escape the expected imposition of a heavy tax burden to finance the reparations required of Germany by the peace treaty, which would diminish their already low standard of living. Because Poland offered no employment opportunities, they saw migration to France and Belgium as their only salvation. The post-war reconstruction going on in France particularly attracted them. The vast majority of Polish miners in the Ruhr wanted better earnings above all, and there seemed little prospect of achieving this in Germany.[70]

The migration, however, began slowly. When rumors spread of a mass migration to France, speakers at Polish meetings in January 1920 urged migrants to wait for news from the community's leaders and warned that conditions in France were worse than in the Ruhr.[71] After the Polish vice-consulate opened in Essen in early January, the vice-consul also advised the migrants at public meetings and in the press not "to sell themselves to the French emigration agents earnestly prowling" the industrial region.[72]

The German citizenship of the Poles of the Ruhr, which made legal entry into France impossible, posed the main obstacle to a mass migration. Therefore they turned in large numbers to the vice-consulate, demanding Polish citizenship and Polish passports. With procedures not yet established for opting for Polish citizenship, the vice-consul refused all assistance, which resulted in some unpleasant scenes. He also saw a problem in the lack of adequate sanitary facilities at French mines. Used to the well-equipped mines in the Ruhr, the Polish migrants, he feared, would be dissatisfied with the conditions at French mines. In any case, he

69. Ponty, *Polonais*, pp. 26–27; Stefan Rejer, "Związek Robotników Polskich we Francji," in *Ćwierć wieku pracy dla Narodu i Robotnika* (Poznań: Nakładem Zarządu Centralnego Zjedn. Zawod. Polskiego, 1927), pp. 493–495.

70. AAN, KGRPB 2, ff. 4–5, 29, vice-consul, Essen, to MSZ, 6 Feb. 1920, 13 May 1920, copies.

71. STAM, Büro Kölpin 296, Group I, Dorsten, 26 Jan. 1920.

72. AAN, KGRPB 2, ff. 19–20, vice-consul, Essen, to MSZ, 13 April 1920, copy.

did not expect migration to France to match the scale of the current migration to the homeland. Mainly miners without resources would go to France because of the better prospects it offered than in Germany or Poland. A yearning for the homeland would draw those with resources to enjoy the fruits of their labor in Poland.[73]

Nevertheless, the vice-consul thought it necessary to prevent a migration to France from taking mainly a "wild" or illegal form. He therefore met with the directorate of the ZZP Miners' Section early in the spring of 1920, and the union leaders decided to send their own representative to France together with the vice-consul to investigate conditions at the mines. On 6 May the vice-consul met with a wider group of community leaders, including the directorate of the ZZP Miners' Section, the Executive Committee, and the leaders of various associations to discuss the matter further and establish guidelines for organizing the migration. Among other things, they agreed to do a precise survey by the middle of June of all those who intended to emigrate or return to the homeland.[74]

By the time he returned from his trip to France, which began on 1 June 1920 in the company of the Polish attaché for emigrant affairs in Berlin and Ignacy Woźniak of the directorate of the ZZP Miners' Section, the Polish vice-consul in Essen evinced a greater enthusiasm for channeling a migration of Polish miners from the Ruhr to France or Belgium. He now saw in this two cardinal virtues, one economic and the other political. The economic virtue had to do with the lack of employment available in the homeland. After less than six months as vice-consul in Essen, he also believed that migration other than to the homeland had a political advantage in that it shielded Poland from "the way of thinking" of the Poles in the Ruhr. "For their demands, although sometimes not very extreme, are unfeasible in today's conditions in the homeland, which will provoke dissatisfaction among them and a reluctance to work, and in this way spread ferment among the wide masses of Polish workers in the fatherland."[75] (The Polish consul in Lille later confirmed this when he characterized the Polish migrants to France from the Ruhr as having "a

---

73. *Ibid.*, ff. 4–5, 19–21, vice-consul, Essen, to MSZ, 6 Feb. 1920, 13 April 1920, copies.

74. *Ibid.*, ff. 20–21, 29, vice-consul, Essen, to MSZ, 13 April 1920, 13 May 1920, copies.

75. *Ibid.*, f. 70, vice-consul, Essen, to MSZ, 17 June 1920.

lack of feeling for Polish statehood, a traditional opposition to government authorities and therefore to the Polish authorities."[76])

In Paris the delegation met with the secretary general of the French mine owners' association (*Comité central des Houillères de France* or CCHF), Jean Duhamel, and the head of the foreign workers' section of the French Ministry of Labor. (Not surprisingly, no French union representative participated.) The French side estimated that the mines needed 5,000–6,000 miners. At the meeting it was agreed that the contracting agencies would be the CCHF and the ZZP Miners' Section. Individuals who receive a contract would present it at the Polish vice-consulate in Essen together with the necessary documents to obtain a Polish passport or at least a certificate testifying to their Polish nationality, which in turn they would present at the French consulate in Düsseldorf to receive a visa free of charge. A French-Polish agreement would settle questions of social insurance.[77]

These arrangements depended on a positive verdict after Woźniak's inspection of France's mines, which took place over the next two weeks. He and the Polish vice-consul, who accompanied him for most of his tour, concluded that, although the technical and sanitary facilities did not compare with those in the Ruhr, "they nevertheless are not so bad as is generally believed."[78] Miners worked an eight-hour day, including travel time to and from the coal face. The lack of experienced interpreters, however, posed a major problem. The French canteens adapted their cooking to the taste of Polish workers and satisfied them completely in 75 percent of the cases [*sic!*]. Housing in barracks for bachelors would not suit everyone, but Woźniak and the vice-consul found the housing for families attractive. All in all, they concluded that they could with a clear conscience endorse the growing movement to migrate to France—the vice-consul reported that everywhere they went they met groups of "wild" Polish emigrants—especially of those without resources, primarily because of the better pay and higher prosperity among French miners than among German miners.[79]

76. AAN, Konsulat Rzeczypospolitej Polskiej w Marsylii 314, f. 20, consul, Lille, to MSZ, 19 Feb. 1929; the consul was Dr. Tadeusz Brzezinski, the father of the Polish-American scholar and former government official Zbigniew Brzezinski.

77. AAN, KGRPB 2, ff. 71, 78, vice-consul, Essen, to MSZ, 17 June 1920, protocol, 28 June 1920. Ponty, *Polonais*, p. 62, presents the meeting as occurring on the initiative of the CCHF.

78. AAN, KGRPB 2, ff. 72, 75, vice-consul, Essen, to MSZ, 17 June 1920, protocol, 28 June 1920.

79. *Ibid.*, ff. 72–73, 75–76.

On 26 June 1920 Woźniak and the vice-consul presented their findings at a meeting in the vice-consulate in Essen attended by ZZP chairman Kołpacki, Sołtysiak of the Polish union's directorate, and Duhamel representing French mine owners. Migration to France was still to be regarded as a necessity due solely to the current impossibility of returning to the homeland. Nevertheless, Kołpacki saw a serious difficulty in the ZZP acting as the contracting agent for French mines, which the German authorities and mine owners would view as a hostile act. After some debate, Duhamel proposed that the CCHF open offices in the French-occupied part of the Rhineland, where ZZP agents would work in the employ of the CCHF (at 2,500 marks per month). The CCHF would pay the expenses of Polish miners recruited for migration to France as well as 5 francs per day of unemployment during the move from work in mines in Germany to work in mines in France. A Polish diplomat in attendance added that the migrants would have their religious needs met in France and that the mines would aid in setting up schools and churches.[80]

On the basis of these discussions, the Polish vice-consulate in Essen began issuing "Certificates of Nationality" to Polish miners for 20 marks (to be raised to 30 marks—because French mine owners covered costs), with which they could obtain visas at the French consulate in Düsseldorf and at the Belgian consulate in Cologne. In the latter half of August 1920 the vice-consul reported an average of thirty requests per day for this proof of Polish nationality.[81] According to a Polish consular official in Paris, 700 migrants from the Ruhr arrived in France to work in the mines in the first two weeks of October 1920. By the end of the year, the Polish consuls in Essen and Cologne reported that 2,500 (including 1,900 miners) and 360 migrated to France from their respective jurisdictions.[82]

The migration did not take place without problems. Polish miners migrating to Belgium angrily refused to pay the required 100 marks for a Belgian visa. Those heading for France, where they could earn more than in the Ruhr, eagerly migrated with their families but encountered a hostile reception from French workers, who referred to them as "boches"—a derogatory term for Germans—because they spoke German among themselves. Many of them also wore miners' hats with inscriptions such as "Hindenburg" or "Ludendorff" and became indignant at

80. *Ibid.*, ff. 75–81, protocol, 28 June 1920.

81. *Ibid.*, ff. 90–91, vice-consul, Essen, to MSZ, 20 Aug. 1920; see f. 92 for a bilingual Polish-French sample of the Certificate of Nationality.

82. AAN, ARPP 231, f. 54, to consul, Antwerp, 14 Oct. 1920, copy; ARPB 1626, ff. 14, 40, to MSZ, 14 March 1921, report, n.d., copies.

suggestions that they tear off these names, which they said would ruin the hat—evidence of a lamentable lack of awareness among Polish miners from the Ruhr, according to a Polish consular official.[83]

More seriously, beginning in November 1920, complaints by Polish migrants multiplied that the individual French mines were not living up to the contracts made in their name by the CCHF. The ZZP delegated Woźniak to make a month-long tour of French mines to address the problem. His reports sent to Bochum—dictated, in the eyes of the Polish consul in Essen, more by emotions influenced by the migrants than by the facts and the inevitable deficiencies connected with the migration—led the ZZP to bring a complete halt to the migration. Seeking its resumption, Duhamel of the CCHF reopened negotiations with the ZZP and, together with Polish consular officials, met with the union's leaders at its headquarters in Bochum on 7 March 1921. By this time, most of the problems had been solved, as evidenced by the almost complete disappearance of complaints. Discussion at the meeting focused on the chief remaining problem, the inadequate housing arrangements. All agreed to restart the migration followed by another investigation by a member of the ZZP directorate to remove all sources of dissatisfaction so that the whole migration process would not suffer. To protect the process, they saw the need for greater attention to the needs of the migrants in France, for example, by establishing a newspaper for them, for which Duhamel promised financial assistance.[84]

The Polish consul in Essen continued to attach great importance to the migration to France. With what he regarded as the impossibility of a return to the homeland, he saw migration to France as the sole resort for Polish miners increasingly harassed by their German fellow workers. In the summer of 1921, at a meeting with a German police director, Kołpacki also claimed that anti-Polish manifestations, and not French recruiting agents, stimulated the growing migration to France.[85] The police

83. AAN, ARPP 231, ff. 52–54, to consul, Antwerp, 14 Oct. 1920, copy; Antoni Taront, *Wspomnienia emigranta polskiego z północnej Francji*, ed. by Daniel Beauvois, Kazimierz Ożóg, and Jadwiga Śrutek (Wrocław, Warsaw, Cracow: Zakład Narodowy im. Ossolińskich, 1994), p. 15; Marcin Bugzel, "Wspomnienia starego emigranta," in *Pamiętniki emigrantów 1878–1958* (Warsaw: Czytelnik, 1960), p. 28, reported that the French miners also called the Poles from the Ruhr "pointed helmets," after the helmets worn by German officers during the war.

84. AAN, ARPB 1626, ff. 14–20, consul, Essen, to MSZ, 14 March 1921, copy; *Jubileuszowy Kalendarz Wychodźczy "Wiarusa Polskiego" 1890–1940 na r. 1940* (Lille: "Wiarus Polski," 1940), p. 156.

85. AAN, ARPB 1626, f. 19, consul, Essen, to MSZ, 14 March 1921, copy; ARPB 1836, ff. 296–297, Cezary Kreczy, consular secretary, report, n.d., received 18 July 1921.

counselor in Bochum, in his annual report on the Polish movement in mid-September 1921, repeated the allegation that Polish miners migrated to France to escape the insults and threats of communist and anti-Polish German workers but noted that they preferred to migrate to France or Holland rather than the homeland because of the greater opportunity of finding well-paying jobs in the mines. Based on supposedly reliable sources, he reported that about 700 Polish miners migrated to France in the first eight months of 1921, a lower rate of migration than in the second half of 1920.[86] This together with a decline for 1921 in the number of migrants to France reported by the Polish consulate in Cologne reflects the temporary halt to the migration brought by the ZZP and thereby demonstrates the union's decisive influence on the emigration from the Ruhr.[87]

By the spring of 1922 the ZZP was again fully supportive of the migration to France. At a public meeting of Polish miners, Kołpacki spoke of the unemployment and misery in Poznania and remarked to those intent on leaving Germany,

If you also do not want to migrate to Poland, you can however migrate to France. There you have nothing to lose because the travel and other costs will also be reimbursed by the French mine owners' association. We want to show the German capitalist that we do not need to perform the most difficult work for them and can still find employment elsewhere.[88]

In fact, the first months of 1922 saw the migration to France rise rapidly and reach its peak in the final months of the year with the approach of the expiration on 10 January 1923 of the rights accorded those who opted for Polish citizenship.[89] The Polish consulate in Essen favored migration to France for the 12,000 heads of households in the Ruhr who opted for Polish citizenship and whose departure from Germany the consulate tried to expedite. In November 1923 the consulate reported that 10,000 of them had left Germany.[90] As noted, many of them

86. STAM, RM VII, Nr. 31, Polizeirat, Bochum, 15 Sept. 1921.

87. AAN, ARPB 1632, f. 40, consulate, Cologne, n.d., reported 286 emigrants to France compared with 360 in 1920. Klessmann, *Polnische Bergarbeiter*, p. 162, citing a Polish source gives 4,310 for the total post-war migration to France at the end of 1921, which also confirms that fewer migrated in 1921 than in 1920, when the total surpassed 2,800.

88. STAM, RM VII, Nr. 35, p. 76, Polizeirat, Bochum, report on Polish movement, 1 Oct. 1922.

89. Ponty, *Polonais*, p. 67.

90. AAN, ARPB 2154, ff. 10–11, 117, consul, Essen, to Polish ambassador, Berlin, 6 Nov. 1923, *aide-mémoire*, 19 Nov. 1923, copy.

felt compelled to leave Germany within the year following the option deadline, that is, by 10 January 1923. Those who received "Certificates of Nationality" enabling them to obtain French or Belgian visas may well have come to the same conviction. The Polish consul in Essen later reported that he issued some 5,000 such certificates by 10 January 1922.[91] Meanwhile, the possibility of a return to the homeland seemed more remote than ever. Thus, the deadlines connected with the right to opt for Polish citizenship served to stimulate the migration to France. As a German official reported on the Polish movement on 1 November 1923, "The strongest emigration began after the option in 1922."[92] Facilitating this migration, the CCHF opened a recruitment bureau under the protection of French occupation forces in Duisburg on 1 January 1922.[93]

In the fall of 1922, the Polish consulate in Essen estimated the total migration to France at 9,500 (including 7,500 workers), an increase of more than 5,000 over the total at the end of 1921.[94] For all of 1922 the consulate in Cologne reported a sixfold rise in the migration to France over the previous year.[95] Also, in 1922 the publisher of the *Narodowiec*, one of the two Polish newspapers in the Ruhr, opened a branch of his press in the northern French province of Pas-de-Calais in connection with the establishment of the first Polish colony there, another signal of the transfer of part of the Polish community in the Ruhr to France.[96]

The French occupation of the main centers of the Ruhr in January 1923 did nothing to slow the migration to France. At a meeting of Polish consuls in Berlin in May 1923, the consul in Essen spoke of the Polish colony in the Ruhr as in the process of liquidating itself through migration to France and Belgium.[97] Once Polish miners began work under French direction prior to the end of passive resistance on the part of most German workers, the threat of retribution together with the economic pressures due to the catastrophic inflation and layoffs made their departure from Germany all the more imperative. Faced with unemployment and the need to depart quickly, those who applied to the Polish consulate for Polish

91. AAN, ARPB 3517, ff. 17–20.

92. STAM, RA I, Pa 94, Münster, 1 Nov. 1923, copy.

93. Ponty, *Polonais*, p. 63; Ponty, p. 66, ignores the mood among Polish miners in the Ruhr when she sees the opening of this bureau as the main stimulant of the migration.

94. Klessmann, *Polnische Bergarbeiter*, p. 162.

95. AAN, ARPB 1632, f. 40, consulate, Cologne, n.d., reported 1,797 emigrants to France compared with 286 in 1921.

96. Stéphane Wlocevski, *Le 25e Anniversaire. Les mineurs polonais en France avant, pendant et après la guerre* (Lens: Impr. du Narodowiec, 1935), p. 23.

97. AAN, ARPB 3260, f. 35, Protocol, 25–26 May 1923.

citizenship received temporary Polish passports without having to wait for approval of their citizenship applications—the consulate later claimed to have issued such passports to 10,800 families in the Ruhr.[98] Thus, more Poles from the Ruhr migrated to France in 1923 than in any previous year, though the rate of migration did not match that of the second half of 1922.[99] The pressure to migrate from Germany, however, exceeded France's capacity to accommodate the migrants. Supposedly a lack of housing slowed the migration to France: in November 1923 the Polish consul in Essen referred to the French willingness to accept migrants as a drop in the bucket. A small group of migrants went to Belgium, but the absence of a Belgian-Polish agreement prevented the sending of more migrants there. Moreover, of the 2,000 heads of households who opted for Polish citizenship and had not yet left Germany, the consul estimated that no more than about 300 met the criteria of French employers, the remainder being the elderly, invalids, widows, or underage orphans, whose only hope of departure from Germany lay in repatriation to the homeland.[100]

The migration to France continued into 1924 and even quickened after the lockout in May and the French announcement of the decision to dismantle the occupation.[101] According to the ZZP, 6,033 Polish workers migrated to France from the Ruhr in 1924 and another 2,078 in 1925.[102] From May 1924 part of the migration to France took place under new circumstances as the CCHF bureau began to recruit Polish miners as German citizens, that is, without requiring that they obtain documentation from the Polish authorities, who regarded this as a "wild" or illegal migration. In August 1925 the Polish consulate in Essen estimated that this migration consisted of about 7,000 workers, barely half of whom had a right to opt for Polish citizenship.[103] These included many who should never have been allowed into France, "the worst scum" of the Polish population in the Ruhr, demoralized and denationalized elements who

---

98. AAN, ARPB 3517, f. 51, consul, Essen, to MSZ, 29 May 1925.

99. AAN, ARPB 1632, f. 40, consulate, Cologne, 18 Oct. 1924, reported 1,893 migrants to France in 1923; Ponty, *Polonais*, p. 67.

100. AAN, ARPB 2154, ff. 11, 117, 119, consul, Essen, to Polish ambassador, Berlin, 6 Nov. 1923, *aide-mémoire*, 19 Nov. 1923, copy.

101. Ponty, *Polonais*, p. 67; AAN, ARPB 1632, f. 40, consulate, Cologne, reported a total migration of 846 to France in 1924 from its district.

102. Klessmann, *Polnische Bergarbeiter*, p. 249.

103. AAN, ARPB 3517, ff. 20–21, 34, special report, consul, Essen, 3 Nov. 1924, report, 10 Aug. 1925. Barciszewski, "Z życia," pp. 530–531, later put the figure at over 2,000 workers.

belonged to German organizations, in the view of the consulate, a view later confirmed by leaders of the Polish community in France.[104] But many people whom the consulate regarded as respectable also migrated to France in this way, without going to the consulate and applying for Polish citizenship, skipping what seemed to them an unnecessary bureaucratic formality and travel expense.[105]

Before the end of 1924 numerous individuals returned to the Ruhr because of dissatisfaction with the conditions they found in France. Under the agreement reached in Vienna in August 1924, the German government regarded as Polish citizens those who obtained a "Certificate of Nationality" from the Polish consulate or opted for Polish citizenship, even if they did not register this with the German authorities. Thus, returning to the Ruhr as foreign citizens, they were subject to discrimination in employment and housing and ultimately to expulsion, and therefore some tried to rid themselves of Polish citizenship.[106] At the end of 1925 the returnees from France constituted the majority of the estimated 400 workers in the Ruhr with Polish citizenship, according to information that the ZZP provided to the Polish consul in Essen.[107] Still, in 1926 the Polish embassy in Berlin continued to regard migration to France of Poles in Germany as in the Polish national interest: it saw the greater population density of Germany as a threat to France and therefore to Poland.[108]

The estimated 25,000 Polish workers (ca. 100,000 with dependents) who stayed in France did not necessarily fare better.[109] They, too, were foreigners and therefore subject to discrimination and expulsion. Of great significance for those who had worked some years in the mines of the Ruhr before migrating to France was the question of pension rights. (In his memoirs one Polish miner recounted that he began work in the Ruhr

104. AAN, ARPB 3517, f. 21, special report, consul, Essen, 3 Nov. 1924; *Jubileuszowy Kalendarz*, p. 156.

105. AAN, ARPB 3517, ff. 5, 21, consul, Essen, to ambassador, Berlin, 16 Aug. 1924; special report, 3 Nov. 1924.

106. *Ibid.*, ff. 19, 40, 52, consul, Essen, special report, 3 Nov. 1924, emigration counselor, Berlin, to MSZ, 24 Sept. 1925, copy, consul, Essen, to MSZ, 29 May 1925.

107. AAN, ARPB 1632, f. 24, consul, Essen, 10 Dec. 1925.

108. AAN, ARPB 3517, f. 83, ministerial memorial, Berlin, 30 Oct. 1926.

109. Barciszewski, "Z życia," p. 530, estimated their number at 25,000, which seems reasonable in light of the above statistics; as consul he estimated their number at more or less 30,000 families or 100,000–130,000 individuals, ANN, ARPB 2019, ff. 10–14, to ambassador, Berlin, 15 July 1924, copy; Ponty, *Polonais*, p. 68, estimates the total at 100,000–130,000; Klessmann, *Polnische Bergarbeiter*, p. 166, at 50,000–80,000.

mines in 1905 and migrated to France eighteen years later.[110]) The German-Polish Social Insurance Treaty of 1931 did not cover them, nor did the equivalent French-Polish agreement of 1929. A German-French treaty was never ratified. Thus, their pensions did not include any compensation for the years spent in the mines of the Ruhr.[111]

This question seems not to have concerned the Polish consulate in Essen, which at no time raised the matter in its correspondence relating to the migration to France. Nor is there any evidence that the ZZP, which first brought up the question of the payment of pensions outside of Germany in 1919, took up the matter in its negotiations with the CCHF. Although the ZZP may have hoped that an agreement between Germany and France would eventually settle the question, the union took a firm stand on issues that threatened to undermine the effort to transfer to France a major portion of the Polish community in the Ruhr. The long-term welfare of these migrants seems to have had a lower priority for both the Polish authorities and the ZZP than their migration from Germany.

The Decline of the Polish Miners' Union in the Ruhr

Membership in the ZZP Miners' Section in the Ruhr region reached its peak in the years immediately following the war, surpassing even its pre-war membership. Official recognition of the ZZP as a negotiating partner on behalf of the Ruhr's miners along with the three other pre-war miners' unions made it a viable alternative for Polish-speaking miners at the same time as the independence of Poland raised their national consciousness.[112] Publicly, the union exhibited no sign that the changed circumstances of the Polish community in the Ruhr had affected the union's long-standing goal of organizing all of Germany's Polish miners. Thus, in December 1920, the union's *Głos Górnika* warned its members not to be fooled by attempts of the *Gewerkverein* to recruit them with claims that the ZZP had lost all significance and that therefore as Catholics they should join the

---

110. Quoted in Ponty, *Polonais*, pp. 113–114.

111. Janusz Holdert, *En toi, France: mes racines meurtries* (Paris: La Pensée Universelle, 1977), p. 12; Klessmann, *Polnische Bergarbeiter*, pp. 167–168; Edward Kołodziej, *Wychodźstwo zarobkowe z Polski 1918–1939: Studia nad polityką emigracyjną II Rzeczypospolitej* (Warsaw: Książka i Wiedza, 1982), pp. 167–168. The same was true of Belgium.

112. A worker who spoke at a Polish election meeting in Bochum, 3 June 1920, claimed that he only recently came to the realization that he was a Pole, STAM, OP 5760, report, 4 June 1920.

Christian trade union. Similarly, the ZZP reacted sharply against reports in 1921 of works councils forcing management to fire employees simply for belonging to the Polish trade union.[113] When, however, these firings affected the lignite mines of central Germany, where the ZZP Miners' Section had fewer members, its chairman Kołpacki recommended to a local union leader that the ZZP members join the Christian trade union. Instead, the local leader succeeded in getting a court to intervene on behalf of his members.[114] This incident demonstrates that after the war the leadership of the ZZP Miners' Section in Bochum had set its course on the union's retrenchment. The leadership simply saw no future for the union or its members in Germany. The union program voted at the second congress of the ZZP in Poznań at the end of July 1923 put it this way: "The ZZP recognizes that the terrain for the resolution of the workers' question can only be one's own law-abiding, democratic sovereign Polish state."[115] The program made no reference to those workers who did not find themselves within the borders of that state. This view together with the ambition of playing a role in the new Polish state and its labor movement motivated a large number of activists to return to the homeland and take up positions there. In April 1920 Jan Brejski credited them with having organized the workers of Upper Silesia, Poznania, and Pomerania "under the national banner" and teaching them discipline.[116]

In keeping with this nationalist view, the ZZP became deeply involved in facilitating and expediting the departure from the Ruhr of its own members. It remains only to outline this self-liquidation of the Polish miners' union in the Ruhr. Of course, other developments that we have described also contributed to the decline and eventual disappearance of the union, and we must consider their effects. The ZZP lost members just as the recognized German-led unions did for their support of the status quo established in Germany after the revolution in November 1918. By

113. *Głos Górnika*, No. 22, 10 Dec. 1920, in *Uebersetzungen aus westfälischen und anderen polnischen Zeitungen*, No. 48, 11 Dec. 1920, HSTAD, RD 16021, f. 236; STAM, RM VII, Nr. 31, f. 52, Polizeirat, Bochum, 15 Sept. 1921.

114. AAN, ARPB 1836, ff. 222–223, 299, 353–354, consulate general, attaché for emigration affairs, 14 May 1921; Jan Chrapczak, Welzow, to Kołpacki, 26 May 1921, copy, decision of Amtsgericht, Senftenberg, 11 June 1921, copy.

115. Franciszek Mańkowski, "Historja Z.Z.P.," in *Ćwierć wieku pracy dla Narodu i Robotnika* (Poznań: Nakładem Zarządu Centralnego Zjedn. Zawod. Polskiego, 1927), pp. 34–266; Marjan Chełmikowski, *Związki zawodowe robotników polskich w Królestwie Pruskim (1889–1918)* (Poznań: Fiszer i Majewski, 1925), p. 203.

116. AAN, ARPB 1835, Jan Brejski, to the Ministry of the Formerly Prussian Zone, April 1920, copy.

joining with the German unions in opposing the revolutionary movements that emerged in the years following the war, the ZZP alienated those among its members who found the concessions wrested from the German government and employers inadequate. The overwhelming majority of ZZP members initially seemed more interested in leaving Germany than in changing the worker's status in Germany, but as early as 1920 the economic reality of the new Poland was deferring or even dashing dreams of returning to the homeland. Moreover, those born and raised in the Ruhr had less desire to migrate to the homeland they never knew. Even before the war long-term migrants seem to have thought of the Ruhr region as their home.[117] Many of their children underwent a process of Germanization, which led them to resist emigration from the Ruhr and to join German unions when they came of age.[118]

Nevertheless, the migration out of Germany had a significant impact on the membership of the ZZP in the Ruhr. Moreover, the involvement of the ZZP in the efforts to organize the migration added extra force to this impact. One might argue that the Polish consulate's requirement that individuals obtain an endorsement of a Polish association before being issued a visa, passport, or "Certificate of Nationality" created an incentive for membership in Polish organizations like the ZZP.[119] But it also meant that precisely those who joined Polish organizations like the ZZP had an easier time leaving Germany than the Polish-speaking residents of the Ruhr who distanced themselves from the Polish community and its organizations.

In 1921 the ZZP Miners' Section showed little outward sign that it had embarked on the path of self-liquidation. That year in Bochum it held its first general meeting since before the war.[120] According to his annual

117. John J. Kulczycki, "Uwarunkowania świadomości narodowej polskich górników w Zagłębiu Ruhry przed I wojną światową," in *Pamiętnik XV Powszechnego Zjazdu Historyków Polskich*, ed. by Jacek Staszewski (Gdańsk-Toruń: Wydawnictwo Adam Marszałek, 1995), Vol. I, Part 2, pp. 151–159.

118. AAN, ARPB 2019, ff. 11–14, report, consul, Essen, 15 July 1924, copy; ARPB 2196, f. 68, vice-consul, Essen, 3 Oct. 1927; Michał Lengowski, *Na Warmii i w Westfalii* (Warsaw: Pax, 1972), pp. 109, 111, speaks of the Germanization of children of even those active in the Polish community in the Ruhr; see also Wojciech Wawrzynek, "Polacy westfalsko-nadreńscy w dwudziestoleciu między wojennym," *Kwartalnik Opolski*, IX, No. 4 (1963), 85.

119. AAN, ARPB 1835, Jan Brejski, to the Ministry of the Formerly Prussian Zone, April 1920, copy, noted this practice; ARPB 3517, f. 50, consul, Essen, to MSZ, 29 May 1925, copy, indicates that the practice continued into the following years.

120. Franciszek Kołpacki, "Zjednoczenie Zawodowe Polskie we Westfalji (w Niemczech)," in *Ćwierć wieku pracy dla Narodu i Robotnika* (Poznań: Nakładem Zarządu Centralnego Zjedn. Zawod. Polskiego, 1927), p. 488.

report on the Polish movement, the police counselor in Bochum in September 1921 still regarded the union as one of the strongest and most active organizations in the Polish community in the Ruhr region. In almost all places where a larger number of Polish miners resided, the union had legal aid bureaus and offered classes in Polish language, literature, and history. Meetings organized by the union numbered in the hundreds.[121]

Nevertheless, after reaching a peak immediately after the war, union membership began to decline. Precise figures on the membership of the ZZP Miners' Section after the war are often impossible to establish. Different sources give different figures, particularly as membership dwindled. In August 1921 the Polish consul in Essen reported that for tactical reasons Polish organizations used inflated membership figures in their relations with the German authorities and German organizations. Thus, whereas he confidentially put the membership of the ZZP Miners' Section at 40,000, a month later in September 1921 the police counselor of Bochum reported that it stood at 60,000 in 280 locals.[122] At its first congress held in independent Poland in October 1921, the ZZP allotted the Miners' Union of the Rhineland and Westphalia delegates based on a membership of 45,018 in 286 locals.[123]

Another sign of the decline in importance of the ZZP came in the miners' elections of 1921, despite what the police counselor of Bochum called "very zealous agitation" on behalf of its own candidates. The union's appeal for votes in the *Wiarus Polski* of 10 July 1921 spoke of the election as "a test of strength" with the goal of achieving representation proportional to the number of Polish miners employed in the Ruhr.[124] Yet fewer of the ZZP candidates won than in the first elections after the war for the works councils (110 compared with 190 in 1920) and for the worker chambers (two compared with four in 1919). Also, the union retained only twenty-six of the thirty seats on the pension board that it had won in 1910.[125]

121. STAM, RM VII, Nr. 31, f. 53, Polizeirat, Bochum, 15 Sept. 1921.

122. AAN, ARPB 184, f. 79, consul, Essen, 24 Aug. 1921; STAM, RM VII, Nr. 31, Polizeirat, Bochum, 15 Sept. 1921.

123. Mańkowski, "Historja," p. 187. According to *Dzieje Zjednoczenia Zawodowego Polskiego 1889–1939* (Chorzów: Nakładem Kartelu Zjednoczenia Zawodowego Polskiego na Śląsku, 1939), pp. 80, 91, the Miners' Section had 45,000 members in 1920 and 33,200 in 1921.

124. STAM, RM VII, Nr. 31, ff. 53–54, Polizeirat, Bochum, 15 Sept. 1921.

125. Christoph Klessmann, "Klassensolidarität und nationales Bewusstsein. Das Verhältnis zwischen der Polnischen Berufsvereinigung (ZZP) und den deutschen Bergarbeiter-Gewerkschaften im Ruhrgebiet 1902–1923," *Internationale Wissenschaftliche*

Migration out of Germany may well account for most of the union's decline.[126] As we have seen, not only did thousands of Polish migrants return to the homeland by 1921, but also the migration further West, particularly to France, began. Other factors, however, played a role as well. Kołpacki himself admitted that, following the Kapp Putsch in 1920, "Our members began to have doubts about our organization."[127] In his report on union membership in the Ruhr in 1921, the Polish consul noted that about 5,500 Polish miners did not belong to any union. In addition, he estimated that about 4,500 Polish miners and metalworkers joined German unions to escape the anti-Polish harassment of German workers that prompted many other migrants to leave Germany.[128]

Following the deadline for opting for Polish citizenship in January 1922, emigration from the Ruhr to France increased at the same time as it continued to the homeland. German officials noted a distinct decline in Polish organizational activity.[129] This found reflection in a further decrease in mandates for candidates of the ZZP to the works councils in 1922, from 110 the previous year to 86. (Votes for Polish candidates declined by even more, from 5.93 percent of the total to 4.17 percent.[130])

Although Kołpacki later claimed that the ZZP Miners' Section lost 16,000 members through emigration in 1922, the second congress of the ZZP in Poznań in 1923 allotted the Bochum miners' union nine votes based on a membership of 33,200.[131] Total membership seems to have declined proportionally less than that of other unions: the *Alter Verband* recorded a loss of nearly 30 percent of its members in 1922.[132] Still, a more than 25 percent decline in the number of ZZP union locals from the previous year indicates a significant weakening of the union structure in 1922.

Korrespondenz zur Geschichte der deutschen Arbeiterbewegung, X (1974), 156.

126. AAN, ARPB 356, ff. 16–17, embassy, Berlin, to MSZ, 8 May 1922, attributed the decline in the mandates for the works councils to re-emigration.

127. Kołpacki, "Zjednoczenie," p. 488.

128. AAN, ARPB 184, f. 80, consul, Essen, 24 Aug. 1921.

129. HSTAD, RD 15379, f. 233, Nachrichtenblatt, No. 54, 21 May 1922.

130. AAN, ARPB 356, f. 16, embassy, Berlin, to MSZ, 8 May 1922.

131. Kołpacki, "Zjednoczenie," p. 488; Mańkowski, "Historja," p. 202. AAN, ARPB 1632, f. 28, consul, Essen, 10 Dec. 1925, reported 36,000 members in the miners' union in the Ruhr for 1921–22 and 22,000 for 1922–23, based on incomplete information from the ZZP; ARPB 2019, ff. 14–15, consul, Essen, 15 July 1924, spoke of 38,000 in the ZZP before 1923, but these may include the metalworkers' union and members in all of Germany; STAM, RM VII, Nr. 35, p. 72, Polizeirat, Bochum, 1 Oct. 1922, estimated the membership of the ZZP Miners' Section to be about 40,000 in 208 union locals in the Ruhr.

132. Klessmann, "Klassensolidarität," p. 154.

Nevertheless, the Polish miners' union had not yet yielded its role in the labor movement in the Ruhr nor internationally. Before the war, the ZZP had remained a member of the miners' International even after the *Gewerkverein* split away and joined in the formation of an international association of Christian unions in 1908. But when the old division in the international movement reappeared after the war and the *Gewerkverein* took the initiative to organize an international union of Christian miners in 1922, the ZZP joined it. Kołpacki had the honor of opening its first congress, in Innsbruck in June 1922, and was chosen vice-president of the organization.[133] The Bochum police counselor noted no slackening of union activity in his annual report in 1922 and referred to the ZZP Miners' Section as "the strongest and most active" Polish organization in western Germany after the National Workers' Party.[134] But the premier standing of the party indicated that in taking over some political functions that the ZZP had itself performed before 1914 the party contributed to the lessening of the union's importance.

The Allied occupation of the nerve centers of the Ruhr in 1923 created special problems for the ZZP Miners' Section of the Ruhr. Emigration continued: according to Kołpacki, 14,000 Polish workers left the Ruhr in 1923.[135] Economics, however, posed perhaps a greater threat to the existence of the Polish miners' union than emigration. Inflation and unemployment that stemmed from the rationalization of the mining industry impoverished workers to the point that they could no longer afford to pay their union dues regularly. Deprived of steady income, the unions in turn could not give unemployment benefits to their members. This was especially true of the ZZP, which derived its funds almost solely from members' dues. The Miners' Section of Bochum only survived thanks to subsidies of 800 francs from the International Christian Union of Miners and several million Polish marks from the ZZP central directorate in Poznań. Still, the union could not meet the demands for assistance from its members, who consequently quit in droves and joined German trade unions, including—according to the Polish consulate—communist organizations.[136] As a result the ZZP had what a

---

133. Wolfgang Jäger and Klaus Tenfelde, *Bildgeschichte der deutschen Bergarbeiterbewegung* (Munich: Beck, 1989), pp. 112–113; Kołpacki, "Zjednoczenie," pp. 488–489; AAN, ARPB 2019, ff. 11–14, consul, Essen, 15 July 1924, copy; ARPB 1632, f. 30, consul, Essen, 10 Dec. 1925.

134. STAM, RM VII, Nr. 35, pp. 77–78, Polizeirat, Bochum, 1 Oct. 1922.

135. Kołpacki, "Zjednoczenie," pp. 488–489.

136. AAN, ARPB 1632, ff. 29–30, consul, Essen, 10 Dec. 1925; ARPB 2019, ff. 11–15, consul, Essen, 15 July 1924.

later police report called the worst year in its history as membership in the Miners' Section fell in 1923 by some 60 percent to 13,400 according to the union's own figures.[137]

In 1924 the Miners' Section fared no better than the previous year. Emigration to France continued at a high rate, but again other factors played an important role in undermining the Polish trade union. Dissatisfaction among rank and file miners over the temporary lengthening of the workday agreed to in December 1923 made itself felt in the elections to the works councils in late March 1924. The *Alter Verband* and the ZZP suffered the heaviest losses, the representation of the ZZP dropping to a mere ten seats from the eighty-six garnered in 1922. In the election of pension fund elders later that year, ZZP candidates received 62 percent fewer votes than in the previous election in 1921 and retained only six of their twenty-six mandates.[138]

Worse than the losses, from the point of view of the Polish authorities, the biggest gains went to the communist union. The Polish consulate in Cologne claimed in 1924 that a large portion of the Polish workers in the Rhineland had joined communist organizations, though for economic reasons rather than ideological ones.[139] In his analysis, the consul in Essen also concluded that "ours went massively into communist ranks." He saw this as the result of a series of political failures. First, the leaders of the Polish community in the Ruhr promised that with Polish independence the migrants would be able to return to the homeland and find "mountains of gold" there, which did not come to pass. Then inflation reduced their savings from decades of work to nothing, so they could not return to the homeland. Many were too old to be recruited for work in France. Persecuted as Poles, they followed the old adage of seeing an ally in an enemy—the communists—of their enemy—the German government and the existing socio-economic and political system.[140]

Then in May 1924 the confrontation between the recognized unions and management over the length of the workday led to a lockout that lasted for most of the month. This conflict and the dismissals that followed dealt a catastrophic blow to the ZZP Miners' Section. Its

137. STAM, OP 5758, f. 541, report on the Polish movement, 1 Jan. 1928, based on a report of the ZZP in 1927; AAN, ARPB 2019, ff. 14–15, consul, Essen, 15 July 1924, copy, cited an even lower figure of 12,000 members in 1923.

138. AAN, ARPP 50, ff. 34–36, 113, Political Report, No. I, 7 April 1924, copy, consulate, Essen, n.d.

139. AAN, ARPB 1842, f. 455, consul general, Cologne, to MSZ, 18 Oct. 1924.

140. AAN, ARPP 50, ff. 34–36, Political Report, No. I, 7 April 1924, copy; quotes on f. 34.

reserves virtually destroyed by inflation, the ZZP could not provide its members with any financial support. In search of assistance, many ZZP members joined German unions. As a result ZZP membership, already diminished in 1923, shrank by more than half, to 4,792.[141] In a later analysis the Polish consulate attributed the decline of the ZZP in part to the defeat of 1924 and the resulting opinion that larger strikes had no chance of success and therefore paying dues to a trade union served no purpose.[142]

The Final Phase in the History of the ZZP in the Ruhr

The Polish consuls of Essen and Cologne saw 1924 as a turning point in the history of the Polish community in the Ruhr, one that marked its loss of all importance. In a report in mid-July 1924 on Polish organizations in the Ruhr region, the Polish consul in Essen pointed out that most members were older and that the participation of the younger generation was small. The Polish community's concentration on returning to the homeland led it to neglect the development of Polish schools after the war. In addition, a lack of funds prevented Polish associations from organizing activities that could compete with German associations in attracting young people. Furthermore, the consul noted, membership in a Polish association could result in some everyday difficulties. Thus only a third of Polish workers belonged to the Polish trade union.[143]

But the ZZP could not even compete with other Polish organizations. According to the Polish consul general in Cologne, the Polish Union of [Catholic] Church Associations and Confraternities of the Rosary for Mutual Assistance (*Związek Wzajemnej Pomocy Towarszystw Kościelnych i Bractw Różańcowych*) had 554 members in thirteen associations within his area of jurisdiction whereas the ZZP had 437 members in eight union locals. In Lintfort, where the same person chaired the ZZP union local and the St. Barbara Association—named for the patron saint of miners—the

141. AAN, ARPB 2196, ff. 16, 19, Cultural-Educational Report No. 6, consul, Essen, 21 May 1927; STAM, OP 5758, f. 541, report on the Polish movement, 1 Jan. 1928, based on a report of the ZZP in 1927.

142. AAN, ARPB 2196, f. 68, vice-consul, Essen, 3 Oct. 1927, mistakenly referred to the "strike" as occurring in 1922.

143. AAN, ARPB 2019, ff. 11, 18, consul, Essen, 15 July 1924, copy; ARPB 1842, f. 468, consul general, Cologne, to MSZ, 18 Oct. 1924, copy.

latter Catholic association had sixty members but the union had only forty.[144]

At the end of 1924 the Polish consul in Essen sent an optimistic report to his superiors at the embassy in Berlin stating that Polish organizations in the Ruhr had overcome the crisis caused by the occupation of the Ruhr, inflation, unemployment, and emigration. Citing statistics supposedly from the end of September 1924 that put the membership of the ZZP Miners' Section in the Ruhr at 9,171 (9,421 in all of Germany) in 147 union locals (162 in all of Germany), he claimed that the ZZP was on its way to offsetting its heavy losses in membership, especially in 1923.[145] These statistics, however, may have had an earlier provenance, before the May lockout, from which the Polish consulate later dated the crisis of the ZZP.[146] In any case, in 1925 there was no sign of a supposed reclamation of membership, only that of a steady erosion.

In December 1925 the Polish consulate in Essen issued a long report on the state of the Polish community in the Ruhr region. It claimed that employers valued the Polish worker and as a result laid off proportionally fewer Poles than native workers. This, however, caused friction between German and Polish workers. With unemployment widespread, the German worker tended to see an enemy in every foreigner, and in the Ruhr this meant the Polish worker. Although the report maintained that incidents of harassment were relatively few, they were usually initiated by nationalist-inclined lower officials or envious German workers. The report also blamed anti-Polish campaigns in the press and public meetings, as occurred in August 1925 in connection with the migration to Germany of Germans from Poland and their reports of mistreatment there.[147]

With regard to the ZZP Miners' Section, the report stated it had a current membership of 3,000—the ZZP later gave the more precise figure of 3,180.[148] Despite its shrunken condition, the consulate regarded it as an organization of significance because of its continued status as one of four

144. AAN, ARPB 1842, ff. 469–470, consul general, Cologne, to MSZ, 18 Oct. 1924, copy.

145. AAN, ARPB 2019, ff. 50–54, 57, 70, report, 19 Dec. 1924, consul, Essen, 30 Dec. 1924; note that this report, f. 43, claims to contain more accurate statistics than the report of 15 July 1924, whose statistics seem more credible.

146. AAN, ARPB 2196, f. 16, Cultural-Educational Report No. 6, consulate, Essen, 21 May 1927. The totals given for Sept. 1924 appear again for 1923–1924 in a later listing of membership based on ZZP data, AAN, ARPB 1632, f. 28, Essen, consul, 10 Dec. 1925.

147. AAN, ARPB 1632, ff. 26–27, consul, Essen, 10 Dec. 1925.

148. STAM, OP 5758, f. 541, report on the Polish movement, 1 Jan. 1928, based a report of the ZZP in 1927.

recognized miners' unions with the right to represent workers in negotiations with management. The report reviewed the post-war history of the ZZP and attributed its decline to massive emigration from the Ruhr—in 1925 another 3,000 who opted for Polish citizenship returned to the homeland—and economic pressures caused by inflation and unemployment, unemployment which in 1925 grew to an unprecedented extent in the Ruhr. Here the report linked the impoverishment of the worker in a vicious circle with the weakening of the ZZP as the consulate had previously done: the worker unable to pay his dues, and without dues the union unable to assist the worker.[149]

As for the future the report emphasized that the Polish community in the Ruhr no longer constituted an *"emigration"* but rather a *"naturalized* Polish colony."* Its migratory links with the homeland had withered, and it had acclimated to a foreign environment while maintaining its Polish character. Moreover, the report concluded, *"One needs to consider its liquidation."* The consulate believed the national consciousness of the community strong enough to resist liquidation by Germanization in the near future. Nevertheless, the process of liquidation would inevitably progress, and therefore one should seek to direct it so as to transfer the "moral-social forces" of the community to another terrain where they could again take part in Polish life.[150]

Membership in the ZZP Miners' Section slipped further in 1926, to 2,875.[151] Moreover, the union's financial standing significantly worsened. Some 500 of its members were living on disability or retirement pensions and as such paid dues of only 20 Pfennige per month (compared with as much as 80 Pfennige per week for other members), for which they received free legal assistance and death benefits. Although they thus constituted a drain on the union's resources, it needed their votes in elections in the mines. The total collected in dues of 47,915 marks in 1926 also suggests that many members did not pay their dues regularly or paid lower dues because of low earnings. In addition, the administrative apparatus of the union ate up about two thirds of the income, leaving barely a third to cover the assistance to members foreseen in the statutes.[152]

149. AAN, ARPB 1632, ff. 27–30, consul, Essen, 10 Dec. 1925.

150. *Ibid.*, ff. 30–31, emphasis in original.

151. STAM, OP 5758, f. 541, report on the Polish movement, 1 Jan. 1928, based a report of the ZZP in 1927.

152. AAN, ARPB 2196, ff. 19–20, 68, 78, Cultural-Educational Report No. 6, consulate, Essen, 21 May 1927, vice-consul, Essen, 3 Oct. 1927, consulate general, Berlin, to emigration counselor, 21 Oct. 1927.

Although the Polish consulate regarded the members of the ZZP as predominantly in sympathy with socialism, it recognized the union's Polish national character. Therefore it still saw the ZZP as an important alternative for Polish workers to membership in German unions.[153] In an attempt to solve the union's economic crisis, the consulate proposed that the Polish organizations of the Ruhr region join together in a financial union, which would be subsidized by the Polish government. The consulate would pressure the Polish inhabitants of the Ruhr to support the new central organization by refusing their requests unless accompanied by certification from the organization. In the view of the consulate, if the ZZP could in this way build up its financial reserves, it would be able to attract members from German unions by offering the same protection at considerably less cost to the worker than the 5–6 marks in monthly dues collected by German unions.[154]

This forlorn scheme lost all feasibility as membership in the ZZP Miners' Section fell by nearly a quarter in the first six months of 1927, to 2,200.[155] Also, the proposal encountered resistance from the individual Polish organizations, which competed for membership and valued their autonomy. Indeed, the consulate singled out the Union of Poles in Germany (*Związek Polaków w Niemczech* or ZPwN) as one of the causes for the decline in the importance of the ZZP in the Polish community in the Ruhr.[156] Founded in 1922 as an organization uniting all the Poles of Germany, the ZPwN took over leadership from the regional Polish organizations, including the Executive Committee in the Ruhr. The ZPwN also assumed the national cultural agenda of the ZZP, making the union less central to the life of the Polish community than it had been previously. The Polish consulate in Essen promoted the new organization, creating the impression that "only he who belongs to the Union of Poles is a good Pole."[157] With its lower monthly dues, the ZPwN attracted more members in the Ruhr than the ZZP. In 1927 the consulate estimated that

---

153. *Ibid.*, ff. 34, 78, consulate, Essen, to consul general, Bytom, copy, consulate general, Berlin, to emigration counselor, 21 Oct. 1927.

154. *Ibid.*, f. 26, Cultural-Educational Report No. 6, 21 May 1927.

155. AAN, ARPB 2019, ff. 194–195, archival note, 4 July 1927; ARPB 2196, f. 68, vice-consul, Essen, 3 Oct. 1927.

156. AAN, ARPB 2196, f. 70, vice-consul, Essen, 3 Oct. 1927; Wojciech Wrzesiński, *Polski ruch narodowy w Niemczech w latach 1922–1939* (Wrocław, Warsaw, Cracow: Zakład Narodowy im. Ossolińskich, 1993), p. 85, claims without presenting any evidence that the ZZP was completely subordinated to the ZPwN and yet the latter feared that the ZZP would become a competitor.

157. AAN, ARPB 2196, f. 33, consulate, Essen, to consul general, Bytom, 30 June 1927.

the membership of the ZPwN in the Ruhr included 3,000 potential members of the ZZP who did not belong to the union and instead mostly belonged to the Union of Church Associations for Mutual Assistance.[158] Failing to achieve a financial union of Polish organizations, the Polish consulate promoted the fusion of the Miners' Section with the Metalworkers' Section of the ZZP as a way of preventing their collapse and of lowering administrative costs. The fusion came at a general assembly of the union at the end of October 1927, which also chose a common directorate, with Kołpacki as chairman. The Metalworkers' Section had even fewer members than the Miners' Section—it had 980 members in the Ruhr region at the end of June 1927—so that even after the fusion the membership of the ZZP in the Ruhr stood at just over 3,000.[159]

The new year brought the next blow to the union when the long-time treasurer of the Miners' Section Jan Kot was arrested and charged with embezzlement, a particularly embarrassing accusation in light of the union's financial woes. The trial in February 1928 revealed that Kot, who held his salaried post (290 marks per month in 1928) since 1923, siphoned off union funds from 1924 until January 1928, a total of 8,445 marks, which he allegedly spent on "women of easy virtue."[160] Although this further undermined the standing of the union in the Polish community, it removed a leading opponent of the financial union of Polish organizations advocated by the Polish consulate. Therefore the Polish consul saw this as an opportunity to carry out a thorough reorganization of the union and bring it back to life. The director of the Union of Poles, Dr. Jan Kaczmarek, himself born in Bochum the son of a coal miner, issued a public declaration promising the same.

Although one cannot speak of a revival of the union, its drastic decline halted at least temporarily: in 1929 membership stood at 2,923 miners and metalworkers in the Ruhr region, only slightly less than in 1927.[161] Also, the union claimed to have intervened successfully in over 3,200 cases in defense of the legal rights of Polish workers in the years 1929–1931.[162] The Polish consulate regarded this type of legal assistance as the most

158. *Ibid.*, f. 24, Cultural-Educational Report No. 6, 21 May 1927.

159. *Ibid.*, ff. 68–69, 77, vice-consul, Essen, 3 Oct. 1927, consulate general, Berlin, to emigration counselor, Berlin, 21 Oct. 1927.

160. *Ibid.*, ff. 86–89, consul, Essen, 25 Jan. 1928, 8 March 1928; quote on f. 89.

161. Klessmann, *Polnische Bergarbeiter*, p. 175.

162. *Naród*, No. 151, 3 July 1932, clipping, AAN, ARPB 2196, f. 115.

important service that the ZZP could provide its members.[163] But the worldwide economic depression that began in these years intensified the pressure on the union. Increased unemployment meant paying more benefits to the union's members. As a result, the union ran a deficit of 11,505.20 marks in 1930, which grew by another 4,587.68 marks before the end of April 1931.[164]

In these circumstances, ZZP chairman Kołpacki turned to the Polish consulate in Essen for a financial subsidy. He claimed that the ZZP had a reserve fund in April 1931 of just 6,000 marks, which soon declined to 5,000 marks, at a time when both metalworkers and miners were fighting for higher wages, which in Kołpacki's view might well lead to a strike or a lockout. The consulate feared that the collapse of the ZZP, the oldest Polish organization in Germany, would have a serious negative effect on Polish organizational life in the Ruhr whereas helping it to survive the economic crisis would enable the union to realize its plans for broadening its activities. Therefore the consulate supported a request for 3,000 marks, which apparently was granted.[165] But optimism about the union's survival and even revival assumed an early end to the economic depression.

In addition to the decline in membership and resources of the ZZP, the Polish community in the Ruhr, which constituted the union's main base, was caught in a conflict over its leadership. The Union of Church Associations for Mutual Assistance and the local section of the Union of Poles, the two most important Polish umbrella organizations in the Ruhr region, broke off all contact with each other in 1931.[166] The ZZP could ill afford to become involved in a split within the Polish community. But Kołpacki opposed the hegemony of the Union of Poles over the Polish community and was a bitter enemy of the ZPwN leader Dr. Kaczmarek. Thus, when in May 1932 the ZZP announced that it would hold its triennial general assembly in Bochum on 19 June 1932, rumors circulated that the meeting would result in the liquidation of the ZZP and that the Union of Church Associations would elect Kołpacki as its chairman and take over the union's headquarters in Bochum.[167]

The fourteenth general assembly of the ZZP of Bochum gave no clear signal that it would be the last. Only thirty-eight delegates participated,

163. *Ibid.*, f. 72, vice-consul, Essen, 10 Oct. 1927.

164. *Ibid.*, ff. 96–97, 100, consul, Essen, 25 April 1931.

165. *Ibid.*, f. 96–98, 100, Kołpacki, to consulate, Essen, 9 April 1931, consul, Essen, 25 April 1931.

166. AAN, ARPB 2053, ff. 573–574, vice-consul, Essen, 24 Oct. 1931; Wrzesiński, *Polski ruch*, p. 238.

167. AAN, ARPB 2196, f. 152, consul, Essen, 14 May 1932.

and just two from Berlin came from outside of the region. But the guests included the chairman of the central directorate of the ZZP in Poland and long-time activist in the Ruhr Mańkowski, the chairman of the ZZP Miners' Section of Polish Silesia in Katowice, and Dr. Kaczmarek of the Union of Poles as well as the leaders of the most important Polish organizations in the Ruhr. In an allusion to local quarrels, Mańkowski in his speech noted the unity of the German minority in Poland and urged the same on the Polish community in the Ruhr region. The chairman of the ZZP Miners' Section in Katowice spoke about the economic crisis as evidence of the bankruptcy of the capitalist system and called for unity in the ranks of workers as well as for cooperation among Poles abroad.[168]

In the discussion at the assembly, Kołpacki came in for heavy criticism for his contacts with the Union of Church Associations. The ZZP chairman defended himself, claiming that Union of Church Associations alone of all local Polish organizations supported the ZZP and therefore he would continue to work with it. The Polish consul in Essen, however, reported that the ZZP representatives from Poland, who in a sense were Kołpacki's superiors, assured the consul that they would pressure Kołpacki into supporting national unity and remaining neutral in the local conflict. In any case, the general assembly reelected Kołpacki as chairman of the ZZP in Germany.[169]

Although the rumor that the general assembly would result in the liquidation of the Polish trade union in the Ruhr proved false, the amendments to its statute voted at the meeting indicated its profound weakness. For the duration of the current economic crisis, the changes in the statute suspended benefits for unemployed members and death benefits for the widows of members. Also, instead of the principle of electing one delegate to the general assembly for every 200 members, locals with as few as ten members would have the right to elect a delegate. The report on administration of the union made at the general assembly further demonstrated the union's decline. Whereas in 1928 it employed three officials, it currently had merely one and a typist on its payroll.[170]

Nevertheless, optimism continued to reign. Kołpacki took part in a meeting of the International Christian Union of Miners in Antwerp. Also, the Union of Poles had wide-ranging plans to revive the ZZP, though a lack of funds would remain an obstacle for the near term. The Polish

---

168. *Naród*, No. 151, 3 July 1932, clipping, AAN, ARPB 2196, f. 115.

169. *Ibid.*, ff. 115, 160, *Naród*, No. 151, 3 July 1932, clipping, consul, Essen, 25 June 1932.

170. *Ibid.*

consulate credited the ZPwN with having prevented the liquidation of the ZZP and with covertly introducing more active elements into the directorate of the ZZP capable of raising the quality of its work.[171] But the economic crisis did not ease and took on a new dimension with the appointment of Adolf Hitler as German chancellor in January 1933. In March and April his National Socialist German Workers' Party (NSDAP) undertook a series of actions directed against the Polish minority. At the Prosper mine in Bottrop, the technical director of the mine, a NSDAP member, posted an announcement that warned, "We cannot protect those elements who do not recognize the German language as their own and who in this way give visible expression that their interests do not coincide with the interests of Germany. It is possible that those persons who do not heed this warning will be arrested for their own protection."[172] Elsewhere individuals lost their jobs if they in any way acknowledged their Polish national identity. Although the economic crisis resulted in the laying off of Germans as well, two thirds of the Poles of the Ruhr were still unemployed in 1935, which suggests they constituted a particular target.[173] Before the end of April 1933 the Polish consul in Essen reported,

> the terror directed against the Polish minority not only is unceasing but on the contrary is continually widening, taking the form, on one hand, of a planned struggle against the Polish minority and its organizational life, and, on the other hand, of unplanned terrorist attacks of separate groups and individuals against particular Poles.[174]

This took its toll of the number of Polish activists and membership in Polish organizations in the Ruhr region.[175]

At the beginning of May 1933, the National Socialist *Deutsche Arbeitsfront* (DAF) supplanted the German trade unions. It did not encompass the ZZP, but the Polish trade union lost the right to represent workers in disputes with management, and pressure built on individual Polish workers to join the DAF. Nevertheless, the union's monthly journal

---

171. *Ibid.*, ff. 115, 121, *Naród*, No. 151, 3 July 1932, clipping, chargé d'affaires, Berlin, to MSZ, 22 Aug. 1932.

172. Wrzesiński, *Polski ruch*, p. 251.

173. Christoph Klessmann, "Zur rechtlichen und sozialen Lage der Polen im Ruhrgebiet im Dritten Reich," *Archiv für Sozialgeschichte*, XVII (1977), 182–183.

174. Wrzesiński, *Polski ruch*, p. 253.

175. *Ibid.*, p. 257; Anna Poniatowska, "Organizacja Związku Polaków w Niemczech," in *Związek Polaków w Niemczech w latach 1922–1982*, ed. by Jerzy Marczewski (Warsaw: Wydawnictwo Polonia, 1987), p. 57.

Zjednoczenie maintained an optimistic tone in December 1933, arguing that the German national revolution had no place for Poles and therefore, "if Polish workers do not want to be without protection and provision, they must without fail to the last man pull together and belong to the ZZP."[176] It was a promise on which the ZZP could hardly deliver. Because the Geneva Convention concerning the division of Silesia between Germany and Poland afforded some protection to the national minorities of that region, the ZZP moved its headquarters from Bochum to Zabrze in German Silesia, where it continued to publish its monthly *Zjednoczenie* even after it ceased publication in Bochum in April 1934. A further decline in membership forced the closing of the ZZP office in Bochum as of 1 July 1934, ending with barely a whimper nearly thirty-two years of history of the Polish miners' union in the Ruhr region.[177]

Hitler's coming to power only delivered the *coup de grâce* to the ZZP Miners' Section in the Ruhr region. The birth of an independent Poland following the defeat of Germany in the world war diverted the attention of the leadership of the union from the labor movement in the Ruhr region to the nascent labor movement in Poland. The most experienced and energetic elements in the union leadership moved to occupy leading positions in the ZZP in the homeland and in the new Polish administration.

Meanwhile, the widespread nationalist conviction that the migrants should return to the homeland prompted the ZZP in the Ruhr to work towards that end. When the Polish authorities, particularly the Polish consulate in Essen, argued the impracticality of an early return migration, the union leaders cooperated with the Polish authorities in first restraining and then redirecting the emigration from the Ruhr, even though Polish officials generally put the new state's *raison d'état* ahead of the welfare of the Polish migrants and had a negative view of their potential influence in the new Polish state. A constant stream of new migrants from the East maintained the vitality of Polish organizations in the Ruhr before the war. Migration from the Ruhr compounded the inevitable decline of the Polish community without this source of new recruits.[178]

---

176. Quoted in Klessmann, "Zur rechtlichen und sozialen Lage," p. 183.

177. Wrzesiński, *Polski ruch*, p. 265; Klessmann, *Polnische Bergarbeiter*, pp. 175, 180, 255; *Leksykon Polactwa w Niemczech* (Warsaw: Państwowe Wydawnictwo Naukowe, 1973), p. 63, lists the ZZP as one of the organizations in Bochum at the time of its printing (1939), but any locals still in existence had lost all significance as trade unions.

178. Lengowski, *Na Warmii*, p. 111.

Consciously engaging in a process of self-liquidation, the ZZP nevertheless struggled to maintain itself as long as a Polish community existed in the Ruhr region. In this it did not succeed. It could not effectively compete with other Polish organizations oriented toward sustaining the life of the Polish minority in Germany. Stripped of the political and cultural roles that it performed for the Polish community in the Ruhr before the war, the ZZP had no function except that of a trade union. But, along with the other recognized trade unions, to which it subordinated itself, the ZZP lost the confidence of miners who did not accept the existing working conditions and who turned to other, more radical groups. Moveover, as its membership and financial resources declined, the ZZP could no longer provide the benefits of membership in a trade union. The course the ZZP had chosen doomed it before the Nazis effected its demise.

Too late some of the old activists of the Polish community in the Ruhr realized that they had overlooked the possibility of leading the community in a different direction. In about 1933 they concluded, "Too bad that it happened this way, because we could have created a small Poland in Westphalia, in which we would have fared better than in the fatherland."[179] But just as they could not have foreseen the consequences of encouraging emigration following the war, they could not have known what impact the Nazi regime would have had on a Polish minority in the German heartland. Either way the Polish community in the Ruhr and its trade union seem to have been doomed to destruction.

179. Wawrzynek, "Polacy," p. 83

Conclusion:
National Versus Social Solidarity

The ZZP, which before the war had worked in social solidarity with the other miners' unions, lost its way after the war as it gave priority to the interests of the Polish state even when they did not coincide with those of its own members. In this regard, the post-war history of the ZZP seems to confirm the assumption of a necessary conflict between national and social solidarity.

The pre-war history of the Polish trade union in the Ruhr nevertheless contradicts this assumption. Between its founding in 1902 and the start of the world war, the ZZP put Polish national solidarity at the service of the labor movement in the Ruhr. The Polish national character of the new union attracted Polish-speaking migrants in the Ruhr in a way that the other unions could not. Many of these migrants would have remained unorganized but for the ZZP, and within just a few years it recruited more of the migrants than the German-led unions combined. Yet, at the same time, the ZZP did not fit the mold of a conservative nationalist organization that the Prussian authorities, German trade unionists, and some later historians tried to cast it in. If anything, in its efforts to establish itself as a bona fide representative of working-class interests, the ZZP assumed a demagogic militant stance that played a role in the outbreak of the massive strike of 1905.

During the 1905 strike, the ZZP proved quite capable of working together with the German-led unions, and its influence among Polish miners contributed to the discipline that marked that strike. Following the strike, it cooperated with one of the two major unions more closely than they did with each other. A common perception of working-class interests and how best to achieve them proved more important than the national character of the unions in defining their solidarity. As a result, the ZZP scandalized a major portion of the leadership of the Polish national movement in Prussia by cooperating with a socialist-oriented trade union rather than a predominantly Catholic one. Because the Polish union identified the working-class interests of its members with the interests of the Polish nation, it also did not hesitate to criticize members of that Polish national elite when they violated those interests. Meanwhile, the ZZP absorbed other less militant Polish worker organizations and restructured itself, so that increasingly it resembled the other trade unions.

National differences between the ZZP and the other unions came to the fore following the defeat of the 1912 strike. Renewed pressure by the Prussian authorities on the Polish minority fostered an atmosphere of national polarization at this time that combined with the need to find a scapegoat for the defeat of the strike. The charges and countercharges among the unions took on an unparalleled ferocity, and the ZZP emphasized its Polish character to set it apart from the other unions. The world war came before the situation could play itself out.

Although initially the war brought the unions together more than they had been since the 1905 strike, the war's course irrevocably transformed the Polish question and its meaning for the Polish miners' union. Once the dream of an independent Poland seemed achievable, the prospect affected the priorities and preoccupations of the members of the Polish union in the Ruhr region as well as those of its leaders. The national solidarity on which the union was based turned to serve the prospective Polish nation-state. ZZP leaders saw their place in this state, both as officials of the state and as leaders of one of its major trade unions. They as well as members of the Polish community in the Ruhr accepted the nationalist assumption that the nation-state should gather all members of its nation within its bosom and that therefore the migrants should return to their homeland.

In the Ruhr the ZZP continued the cooperation with the other trade unions that resumed during the war, but primarily as a rear-guard action to cover the retreat of the Polish community to its homeland. Along with the other pre-war unions, the ZZP won official recognition as a negotiating partner with management. But it abandoned all efforts at protecting the independence of action that it had jealously guarded before the war. Viewing its participation in the labor movement in the Ruhr as a temporary evil to protect itself and its members, the ZZP subordinated itself to the German-led unions. The Polish union's lower level of concern with developments in the Ruhr mirrored the lack of extensive involvement on the part of Polish migrants in the various movements that affected the Ruhr region in the early years following the war.

The assumption of an imminent departure as well as of an identity of interests with those of the new Polish state sometimes blinded the union leadership to the long-term interests of its members. A willingness to serve the French authorities during the occupation of the Ruhr clearly endangered the future of the Polish migrants in the Ruhr. Efforts to promote emigration also did not always benefit the migrants, as illustrated by the number who returned to the Ruhr and by the unknown number who came to regret their departure from what many of them had come to think of as their home, if not their homeland. Officials of the new Polish state saw their fellow nationals in the Ruhr as a threat to the stability of the state and therefore obstructed their return migration as much for this reason as for economic reasons. Polish officials saw the migrants in instrumental terms of how they might be best used to serve Polish *raison d'état*. If a Polish trade unionist complained that the predominantly German trade unions treated the Polish migrants in a stepmother-like fashion, the Polish state did not behave toward them as a true mother would either.

With neither the leadership of the Polish Miners' Union nor the Polish state firmly dedicated to the preservation of the union in the Ruhr region, it inevitably declined. All the unions of the region suffered from the economic and eventually the political changes that Germany underwent in the first one and a half decades after the war. Hitler's coming to power would have deprived the Polish union of a future in the Ruhr in any case, but the ZZP had set its course on its own liquidation much earlier. The union's belated efforts to survive could not undo what it had done to itself with the support and encouragement of officials of the Polish state.

No easy generalization about how a trade union organized by and for a national minority will behave springs from this study. Such a union can enhance working-class solidarity: there is no necessary conflict between national and social solidarity. Instead, one can reinforce the other as when a class claims the status of a national class whose interests coincide with those of the nation. A trade union of a national minority can, however, also direct its primary attention to the homeland and subordinate its activities to the goals of a political leadership representing a different national class. This seems especially likely if the national minority perceives itself as persecuted or discriminated against and sees the homeland as a haven from its suffering. Thus, the authorities of both the host country and the homeland may define the choices available to the national minority and thereby impinge upon its decisions more than its own leaders. In this sense our findings may suggest a wider application.

Finally, one must pay tribute to the achievements of the ZZP and its leaders, nearly all of whom were at best self-educated. This was an organization almost exclusively formed by and for members of the working class who also belonged to an unwelcome national minority. As such the ZZP also shared in the painful paradox of many a national minority. When before 1914 the ZZP demonstrated a willingness to put national solidarity at the service of the labor movement in the Ruhr, the other unions often accused it of being nationalist and separatist. When after the war the ZZP proved willing to subordinate itself to the interests of the Polish state, most officials of that state regarded it as insufficiently patriotic and overly concerned with working-class interests. Unrequited love may well define the fate of most national minorities.

Appendix 1:
Membership in the ZZP[1]

Year	ZZP Total	Miners' Section Total	Miners' Section Ruhr	Ruhr Total	Metal Workers' Section Ruhr	Metal Workers' Section Total
1903	4,616			4,616		
1904[2]	10,081			9,916		
1905[3]	30,875			> 28,250		
1906	40,962			35,863		
1907	47,926			29,526		
1 April 1908	48,952[4]		40,842			
1909	57,000	22,243	17,772			5,749[5]
1910	66,970	38,387	26,309			
1911	66,970	38,387	26,309			
1912	77,322	50,903	30,354			
1913	75,171	50,047	28,936			
1914	50,512	29,512	16,137			
1915	34,590	17,295	9,130			
1916	33,884	16,942	9,027			
1917	43,984	21,992	12,746			
1918	73,720	36,860	20,834			
1919	466,636[6]	51,722[7]	46,261			
1920	570,537	67,000	45,000		11,140	
1921			45,018			
1922		60,000	33,200			
1923		13,400				
1924			4,792[8]		3,017	
1925			3,180		2,880	
1926			2,875		1,500	
30 June 1927			2,200[9]		980	
1929				2,923		

1. Christoph Klessmann, *Polnische Bergarbeiter im Ruhrgebiet 1870–1945: Soziale Integration und nationale Subkultur einer Minderheit in der deutschen Industriegesellschaft* (Göttingen: Vandenhoeck & Ruprecht, 1978), pp. 175, 283, with modifications based on the sources noted. The sources frequently give contradictory information; the figures given here, which are sometimes only estimates, seem the most accurate.
2. STAM, RM VII, 35b, Polizei-Verwaltung, Bochum, copies of reports, 8 July, 3 Oct. 1904, 5 Jan. 1905; see also HSTAD, RD 874, ff. 266–267.
3. Jerzy Kozłowski, "Polnische Berufsvereinigung (ZZP). Einflussbereich und Tätigkeit der polnischen Gewerkschaft in Deutschland 1902-1919," *Fremdarbeiterpolitik des Imperialismus*, XX (1988), 44, 50; Franciszek Mańkowski, "Historja Z.Z.P.," in *Ćwierć wieku pracy dla Narodu i Robotnika* (Poznań: Nakładem Zarządu Centralnego Zjedn. Zawod. Polskiego, 1927), pp. 34–266; Marjan Chełmikowski, *Związki zawodowe robotników polskich w Królestwie Pruskim (1889–1918)* (Poznań: Fiszer i Majewski, 1925), p. 67, gives the membership total at the end of 1905 as 25,684 and at the end of Jan. 1906 as 32,364; it seems improbable that the membership grew so rapidly in one month, but the total given here for the end of 1905 lends the latter figure greater credibility.
4. STAM, OP 5365, RPA, 18 April 1908; Joh. Victor Bredt, *Die Polenfrage im Ruhrkohlengebiet. Eine wirtschaftspolitische Studie* (Leipzig: Duncker & Humblot, 1909), p. 52.
5. Mańkowski, "Historja," pp. 99–100.
6. *Ibid.*, pp. 157–158.

7. Kozłowski, "Polnische Berufsvereinigung," p. 51, gives 132,462 as the total membership of the Miners' Section in both the Ruhr and Upper Silesia, which apparently includes members both in Poland and Germany, whereas the figure given here seems to include only the membership in Germany.

8. STAM, OP 5758, f. 541, report on the Polish movement, 1 Jan. 1928, based on a report of the ZZP in 1927, seems more accurate for the Miners' Section in the Ruhr for the years 1924–1926 than round numbers cited in AAN, ARPB 2196, ff. 33, 67, consulate, Essen, to consulate general, Bytom, 30 June 1927, copy, 3 Oct. 1927, on which the figures for the Metalworkers' Section are based.

9. AAN, ARPB 2019, ff. 194–195, archival note, 4 July 1927; ARPB 2196, f. 68, vice-consul, Essen, 3 Oct. 1927.

Appendix 2:
The Program and Demands of the ZZP,
27 October 1917

The Program of the ZZP[1]

I

(a) The ZZP, as the representative of the working class, aspires to a close link with Polish society with all the obligations and rights stemming therefrom. For this reason the ZZP rejects the so-called class struggle, based on internationalism, as harmful for the development of a healthy society. The existence and the favorable development of the whole nation will be ensured only when one uses one's best possible endeavors to raise and utilize the abilities of all, including the lowest social strata, in the service of the public welfare. The aspiration for the moral and material elevation of the existence of the worker, ensuring him due respect and status in society, as the goal and task of the ZZP, is not just a demand of a certain class of society, but rather serves the interests of the whole of society.

(b) As long as the Polish nation in whole or in part is included in a state structure alien to it, the ZZP bases its activity on the constitution and laws of that state and urges the Polish working class within the framework of the labor movement to fulfill the obligations and take advantage of the rights deriving from belonging to the state. Regarding the nation, with which we are united by the state to which we belong, the ZZP applies the same principles as those that constitute the guidelines of the Polish labor movement. A cooperative relationship with the state and the nation, together with whom we happen to live, is possible—if the state does not block the cultural and economic development of the Polish nation.

II

The ZZP has been and remains faithful to the principle that actuated its founders, that in the process of achieving its chosen goals, it will use means allowed by Christian teaching, and that religious and political controversies and all agitation in the spirit of social democracy are excluded.

---

1. Marjan Chełmikowski, *Związki zawodowe robotników polskich w Królestwie Pruskim (1889–1918)* (Poznań: Fiszer i Majewski, 1925), pp. 273–276.

III

The ZZP regards private property as the arrangement indissolubly linked with the disposition of a diligent and thrifty person and with the needs of social life. Private property and [a free market] economy, free enterprise, but also state, communal and cooperative businesses are useful arrangements of economic life. The ZZP nevertheless turns sharply and decidedly against abuse of economic freedom, by which the fruits of cultural and economic progress are frequently wasted in a manner contrary to the good of society, and by which is created an unbearable relation of dependency in general and of the individual on the owner. Every property is connected with a fund of moral responsibility, which sets the limits on the expansion and utilization of property.

IV

Based on the principle that to a certain degree entrepreneurs and workers have common interests, the ZZP declares its readiness for action in common of workers with entrepreneurs for the purpose of maintaining and elevating trade and industry but nevertheless demands for the working class suitable participation in the profits of production. Because the current state juridical and economic system does not guarantee the working class the participation in profits that belongs to it, the ZZP definitely stresses the absolute need for an independent labor organization, which within the limits set by state laws and consideration for public welfare tries to remove deficiencies stemming from the working class being the weaker side in the so-called free labor contract.

V

Relying above all on self-help methods derived from an occupational association, the ZZP regards social protection provided by the state, communal associations, and communities as an indispensably necessary means of assistance to compensate the wage-earning strata for the deficiencies and damage due to the defective economic system and labor relations. To be able to present its wishes and demands in a proper way, the ZZP maintains close contact with the representatives recognized by Polish society in parliaments and communes.

Demands of the ZZP[2]

1 Equality of Rights

Because work, in which a person puts his whole being and his physical and spiritual abilities, cannot be regarded as less valuable than property or titles, equality of rights in all areas of social life is an indispensable necessity. Therefore we demand:

(a) the removal of all estate and property privileges from electoral, state, and communal laws;

(b) the enabling of all talented individuals to attain higher education regardless of their state of wealth or origin;

(c) the admission of individuals of all social strata to all offices;

(d) the recognition of trade unions, by the authorities, the law, and employers, as the chosen representative of the workers; the development and expansion of the right of association together with the removal of constraining laws (such as § 153 of the trade regulations and impediments to the setting up of strike pickets, etc.); the creation of workers' committees;

(e) the reform of work laws with special regard to journeymen, state and agricultural workers, as well as sufficient protection for those who are called to represent the interests of workers in labor courts, workers' sections, etc.;

(f) co-management of insurance arrangements, employment offices, etc.

2 Protection of the Lives, Health, and Morality of Workers

(a) The introduction of a maximum workday;

(b) the protection of juvenile workers;

(c) the protection of women;

(d) the supplementation and amplification of laws regarding Sunday as a day of rest.

2a Regulation of Wages

(a) The guarantee of a minimum wage;

(b) the development of the structure of wage scales and its extension to all occupations;

(c) the creation of courts of arbitration and offices of conciliation with the power to make legally binding decisions;

(d) recognition of the principle that the work of male, female, and juvenile workers should be of equal value.

2. *Ibid.*, pp. 240–242.

Appendix 2: Program and Demands of the ZZP

3 Workers' Insurance

(a) The adaptation of insurance benefits to the cost of living;
(b) the extension of obligatory benefits of sick funds to the family of the insured;
(c) the extension of insurance against injury to other occupations and to so-called occupational diseases;
(d) the reform of the *Knappschaften* [miners' pension and insurance funds], above all their unification and regulation by the laws of the Reich;
(e) the unification and reform of foundry and factory pension funds;
(f) the introduction of state unemployment insurance.

4 Housing Reform

(a) The avoidance of the construction of large barrack-like apartment buildings lacking light and air, and further facilitation of the building of small (garden) houses;
(b) combating the foul custom of excluding families with many children;
(c) guaranteeing the inhabitants of so-called government housing an appropriate period of time before eviction and the prohibition of the abridgement of the civil rights of the inhabitants (concerns the prohibition of the peddling of certain newspapers and the collection of dues, obligatory purchases in certain stores, etc.);
(d) state health supervision of housing.

5 Tax Reform

(a) The lifting of the income level free from taxation;
(b) the development of privileges for children and higher taxes for single persons and those without children;
(c) no encumbering of indispensable food items and items of everyday necessity with taxes;
(d) progressive gradation of taxation of the highest incomes and properties.

Bibliography

Archival Sources

Archiwum Akt Nowych, Warsaw
ARPB 179
ARPB 182
ARPB 183
ARPB 184
ARPB 268
ARPB 356
ARPB 1626
ARPB 1627
ARPB 1632
ARPB 1835
ARPB 1836
ARPB 1839
ARPB 1842
ARPB 2018
ARPB 2019
ARPB 2053
ARPB 2154
ARPB 2196
ARPB 3260
ARPB 3517
ARPB 3524
ARPB 3688
ARPP 50
ARPP 51
ARPP 53
ARPP 231
KGRPB 2
Konsulat Rzeczypospolitej Polskiej w Marsylii 314
Archiwum Państwowe Miasta Poznania i Województwa Poznańskiego
Polizeipräsidium 2692
Polizeipräsidium 4939
Polizeipräsidium 4964
Polizeipräsidium 6272
Polizeipräsidium 6639
Polizeipräsidium 27256

Bibliography

Biblioteka Raczyńskich, Poznań, Manuscript Division
MS. 800
MS. 785
Nordrhein-Westfälisches Hauptstaatsarchiv, Düsseldorf
LR Moers 788
RD 874
RD 9081
RD 15032
RD 15379
RD 15554
RD 15740
RD 15915
RD 15921
RD 15924
RD 15925
RD 15933
RD 15934
RD 15935
RD 15939
RD 15945
RD 15975
RD 15980
RD 16021
RD 16022
RD Präs 841
RD Präs 846
RD Präs 851
RD Präs 871
RD Präs 874
RD Präs 877
Staatsarchiv Münster
BA Herne A8, Nr. 16
Büro Kölpin 19
Büro Kölpin 128
Büro Kölpin 147
Büro Kölpin 179
Büro Kölpin 192
Büro Kölpin 193
Büro Kölpin 210
Büro Kölpin 230
Büro Kölpin 294
Büro Kölpin 296
Büro Kölpin 327
Findbuch B 138

Bibliography

Generalstaatsanwaltschaft Hamm 3573.
OBAD 883
OBAD 884
OBAD 887
OBAD 888
OBAD 1843
OP 2748, Bd. 4
OP 2847, Bd. 7, 9
OP 2849, Bd. 1, 5, 6, 7
OP 5365
OP 5370
OP 5435
OP 5758
OP 5760
OP 5844
OP 6007
OP 6201
OP 6350
OP 6351
OP 6396
OP 6523
OP 6617
RA I, Nr. 63, 64, 66, 149, 152, 1476
RA I, Pa 94
RM VII, Nr. 17, Bd. 1, 2
RM VII, Nr. 18, Bd. 1
RM VII, Nr. 31
RM VII, Nr. 35
RM VII, Nr. 35b
RM VII, Nr. 36c
Stadtarchiv Bochum
   LR 1276
   LR 1277
Stadtarchiv Bottrop
   A V - 3, Nr. 3

Other Primary Sources

Adamek, J., "Die Kampfesweise der polnischen Reichsfraktion," *Die Neue Zeit*, XXVII, No. 2 (1909), 772–782.
Adelmann, Gerhard, ed., *Quellensammlung zur Geschichte der sozialen Betriebsverfassung. Ruhrindustrie unter besonderer Berücksichtigung des Industrie- und Handelskammerbezirks Essen*, Vol. I: *Überbetriebliche*

Bibliography

Einwirkung auf die soziale Betriebsverfassung der Ruhrindustrie (Bonn: Peter Hanstein, 1960); Vol. II: *Soziale Betriebsverfassung einzelner Unternehmen der Ruhrindustrie* (Bonn: Pub. der Gesellschaft für Rheinische Geschichtskunde, 1965).

Altkemper, Johannes, *Deutschtum und Polentum in politisch-konfessioneller Bedeutung* (Leipzig: Duncker & Humblot, 1910).

Arbeitsmaterialien des XIX. Betriebsräteseminars an der Ruhr-Universität Bochum zum Thema: "Ausländer, Gastarbeiter: Integrationsprobleme und ihre Lösungsansätze in historischer und Aktueller Perspektive" (Bochum: Ruhr-Universität Bochum and Industriegewerkschaft Metall, 1985).

Banaszak, Antoni, "Z.Z.P. a policja pruska i sądy w ostatnich latach przed wojną światową," in *Ćwierć wieku pracy dla Narodu i Robotnika* (Poznań: Nakładem Zarządu Centralnego Zjedn. Zawod. Polskiego, 1927), pp. 541–553.

Barciszewski, Leon, "Z życia emigracji polskiej w Niemczech i Francji," in *Ćwierć wieku pracy dla Narodu i Robotnika* (Poznań: Nakładem Zarządu Centralnego Zjedn. Zawod. Polskiego, 1927), pp. 517–535.

Brandt, Hans Jürgen, ed., *Die Polen und die Kirche im Ruhrgebiet 1871–1919: Ausgewählte Dokumente zur pastoral und kirchlichen Integration sprachlicher Minderheiten im deutschen Kaiserreich*, (Münster: Aschendorff, 1987).

Bredt, Joh. Victor, *Die Polenfrage im Ruhrkohlengebiet. Eine wirtschaftspolitische Studie* (Leipzig: Duncker & Humblot, 1909).

Brejski, Jan, "Dlaczego powstało 'Zjednoczenie Zawodowe Polskie?'—Bo chciał tego lud polski," in *Ćwierć wieku pracy dla Narodu i Robotnika* (Poznań: Nakładem Zarządu Centralnego Zjedn. Zawod. Polskiego, 1927), pp. 511–515.

Broesike, Max, "Die Polen im westlichen Preussen 1905," *Zeitschrift des Königlich Preussischen Statistischen Landesamts*, XLVIII (1908), 251–274.

Bruhns, Julius, "Polenfrage und Sozialdemokratie," *Die Neue Zeit*, XXVI (1908), 707–714, 757–765.

Brust, August, "Der Bergarbeiterstreik im Ruhrrevier," *Archiv für Sozialwissenschaften und Sozialpolitik*, XX, No. 2 (1905), 480–506.

Bugzel, Marcin, "Wspomnienia starego emigranta," in *Pamiętniki emigrantów 1878–1958* (Warsaw: Czytelnik, 1960), pp. 21–72.

Closterhalfen, Karl, "Die polnische Bevölkerung in Rheinland und Westfalen," *Deutsche Erde*, X, No. 5 (1911), 114–120.

Drygas, Stanisław, *Czas Zaprzeszły: Wspomnienia 1890–1944* (Warsaw: Czytelnik, 1970).

Engel, Konrad, *Zum Ausstande der Bergarbeiter im Ruhrbezirk* (Berlin: Springer Verlag, 1905).

Bibliography

Fischer-Eckert, Li, *Die wirtschaftliche und soziale Lage der Frauen in dem modernen Industrieort Hamborn im Rheinland* (Hagen: Karl Stracke, 1913).

"Geschichte einer polnischen Kolonie in der Fremde: Jubiläumsschrift des St. Barbara-Vereins in Bottrop" (Bottrop, 1911), *Kirche und Religion im Revier: Beiträge und Quellen zur Geschichte*, Vol. IV (Essen: Sozialinstitut des Bistums Essen, 1968).

Habrowski, Władysław, "Do was się zwracam, młodzi górnicy...," in *Pamiętniki Górników*, ed. by Bronisław Gołębiowski (Katowice: Wydawnictwo "Śląsk," 1973), pp. 96–105.

Holdert, Janusz, *En toi, France: mes racines meurtries* (Paris: La Pensée Universelle, 1977).

Hue, Otto, *Die Bergarbeiter: Historische Darstellung der Bergarbeiter-Verhältnisse von der altesten bis in die neueste Zeit*, Vol. II (Stuttgart: I.H.W. Dietz Nachf. G.m.b.H., 1913).

_____, "Über den Generalstreik im Ruhrgebiet," *Sozialistische Monatshefte*, Feb. 1905, pp. 201–210.

_____, "Die Väter des Sprachenparagraphen," *Die Neue Zeit*, XXVI (1908), 445–453.

Hulanicki, Stefan, "Reemigracja Polaków z Niemiec i Ameryki," *Strażnica Zachodnia*, I, Nos. 5–6 (1922), 73–78.

Imbusch, Heinrich, *Arbeitsverhältnisse und Arbeiterorganisationen im deutschen Bergbau* (Essen: Verlag des Gewerkvereins christlicher Bergarbeiter, 1908).

_____, *Bergarbeiterstreik im Ruhrgebiet im Fruhjahr 1912* (3rd ed.; Cologne: Christl. Gewerkschaftsverlag, n.d. [1912]).

Jakóbczyk, Witold, ed., *Wielkopolska (1851–1914): Wybór źródeł* (Wrocław: Ossolineum, 1954).

Jubileuszowy Kalendarz Wychodźczy "Wiarusa Polskiego" 1890–1940 na r. 1940 (Lille, France: "Wiarus Polski," 1940).

Kołpacki, Franciszek, "Polnische Berufsvereinigung," *Internationales Handwörterbuch des Gewerkschaftswesens* (Berlin: 1932), II, 1274, reprinted in *Arbeitsmaterialien des XIX. Betriebsräteseminars an der Ruhr-Universität Bochum zum Thema: "Ausländer, Gastarbeiter: Integrationsprobleme und ihre Lösungsansätze in historischer und Aktueller Perspektive"* (Bochum: Ruhr-Universität Bochum and Industriegewerkschaft Metall, 1985), p. 23.

_____, "Zjednoczenie Zawodowe Polskie we Westfalii (w Niemczech)," in *Ćwierć wieku pracy dla Narodu i Robotnika* (Poznań: Nakładem Zarządu Centralnego Zjedn. Zawod. Polskiego, 1927), pp. 483–489.

Leimpeters, Johann, "Die Taktik des Bergarbeiterverbandes," *Sozialistische Monatshefte*, June 1905, pp. 485–495.

Leksykon Polactwa w Niemczech (Warsaw: Państwowe Wydawnictwo Naukowe, 1973).

Bibliography

Lengowski, Michał, *Na Warmii i w Westfalii* (Warsaw: Pax, 1972).

Mańkowski, Franciszek, *Za chlebem w świat* (Bochum: Oddział Górnikow Zjednoczenia Zawodowego Polskiego, n.d. [ca.1913]).

_____, "Geschichte der polnischen Verbände," *Kalendarz Górniczy*, 1913, in German translation, STAM, RM VII, Nr. 36c.

_____, "Historja Z.Z.P.," in *Ćwierć wieku pracy dla Narodu i Robotnika* (Poznań: Nakładem Zarządu Centralnego Zjedn. Zawod. Polskiego, 1927), pp. 34–266.

_____, "Związki zawodowe na wychództwie," *Pamiętnik wystawy przemysłowej w Bochum od 19–27 lipca 1913 roku* (Oberhausen: Nakładem Komitetu Wystawowego, n.d. [1913]), pp. 28–35.

Marchlewski, Julian, "Gorzałka a patriotyzm Koła Polskiego w Berlinie," in Julian Marchlewski, *Pisma wybrane*, Vol. II (Warsaw: Książka i Wiedza, 1956), pp. 401–409.

Połomski, Franciszek, "Ze wspomnień starego 'Westfaloka'—A. Podeszwy," *Studia Śląskie*, I (1958), 253–264.

Rejer, Stefan, "Związek Robotników Polskich we Francji," in *Ćwierć wieku pracy dla Narodu i Robotnika* (Poznań: Nakładem Zarządu Centralnego Zjedn. Zawod. Polskiego, 1927), pp. 491–510.

Schulze, Franz, *Die polnische Zuwanderung im Ruhrrevier und ihre Wirkung* (Munich: Josefs Druckerei, Bigge, 1909).

Statistisches Jahrbuch für den Preussischen Staat, Vol. XI (Berlin: Herausgeben vom Königlich Preussischen Statistischen Landesamt, 1914).

Stenographische Berichte über die Verhandlungen des Preussischen Hauses der Abgeordneten.

Stenographische Berichte über die Verhandlungen des Reichstags.

Taeglichsbeck, O., *Die Belegschaft der Bergwerke und Salinen im Oberbergamtsbezirk Dortmund nach der Zahlung vom 16. Dezember 1893* (2 vols.; Dortmund: Bellman & Middendorf, 1895–96).

Taront, Antoni, *Wspomnienia emigranta polskiego z północnej Francji*, ed. by Daniel Beauvois, Kazimierz Ożóg, and Jadwiga Śrutek (Wrocław, Warsaw, Cracow: Zakład Narodowy im. Ossolińskich, 1994).

Tenfelde, Klaus, and Trischler, Helmuth, eds., *Bis vor die Stufen des Throns: Bittschriften und Beschwerden von Bergleuten im Zeitalter der Industrialisierung* (Munich: Verlag C.H. Beck, 1986).

Der Verrat des schwarz-gelben Gewerkvereins der Bergarbeiter: Eine Darstellung der Bergarbeiterbewegung und -kämpfe in der Zeit nach dem Ruhrbergarbeiterstreik im Jahre 1905 bis einschliesslich des Streiks im Jahre 1912 (2nd rev. ed.; Bochum: Vorstand des Verbandes der Bergarbeiter Deutschlands, 1912).

Wachowiak, Andrzej, "Wspomnienia z polskiej, robotniczej emigracji do Westfalii i Nadrenii oraz do Francji z konca XIX i początku XX wieku" (Typed manuscript, 1965), Wspomnienie No. 839, Zakład Historii i Teorii

Bibliography

Ruchu Zawodowego, Centrum Studiów Związków Zawodowych, Ogólnopolskie Porozumienie Związków Zawodowych, Warsaw.

_____, ed., *Przewodnik po Westfalii i Nadrenii. Podręcznik dla osób prywatnych i towarzystw* (Oberhausen: Drukiem J. Kawalera i Sp., 1913).

Wachowiak, Stanisław, *Czasy, które przeżyłem: Wspomnienia z lat 1890–1939* (Warsaw: Czytelnik, 1983).

_____, "Wychodźtwo polskie westfalsko-nadreńskie," in *Ćwierć wieku pracy dla Narodu i Robotnika* (Poznań: Nakładem Zarządu Centralnego Zjedn. Zawod. Polskiego, 1927), pp. 7–33.

"Waffenstillstand. Aus dem Streikgebiet," *Soziale Praxis*, 16 Feb. 1905, columns 500–503.

Wojciechowski, Jakub, *Życiorys własny robotnika*, Vol. I (Poznań: Wydawnictwo Poznańskie, 1971).

Związek Zawodowy Górników, *Życiorysy górników* (Katowice: Wydawnictwo Związku Zawodowego Górników w Polsce, 1949).

Secondary Sources

Adelmann, Gerhard, "Die Beziehungen zwischen Arbeitgeber und Arbeitnehmer in der Ruhrindustrie vor 1914," *Jahrbücher für Nationalökonomie und Statistik*, Bd. 175 (1963), pp. 412–427.

_____, *Die soziale Betriebsverfassung des Ruhrbergbaus vom Anfang des 19. Jahrhunderts bis zum Ersten Weltkrieg unter besonderer Berücksichtigung des Industrie- und Handelskammerbezirks Essen* (Bonn: Ludwig Röhrscheid Verlag, 1962).

Blecking, Diethelm, *Die Geschichte der nationalpolnischen Turnorganisation "Sokół" im Deutschen Reich 1884–1939* (Dortmund: Forschungsstelle Ostmitteleuropa an der Universität Dortmund, 1987).

Bock, Hans Manfred, *Syndikalismus und Linkskommunismus von 1918–1920: Zur Geschichte und Soziologie der Freien Arbeiter-Union Deutschlands (Syndikalisten), der Allgemeinen Arbeiter-Union Deutschlands und der Kommunistischen Arbeiter-Partei Deutschlands* (Meisenheim am Glan: Verlag Anton Hain, 1969).

Brandt, Hans Jürgen, "Das Kloster der Redemptoristen in Bochum und die Polenseelsorge im westfaelischen Industriegebiet (1883–1918)," *Spicilegium Historicum Congregationis SSmi Redemptoris*, Jg. XXIII, Fasc. 1 (1975), 131–199.

Brauckmann, Gerhard, "Der Einfluss des Konjunkturverlaufs auf die gewerkschaftlichen Mitgliederbewegung" (Unpublished Ph.D. Dissertation, University of Bochum, 1972).

Braunthal, Gerard, *Socialist Labor and Politics in Weimar Germany: The General Federation of German Trade Unions* (Hamden, Connecticut: Archon Books, 1978).

Bibliography

Brose, Eric Dorn, *Christian Labor and the Politics of Frustration in Imperial Germany* (Washington, D.C.: The Catholic University of America Press, 1985).

Brüggemeier, Franz-Josef, "Bedürfnisse, gesellschaftliche Erfahrung und politisches Verhalten: Das Beispiel der Bergarbeiter im nordlichen Ruhrgebiet gegen Ende des 19. Jhs.," *Sozialwissenschaftliche Informationen für Unterricht und Studium*, VI, No. 4 (1977), 152–159.

_____, *Leben vor Ort. Ruhrbergleute und Ruhrbergbau 1889–1919* (Munich: C.H. Beck, 1983).

Buzek, Józef, *Historya polityki narodowościowej rządu pruskiego wobec Polaków od traktatów wiedeńskich do ustaw wyjątkowych z r. 1908* (Lwów: Nakład H. Altenberga, 1909).

Chełmikowski, Marjan, *Związki zawodowe robotników polskich w Królestwie Pruskim (1889–1918)* (Poznań: Fiszer i Majewski, 1925).

Chlebowczyk, Józef, *On Small and Young Nations in Europe: Nation-Forming Processes in Ethnic Borderlands in East-Central Europe* (Wrocław: Ossolineum, 1980).

Chojnacki, Wojciech, "Bibliografia czasopism i kalendarzy wydawanych w języku polskim w Westfalii i Nadrenii w latach 1890–1918," *Przegląd Polonijny*, III, No. 1 (1977), 191–200.

Cieślak, Tadeusz, "'Gazeta Grudziądzka' 1894–1918. Fenomen wydawniczy," *Studia i materiały do dziejów Wielkopolski i Pomorza*, III, No. 2 (1957), 175–188.

_____, "Pismo polskich robotników w Westfalii 'Wiarus Polski' (1890–1923)," *Rocznik historii czasopiśmiennictwa polskiego*, XI, No. 2 (1972), 223–236.

Clark, Edwin Jared, "Industry, Society, and Politics in the Ruhr: National Liberalism in Dortmund, 1848–1913" (Unpublished Ph.D. Dissertation, University of Illinois at Chicago, 1990).

Crew, David F., "Class and Community. Local Research on Working-Class History in Four Countries," in *Arbeiter und Arbeiterbewegung im Vergleich. Berichte zur internationalen historischen Forschung*, ed. by Klaus Tenfelde, *Historische Zeitschrift*, Sonderheft, Vol. XV (Munich: R. Oldenbourg Verlag, 1986), 279–336.

_____, *Town in the Ruhr: A Social History of Bochum, 1860–1914* (New York: Columbia University Press, 1979).

Czubiński, Antoni, "Działalność polityczna władz powstańczych," in *Powstanie wielkopolskie 1918–1919: Zarys dziejów*, ed. by Antoni Czubiński, Zdzisław Grot, and Benon Miśkiewicz (3rd ed., rev.; Warsaw, Poznań: Państwowe Wydawnictwo Naukowe, 1988), pp. 393–493.

_____, "Rewolucja 1918–1919 w Niemczech wobec kwestii polskiej w listopadzie i grudniu 1918 roku," in *Powstanie wielkopolskie 1918–1919*, ed. by Zdzisław Grot (Poznań: Wydawnictwo Poznańskie, 1968), pp. 67–88.

Bibliography

_____, "Sytuacja polityczna w zaborze pruskim po rewolucji listopadowej w Niemczech (listopad-grudzień 1918 roku)," in *Powstanie wielkopolskie 1918–1919: Zarys dziejów*, ed. by Antoni Czubiński, Zdzisław Grot, and Benon Miśkiewicz (3rd ed., rev.; Warsaw-Poznań: Państwowe Wydawnictwo Naukowe, 1988), pp. 98–165.

Dörnemann, Manfred, *Die Politik des Verbandes der Bergarbeiter Deutschlands von der Novemberrevolution 1918 bis zum Osterputsch 1921 unter besonderer Berücksichtigung der Verhältnisse im rheinisch-westfälischen Industriegebiet* (Bochum: Berg-Verlag, n.d. [1966]).

Dowe, Dieter, "The Workingmen's Choral Movement in Germany before the First World War," *Journal of Contemporary History*, XIII, No. 2 (1978), 269–296.

Dzieje Zjednoczenia Zawodowego Polskiego 1889–1939 (Chorzów: Nakładem Kartelu Zjednoczenia Zawodowego Polskiego na Śląsku, 1939).

Eley, Geoff, *From Unification to Nazism: Reinterpreting the German Past* (Boston: Allen & Unwin, 1986).

Elsner, Lothar, "Foreign Workers and Forced Labor in Germany during the First World War," in *Labor Migration in the Atlantic Economies: The European and North American Working Classes During the Period of Industrialization*, ed. by Dirk Hoerder (Westport, Connecticut: Greenwood Press, 1985), pp. 189–222.

Evans, Richard J., "Introduction: the Sociological Interpretation of German Labour History," in *The German Working Class 1888–1933: The Politics of Everyday Life*, ed. by Richard J. Evans (London: Croom Helm, 1982), pp. 15–53.

Feige, Ullrich, *Bergarbeiterschaft zwischen Tradition und Emanzipation: Das Verhältnis von Bergleuten und Gewerkschaften zu Unternehmern und Staat im westlichen Ruhrgebiet um 1900* (Düsseldorf: Schwann, 1986).

Feldman, Gerald D., "German Business Betwen [sic] War and Revolution: The Origins of the Stinnes-Legien Agreement," in *Entstehung und Wandel der modernen Gesellschaft*, ed. by Gerhard A. Ritter (Berlin: Walter de Gruyter & Co., 1970), pp. 312–341.

Filipiak, Tadeusz, *Dzieje związków zawodowych w Wielkopolsce do roku 1919: Studium porównawcze z historii gospodarczo-społecznej* (Poznań: Wydawnictwo Poznańskie, 1965).

Fricke, Dieter, *Der Ruhrbergarbeiterstreik von 1905* (Berlin: Rütten & Loening, 1955).

Fulde, Herbert, *Die polnische Arbeitergewerkschaftsbewegung* (Weinfelden: A.-G. Neuenschwander'sche Verlagsbuchhandlung, 1931).

Geary, Dick, "The Ruhr: From Social Peace to Social Revolution," *European Studies Review*, X (1980), 497–511.

Gębik, Władysław, *Pod warmińskim niebem (O Michale Lengowskim)* (Warsaw: Ludowa Spółdzielnia Wydawnicza, 1974).

Bibliography

Gillis, John R., "The Future of European History," *Perspectives: American Historical Association Newsletter*, XXXIV, No. 4 (April 1996), 1, 4–6.

Goch, Stefan, "Radical Left-Wing Miners' Organizations in the Ruhr Area 1917 to 1925," paper presented at the Third International Mining History Conference, Golden, Colorado, 6–10 June 1994.

_____, *Sozialdemokratische Arbeiterbewegung und Arbeiterkultur im Ruhrgebiet: Eine Untersuchung am Beispiel Gelsenkirchen 1848–1975* (Düsseldorf: Droste Verlag, 1990).

Greene, Victor R., *American Immigrant Leaders 1800–1910: Marginality and Identity* (Baltimore: Johns Hopkins University Press, 1987).

Halperin, S. William, *Germany Tried Democracy: A Political History of the Reich from 1918 to 1933* (New York: W.W. Norton & Company, 1946).

Hartewig, Karin, *Das unberechenbare Jahrzehnt: Bergarbeiter und ihre Familien im Ruhrgebiet 1914–1924* (Munich: Verlag C.H. Beck, 1993).

Hemmerling, Zygmunt, *Posłowie polscy w parlamencie Rzeszy niemieckiej i sejmie pruskim (1907–1914)* (Warsaw: Ludowa Spółdzielnia Wydawnicza, 1968).

Herbert, Ulrich, *A History of Foreign Labor in Germany, 1880–1980: Seasonal Workers/Forced Laborers/Guest Workers* (Ann Arbor: The University of Michigan Press, 1990).

Herre, Günther, "Arbeitersport, Arbeiterjugend und Obrigkeitsstaat 1893 bis 1914," in *Sozialgeschichte der Freizeit. Untersuchungen zum Wandel der Alltagskultur in Deutschland*, ed. by Gerhard Huck (Wuppertal: Peter Hammer Verlag, 1980), pp. 187–205.

Hickey, S.H.F., *Workers in Imperial Germany: The Miners of the Ruhr* (Oxford: Clarendon Press, 1985).

Hobsbawm, E.J., "What is the Workers' Country?" in *Workers: Worlds of Labor*, ed. by Eric Hobsbawm (New York: Pantheon Books, 1984), pp. 49–65.

Jakóbczyk, Witold, *Studia nad dziejami Wielkopolski*, Vol. III: *1890–1914* (Poznań: Państwowe Wydawnictwo Naukowe, 1967).

Janowska, Halina, *Emigracja zarobkowa z Polski 1918–1939* (Warsaw: Państwowe Wydawnictwo Naukowe, 1981).

Kaczmarek, Johannes, "Die polnischen Arbeiter im rheinisch-westfälischen Industriegebiet, eine Studie zum Problem der sozialen Anpassung" (Unpublished Ph.D. Dissertation, Cologne, 1922).

Kaelble, Hartmut, and Volkmann, Heinrich, "Konjunktur und Streik während des Übergangs zum Organisierten Kapitalismus," in *Arbeiter in Deutschland. Studien zur Lebensweise der Arbeiterschaft im Zeitalter der Industrialisierung*, ed. by Dieter Langewiesche and Klaus Schönhoven (Paderborn: Ferdinand Schöningh, 1981), pp. 269–295.

Kirchhoff, Hans Georg, *Die staatliche Sozialpolitik im Ruhrbergbau 1871–1914* (Cologne: Westdeutscher Verlag, 1958).

Klessmann, Christoph, "Klassensolidarität und nationales Bewusstsein. Das Verhältnis zwischen der Polnischen Berufsvereinigung (ZZP) und den

Bibliography

deutschen Bergarbeiter-Gewerkschaften im Ruhrgebiet 1902–1923," *Internationale Wissenschaftliche Korrespondenz zur Geschichte der deutschen Arbeiterbewegung*, X (1974), 149–178.

_____, "Polish Miners in the Ruhr District: Their Social Situation and Trade Union Activity," in *Labor Migration in the Atlantic Economies: The European and North American Working Classes During the Period of Industrialization*, ed. by Dirk Hoerder (Westport, Connecticut: Greenwood Press, 1985), pp. 253–275.

_____, *Polnische Bergarbeiter im Ruhrgebiet 1870–1945: Soziale Integration und nationale Subkultur einer Minderheit in der deutschen Industriegesellschaft* (Göttingen: Vandenhoeck & Ruprecht, 1978).

_____, "Zur rechtlichen und sozialen Lage der Polen im Ruhrgebiet im Dritten Reich," *Archiv für Sozialgeschichte*, XVII (1977), 175–194.

_____, "Zjednoczenie Zawodowe Polskie (ZZP—Polnische Berufsvereinigung) und Alter Verband im Ruhrgebiet," *Internationale Wissenschaftliche Korrespondenz zur Geschichte der deutschen Arbeiterbewegung*, XV (1979), 68–71.

Koch, Max Jürgen, *Die Bergarbeiterbewegung im Ruhrgebiet zur Zeit Wilhelms II. (1889–1914)* (Düsseldorf: Droste, 1954).

Kołodziej, Edward, *Wychodźstwo zarobkowe z Polski 1918–1939: Studia nad polityką emigracyjną II Rzeczypospolitej* (Warsaw: Książka i Wiedza, 1982).

Kotłowski, Tadeusz, *Zjednoczenie Zawodowe Polskie: Zasięg wpływów i działalność społeczno-polityczna w latach 1918–1939* (Poznań: Uniwersytet im. Adama Mickiewicza, 1977).

Kozłowski, Jerzy, "Polnische Berufsvereinigung (ZZP). Einflussbereich und Tätigkeit der polnischen Gewerkschaft in Deutschland 1902–1919," *Fremdarbeiterpolitik des Imperialismus*, XX (1988), 43–52.

_____, *Rozwój organizacji społeczno-narodowych wychodźstwa polskiego w Niemczech w latach 1870–1914* (Wrocław: Ossolineum, 1987).

Kroker, Evelyn, "Arbeiterausschüsse im Ruhrbergbau zwischen 1906 und 1914," *Der Anschnitt*, XXX, No. 6 (1978), 204–215.

Kulczycki, John J., "The First Migrants' Miner Associations in the Ruhr," in *Essays in Russian and East European History: Festschrift in Honor of Edward C. Thaden*, ed. by Leo Schelbert and Nick Ceh (Boulder, Colorado: East European Monographs, 1995), pp. 101–115.

_____, *The Foreign Worker and the German Labor Movement: Xenophobia and Solidarity in the Coal Fields of the Ruhr, 1871–1914* (Oxford, Providence, USA: Berg Publishers, 1994).

_____, "The Herne 'Polish Revolt' of 1899: Social and National Consciousness among Polish Coal Miners in the Ruhr," *Canadian Slavonic Papers*, XXXI, No. 2 (1989), 146–169.

Bibliography

_____, "Nationalism over Class Solidarity: The German Trade Unions and Polish Coal Miners in the Ruhr to 1902," *Canadian Review of Studies in Nationalism*, XIV, No. 2 (1987), 261–276.

_____, "Polish Economic Immigration in Western Germany and France, 1895–1935," in *Russian and Eastern European History: Selected Papers from the Second World Congress for Soviet and East European Studies*, ed. by R.C. Elwood (Berkeley, California: Berkeley Slavic Specialties, 1984), pp. 261–276.

_____, "The Prussian Authorities and the Poles of the Ruhr," *The International History Review*, VIII, No. 4 (1986), 593–603.

_____, "Scapegoating the Foreign Worker: Job Turnover, Accidents, and Diseases among Polish Coal Miners in the German Ruhr, 1871–1914," in *The Politics of Immigrant Workers: Labor Activism and Migration in the World Economy Since 1830*, ed. by Camille Guerin-Gonzales and Carl Strikwerda (New York: Holmes & Meier, 1993), pp. 133–152.

_____, "Uwarunkowania świadomości narodowej polskich górników w Zagłębiu Ruhry przed I wojną światową," in *Pamiętnik XV Powszechnego Zjazdu Historyków Polskich*, ed. by Jacek Staszewski (Gdańsk-Toruń: Wydawnictwo Adam Marszałek, 1995), Vol. I, Part 2, pp. 151–159.

Lawaty, Andreas, *Das Ende Preussens in polnischer Sicht: Zur Kontinuität negativer Wirkungen der preussichen Geschichte auf die deutsch-polnischen Beziehungen* (Berlin: de Gruyter, 1986).

Levy, Richard S., "Introduction: The Political Career of the *Protocols of the Elders of Zion*," in Binjamin W. Segel, *A Lie and a Libel: The History of the Protocols of the Elders of Zion*, trans. and ed. by Richard S. Levy (Lincoln, Nebraska, and London: University of Nebraska Press, 1995), pp. 1–47.

Marczewski, Jerzy, *Narodowa Demokracja w Poznańskiem 1900–1914* (Warsaw: Państwowe Wydawnictwo Naukowe, 1967).

Marssolek, Inge, "Sozialdemokratie und Revolution im östlichen Ruhrgebiet. Dortmund unter der Herrschaft des Arbeiter- und Soldatenrates," in *Arbeiter- und Soldatenräte im rheinisch-westfälischen Industriegebiet: Studien zur Geschichte der Revolution 1918/19*, ed. by Reinhard Rürup (Wuppertal: Peter Hammer Verlag, 1975), pp. 239–314.

Martiny, Martin, "Arbeiterbewegung an Rhein und Ruhr vom Scheitern der Räte- und Sozialisierungsbewegung bis zum Ende der letzten parlamentarischen Regierung der Weimarer Republik (1920–1930)," in *Arbeiterbewegung an Rhein und Ruhr: Beiträge zur Geschichte der Arbeiterbewegung in Rheinland-Westfalen*, ed. by Jürgen Reulecke (Wuppertal: Peter Hammer, 1974), pp. 241–273.

Mogs, Fritz, "Die sozialgeschichtliche Entwicklung der Stadt Oberhausen (Rhld.) zwischen 1850 und 1933" (Unpublished Dissertation, University of Cologne, 1956).

Bibliography

Mommsen, Hans, "Die Bergarbeiterbewegung an der Ruhr 1918–1933," in *Arbeiterbewegung an Rhein und Ruhr: Beiträge zur Geschichte der Arbeiterbewegung in Rheinland-Westfalen*, ed. by Jürgen Reulecke (Wuppertal: Peter Hammer, 1974), pp. 275–314.

_____, "Soziale Kämpfe im Ruhrbergbau nach der Jahrhundertwende," in *Glück auf, Kameraden! Die Bergarbeiter und ihre Organisationen in Deutschland*, ed. by Hans Mommsen and Ulrich Borsdorf (Cologne: Bund-Verlag, 1979), pp. 249–272.

Mommsen, Hans, *et al.*, *Bergarbeiter. Ausstellung zur Geschichte der organisierten Begarbeiterbewegung in Deutschland* (Bochum: Berg-Verlag GmbH, 1969) (unpaged).

Moses, John A., *Trade Unionism in Germany from Bismarck to Hitler 1869–1933*, Vol. I: *1869–1918* (Totowa, New Jersey: Barnes & Noble, 1982), Vol. II: *1919–1933* (London: George Prior Publishers, 1982).

Müllers, Robert, "Die Bevölkerungsentwicklung im Rheinisch-Westfälischen Industriegebiet (in der Abgrenzung des Siedlungsverbandes Ruhrkohlenbezirk) von 1895 bis 1919" (Unpublished Ph.D. Dissertation, University of Münster, 1920).

Murphy, Richard Charles, *Guestworkers in the German Reich: A Polish Community in Wilhelmian Germany* (Boulder, Colorado: East European Monographs, 1983).

Murzynowska, Krystyna, *Polskie wychodźstwo zarobkowe w Zagłębiu Ruhry w latach 1880–1914* (Wrocław: Ossolineum, 1972).

_____, "Ruch zawodowy robotników polskich w Zagłębiu Ruhry," in *Ruch zawodowy w Polsce: Zarys dziejów*, ed. by Stanisław Kalabiński, Vol. I (Warsaw: Instytut Wydawniczy CRZZ, 1974), pp. 477–521.

_____, "Związki polskiego wychodźstwa zamieszkałego w Zagłębiu Ruhry z krajem w latach 1870–1918," in *Polska klasa robotnicza: Studia historyczne*, ed. by Elżbieta Kaczyńska, Vol. X (Warsaw: Państwowe Wydawnictwo Naukowe, 1983), pp. 101–133.

Nadolny, Anastazy, "Polskie duszpasterstwo w Zagłębiu Ruhry (1871–1894), *Studia Pelplinskie* (1981), pp. 239–315.

Neumann, Walter, *Die Gewerkschaften im Ruhrgebiet. Voraussetzungen, Entwicklung und Wirksamkeit* (Cologne: Bund Verlag, 1951).

Oertzen, Peter von, "Die grossen Streiks der Ruhrbergarbeiterschaft im Frühjahr 1919. Ein Beitrag zur Diskussion über die revolutionäre Entstehungsphase der Weimarer Republik," *Vierteljahrshefte für Zeitgeschichte*, 6. Jg. (1958), 231–262.

Orzechowski, Marian, "Akcja plebiscytowa na rzecz Górnego Śląska w Nadrenii i Westfalii," *Zaranie Śląskie*, XXVIII, No. 2 (1965), 473–493.

_____, "Z dziejów polskiego ruchu robotniczego w Nadrenii-Westfalii w latach 1918–1933," mimeographed (Poznań: Instytut Zachodni, 1969).

_____, *Narodowa demokracja na Górnym Śląsku (do 1918 roku)* (Wrocław: Zakład Narodowy im. Ossolińskich, 1965).

Bibliography

Panzera, Donald P., "Organization, Authority, and Conflict in the Ruhr Coal Mining Industry: A Case Study of the Gutehoffungshütte, 1853-1914" (Unpublished Ph.D. Dissertation, Northwestern University, 1980).

Piotrowski, Adam, *Powstanie i rozwój polskich związków zawodowych pod zaborem pruskim* (Poznań: Nakładem i drukiem "Pracy" Sp. z ogr. p., 1910).

Poniatowska, Anna, "Działalność społeczno-polityczna," in *Związek Polaków w Niemczech w latach 1922-1982*, ed. by Jerzy Marczewski (Warsaw: Wydawnictwo Polonia, 1987), pp. 65-118.

_____, "Organizacja Związku Polaków w Niemczech," in *Związek Polaków w Niemczech w latach 1922-1982*, ed. by Jerzy Marczewski (Warsaw: Wydawnictwo Polonia, 1987), pp. 37-64.

_____, *Polacy w Berlinie 1918-1945* (Poznań: Wydawnictwo Poznańskie, 1986).

Ponty, Janine, *Polonais méconnus: Histoire des travailleurs immigrés en France dans l'entre-deux-guerres* (Paris: Publications de la Sorbonne, 1988).

Popiołek, Kazimierz, ed., *Dzieje górniczego ruchu zawodowego w Polsce (do 1918 R.)*, Vol. I (Warsaw: Wydawnictwo Związkowe CRZZ, 1971).

Potthoff, Heinrich, *Gewerkschaften und Politik zwischen Revolution und Inflation* (Düsseldorf: Droste Verlag, 1979).

Reulecke, Jürgen, "Der Erste Weltkrieg und die Arbeiterbewegung im rheinisch-westfälischen Industriegebiet," in *Arbeiterbewegung an Rhein und Ruhr: Beiträge zur Geschichte der Arbeiterbewegung in Rheinland-Westfalen*, ed. by Jürgen Reulecke (Wuppertal: Peter Hammer, 1974), pp. 206-239.

Ritter, Gerhard A., "Workers' Culture in Imperial Germany: Problems and Points of Departure for Research," *Journal of Contemporary History*, XIII, No. 2 (1978), 165-190.

Rosenberg, Donald, "The Ruhr Coal Strike and the Prussian Mining Law of 1905: A Social and Political Conflict of Working Class Aspirations and Industrial Authoritarianism" (Unpublished Ph.D. Dissertation, University of California, Los Angeles, 1971).

Roth, Günther, *The Social Democrats in Imperial Germany: A Study of Working-Class Isolation and National Integration* (Totowa, N.J.: Bedminster Press, 1963).

Saul, Klaus, *Staat, Industrie, Arbeiterbewegung im Kaiserreich: Zur Innen- und Aussenpolitik des Wilhelminischen Deutschland 1903-1914* (Düsseldorf: Bertelsmann Universitätsverlag, 1974).

Schmidtchen, Volker, "Arbeitersport - Erziehung zum sozialistischen Menschen? Leitwerte und Jugendarbeit in zwei Ruhrgebietsvereinen in der Weimarer Republik," in *Fabrik, Familie, Feierabend: Beiträge zur Sozialgeschichte des Alltags im Industriezeitalter*, ed. by Jürgen Reulecke and Wolfhard Weber (Wuppertal: Peter Hammer Verlag, 1978), pp. 345-375.

Schneider, Michael, "Christliche Arbeiterbewegung in Europa. Ein vergleichender Literaturbericht," in *Arbeiter und Arbeiterbewegung im Vergleich. Berichte*

Bibliography

zur internationalen historischen Forschung, ed. by Klaus Tenfelde, *Historische Zeitschrift,* Sonderheft, Vol. XV (Munich: R. Oldenbourg Verlag, 1986), pp. 477–505.

_____, *Die Christlichen Gewerkschaften 1894–1933* (Bonn: Verlag Neue Gesellschaft, 1982).

_____, "Religion and Labour Organisation: The Christian Trade Unions in the Wilhelmine Empire," *European Studies Review,* XII, No. 3 (1982), 345–369.

Schönhoven, Klaus, *Expansion und Konzentration. Studien zur Entwicklung der Freien Gewerkschaften in Wilhelminischen Deutschland 1890 bis 1914* (Stuttgart: Klett-Cotta, 1980).

_____, "Die Gewerkschaften als Massenbewegung im Wilhelmischen Kaiserreich 1890 bis 1918," in *Geschichte der deutschen Gewerkschaften von den Anfängen bis 1945,* ed. by Ulrich Borsdorf (Cologne: Bund-Verlag, 1987), pp. 167–278.

Schröder, Wilhelm, ed., *Handbuch der sozialdemokratischen Parteitage von 1863 bis 1909* (Munich: G. Birk & Co.m.b.H., 1910).

Schrumpf, Emil, *Gewerkschaftsbildung und -politik im Bergbau (Unter besonderer Berücksichtigung des Ruhrbergbaus)* (Bochum: Industriegewerkschaft Bergbau mbH, 1958).

Severing, Carl, *1919/1920 im Wetter- und Watterwinkel* (Bielefeld: Buchhandlung Volkswacht, 1927).

Smith, Anthony D., *The Ethnic Revival* (Cambridge: Cambridge University Press, 1981).

Spencer, Elaine Glovka, "West German Coal, Iron and Steel Industrialists as Employers, 1896–1914" (Unpublished Ph.D. Dissertation, University of California at Berkeley, 1969).

Spethmann, Hans, *Zwölf Jahre Ruhrbergbau,* Vols. I–IV (Berlin: Verlag von Reimar Hobbing, 1928–1930).

Stearns, Peter N., "The European Labor Movement and the Working Classes, 1890–1914," in *The European Labor Movement, the Working Classes and the Origins of Social Democracy, 1890–1914* by Harvey Mitchell and Peter N. Stearns (Itasca, Illinois: F.E. Peacock Publishers, Inc., 1971), pp. 118–221.

Stefanski, Valentina-Maria, *Zum Prozess der Emanzipation und Integration von Aussenseitern: Polnische Arbeitsmigranten im Ruhrgebiet* (Dortmund: Forschungsstelle Ostmitteleuropa an der Universität Dortmund, 1984).

_____, "Tożsamość i integracja. Polskie wychodźstwo zarobkowe w Zagłębiu Ruhry," in *Organizacje polonijne w Europie Zachodniej—Współczesność i tradycje. Materiały z konferencji naukowej w dniach 2 i 3 kwietnia 1987 r. w Poznaniu,* ed. by Barbara Szydłowska-Ceglowa and Jerzy Kozłowski (Poznań: Uniwersytet im. Adama Mickiewicza, 1991), pp. 103–113.

Bibliography

Steinisch, Irmgard, "Der Gewerkverein Christlicher Bergarbeiter," in *Glück auf, Kameraden! Die Bergarbeiter und ihre Organisationen in Deutschland*, ed. by Hans Mommsen and Ulrich Borsdorf (Cologne: Bund-Verlag, 1979), pp. 273–299.

Tenfelde, Klaus, "Die Bergarbeiter, ihre Gewerkschaften und der Kapp-Putsch," in *Ruhrkampf 1920*, ed. by Johannes Gorlas and Detlev J.K. Peukert (Essen: Klartext, 1987), pp. 40–58.

_____, "Bergmännisches Vereinswesen im Ruhrgebiet während der Industrialisierung," *Fabrik, Familie, Feierabend: Beiträge zur Sozialgeschichte des Alltags im Industriezeitalter*, ed. by Jürgen Reulecke and Wolfhard Weber (Wuppertal: Peter Hammer Verlag, 1978), pp. 315–344.

_____, "Gewalt und Konfliktregelung in den Arbeitskämpfen der Ruhrbergleute bis 1918," in *Gewalt und Gewaltlosigkeit: Probleme des 20. Jahrhunderts*, ed. by Friedrich Engel-Janosi *et al.* (Munich: R. Oldenbourg Verlag, 1977), pp. 185–236.

_____, "Linksradikale Strömungen in der Ruhrbergarbeiterschaft 1905 bis 1919," in *Glück auf, Kameraden! Die Bergarbeiter und ihre Organisationen in Deutschland*, ed. by Hans Mommsen and Ulrich Borsdorf (Cologne: Bund-Verlag, 1979), pp. 199–223.

_____, "Mining Festivals in the Nineteenth Century," *Journal of Contemporary History*, XIII, No. 2 (1978), 377–412.

_____, *Sozialgeschichte der Bergarbeiterschaft an der Ruhr im 19. Jahrhundert* (Bonn-Bad Godesberg: Verlag Neue Gesellschaft GmbH, 1977).

Teuteberg, Hans Jürgen, *Geschichte der industriellen Mitbestimmung in Deutschland. Ursprung und Entwicklung ihrer Vorläufer in Denken und in der Wirklichkeit des 19. Jahrhunderts* (Tübingen: J.C.B. Mohr [Paul Siebeck], 1961).

Thompson, E.P., *The Making of the English Working Class* (New York: Vintage, 1966).

Wachowiak, Stanisław, *Polacy w Nadrenii i Westfalii* (Poznań: Nakładem Zjednoczenia Zawodowego Polskiego, 1917).

Walaszek, Adam, "Emigranci polscy wśród Robotników Przemysłowych Świata, 1905–1917," *Przegląd Polonijny*, XIV, No. 2 (1988), 41–55.

Wandycz, Piotr S., *The Lands of Partitioned Poland, 1795–1918* (Seattle: University of Washington Press, 1974).

Wawrzynek, Wojciech, "Polacy westfalsko-nadreńscy w dwudziestoleciu między wojennym," *Kwartalnik Opolski*, IX, No. 4 (1963), 75–90.

Wehler, Hans-Ulrich, *Sozialdemokratie und Nationalstaat: Die deutsche Sozialdemokratie und die Nationalitätenfragen in Deutschland von Karl Marx bis zum Ausbruch des Ersten Weltkrieges* (Würzburg: Holzner-Verlag, 1962).

Bibliography

Wielkopolski słownik biograficzny (Warsaw: Państwowe Wydawnictwo Naukowe, 1981).

Wlocevski, Stéphane, *Le 25e Anniversaire. Les mineurs polonais en France avant, pendant et après la guerre* (Lens: Impr. du Narodowiec, 1935).

Wrzesiński, Wojciech, *Polski ruch narodowy w Niemczech w latach 1922–1939* (Wrocław, Warsaw, Cracow: Zakład Narodowy im. Ossolińskich, 1993).

Index

Index

Index

Index

Mine Owners Association 51, 99, 108
miners:
  blacklisting 91, 99, 100, 126
  firings 91, 140, 183, 188, 189, 222, 232
  layoffs 75, 198, 218, 228, 239
  lockout 201, 203, 229, 237, 239, 243
  overtime 140, 172, 191
  unemployment 182, 185, 187, 227, 228, 236, 239, 240, 245, 258
  workday, length of 39, 45–48, 90, 132, 146, 160, 166, 173, 199–201, 224, 237, 257
miners' elected representatives:
  assessors in mining courts (Berggewerbegerichte) 108, 111
  safety inspectors 100, 107, 109, 141
  workers' committees 107–110, 140, 146, 168, 257
  works councils 189, 196, 232, 234, 235, 237
  see also elders, under miners' pension and insurance fund and pensions
miners' pension and insurance fund and pensions 25, 82, 90–92, 98, 127, 209, 213, 217, 230, 231, 240, 258
  elders 22, 25, 30, 36–38, 75, 84, 90, 107, 108, 110, 234, 237
mining legislation 10, 47, 58, 97, 98, 100, 107, 109
Moers 56, 186, 188
Mönchen-Gladbach 103
Monte Carlo 122
Moravians 98
Munich 102
Münster 39, 52, 53, 76, 77, 80, 119, 142, 143, 145, 163, 164, 167, 169, 171, 185, 186, 206

Napieralski, Adam 71
Narodowiec 80, 113, 117, 118, 122, 148, 205, 228
National Council 129, 130, 205, 206
National Democrats 69
nationalization of the mines 102, 151, 159, 160, 166
National Liberals 113, 120
National Socialist German Workers' Party (NSDAP) and Nazi 245, 247
national solidarity 1, 2, 4, 5, 31, 85, 92–94, 137, 249, 251
National Workers' Party (NPR) 153, 154, 187, 215, 216, 236

National Workers' Party (NSR) 151–153, 207, 208, 211
National Workers' Union 153
Neumühl mine 50, 51, 60, 112, 114
November revolution in Germany (1918) 146, 159, 160, 162, 163, 167, 173, 232, 246
Nowicki, Stanisław 70, 79, 96
NPR, see National Workers' Party (NPR)
NRL, see Main People's Council
NSR, see National Workers' Party (NSR)

Oberhausen 17, 25, 33, 35, 48, 50, 53, 62, 84, 91, 167, 171, 172
Oberhausen mine 45, 46, 109
Oberhausen-Vondern 176
Obermarxloh 108, 165
opting for Polish citizenship 157, 212–221, 227–230, 235, 240
Orędownik 57
Osterfeld 50, 168
Ostmarkenverein 85
Oświata educational association 29

Paderborn 13
papal encyclical 81, 102
Parceling Bank 206
pastoral care, Polish demand for 13, 19, 79, 128
Piecha, Stanisław 147
Piecha, Szczepan 207
Piłowski, Jan 13
Pius X 102
plebiscite in Upper Silesia 185–188, 190
Poland, Kingdom of 144, 147
Poland and Polish state 1, 2, 4, 139, 146–151, 153–158, 162, 163, 169, 177, 179–189, 191–193, 195–199, 202, 205, 206, 208–219, 221–223, 227, 230–234, 239, 244, 246, 249–251
Polish anti-German hostility 34, 116, 117, 138, 167, 168, 185, 190
Polish Circle and parliamentary deputies 38, 68, 87, 90–92, 94, 95, 100, 123, 131, 256
Polish consulate in Cologne 181, 199, 208, 225, 227, 228, 237, 238
Polish consulate (vice-consulate) in Essen 172–176, 181, 183, 184, 186–188, 190–200, 208–216, 218–246
Polish embassy in Berlin 197, 210, 211, 221, 235, 239
Polish Ministry of Foreign Affairs 5, 173, 193, 211, 217, 221

Index

Index

Index